Piedmont
College Library

Demorest, Ga.

77209

Class   Book
372.6   L168

Guiding Children's Language Learning

Guiding Children's

Contributing Authors

Joe L. Frost
  University of Texas
  Austin, Texas

Helen Heffernan
  State Department of Education
  Sacramento, California

Ralph E. Kellogg
  Palm Springs Unified School District
  Palm Springs, California

Robert M. Bloom
  James A. Garfield School
  Brighton, Massachusetts

H. Beresford Menagh
  Beresford Associates
  McLean, Viriginia

Donald R. Ferris
  Purdue University
  West Lafayette, Indiana

Pose Lamb
  Purdue University
  West Lafayette, Indiana

Edith Trager Johnson
  University of California at Santa Barbara
  Santa Barbara, California

Ruth Hochstetler
  Ball State University
  Muncie, Indiana

Elizabeth H. Ratté
  Boston University
  Boston, Massachusetts

Mary Montebello
  State University of New York at Buffalo
  Buffalo, New York

Language Learning

Planning Editor

POSE LAMB
Purdue University
West Lafayette, Indiana

WM. C. BROWN COMPANY PUBLISHERS
Dubuque, Iowa

EDUCATION SERIES

Consulting Editors
Pose Lamb
Purdue University

Lowry W. Harding
The Ohio State University

contents

introduction

Language Arts is a rapidly changing facet of the curriculum of the elementary school. Since the first edition of *Guiding Children's Language Learning* was written, new developments in the field of linguistics (approaches to the study of grammar and syntax, in particular) have come to the attention of teachers. The position of Foreign Language in the Elementary School has changed. The influence of the "behavioral objectives" movement has been felt in language arts as it has in every other curricular area. A great deal of controversy currently surrounds the area of language acquisition and development as well as the issues related to the extent of racial and cultural influences on these significant human characteristics. Evolution (if not revolution) is expected and accepted today, and growth, change, and development are apparent to careful observers of the educational process. Along with other curriculum fields, the English Language Arts has changed. Thus, a new edition of *Guiding Children's Language Learning*, with references to recent research and reflecting current trends and issues seems not only justified but necessary.

The authors and editor have attempted to bring together material which will help the prospective teacher and those now teaching. Certain features of the previous edition have been maintained; chapters have been prepared by specialists within the general field of language arts. This revised edition is the product of the thinking and practical experience of eleven specialists, each contributing in one area of particular competence and interest. The end-of-chapter suggestions, "Extending Your Learning" have been revised in an effort to better meet the needs of today's and tomorrow's teachers of the English Language Arts.

A brief introduction to each chapter has been included in an effort to stress the interrelatedness of the language arts. None of the eleven authors who contributed to this text believes that his area of specialization exists in a vacuum. It is obvious that the language arts are interrelated, that listening influences speaking, speaking writing, and writing reading. The selection of specialists to write separate chapters is not a denial of this. However, the reader's task of integrating and relating separate chapters may be facilitated by the brief introductory sections before each chapter.

The study of language and the utilization of the results of that study should be challenging, rewarding, and pleasant for children. The authors of this textbook and the editor hope they have been successful in presenting to teachers some suggestions for achieving these goals.

Focus

The manner in which a child acquires and gains maturity in using language has been the focus of a great deal of interest, scientific and non-scientific. It is currently a topic of some controversy; Lenneberg* reminds us that man is a biological organism and has much in common with other biological organisms; Jensen,** and others, have presented evidence suggesting that there are cultural and racial influences on cognitive development (including language acquisition) which it is not wise to ignore. It appears that the well known nature vs. nurture controversy has gained new life and is being debated and discussed again, although this time at a more sophisticated and scholarly level.

Regardless of the evidence suggesting that other biological species possess signal systems of a rudimentary nature, it seems fairly clear that only man possesses language in its fullest, most complete dimensions. It is because the manner in which a child learns to use language is of crucial importance to his success in acquiring skill in any facet of it that this chapter has been placed first. The responses made to an infant's babbling, the reinforcement given a pre-school child's efforts to name and classify, all have direct and significant relationships to the child's later efforts to spell and to write.

Dr. Frost devotes a significant portion of this chapter to detailing the progress of most human beings as they acquire language. He also suggests that there are deviations from the norm; Institutionalized children, children from backgrounds labeled "culturally different," and he takes the position that the school can and should make special efforts to help such children. In other words, what Frost terms "environmental manipulation" can produce beneficial results with children whose language development has not been what society terms "normal" or average.

Throughout *Guiding Children's Language Learning* the reader will find reinforcement for an important concept introduced in this first chapter. The child brings to school the language he knows. It is the best he has to offer. It is that language used by those he knows and loves—those who give him his security. Little of a positive nature will be accomplished if the school labels this language as unacceptable and sub-standard. To begin where the child is is an educational truism, almost a cliche; it does not imply that nothing can be done. However, it is extremely important that the child's first away-from-family contacts be with those who recognize his value and worth as a human being, and see the close relationship which exists between accepting the child's language and accepting the child.

---

*Eric H. Lenneberg, "A Biological Perspective of Language," *New Directions in the Study of Language* (Cambridge, Massachusetts: The M.I.T. Press, 1964), p. 71.
**Arthur R. Jensen, "How Much Can We Boost IQ and Scholastic Achievement," *Harvard Educational Review* 39 (Winter, 1969):1-123.

Joe L. Frost

chapter one

language development
in children

Throughout the history of man language has evolved to its present sophisticated state. In the beginning the systems and sounds of language were relatively simple, serving to communicate the thoughts, feelings, and emotions of primitive peoples seeking sustenance from a threatening environment. The perennial test of matching wits with the lesser animals sharpened the language powers of man and he reigned supreme, distinct and apart from all other forms of life. From the original face-to-face confrontation of primitive eras man's prevailing needs spurred the development of increasingly sophisticated communicative devices and he expanded his influence beyond his mother planet. The movement of man toward communicative excellence is quite a story, not unmarked by tragedy, for the very tools that allow the assault on our neighboring planets hold the threat of mankind's destruction. Unfortunately, it seems, our abilities to control and consequently to humanize have failed to keep pace with our abilities to construct and our drives to destroy. Herein lies the challenge to the schools, those institutions charged with the responsibility of shaping the language and thought of the young toward the charitable goals of a democratic society.

The power of the schools is tempered by the communicative patterns of family and neighborhood. Just as the sounds and symbols of language differ from country to country, the patterns of communities, sub-communities and ethnic groups within a country hold great variations. Dialectal differences are everywhere obvious but each pattern is shaped by the needs and necessities of a particular societal group and generally serves quite admirably within that context. The notion of dialectal superiority represents no less a devious argument than the pretentious notion of racial superiority for both are presently humiliating and destructive in their effects, particularly upon the young who must bear the brunt of misguided teacher expectation and method. The task of the teacher is to *construct*, not to *destruct*, and construction always begins from a base or foundation. *The foundation for language teaching is the language which the child brings to school*, and this point must be central if teaching is to be humane and sound.

The growing child makes the language of family and neighborhood his language. "Differences in accents, usage and structure, colloquialisms of family or regional origin, add spice to language and deepen the appreciation of those who learn to understand and enjoy it."[1] Just how language develops and differences emerge is quite a story, involving numerous interrelationships between the structure of language and the nature of the child.

Language Development During Infancy

From the moment of birth the child begins to learn from the world around him. For the first few weeks he is a more or less passive recipient of the attention given him by the significant adults in his life. But he quickly learns that he can modify his immediate world and his skill in doing this grows. The primary means for effecting change or activity in the infant's environment is through vocalization, although movement of the extremities may also have some effect. The earliest vocalizations are reflexive and have no pattern of meaning; no particular sound is connected to any one situation.

During the first three or four months adult responses to cooing and crying make it possible for the infant to learn that vocalization has an effect on his immediate comfort. Crying brings relief from pain and hunger; cooing solicits smiles and comforting pats. As a result of continuous reinforcement, the infant begins to associate vocal sounds with the satisfaction of needs. The alert mother is able to determine the significance of early sounds and through her responses plays an important

1. Helen K. Mackintosh, editor, *Children and Oral Language* (A joint publication of ACEI, ASCD, IRA, and NCTE, 1964), p. 6.

role in the initial language development of the child. In addition to need satisfaction early vocalization appears to give the infant personal pleasure; exercises the maturing speech apparatus, and as Carroll stated, "Certain it is that the infant early develops the capacity of reacting differentially to adult voices."[2] Thus through increasingly meaningful interaction the infant develops simple but effective means of communication.

Early Forms of Communication

The "cooing" of the first few months gradually develops into the "babbling" stage, which continues through most of the first year. During the latter part of the babbling stage the child begins to recognize and understand words and phrases. A more flexible and differentiated language system than vocalization alone is emerging. The vocal sounds of cooing and babbling become more meaningful through the use of intonation and inflexion. The child associates rising inflexion and tempo with pleasure or surprise and lower inflexion and tempo with discomfort or disappointment. In addition, expressive behavior—smiling, frowning, speed of movement, and softness or roughness of physical contacts—begins to have more meaning. Opportunity for use of these communicative forms, independently and in combination, is an indispensable prerequisite to later, more articulate use of language. Individual differences in rate and quality of language development are evident during this period. Recently much attention is focused upon the effects of amount and variety of the child's early linguistic experiences.

Near the beginning of the second year of life, genuine talking usually begins. Many eager parents, upon hearing sound duplications which may only remotely resemble "ma-ma" or "da-da," are confident that their child is now talking, but mere repetition of sounds in absence of meaning is only a prelude to genuine speech. It is some time later, when verbal sounds are closely associated with objects, people or activities, that the first true words are spoken. From this point on language is commonly used as an indication of mental development. According to Watts, "it is pretty well agreed that linguistic development is a good index, though, of course, not a complete one, of the general powers of children in their earlier years."[3]

---

2. John B. Carroll, "Language Acquisition, Bilingualism, and Language Change," *Encyclopedia of Educational Research* (New York: The Macmillan Co., 1960), p. 337.

3. A.F. Watts, *The Language and Mental Development of Children* (New York: D.C. Heath, 1948), p. 34.

McCarthy and other writers stress that linguistic development during the second year of life is dependent largely upon imitation, which is quite prominent during this period.[4] This is evidenced by the fact that the normal child learns the language of his environment but the congenitally deaf child does not learn to speak at all because he is deprived of opportunity for imitation. It also is general knowledge that the child of English speaking parents learns English to the exclusion of all other languages, the Japanese child learns Japanese, etc., if the parents speak only one language.

Near the end of the second year the child makes rapid vocabulary growth. Single words often represent numerous meanings and may be used in many different contexts. "Drink" may mean water or milk. "Dog" often refers to every walking creature even remotely resembling a dog; "car" means car, truck, bus, or even train. Quite frequently the child, instead of using the single sound "dog" or "car" will say "dog-dog" or "car-car." This appears to be a natural tendency. Occasionally a child will become "fixated" at this stage described by Gardner as the "grunt and point" stage.[5] Although mental development or vocal and auditory mechanism *could* be causative factors, most often the reason is simply that the child feels no need for further language sophistication. A crude "grunt" coupled with a pointed finger serves his desires remarkably well. "Language, like other important human skills, is learned. In order for the learning to occur, there must be motivation on the part of the child. The child must somehow discover that he can satisfy his own needs better by talking than by not talking, and by talking well rather than poorly."[6] Between the ages of one and five years mastery of spoken language is normally acquired very rapidly, and " . . . the child whose language development is seriously delayed for any reason labors under an almost unsurmountable handicap in his social and academic relationships."[7] On the basis of numerous investigations it appears extremely important that children acquire skill in linguistic expression at an early age. Parents play a significant role in this development. Watts recorded an illustrative incident " . . . of one small child who was told in a public place to look at the 'bow-wow.' " The child

---

4. D. McCarthy, "Language Development in Children," in L. Carmichael, editor *Manual of Child Psychology,* 2nd edition (New York: Wiley, 1954).
5. Gardner, *op. cit.,* p. 170.
6. Gardner, *op. cit.,* p. 170.
7. McCarthy, *op. cit.,* p. 494.

replied, "Don't say 'bow-wow,' mother; people will think that you can't say 'dog.' "[8]

Language Development During the Preschool Period

The preschooler is primarily a self-centered or egocentric person. Language exists for him as a means for getting what he wants. Through meeting and coping with many minor difficulties and through receiving affection and recognition for his early attempts to please, the child begins to recognize the value of interaction with others. Piaget recognizes in addition to egocentric speech a second type which he calls socialized speech.[9] In egocentric speech the child makes no attempt to address himself to a person, does not appear to care if anyone is listening, but talks for himself or anyone who happens to be in his presence. In socialized speech which is usually quite evident at seven to eight years of age the child addresses himself to a particular person, considers his point of view and actually exchanges ideas with him. Considering that each person must perceive, think, and interpret only in terms of his own unique experiences, some degree of self-centered vocalizing is expected for people of all ages. Piaget's findings concerning the functions of language and language as a means of revealing thought have been tested by other investigators with varying amounts of agreement. The differences can be attributed to variability in rate of development which is characteristic for children in any age group, though the sequence of development except under extreme conditions is invariant.

The Nature of Development

We have seen that language development of the child, in its many forms, progresses in an orderly fashion. By the time the child is in kindergarten his vocabulary has usually reached several thousand words, and he clearly demonstrates skill in sentence usage, listening, and other communicative skills. This has come about through trial and error and is dependent largely upon imitation of those around him. First words deal with concrete objects and events but the child's speech is rapidly expanded to include more abstract terms and finally complete sentences. All this has been achieved in absence of any formal lessons in

---

8. Watts, *op. cit.*, p. 35.
9. Jean Piaget, *The Language and Thought of the Child* (New York: Humanities Press, 1955).

grammar. The wide variation in achievement of a particular language task—learning to talk, to use expressive behavior effectively, etc.—is dependent upon many factors. These factors are internal and external, innate and environmental, but always multiple. Continuous but irregular patterns of development dependent upon multiple factors is characteristic of child growth and development in general. Not only does major achievement of language tasks follow an orderly pattern but as Olson stated,

> Although children growing up in various environments learn to speak many different languages, the time sequence in the acquisition of sound elements is surprisingly constant ... There is some evidence that gross motor developments precede fine motor coordination in the speech musculature ... There appears to be some coincidence in linguistic development with phases of motor development ... There are also anatomical, social, and feeding correlates.[10]

At least four major factors are important to growth in language: "(1) mental, (2) physical, (3) social and emotional, and (4) educational."[11] Growth in any of these areas is supplementary to language growth. Total growth of the child generally occurs in a sequential manner with marked variation between individuals and also between separate but related areas of growth. The wise adult does not necessarily buy a size 8 dress for her eight-year-old daughter. She may find that size 6 or size 10 fits better. But adults are not always pillars of wisdom when pacing instruction and learning materials to the educational needs of the child and the idea that children achieving below "average" represent failures in teaching persists to this day. The practices of many schools suggests that it is easier for the child to change his needs than for the school to modify its demands.

The knowledge that growth is modifiable also has powerful implications for the schools. The degree of care and affection given the young child has an impact on the development of a mature personality. Fear and anxiety, rooted in the culture of the home and reinforced by inappropriate school expectations, makes an indelible mark on the personality of the child. An enriched school environment does not erase the effects of a debilitating home environment but enrichment can make a significant difference. The child who arrives at school unhealthy, unhappy, and unready to learn will remain unhealthy, un-

10. Willard C. Olson, *Child Development* (Boston: D.C. Heath, 1959), p. 124.
11. Glenn R. Hawkes and Damaris Pease, *Behavior and Development from 5 to 12* (New York: Harper, 1962), p. 225.

happy, and unready to learn unless the school modifies its expectations and broadens its role in the educative process. Good health—mental, emotional and physical—is prerequisite to school progress. It follows that the school must direct its attention to these needs before teaching-learning proceeds.

Evidence of Language Growth

Language growth in the past has often been determined by investigators in two ways: (1) by the increase in size of vocabulary and (2) by the length of sentences.

There is a wide range of individual differences in vocabulary increase, causing variation in the results of different investigators. Only during the preschool period is it practical to use the complete vocabularies of children in assessment of growth. The wider range of experiences of older children makes necessary the use of sampling.

One widely quoted estimation of vocabulary increase is that of Madorah Smith.[12] Notice (Table 1) that vocabulary increases very slowly during infancy, quite rapidly during the preschool period, and drops off again at about five to six years of age. Using a different set of criteria involving various methods to determine whether a child understood a word, Mary Smith[13] found markedly different results (Table 2). Instead of having a vocabulary of 2,562 words upon entry to first grade (Madorah Smith, 1926) the child may have a vocabulary of 24,000 words (Mary Smith, 1941).

The results of a more recent study by Shibles supports the *larger* general size of first grade children's understanding vocabulary.[14] Furthermore, recent follow-up studies, (Templin[15]) using the same methods as early investigations, have shown that children are currently talking in longer sentences and using larger vocabularies. McCarthy believes that this may be due to

> . . . the advent of radio and television, fewer foreign born and bilingual children, the rise of nursery schools affording more opportunities for language stimulation outside the home for the formerly underprivileged groups of

12. Madorah E. Smith, "An Investigation of the Development of the Sentence and the Extent of Vocabulary in Young Children," *University of Iowa, Student Child Welfare* 3 (1926): 5.

13. Mary K. Smith, "Measurement of the Size of General English Vocabulary through the Elementary Grades and High School," *Genetic Psychology Monographs* 24 (1941): 311-345.

14. Burleigh H. Shibles, "How Many Words Does a First-Grade Child Know?" *Elementary English* 41 (January, 1959): 42-47.

15. Mildred Templin, *Certain Language Skills in Children, Their Development and Relationship*, University of Minnesota, Institute of Child Welfare, Mono. Ser. No. 26, 1957.

TABLE 1.1

Average Size of Vocabularies of 273 Children From 8 Months to 6 Years

Age Group		Number of Children	Average IQ	Vocabulary	
Years	Months			Number of Words	Gain
	8	13		0	
	10	17		1	1
1—	0	52		3	2
1—	3	19		19	16
1—	6	14		22	3
1—	9	14		118	96
2—	0	25		272	154
2—	6	14		446	174
3—	0	20	109	896	450
3—	6	26	106	1,222	326
4—	0	26	109	1,540	318
4—	6	32	109	1,870	330
5—	0	20	108	2,072	202
5—	6	27	110	2,289	217
6—	0	9	108	2,562	273

SOURCE: M.E. Smith, "An Investigation of the Development of the Sentence and Extent of Vocabulary in Young Children," *Univ. of Iowa Stud. Child Welf.*, 1926, 3 (5): 54. Reprinted by permission.

TABLE 1.2

The Growth of Vocabulary

Grade	Basic	Derived	Total
1	16,900	7,100	24,000
2	22,000	12,000	34,000
3	26,000	18,000	44,000
4	26,200	18,800	45,000
5	28,500	22,500	51,000
6	31,500	18,000	49,500

SOURCE: Mary K. Smith. "Measurement of the Size of General English Vocabulary through the Elementary Grades and High School." *Genetic Psychology Monographs* 24:311-345, 1941. Reprinted by permission.

children, more leisure time for parents to spend with their children, reduced amount of time that children are cared for by nurse-maids of limited verbal ability, better economic conditions allowing parents even in lower income brackets to provide stimulating environments for children to be treated more permissively and to find greater acceptance in the modern home.[16]

Obviously, some degree of artificiality enters into the study of vocabulary because of the degrees of meaning that can be attached to any word. Is the child able to say the word, use it in his speech, read it, define it? How well can he do this? At best, vocabulary estimations are useful as very general estimations for what the child actually knows. The degree of knowing about a word and the related meanings that word holds for a child is very personal, not to be fully understood or completely shared by another.

The average age of the child upon speaking his first sentence is about seventeen and five-tenths months with complete sentences appearing at about four years.[17] McCarthy compiled data from ten investigations of mean length of sentences for one to nine-year-old children.[18] There was quite striking agreement among the investigators, each employing different subjects and methods. McCarthy therefore concluded that mean sentence length is the most . . . "reliable, easily determined, objective, quantitative, and easily understood measure of linguistic maturity."[19] But Watts draws attention to the range and quality of the words which children use.[20] The child who writes or speaks, "He did not know which place he would have to go in the end," has not shown that he possesses a richer or fuller vocabulary by using 13 words than the child who stated, "His ultimate destination was uncertain." It is clear that study of the child's language growth must take into account range and quality in addition to quantity.

The current emphasis on restricting the vocabulary of instructional materials, particularly basal readers, is unrealistic and harmful. Most young children have developed extremely large vocabularies as a result of increased travel, television, and children's books. The basic vocabulary for the beginner in school is that which he has, understands, and uses. Clearly this is a highly individual matter.

16. Dorothea A. McCarthy, "Research in Language Development: Retrospect and Prospect," *Child Development Monographs* 24 (1959): 13-15.

17. M.M. Nice, "Length of Sentences as a Criterion of a Child's Progress in Speech," *Journal of Educational Psychology* 16 (1925): 370-379.

18. McCarthy, *op. cit.* (1954), p. 546-547.

19. McCarthy, *Ibid.*, p. 551.

20. Watts, *op. cit.*, p. 31.

Attention to the size of vocabulary and length of sentences as an index of language power has recently been supplemented by attention to structure of language and the familiarity of the child with these structures.

Strickland divided the talk of 575 children into units according to rising and falling intonation, pause, and meaning.[21] A unit of speech ending with a distinct falling intonation was called a phonological unit (indicated by #). Each phonological unit contains one or more meaning or structural units, spoken with varying intonation, and partial pauses (indicated by /). For example:

> I have to be saving my money/you know/ because we're going to be gone//let's see//I guess it is four or five months# I'm saving my money for that and then afterward // I'm keeping it for what I want #.

This study revealed that the length of phonological units used is *not* an indication of language maturity; that some basic patterns appear with great frequency (Table 3), the most used appearing with high frequency at all grade levels; that these structures, learned at an early age, appear to be basic building blocks of children's language.

Difficulties with language appear to involve more than learning hard words and speaking, reading, or writing long sentences. Linguists emphasize the role of vocabulary in later learning of reading and writing, but they also recognize that the learning of oral language *patterns* facilitates the use of printed materials.

Language Development in Nursery School and Kindergarten

For most children school experiences begin upon entry to kindergarten or first grade but many others are fortunate in attending good nursery schools. The nursery school is carefully planned to give the child many rich, stimulating experiences with materials and other children. These experiences are desirable for *all* children but especially for those from impoverished families. The stimulation provided by peers and understanding teachers, manipulation of many-shaped and many-colored objects, and listening to good children's stories, etc. are essential to language, social, and intellectual development. During recent years, educators and others concerned with children have begun

---

21. Ruth G. Strickland, *The Language of Elementary School Children: Its Relationship to the Language of Reading Textbooks and the Quality of Reading of Selected Children*, vol. 38 (Bloomington: Indiana University, School of Education, 1962).

to emphasize, with renewed vigor, the importance of these experiences and are currently active toward making them available. Operation "Headstart" is a direct result of the clearly established need for compensatory preschool enrichment programs for culturally disadvantaged children.

TABLE 1.3

Total Number of Structural Patterns Used and Frequency of Use
of Each at Four Grade Levels

Grade	Total number	Frequency of use		
		1 - 4 times	5 - 10 times	More than 10 times
1	658	588	53	47
2	747	652	39	51
4*	722	620	50	52
6	1041	918	69	54

*Based on 75 cases (other grades 100 cases each).
SOURCE: Ruth G. Strickland, *The Language of Elementary School Children:* Its Relationship to the Language of Reading Textbooks and the Quality of Reading of Selected Children. Bloomington: Indiana University, School of Education, 38:16. Reprinted by permission.

These early nursery school years of the twos, threes, and fours bring rapid growth in language skills. Funds of knowledge and ranges of interests broaden to include real conversation and social interaction, resulting in an ever-widening range of interests and skills. The nursery school child is bright-eyed at the wonders of his world. He explores, he looks, he feels, he hears, he tries it all on for size and, curiously enough, the healthy child takes off and discards the parts that don't fit.

Still wide-eyed with the wonder of it all, the child comes to kindergarten. Here he lives in a world that too often resembles the more formal scene that will come next year upon entry to first grade. The days are too short, the room too small to contain his enthusiasm and exploratory activity. Guidance is no longer dependent upon physical handling. The child responds to verbal suggestions and directions and may offer some of his own. He often substitutes language for force, suggesting to another child, "Let me show you how to do it." On the playground he may resort to name calling rather than hitting and kicking to make his point.

The teacher makes provisions for the social development of children through cooperative group planning, goal setting, working in small and large groups and evaluating behavior and work habits. Planning with the teacher gives opportunity to express ideas, have them tested in practice, and finally revise plans for more effective results.

Parents, siblings, radio and television have all contributed to the background of ideas the child brings to school, but many gaps still exist. He defines words only in terms of their function: "A car is to ride in." "Candy is to eat." He generalizes readily: of the two rabbits in the classroom, one white and one spotted, only the white one had babies so, "All white rabbits are mother rabbits." His speech closely resembles that of the adults in his home; if a child's parent says "We may have precipitation today, so take your raincoat," any discussion of weather in school is likely to bring forth the word, "precipitation," not "rain." "It's a cool day" may call up no image of weather for the slum child who views "cool" as "great," "smooth," or "sharp." The teacher recognizes that growth in language skills is fostered by observing, listening, feeling, tasting, comparing, classifying and generalizing in a social context that values freedom and requires responsibility.

Interrelationships Among Various Aspects of Language Development

The natural sequence of language skills development is listening with some degree of comprehension, speaking with meaning, reading with understanding and finally writing. The interrelated nature of language growth is evident even before the child starts to school. Through interaction with others he has developed speech sounds resembling those that he has heard. The fact that deaf children do not learn to speak during this period is ample evidence that speaking is closely related to listening.

Reading and writing are essential tools for communication in our culture. Some understanding of sharing ideas, feelings and wants, plus the acquisition of certain skills—enunciation and articulation, auditory discrimination, comprehension—is necessary for effective reading. Billy commented to the teacher, "I see a boid in the tree outside the window." The teacher answered, "That isn't a boid, Billy, that's a bird." "Well it looked like a boid to me," said Billy, may reflect a problem of articulation, comprehension, auditory discrimination or a combination of these. The alert teacher daily observes many minor *effects of* language difficulty but must be very skillful indeed to isolate specific *causes.*

A clearer view of the underlying relationships existing for each of the language arts can be gained by examination of available research findings. Hughes studied 332 fifth grade children and found high relationships among reading, spelling, word meaning, general usage, capitalization, punctuation, sentence sense, and paragraph organization.[22] Hildreth reported several studies that pointed out the interrelationships that exist among oral and written communication, reading, spelling, handwriting.[23] Writing, usually the last of the common communication forms to be developed, is dependent upon oral language and comprehension; it is related to skill in reading and growth in spelling and handwriting. Because of the relatedness that exists among these different phases of language expression, Hildreth believes that more integration should be achieved for language instruction in schools.

Much remains to be learned about the extent of interrelations among aspects of language. Loban's longitudinal study has recently yielded important evidence about interrelations for the following factors; oral language with written language; oral language with reading; reading with written language; and health with general language ability.[24] These interrelations extend through the elementary grades and are positive for the intermediate and upper grades.

In successive years third grade pupils who wrote well also ranked high in use of oral language and reading. Children who scored below average on any one of the measures were below average on the other two.

As the children continued into the upper grades a higher relationship was found between writing and reading. By grade six (Table 4),

> The superior group in writing has by far the highest teacher's rating. Even more striking is the fact that every subject ranked superior in writing is *reading above* his chronological age; *every* subject ranked illiterate or primitive in writing is *reading below* his chronological age. (p. 75).

22. Vergil H. Hughes, "A Study of the Relationships Among Selected Language Abilities," *Journal of Educational Research* 47 (October, 1953): 97-105.

23. Gertrude H. Hildreth, "Interrelationships Between Written Expression and the Other Language Arts," in *Interrelationships Among the Language Arts* (Research Bulletin of the National Conference on Research in English, 1954), pp. 4-12.

24. Walter D. Loban, *The Language of Elementary School Children* (Champaign: National Council of Teachers of English, 1963).

TABLE 1.4

Interrelations among Reading, Writing, and Oral Language
Grade Six

Written language: classification of subjects		Number in group	Number reading above chronological age	Number reading below chronological age	Average reading achievement above or below expected age norm	Oral language: average teachers' ratings
I	Superior group	21	21	0	+3 yr. and 6 mo.	4.08
II	Good group	102	83	19	+1 yr. and 6 mo.	3.52
III	Inferior group	73	20	53	−0 yr. and 9 mo.	3.01
IV	Illiterate group	22	0	22	−2 yr. and 7 mo.	2.61
V	Primitive group	4	0	4	−3 yr. and 6 mo.	2.53
TOTAL GROUP		222	124	98	+0 yr. and 5 mo.	3.15

SOURCE: Walter D. Loban. *The Language of Elementary School Children.* Champaign; National Council of Teachers of English, 1963, p. 74. Reprinted by permission of the National Council of Teachers of English and Walter D. Loban.

In addition to reading and writing, there was a positive relation between reading and oral language, oral language and listening, and a low positive relation for health and language ability (speaking, writing or reading). "Apathy, lassitude, and low vitality appear to be concomitants of low language ability for some subjects." (p. 75)

These relationships suggest that growth in one area reinforces growth in others. It is logical and necessary, then, that language activities be rich and varied for assuring optimum growth in each. At the same time, accurate assessment of the child's present language status and future needs is highly dependent upon evaluation of other facets of total development; in order to understand the child's pattern of language growth it is necessary first to know about his physical equipment and his social and emotional development. In short, we must know his personality structure.

Speech itself, highly related to other aspects of language, is also closely related to personal development. "A speech disorder is a disorder of the person as well as a disorder in the reception and transmission of spoken language."[25] Present day language authorities are largely in agreement that personality problems nearly always accompany language disabilities. If we are to understand speech we must understand the person, for the child in need of psychological help usually has symptoms of language difficulty. Most speech disorders such as baby talk and lisping are associated with poor human relations in the home.[26] This, of course, does not refer to children with organic difficulties. Aside from organic causes, language disability appears to be a symptom of emotional disorder.

Maladjusted and backward children are frequently observed to have trouble with speech, and when allowed to continue without correction are commonly regarded by peers, parents, and teachers as "retarded." This form of discrimination is perhaps more subtle in nature than more common forms but the effects on the growing child are equally devastating. Another cause for concern among adults is the late-speaking child. Although all mentally defective children are late in learning to speak, all bright children do not speak early and all late speakers are not mentally retarded.[27] Gifted children *usually,* however, speak early and early speech is a good index of mental ability.

Beck has discovered that children who later have reading disabilities can be identified in the nursery school.[28] Slow readers in fifth grade had shown signs of emotional disturbance as preschoolers at six times the rate for normal readers. Educative procedure for the child with a language disorder " . . . is to help him organize incoming stimuli so that useful concepts can result."[29] Neither rote production and recognition of words nor the memorization of principles will serve this end. Rather, it is understanding the *meaning* of principles that makes them useful.

It is true that speech mirrors the personality of the child. Image of self and others is closely interwoven with family language patterns and has its roots in early childhood. From early in the child's life the two facets of language which precede reading and writing, namely listening and speaking " . . . are intricately interrelated—neurologically, intellec-

25. L.E. Travis, editor, *Handbook of Speech Pathology* (New York: Appleton-Century-Crofts, 1957), p. 5.
26. McCarthy, *op. cit.* (1959).
27. Dorothea McCarthy, "Language Development," *Child Development Monographs* 25 (1960).
28. Harriet K. Beck, "Relationship of Emotional Factors in Early Childhood to Subsequent Growth and to Achievement in Reading" (Doctoral Dissertation; University of Michigan, 1951).
29. Nancy E. Wood, "Language Disorders in Children," *Child Development Monographs* 25 (1960).

tually and socially . . . continually modified by people and events."[30] Like personality development, social growth is closely interwoven with language power. The quality of the child's social relationships will in large measure determine the level of language power he will attain.

Language, Thought and Intelligence

Because of previous experiences, the child has accumulated certain raw materials—percepts, images, memories, and concepts—that he manipulates during thinking. His *ability* to manipulate these raw materials is called intelligence. Exactly how language fits into this framework is not clear, but language is so closely related to thinking that many psychologists regard them as identical.

> . . . . some members of the behaviorist school of psychology regard thinking as subvocal speech. They have pointed out that, during thinking movements of the throat and tongue are observable, and therefore that thinking may be termed "internal speech." On the other hand, certain experimental evidence contradicts this point of view. Animals cannot speak in the usual sense of the term, but there seems little doubt that they engage in some forms of thinking. An infant understands language before he actually uses it himself. As early as the eighth or ninth month he can understand gestures, look for a dropped object, or reach for an attractive object, before he can talk about them. Furthermore, some thought seems to be based rather directly on kinesthetic, tactual, auditory, and other sensations and images. It seems reasonable, therefore, to consider language and thought as closely related but not identical.[31]

". . . during the later preschool years and in subsequent development throughout childhood, over-all language development is the best single index of intelligence available to psychologists."[32] In addition to measuring other standard items, many tests of intelligence measure vocabulary. It is one of the most valid measures of intelligence.

Russell has developed a schema for thinking (Figure 1) which illustrates the processes which occur from the time a stimulus is received by the child until a conclusion is reached.[33] The four main factors involved are: (1) the materials for thinking—sensations perception, etc., (2) the motives for thinking—feelings, needs, attitudes, etc., (3) the processes in thinking—patterns of activity, such as selecting, eliminat-

---

30. Mackintosh, *op. cit.,* p. 4.
31. David H. Russell, *Children's Thinking* (Boston: Ginn, 1956), p. 24, 25.
32. Gardner, *op. cit.,* p. 182.
33. Russell, *op. cit.*

ing, searching, manipulating and organizing, and (4) the abilities in thinking—habits, techniques and guides which can be acquired and developed.

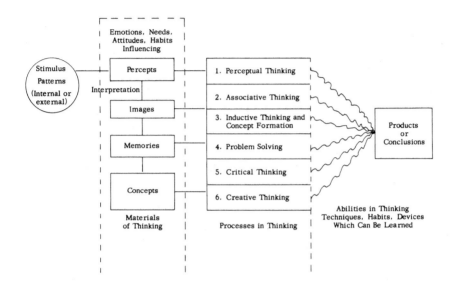

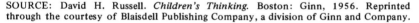

SOURCE: David H. Russell. *Children's Thinking.* Boston: Ginn, 1956. Reprinted through the courtesy of Blaisdell Publishing Company, a division of Ginn and Company.

FIGURE 1.1. Schema for Thinking.

The raw materials for thinking have been described by Carin and Sund:

> *Sensations* develop an awareness of stimuli without much interpretation. *Percepts* are what is known about an object, a quality, or a relationship as a result of sensations. Percepts are the fabric from which concepts are formed. *Images* are previous percepts. *Concepts* are abstractions which organize objects and events into categories. *Generalizations* or *principles* are concepts involving relationships between two or more abstractions, objects or events.[34]

34. Arthur Carin and Robert B. Sund, *Teaching Science Through Discovery* (Columbus: Charles E. Merrill, 1964).

The steps or sequence of thinking are described by Russell.

> ... the environment stimulates thinking; the thinking takes its initial direction; there is some search for related materials; these materials are organized into tentative patterns or hypotheses; the hypotheses are examined critically; and some tentative conclusion or goal is reached which may eventuate in overt action.[35]

The first three types of thinking are:

> ... perceptual thinking, associative thinking, and inductive-deductive learning. Problem solving, critical thinking, and creative thinking—the next higher order of thinking which is commonly compared to scientific processes— depend upon the proper formulation of percepts, concepts, and generalizations for their foundation.[36]

The operative efficiency of the child's mental or cognitive structure (schema) appears to be dependent upon opportunity for use.[37] The mental schema becomes more flexible through adjustment to varieties of situations and the child consequently develops a wider range of interests. Further, gradual change in mental structures seems to occur as a result of continuous interaction of the child and his environment.[38]

For many years the concept of unchanging intelligence was a common guide for school practice, but Hunt has compiled evidence of a contradictory nature.[39,40] He has asserted, with extensive supportive evidence, that the concepts of fixed intelligence and predetermined intelligence are no longer tenable. Psychologists have attempted to explain learning in terms of stimulus response bonds, using the telephone as a mechanical model of the brain's operation. Thus they have all too often envisioned the brain as a static switchboard through which each stimulus could be connected with a variety of responses, which in turn could become the stimuli for still other responses.

But Hunt cites research demonstrating that a more active kind of process goes on between the ears. The programming of electronic computers clarifies the general nature of the requirements for solving logical problems. Three major components of these requirements have been described: (1) memories, or information, coded and stored; (2) opera-

---

35. Russell, *op. cit.*, p. 28.

36. Carin and Sund, *op. cit.*, p. 40.

37. Jean Piaget, *The Origins of Intelligence in Children*, Trans. Margaret Cook (New York: International Universities Press, 1936, 1952).

38. J. McV. Hunt, *Intelligence and Experience* (New York: Ronald, 1961).

39. *Ibid.*

40. J. McV. Hunt, "How Children Develop Intellectually," *Children* 11 (May, 1964): 83-91.

tions of a logical sort which can act upon the memories; and (3) hierarchically arranged programs of these operations for various purposes.

A likely place for equivalents of these components within the brain is the intrinsic portions of the cerebrum which have no direct connections with either incoming fibers from the receptors of experience or outgoing fibers to the muscles and glands. The intrinsic portion of the brain is very small in such animals as the frogs and salamanders used as subjects in some of the early experiments on the embryology of behavior; consequently belief in predetermined development appeared to be consonant with the data on behavioral development. The increasing proportion of the brain constituting the intrinsic portion in higher animals suggests an anatomic basis for the increasing role of infantile experience in development.

Experience may be regarded as programming the intrinsic portions of the cerebrum for learning and problem solving, and the intellectual capacity of a person at any given time may be conceived to be in very considerable part a function of the nature and quality of this experimental programming.[41] Consequently, the I.Q. score may vary as much as 20 to 40 points as a result of environmental stimulation or lack of environmental stimulation.[42]

It is not clear whether the child gains language power as a result of high intelligence or gains high intelligence as a result of language power. In either event, the close relationship between language and intelligence suggests that conditions facilitative for the growth of either are essential for the growth of both. Furthermore these conditions are highly dependent upon the degree and quality of the child's daily listening, speaking, manipulating and interacting.

The prevailing controversy as to the relative importance of nature and nurture in the development of children naturally arises here. It is clear that nature and nurture always operate together; they are mutually interdependent; one in absence of the other has no meaning. In fact, without either there would be no life. Nature ordinarily endows the child with a complete set of equipment ensuring the potential for growth, but that potential is achieved only in the course of the child's interaction with his circumstances. The rate and quality of his growth

41. Hunt, *op. cit.*, (1964).
42. Joe L. Frost and Glenn R. Hawkes, *The Disadvantaged Child* (Boston: Houghton Mifflin, 1966).

can be accelerated, retarded or even stopped by the conditions of his circumstantial nurture.

Arthur Jensen has concluded that intelligence is determined largely by heredity and cannot be altered significantly by improving environment.[43] He also postulates genetic differences between Negroes and whites in intellectual ability. Analysis of the arguments generated by Jensen's voluminous study shows considerable disagreement but the bulk of these arguments appear to support the thesis that we are not in a position to say with certainty that there are genetic racial differences in intelligence nor have we sufficient evidence to assert with confidence the degree of impact upon intellectual development that is possible through environmental manipulation. (See *Harvard Educational Review,* Spring 1969, Summer 1969 for opposing arguments.)

Language and Experience

Considerable evidence exists to support the view that socioeconomic status of the family is closely related to the child's linguistic development. McCarthy's review of research related to environment and language shows that children from a restricted environment are retarded in all areas of development but the degree of retardation is greater in language development.[44] They use fewer words, less mature sentences, have greater difficulty in interpreting the language of others, and generally have poorer articulation. The greatest degree of language sophistication is found among children of professional men, with differences increasing as age increases. Several investigators have reported that travel and other events which give opportunities for varied experiences are followed by increase in vocabulary, particularly nouns. It appears reasonable to assume that this increase is accompanied by growth in meaning.

Hildreth reported that "a large proportion of reading disability cases come from homes where language is used for every day, or not particularly intellectual subjects or where a substandard dialect is used: Children that move from one dialect area to another have considerable difficulty adjusting to school. A substantial relationship exists between

---

43. Arthur R. Jensen, "How Much Can We Boost IQ and Scholastic Achievement?" *Harvard Educational Review* 39 (Winter, 1969): 1-123.
44. McCarthy, *op. cit.,* (1954).

reading problems and other linguistic deficiencies which appear to be characteristic of children who move from school to school frequently."[4][5]

Young compared "regular" and "relief" children attending the same school.[4][6] Regular children surpassed the "relief" children on all aspects of language which were analyzed. "Relief" boys showed greatest retardation. "Regular" girls were the most advanced. As a rule girls surpass boys in language power during the elementary school years. This may be due in part to their more rapid rate of physiological development. Classes for retarded readers usually contain more boys than girls.

Potential intelligence cannot be assessed in terms of linguistic skill, for potentiality can be considerably altered by the experiences of the child. It is unreasonable to assume that merely because a child has been reared in an impoverished home he is restricted by hereditary factors; this conceivably could be true of any child regardless of choice of parentage. Rather it appears that different environments affect language development and the impoverished child lacks opportunities which contribute to development. Bernstein has found that the middle class uses "formal" modes of speech which varies between individuals.[4][7] This makes possible greater clarification of meaning. The lower class family uses a more "restricted" speech. This places children at a decided disadvantage in the middle-class oriented school which values the verbal linguistic skills and patterns of the middle class. Consequently, children of lower class homes may meet progressive failure in oral communication and in the related areas of listening, reading, and writing. It is clear, then, that restrictions imposed by deprivation of stimulating experiences, especially during infancy and early childhood, commonly delimit the progress of children in school.

Restriction of stimulating experiences during early life can also seriously affect growth in areas other than language. This has been established by numerous studies of both animals and humans.

Studies of animal behavior, which established conditions closely paralleling the problem of cultural deprivation or sensory restriction of humans, reveals that animals (dogs or chimpanzees) reared in darkness

---

45. Gertrude Hildreth, "Linguistic Factors in Early Reading," *The Reading Teacher* 18 (December, 1964): 172-178.

46. F.M. Young, "An Analysis of Certain Variables in a Developmental Study of Language," *Genetic Psychology Monographs* 23 (1941): 3-141.

47. Basil Bernstein, "Language and Social Class," *British Journal of Sociology* 21 (1958): 159-174.

or isolation were greatly restricted in performance of social functions or the solving of problems at maturity.[48]

Although we do not subject children to conditions of deprivation for purposes of experimentation, fate and neglect have provided ample cases for study. In a Teheran orphanage, where children had little opportunity for stimulation, 60 percent could not sit alone at two years of age and 85 percent could not walk alone at four years of age.[49] This illustrates the effect that early experience can have on even the rate of locomotor development and, when compared to other evidence, suggests that retardation in one area of development may be accompanied by retardation in other areas. For example, Goldfarb compared a group of adolescents that had been placed in institutions as infants with a group of adolescents that had been institutionalized much later.[50] The early institutionalized group was much more apathetic and *generally immature* during adolescence.

One of the most dramatic illustrations of the effects of sensory stimulation or enriched living on intellectual development is a study of Skeels.[51] Thirteen mentally retarded infants were placed in an institution that provided person-to-person contacts; later eleven of these were placed in adoptive homes. A contrast group of twelve children, with higher intelligence initially, remained in a relatively nonstimulating environment over a prolonged period. This contrast group showed progressive mental retardation while the "enriched" group showed progressive mental growth.

A follow-up study after these children had reached adulthood showed that all of the children who had been placed in stimulating environments were self-supporting; none was institutionalized. Eleven of the thirteen married and nine had children. The median grade completed in school was twelve. One girl with an initial I.Q. of 35 graduated from high school and completed a semester in college.

Of the twelve who remained in the "nonstimulating" environment,

48. Ronald Melzack and William R. Thompson, "Effects of Early Experience on Social Behavior," *Canadian Journal of Psychology* 10 (1956): 82-90; Austin H. Riesen "The Development of Visual Perception in Man and Chimpanzee," *Science* 106 (1947): 107-108; W.R. Thompson and W. Heron, "The Effects of Restricting Early Experience on the Problem-Solving Capacity of Dogs," *Canadian Journal of Psychology,* 8 (1954): 17-31.

49. W. Dennis, "Causes of Retardation Among Institutional Children," *Journal of Genetic Psychology* 96 (1960): 47-59.

50. W. Goldfarb, "The Effects of Early Institutional Care on Adolescent Personality," *Journal of Experimental Education* 12 (1953): 106-129.

51. Harold M. Skeels, "Effects of Adoption on Children From Institutions," *Children* 12 (January-February, 1965): 33-34.

one died after continued residence in a state institution for the mentally retarded; four are still wards of mental institutions. Two of the four females were sterilized. Median school grade completed was three. Cost to the state for this group has been about $100,000.

Lenneberg[52] recently caused quite a stir in educational and psychological circles through his discussion of relationships of language development and physical indications of brain maturation. He points out that these correlations do not prove causal connections, but they do suggest that a purely environmental explanation of language development would be open to severe question. In interpreting Lenneberg it seems important to note that he stresses the differences between *what children actually do* and *what they can do*. He is interested in the underlying capacity for language and it is in this context that he forms his arguments. He recognized that "certain aspects of the environment are absolutely essential for language development."

In studies of children from many different societies Lenneberg found no evidence of variation in developmental rate, despite enormous differences in social environment. He believes that "language development follows its own natural history. The child can avail himself of this capacity if the environment provides a minimum of stimulation and opportunity." Although impoverished environments are not conducive to good language development, specific training measures are not necessary, according to Lenneberg, for "a wide variety of rather haphazard factors seems to be sufficient." This contention is contradictory to conclusions from numerous experimental compensatory preschool programs enrolling disadvantaged Afro-American and Mexican-American children (American Institutes for Research,[53] Southwest Educational Development Laboratory[54]). These studies indicate that haphazard approaches or "verbal bombardment" approaches fail to achieve language gains as rapidly as structured, systematic approaches.

A Holistic Analysis of Human Development

The interrelationships that exist among language, intelligence, thinking and social, physical, and emotional factors imply that the effective language arts program will be holistically based. Although this "holis-

---

52. Eric H. Lenneberg, "On Explaining Language," *Science* 164 (May, 1969): 635-643.
53. American Institutes for Research, *A Study of Selected Exemplary Programs for the Education of Disadvantaged Children,* (Palo Alto: September, 1968).
54. Southwest Educational Development Laboratory, *Annual Evaluation Report,* (1968-1969, San Antonio Urban Educational Development Center: Austin, Texas, 1970).

tic" concept has maintained theoretical consideration for many years, practical application has lagged. As a consequence, more attention is commonly given to what is "taught" than to how learning occurs. This results in superficial learner commitment and shallow thinking. The child, expected to adjust his needs to the school's goals, modify his goals to grade-level standards, and gear his thinking toward accumulation of facts, has limited opportunity for growth in language power.

The process of language development may be described through an illustration (Figure 1.2) which offers a general scheme for a developmental outlook on the processes through which the child gains language power. He comes to school with a unique set of learnings and potentialities that have been shaped by nature and nurture. The school environment continues to be influential in further language growth which is shaped largely by the quality of experiences offered by the home prior to school entrance.

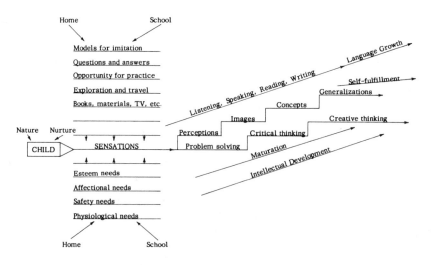

FIGURE 1.2. Schema for human development.

The child has certain inborn needs, reinforced by the culture of his home and neighborhood, which seek fulfillment: physiological needs—food, clothing, and health; safety needs—freedom from physical harm and mental stress; affectional needs—loving people around him, and esteem needs—favor and appreciation of his peers. While most children's physiological and safety needs are met by the home, fewer receive the affection and esteem so essential to a high degree of self-fulfillment. Despite contradictory practice, these are essential ingredients for effective school functioning and language development. "Failure of need satisfaction produces narrowness and rigidity of perceptual organization."[55] It follows, then, that the effective educational system will consider these needs ". . . in ways that allow the child to preserve dignity."[56]

Upon arrival at school, the child exhibits language patterns very similar to those used in his home. This has resulted from imitation of models—the adults in his life—and the opportunities he may have had to explore on his own, his freedom to ask questions and get answers which encourage thinking and further questioning, and the variety of manipulative materials available for comparison and discrimination. The variety and quality of reading materials *on the shelf* make little impact on language development. Active use and demonstrated enjoyment of books by significant people in the child's world make a great deal of difference.

As the child grows through time he gains skill in language and thinking. As he experiences widely, he engages in more complex thinking. He makes difficult choices which involve more than 2 plus 2 or a distinction between more or less.

He begins to formulate procedures which are widely recognized as scientific problem solving—isolating a problem, gathering information about possible solutions, taking action aimed toward solution, and finally drawing tentative conclusions based upon the evidence available.

Critical thinking emerges as the child becomes aware of, and makes the values and norms of society a part of himself. He judges events and situations in terms of these commonly held values and, hopefully, begins to apply these in varied situations. As he builds backgrounds of meanings, values and norms are called up automatically without undue consideration of consequence or effect. He needs "telling" less often, and weighs information to reach the "best" conclusion.

This growth in thinking is largely dependent upon parallel growth in

55. Arthur W. Combs, "A Perceptual View of the Adequate Personality," in: *Perceiving, Behaving, Becoming* (Washington: Association for Supervision and Curriculum Development, 1962), p. 61.
56. Frost and Hawkes, *op. cit.*

language. Percepts and concepts must be thrown into fresh combinations to accommodate the child's enlarged world of thinking. This leads to the emergence of the highest form of language and thought activity—creativity.

All children have the potential for creative thinking but conditions of teaching rarely ensure, or even allow, its emergence. The quantity and quality of ideas can be improved through teaching, but pedagogy usually demands facts, and ideas often don't count. The production of new ideas and application through speaking, writing, art, etc. are enhanced or restricted by the structure of the school situation.

Finally, emphasis upon the "whole child" implies that conditions facilitative to creative thinking contribute to self-fulfillment. Adequate persons ". . . not only possess more information or understanding; they are able to produce these when needed and to put them to effective use."[57] In the past creative activity implied only tangible products but this misconception is being replaced by a more dynamic view.

> We still search for and encourage the tangible, but the concept of creativity has been enlarged to include ideas, decisions, relationships, problem solving— results of man's cognitive powers. The product, whatever form it may take would not evolve without the process. The growing realization of the universality of creativity, of man's heretofore unsuspected capacity for creativeness, of the uniqueness of every individual, places the idea of creativity in new perspective . . . Creativity is necessary for a fully adequate personality.[58]

Language and Teaching

At age five or six the child goes to school. The school now shares the home's continuing responsibility for his language development. If the home has done its job well, the school's role is usually uncomplicated. If a course of failure has been established, however, much insight and skill will be needed for alteration. School success hinges upon home success and home support. Consistency of expectations, demands, values, and language patterns between home and school reinforces the behavioral patterns of the child and facilitates school progress. The culturally disadvantaged child often finds that the language patterns of his home are unacceptable by the school and that his usual ways of communicating are ineffective. He finds that books are written about people he has never seen using language patterns he has never heard. He

57. Combs, *op. cit.,* p. 60.

58. *Perceiving, Behaving, Becoming, A.S.C.D.* (Washington: Association for Supervision and Curriculum Development, 1962), p. 142.

therefore has little chance of "catching up" with those who have made this "foreign" language their language since infancy.

The school must not allow the obvious deficiencies of the few to unduly detract its attention from those who seek and require continuous direction toward ever higher levels of language functioning. The gifted, for example, often comprise the most retarded group in a school. Their level of functioning is sufficiently high to get along quite well—even to make the honor rolls—but the depths of their linguistic ability remain untapped. Too little incentive and opportunity for high order thinking exists in their school world of facts and averages. Knowledge of language development and human behavior offers guidelines for teacher action. Among those principles discussed in this chapter that should influence language teaching are:

1. The growing child makes the language of family and neighborhood his language.
2. Linguistic development is dependent largely upon imitation.
3. There are wide individual differences in rate and quality of language development.
4. It is extremely important that children acquire skill in linguistic development at an early age.
5. Good health—mental, emotional, and physical—is prerequisite to success in language.
6. At best, vocabulary estimations are useful as very general estimations for what the child actually knows.
7. Assessment of the child's language growth must take into account range and quality in addition to quantity.
8. The basic vocabulary for the beginner in school is that which he has, understands, and uses.
9. Difficulties with language appear to involve more than learning hard words and speaking, reading, or writing long sentences; meaning units, learned at an early age, appear to be basic building blocks of children's language.
10. Expressive behavior—gestures, drawing, painting, dramatization—are important facets of language which enrich and deepen communicative meanings.
11. Language development is intricately interrelated with mental, social, and personal development.
12. Language and thought are inextricably interrelated.

13. Efficiency of thinking structures is dependent upon use.
14. Attainment of higher levels of thinking requires corresponding growth in language.
15. Language and thinking can be improved through teaching.
16. Language and intellectual growth are highly dependent upon the degree and quality of the child's daily listening, speaking, manipulating, and interacting.
17. Restrictions imposed by deprivation of stimulating experiences, especially during infancy and early childhood, commonly delimit language development.
18. The child has certain inborn needs, reinforced by the culture of home and neighborhood, which seek fulfillment.
19. The process through which language grows is the process that unleashes creativity and promotes growth toward self-fulfillment.
20. The effective language arts program will have bases in the major dimensions of human development.

The role of the teacher in the language development of the child has long been regarded as one of providing instruction in skills and prescribing assignments in workbooks. As a result, it was hoped, the child would naturally integrate the knowledge thus gained into his language learning structure and growth would logically occur. But language is much more dynamic than this. It is psychological, not logical, and it attains function and power from deep personal meanings gained through living with others, not from external rules and restrictions. As Sylvia Ashton Warner masterfully states,

> What a dangerous activity ... teaching is. All this plastering on of foreign stuff. Why plaster on at all when there's so much inside already? So much locked in? If only I could get it out and use it as working material. And not draw it out either. If I had a light enough touch it would just come out under its own volcanic power.[59]

Teachers Must Provide Freedom for Exploration

Children are constantly engaged in searching for truth through exploring, manipulating, testing, tasting, feeling—even groping. They learn from mistakes. Even the most creative adults make false starts and test many wrong assumptions for each really productive idea. The fact that children learn to speak about as well as the adults in their lives before

59. Sylvia Ashton Warner, *Spinster* (New York: Simon and Schuster, 1958).

encountering the more formal language teaching of the school tells us that this inborn searching and trying on for size has been remarkably effective. Recent studies by Torrance suggest that mental abilities involved in creative thinking and learning are different than those used in learning by authority.[60] In addition, creative thinking and learning depend upon opportunity for active exploration. Fewer than 10 percent of a group of elementary language arts teachers selected a creative thinking category as the most important type of mental operation. Certainly we cannot say that a child is growing toward mental self-fulfillment ". . . if the abilities involved in learning and thinking creatively remain undeveloped or are paralyzed by excessive prohibitions."[61]

Consider a group of first grade children on their first day of using rhythm band instruments.

> On this occasion most teachers are driven to distraction. Wanting to talk about the instruments and how they work, they usually fail to hold the attention of the children. Not so, the teacher of this first grade class. She has learned that the children must first be permitted to encounter their instruments creatively. They want to feel them, smell them, look at them, tap them, and sense them in every way possible. They must find out at once what the instruments will do. After this they are *ready* to learn by authority.[62]

Teachers Must Provide Time for Solitary Thought

In addition to the requirement of exploratory freedom for the release of creativity and the growth of language is the need for solitary thought. Jimmy, two years behind (achievement tests), went to fifth grade. Quiet but not particularly studious, Jimmy had never seemed to fit into the usual scheme of classroom activity. Here, in fifth grade, the teacher introduced group planning. One morning during the regular planning of ongoing activities, Jimmy stated that he needed to use a period of time for *thinking.* The teacher had never heard such a request. What would the principal *think* if he came into the room and found a child *thinking?* (Robert Frost was once dropped from school for such activity!) Jimmy was allowed to have a quiet thinking period regularly that school year. His reflection led to searching through reference materials for information on his previously unrevealed interest—science.

60. E. Paul Torrance, *Education and the Creative Potential* (Minneapolis: The University of Minnesota Press, 1963).
61. Torrance, *op. cit.,* p. 46.
62. *Ibid.,* p. 48.

He built models; his parents gave him space in the basement for a laboratory; his peers gained a new respect for him. At the end of the school year he scored two to four years above his grade level (standardized tests). Three years later, Jimmy continued his search for truth. Oh yes, he regularly makes the honor roll.

Teachers Must Be Good Models

Children learn the language pattern of their geographical region, their community, their family; and these are relatively permanent. But the everyday model set by teachers and other adults can help children correct common errors in language usage. As they hear, see and read good language, changes are made in their own. Some children commonly practice better language than their teachers and demand correctness in both speech and written communication. Bobby, eleven years old, was selected to edit the room newsletter. He carefully reviewed each article and corrected grammatical errors. The material was then typed by the teacher (first year). When completed and handed to the class to take home, Bobby located and drew big circles around twenty-four spelling (typographical) errors. He was so distraught that he refused to have a copy in his possession. For there on page one was the statement—Proofreader, Bobby Jones. Needless to say this was a grievous teaching error.

Teachers Must Provide Many Materials

The provision of basal textbooks is merely a beginning. To accommodate the wide range of abilities within any classroom the teacher makes available numerous books and other printed materials on many levels of difficulty. Many manipulative materials are made available for the child's use. The real object leaves a more vivid mental impression than any amount of reading, hearing about, or looking at pictures. Real objects are also useful for developing vocabulary and concepts of size, color, shape, texture, etc. Accurate oral or written description of objects depends upon opportunity to discover their properties just as accurate description of events depends upon direct involvement in them. One second grade teacher had a workbench, complete with vise, hammer, saws, nails, screws, and scrap lumber available for children's use. The ability to use these tools and the possession of words to describe them are not innate—they have to be learned. Many basic concepts which must be developed before more complex learning and thinking is possible are rooted within such simple manipulative activities as these.

Teachers Must Provide Environments Which Foster Security

The absence of emotional security affects langauge development and learning in general. Lack of security leads to misdirection of drives normally used for desirable learning. The child, of course, continues to learn but these are "failure" learnings, not "success" learnings. His extreme efforts to win approval and security often result in rejection by peers and adults and reinforce the pattern of failure. Thus as the personality is shaped, potentially constructive energy becomes destructive energy. The "creative" writing of Jay reveals the direction of thought and energy commonly resulting from broken homes and lack of parental affection.

THE BEST FRIEND
By Jay Smith

Once I knew a friend. A kind considerate friend and the best one I had. He was a sixth grader and I was a fifth grader. He was the best friend I had.

And later:

THE SECOND BEST FRIEND
By Jay Smith

When I was in the fifth grade I had a friend and a kind one too. She encouraged me and I won't forget her . . .

Fortunately, Jay's second best friend was an understanding teacher who was able to "substitute" for parents and help him gain acceptance with the peer group.

Teachers Must Provide for Stimulating Inquiry

Two prevalent practices which stifle inquiry are emphasis on facts emphasis on competition. Although there are few right answers, only better or worse ones, schools actively seek to instill in children ability to recall quantities of facts upon demand. Studies of the questions teachers ask reveal that over 90 percent require factual answers. This behavior tells the child that what he *thinks* is less important than what other people tell him: that he doesn't have to think to be successful as long as he has a good memory. When asked what she considered the most significant about John Glenn's orbital flight, one wise teacher replied, "The fact that it was associated with a date. Children for decades will have another 1492 to remember."

Teachers should ask questions that require thinking responses and should encourage and respect the questions children ask. Unusual questions and answers lead to deeper thinking. Deeper thinking requires greater communicative ability and greater communicative ability means language growth. All this is learned through inquiry and inquiry cannot function in a restrictive classroom.

Inquiry functions best in a cooperative classroom which values freedom and demands responsibility. It functions least in a highly competitive classroom which values success at the expense of those who fail. Combs[63] derives our false beliefs about competition:

> Myth: We live in a competitive society.
> Fact: We live in the most cooperative, interdependent society the world has ever known.
> Myth: Competition is a powerful motivating force.
> Fact: Only those compete who think they have a chance of winning. The rest ignore the competition.
> Myth: Competition is a useful device for controlling and improving quality.
> Fact: Competition is inefficient and outmoded as a means for quality production.

It comes as quite a surprise, indeed, for Americans who see people in other cultures of the world playing the game of baseball with all the energy and zest of a major league team but refusing to keep score! Some of the children in American classrooms don't keep score but they are the losers and they don't participate in the game. As a result we have more dropouts in school than out—losers, uncommitted to the school's purposes.

Teachers Must Be Diagnosticians

If teachers could accurately diagnose the learning difficulties of children and provide appropriate remediation there would be no "slow" learners. But a high degree of skill is involved in accurately diagnosing the most common learning deficiencies and even greater skill is needed to equate cause and correction. Causes of learning deficiencies are usu-

---

63. Arthur W. Combs, "The Myth of Competition," *Childhood Education* 33 (February, 1957): 364-69.

ally multiple and differ from child to child. Often underlying causes are evident only to trained specialists, particularly organic deficiencies. Correction also may require the services of specialists. But within the domain of the classroom many common deficiencies can be discovered and corrected by alert teachers.

In fourth grade, Sue was unable to read or write beyond a very elementary level. Her paintings however, revealed great insight and appreciation for beauty. An alert teacher discovered through a simple eye test that her vision was faulty (she had missed school when regular eye exminations were given). Seven months later she was reading at grade level with corresponding improvement in writing. Now she could match the beauty of her artistic creations with that of her poetry:

THE FLOWERS

The flowers are the prettiest thing,
I think.
To see in the Spring,
A most beautiful thing.
Their petals quiver when a breeze
    passes by.
And birds sing their happy song that
    winter has gone by.

In the morning all covered with dew,
The flowers sing a beautiful tune.
Of the sky, and the sea, and of the
    beautiful day.

Diagnosis refers not only to deficiencies but also to the regular procedure whereby teachers determine readiness levels for instruction. Instruction should naturally follow diagnosis. Teaching prior to assessment of needs is analogous to the medical doctor proceeding to operate without examining the patient. An individualized classroom program under conditions of *true* nongradedness is most conducive to success in diagnostic teaching.

Teachers Must Provide Intensive Periods of Language Instruction for Disadvantaged Children

The research and experimentation of compensatory language programs of the late 1960's support the need for providing short periods of intensive language instruction as a part of the total program. Frost and Rowland[64] analyzed many of the major experimental compensatory

---

64. Joe L. Frost and G. Thomas Rowland, *Compensatory Programming: The Acid Test of American Education,* (Dubuque, Iowa: Wm. C. Brown Company Publishers, 1971).

programs and they reviewed the analyses of others to conclude that "verbal bombardment" and "social contact" approaches are not as effective as structured approaches involving intensive adult-child communication using specific objectives, questioning and modeling techniques for teaching-learning "standard English."

Teachers Must Themselves Seek Self-Fulfillment

Teachers cannot long conceal their true beliefs from children. They show in day-by-day decisions. Even the infant knows whether adults are doing things *for* him or *to* him and this will have its effects. The teacher's behavior reveals his values and beliefs about training children. If teachers are to maximize the creative potential of children they must be actively seeking growth for self. Creative tendencies of teachers are revealed through the provisions of a classroom atmosphere in which creative language and thought may flourish in children.

Conclusion

The writer began by drawing attention to the importance of language; stated early that language is complex; proceeded to describe interrelated factors; concluded by describing the roles of effective teachers.

The underlying current throughout emphasized the need for a more dynamic view of language development: . . . The degree of knowing about a word and the related meanings that word holds for a child is very personal, not to be fully understood or completely shared by another . . . In order to understand the child's pattern of language growth we must know his personality structure . . . It is understanding the *meaning* of principles that makes them useful . . . The *quality* of the child's social relationships will in large measure determine the level of language power he will attain . . . Language is psychological, and it attains function and power from deep personal meanings gained through living with others, not from external rules and restrictions.

We are uncertain about what facts will be required of tomorrow's adult, so we are insecure about what to teach today's child. But we can be confident that diversity of skill in language and thought will serve the child well in whatever condition of living he may find himself. Consequently, teachers may well examine their hierarchy of beliefs about teaching—activity or passivity? inquiry or rote? lives or lessons? This writer was speaking to teachers and teachers-to-be when she said:

The thread which interlaces all of the richness of growth, which becomes one in today and tomorrow, is that of inner personal growth . . . Surely there is time for this kind of looking toward tomorrow. There is always *some* time; never *enough* when life is full. Perhaps when we see tomorrow look at us from little children's eyes we will think, "how carefully we'd teach if we were wise!"[65]

EXTENDING YOUR LEARNING

1. Listen to the speech of two three-year-olds, two six-year-olds. What differences in speech did you notice between the individuals? between the two couples?
2. Observe an elementary class. On the basis of speech try to select a child whom you think may be a slow learner or a fast learner. Select a child who may have emotional problems—fearful, insecure, etc. Note behavior other than speech that influenced your selection. Discuss your observations with the child's teacher. How do your observations differ? Why do they differ?
3. If possible, make a case study of the language development of one child (you may examine existing case studies). How does the evidence presented compare with ideas previously held?
4. Compare two or more case studies. What are the implications of your findings to language teaching?
5. Observe a class of slow learners. Compare the quantity and quality of language with that of a "typical" class; with a gifted class. Note the incidence of creative activity (including verbal response) in each group. Study the cumulative records—health, tests, teacher observations—of several children.
6. During observations note the extent and kind of intellectual stimulation and the general learning atmosphere (facilitative or restrictive) in each classroom. Does the teacher emphasize creativity or conformity? How does she communicate with the children? What effects do various ways of teacher communication have on the behavior of children? How does the teacher provide for the development of language power? Is this done subtly or overtly?

BIBLIOGRAPHY

American Institutes for Research, *A Study of Selected Exemplary Programs for the Education of Disadvantaged Children,* (Palo Alto: September, 1968).

Beck, Harriet K. "Relationship of Emotional Factors in Early Childhood to Subsequent Growth and to Achievement in Reading." Unpublished Doctoral Dissertation. University of Michigan, 1951.

Bernstein, Basil. "Language and Social Class." *British Journal of Sociology.* 21:159-174, 1958.

Carroll, John B. "Language Acquisition, Bilingualism, and Language Change." *Encyclopedia of Educational Research.* New York: The Macmillan Co., 1960.

Combs, Arthur W., "A Perceptual View of the Adequate Personality." In: *Perceiving, Behaving, Becoming.* Washington: Association for Supervision and Curriculum Development, 1962.

Combs, Arthur W. "The Myth of Competition." *Childhood Education. 33*:364-69, February, 1957.

---

65. Lena Rexinger, "How Carefully We'd Teach If We Were Wise," *Childhood Education* 35 (May, 1959): 391-393.

Frost, Joe L. and Glenn R. Hawkes. *The Disadvantaged Child*. Boston: Houghton Mifflin, 1966.

Frost, Joe L. and G. Thomas Rowland. *Compensatory Programming: The Acid Test of American Education*. Dubuque, Iowa: Wm. C. Brown Company Publishers, 1971.

Gardner, Bruce D. *Development in Early Childhood*. New York: Harper and Row, 1964.

Goldfarb, W. "The Effects of Early Institutional Care on Adolescent Personality." *Journal of Experimental Education*. 12:106-129, 1953.

Hawkes, Glenn R. and Damaris Pease. *Behavior and Development from 5 to 12*. New York: Harper, 1962.

Hildreth, Gertrude. "Interrelationships Between Written Expression and the Other Language Arts." In *Interrelationships Among the Language Arts*. Research Bulletin of the National Conference on Research in English. 4-12, 1954.

Hildreth, Gertrude. "Linguistic Factors in Early Reading." *The Reading Teacher*. 18:172-178, December, 1964.

Hughes, Vergil H. "A Study of the Relationships Among Selected Language Abilities." *Journal of Educational Research*. 47:97-105, October, 1953.

Hunt, J. McV. *Intelligence and Experience*. New York: Ronald, 1961.

Hunt, J. McV. "How Children Develop Intellectually." *Children*. 11:83-91, May, 1964.

Jensen, Arthur R. "How Much Can We Boost IQ and Scholastic Achievement?" *Harvard Educational Review* 39: 1-123.

Lenneberg, Eric II. "On Explaining Language." *Science* 164 (May, 1969).

McCarthy, Dorothea. "Language Development." *Child Development Monographs*. 25: 1960.

McCarthy, Dorothea. "Language Development in Children." In L. Carmichael (ed.) *Manual of Child Psychology*. 2nd ed. New York: Wiley, 1954.

McCarthy, Dorothea. "Research in Language Development: Retrospect and Prospect." *Child Development Monographs*. 24: 1959.

Mackintosh, Helen K. (ed.) *Children and Oral Language*. A joint publication of ACEI, ASCD, IRA, and NCTE. 1964.

Melzack, Ronald and William R. Thompson. "Effects of Early Experience on Social Behavior." *Canadian Journal of Psychology*. 10:82-90, 1956.

Nice, M.M. "Length of Sentences as a Criterion of a Child's Progress in Speech." *Journal of Educational Psychology*. 16:370-379, 1925.

Olson, Willard C. *Child Development*. Boston: D.C. Heath, 1959.

Piaget, Jean. *The Language and Thought of the Child*. New York: Harcourt Brace, 1926.

Piaget, J. *The Origins of Intelligence in Children*. (Margaret Cook, trans.) New York: International Universities Press, 1952. (Originally published 1936).

Rexinger, Lena. "How Carefully We'd Teach If We Were Wise." *Childhood Education*. 35:391-393, May, 1959.

Shibles, Burleigh H. "How Many Words Does a First-Grade Child Know" *Elementary English*. 41:42-47, January, 1959.

Skeels, Harold M. "Effects of Adoption on Children From Institutions." *Children*. 12:33-34, January-February, 1965.

Smith, M.E. "An Investigation of the Development of the Sentence and the Extent of Vocabulary in Young Children." University of Iowa, Stud. Child Welfare, 3:1926.

Smith, Mary K. "Measurement of the Size of General English Vocabulary through the Elementary Grades and High School." *Genetic Psychology Monographs. 24*:311-345, 1941.

Southwest Educational Development Laboratory. *Annual Evaluation Report.* (1968-1969, San Antonio Urban Educational Development Center: Austin, Texas, 1970).

Strickland, Ruth G. *The Language of Elementary School Children: Its Relationship to the Language of Reading Textbooks and the Quality of Reading of Selected Children.* Bloomington: Indiana University, School of Education. *38:* 1962.

Thompson, W.R. and W. Heron. "The Effects of Restricting Early Experience on the Problem-Solving Capacity of Dogs." *Canadian Journal of Psychology. 8*:17-31, 1954.

Torrance, E. Paul. *Education and the Creative Potential.* Minneapolis: The University of Minnesota Press, 1963.

Travis, L.E. (Ed.) *Handbook of Speech Pathology.* New York: Appleton-Century-Crofts, 1957.

Warner, Sylvia Ashton. *Spinster.* New York: Simon and Schuster, 1958.

Watts, A.F. *The Language and Mental Development of Children.* New York: D.C. Heath, 1948.

Wood, Nancy E. "Language Disorders in Children." *Child Development Monographs 25:* 1960.

Young, F.M. "An Analysis of Certain Variables in a Developmental Study of Language." *Genetic Psychology Monographs. 23*:3-141, 1941.

Focus

Frost has noted that the school has definite responsibilities for both building upon the linguistic *strengths* of a pupil and providing compensatory programs where *weaknesses* are observed. The school *can* and *should* become an active agent, facilitating language growth and development.

In this chapter, Helen Heffernan details what types of programs, and what content, will accomplish the general objective of guiding a child toward more effective use of his language.

Miss Heffernan believes very strongly in the importance of an integrated approach to learning. Her ideas are unusually stimulating and provocative in this era of specialists, team teaching and the questions currently being raised about the validity of the self-contained classroom concept. It cannot be denied that responsibility for guiding children's growth and development in language must not be the responsibility of the "English" or "Language Arts" teacher alone. It very well may be that while something is gained, in a cognitive sense, by assigning primary responsibility for the curriculum in English to one member of a team who possesses special competence in this field, something may be lost, in that children may come to believe that knowledge can be compartmentalized, sectioned, and divided. The author of this chapter has worked with teachers and with children for many years. She has not arrived at her philosophical position without much thought, and a great deal of practical experience.

The sample daily schedules the author includes are the outgrowth of this belief in an integrated approach to teaching and learning. They also provide evidence of her belief in the ability of teachers and children to accept responsibility for developing a sound and effective teaching-learning environment in the classroom. No "teacher proof" materials (or curricula) here!

Reading is a complex act; experts do not agree on a definition of the term, much less its limits (Does one *read* the expression on another person's face? Is stopping for a red traffic light, responding to a signal, *reading?*) A decision was made not to include a detailed discussion of reading in this text, since the body of knowledge and literature related to reading appears to be large enough to warrant separate and equal treatment. It was feared that any treatment of reading in a general book of this nature would be superficial. Nevertheless, and without going into great detail, Helen Heffernan does an excellent job of indicating the close relationship of reading to the other Language Arts. Expecting a child to read what he has not experienced, heard, and said, is expecting something which cannot be done easily, if, in fact, it can be done at all.

This chapter reflects the author's sincere belief in the value of each human being, (to be specific, teachers and pupils) and the importance of developing effective communication skills in order that each child may grow toward a richly satisfying life as an adult.

Helen Heffernan

chapter two

language arts programs in elementary schools

Language is man's most distinctive human characteristic. During the centuries of human history, communication has progressed from gestures and monosyllables to a complex system of spoken and written language using sounds and symbols unique to the particular culture in which it developed. Every human society has developed language. Susanne K. Langer describes language as "the most momentous and at the same time the most mysterious product of the human mind."[1] She further defines language "as primarily a vocal actualization of the tendency to see reality symbolically."[2]

Because communication is vital in the life of every person, elementary schools allot a considerable amount of time to instruction in the language arts. Proficiency in listening, speaking, reading and writing contributes to the development of personality. Language is a critical factor in cognitive development. The acquisition of the various skills in the art of communication is essential to the child's progress throughout his entire educational program and to his successful functioning as an adult.

Before the child enters school language behaviors are well established and teachers are challenged to adapt instruction to the type of language facility and fluency the child brings to the tasks of the school.

1. Susanne K. Langer, *Philosophy in a New Key* (Cambridge, Massachusetts: Harvard University Press, 1951), p. 103.
2. *Ibid.*, p. 109.

Early Language Development

The importance of the early language development of infants and young children is clarified by Susanne Langer when she says:

> ... There is *an optimum period* of learning, and this is a stage of mental development in which several impulses and interests happen to coincide: The lalling instinct, the imitative impulse, a natural interest in distinctive sounds, and a great sensitivity to "expressiveness" of any sort.[3]

Langer points out that if language is not developed during infancy and the early years of life (1) by experimentation with "spontaneous phonetic material" and (2) by receiving approval and satisfaction from adults in the environment for producing vocal symbols that represent meaningful words in the language of his culture, language development either fails to take place or is seriously arrested. Constant vocalization according to Langer is "a passing phase in our instinctive life."[4]

In support of her point of view, Langer cites the cases of lost or deserted children who incited the maternal instinct of animals, were reared by them, and thus were separated from human speech. Among others she cites the case of Kamala, reported originally by Arnold Gesell.[5] Kamala, the "wolf-girl" was found in Midnapur, India, in 1920. After six years in human surroundings, she had learned only forty words and never learned to use sentences of more than two or three words. Significantly, she never spoke unless spoken to. Langer concludes that

> The impulse to chatter had been outgrown without being exploited for the acquisition of language.[6]

Children who come from socially and economically impoverished environments are frequently two or more years retarded in language development. Such children are immeasurably handicapped in meeting the traditional learning tasks of the school and particularly that important segment of the educational program involving verbal symbolization.

Jerome Kagan agrees that

> The most dramatic differences between lower- and middle-class children of preschool or school age involve language skills.[7]

---

3. *Ibid.,* p. 109.

4. *Ibid.,* pp. 121-122.

5. Arnold Gesell, "The Biography of a Wolf Child," *Harper's Magazine* (January, 1941).

6. Langer, *op. cit.,* pp. 121-122.

7. Jerome Kagan, "The Child: His Struggle for Indentity," Part 5 in a symposium on the Child, *Saturday Review* (December 7, 1968), p. 82.

He takes exception, however, to the belief that this results from lower-class parents talking less frequently to their children. He maintains that the deprivation is not so much an absence of vocalization as a lack of *distinctive vocalization.*

The lower-class child may actually be surrounded by an excessive amount of sound with the television going, other children playing and talking close at hand, and loud sounds from nearby streets. The mother may approach the child from time-to-time and actually speak to the child as often as the middle-class mother would speak to her child. The lower-class child does not attend because of the background noise and does not respond as he would if he were able to separate the distinctive vocalization from his noisy and confused environment. The question of language retardation then, according to Kagan, may well be influenced by the degree of distinctiveness of the vocalization and the presence or absence of background distraction.

Planned intervention on the part of appropriate societal institutions to improve the home environment and child rearing practices and to provide nursery schools, kindergartens and day-care centers in which young children can hear and are encouraged to use speech no doubt promises some amelioration of this handicap. Participation in a wide variety of rich, developmental activities, unrestricted opportunity to talk and play with other children, the sympathetic attention of understanding adults who have time to listen are promising forms that intervention may take to lessen this language handicap which is too frequently interpreted as limited intellectual endowment rather than deprivation of essential conditions for conceptual and language development.

The poor school progress of economically disadvantaged children, as Kagan points out

> . . . is probably the result of many factors including low income, residence in a slum neighborhood, an unstable family organization, absence of a father, a peer group that does not value school success and, in some cases, inadequate nutrition of the individual child.[8]

In working with children from deprived environments, teachers must be watchful about developing a fixed idea about the children's inability to learn. Such an idea on the part of the teacher becomes a "self-fulfilling prophecy" for many a child.[9]

---

8. *Ibid.,* p. 88.

9. See also Rodger Hurley, *Poverty and Mental Retardation: A Causal Relationship* (New York: Random House, 1970); Robert Rosenthal and Lenore Jacobson, *Pygmalion in the Classroom* (New York: Holt, Rinehart and Winston, Inc., 1968).

Teachers must never forget what Langer has stated so well

Language though normally learned in infancy without any compulsion or formal training is none the less a product of sheer learning an art handed down from generation to generation.[10]

No one disputes the necessity for satisfying the dependency needs of the young child. Physical survival depends on such nurturance. If these needs are not met, the child's development terminates. It is equally important for parents to understand that the baby's babbling and the mother's and father's happy response to his successful effort to imitate words constitute the foundation of his language and to a considerable degree his later success in life. Children whose early language development has had the joyous guidance of parents who were delighted at their baby's effort, enter school with excellent vocabularies, with most of the patterns of language and with readiness for further language development firmly established. Parents, the child's first teachers, thus play paramount roles in establishing the child's ability to cope with early school demands.

This is not to say that the parents' responsibility for the child's language development ends with his entrance into school. Parents who take ample opportunity to talk with their children on subjects of mutual interest contribute steadily to their expanding interest in their world and in the language they need to express their ideas and feelings. Children learn to talk and listen by talking and listening and the more experience they have the greater will be their facility.

At a parent teacher meeting where this topic was under discussion, a mother of a family of four said:

I was brought up in a home where my father and mother didn't know about baby-sitters; my mother saw her role as taking care of her children and when I began my family, I naturally followed her example. Wherever I went, I took my children with me. We reduced much of the family living to routine so we had more time for the things that were important.

I let the children help with the cooking; when we made rolls all five of us work at it, even the youngest one. I think many parents are actually afraid of their children, but we do everything with them and have really come to know, appreciate and work with the uniqueness of each child.

We watch programs on TV together and decide which ones are valuable and which are a waste of our precious time. My husband and I watch carefully for announcements to see that we do not miss any important special programs but we rule out firmly in family council the ones we consider of less value.

10. Langer, *op. cit.*, p. 108.

We try to have the children meet, if possible, or at least see face-to-face important people who come to our town. My husband took time off from work recently so the boys could meet a famous baseball player who was speaking to a local service club.

While the children were still babies in arms, we read stories and recited poetry to them every day.

We had a student from Ethiopia as a guest in our home during her last two years in high school. Our children are as eager about her letters from college as they would be if she were an older sister.

This parent reflected a pattern of family life of inestimable value in helping young children to grow in power to live successfully in a social group held together by communication.

Interrelationships Among the Language Arts

The language arts include listening, speaking, reading and written language comprising handwriting and spelling, all of which involve the use of words. In listening and speaking, ideas are received through words. In reading, writing and spelling ideas are expressed and communicated through words. The ways in which ideas are received and expressed are interrelated. Listening and reading stimulate speaking and writing. Speaking and writing encourage listening and reading. All of the language arts are inextricably interdependent and interrelated.

Listening

Listening is basic to language development. The young child listens to his own babbling and responds joyously as his phonetic experimentation wins smiles of approval from his parents. He listens to the words his parents repeat for him again and again and imitates the use the adult makes of tongue, lips and teeth in producing sounds. His gratification in his success is spontaneous and extravagant. Stimulated by his success, his sounds become more accurate, he combines several words, he uses short sentences and then longer sentences. As he moves into an expanding environment his need for communication increases until there are few minutes in his waking day when he is not experimenting with speech.

Young children who have been read to and have followed with an adult the pictures and even the symbols on the printed page soon note any omission designed by the adult to shorten the story-reading period. Children who have enjoyed these reading sessions with a loved parent or friend have less difficulty in learning to read than those who have not had such listening experiences. Listening to stories or poems read or told fills an important segment of the educational program in nursery school and kindergarten and should continue through the entire elementary school.

The reading vocabulary of children is much smaller than their understanding vocabulary. Constant visions of literary treats ahead motivate children's efforts to learn when teachers continually enhance their experience with well-interpreted material which the child can understand and enjoy when read to him but which he may be unable to read for himself.

The child must comprehend ideas in the spoken language if he is to recognize them in reading symbols. He can read only what he already knows. A government-sponsored motion picture: *Children Without*, produced by the Division of Press, Radio and TV Relations, National Education Association, shows a group of children puzzling over a word. When the difficulty was resolved, one boy said, "Oh, that's how 'sompin' looks in print." No child can read correctly a word he does not understand or which he has not heard spoken correctly.

As the child hears words spoken in context, his stock of word meanings increases. Repeated hearing of an expression that occurs in reading helps the child to read it. The teacher who works on different words the child will later encounter in reading helps him to hear the word correctly and to understand its meaning.

Throughout the child's school experience and in his out-of-school life as a child and as an adult it is important that he be a good listener. Listening implies more than hearing. Listening involves comprehending, interpreting and evaluating. Listening is, of course, a social courtesy to the speaker but its purpose is much broader. Listening critically to what is heard, evaluating the facts, determining the speaker's purpose, and comparing what is said with information from other sources are all a part of intelligent listening. The child can be helped to learn that all communication with other people depends as much on listening as on speaking.

Speaking

One of the basic drives to learning is the desire to share and communicate. Man is gregarious. Since from 75 to 90 percent of communication is oral, it is of the utmost importance that children have ample opportunity for speaking and considerable instruction in the more formal aspects of speaking such as sharing experiences, story telling, conversing, discussing, making reports, making introductions, interviewing, using the telephone, and participating in meetings. Listening to others and telling about his experience helps the child develop a conceptual background essential to learning to read. Competence in telling about the episodes in his experiences in correct sequence is one evidence of a child's readiness to read.

Children read with greater ease what they have experienced and talked about. The primary teacher frequently records what the children have said following a study trip to the supermarket, the zoo, the harbor, the dairy farm. Children have no difficulty reading these "experience stories" through which they have lived at firsthand and which contain the actual words with which they have expressed their ideas. Teachers skillful in the experience or language approach to the teaching of reading anticipate words and phrases the children will encounter later in preprimers and primers and thus pave the way to success when children begin reading in a book.[11]

What a child has experienced and enjoys talking about may actually open the door to reading. Ten-year-old Harry, who had experienced much difficulty in learning to read, became the proud possessor of a pair of carrier pigeons. Interest led to Harry's interviewing more mature pigeon fanciers who in turn shared with Harry the books and magazines published for people with this particular hobby. Motivation for reading was established. Harry's need to learn more about pigeons transformed his negative attitude toward reading and produced the eager motivation essential to mastery.

As reading instruction becomes more highly individualized children give oral reports on what they have read, thus revealing to the teacher their level of comprehension as well as their facility in oral language.

Discussion of books, recording brief book reports on the tape recorder or simple pupil-directed dramatization of a story or a dramatic episode from a book several children have read show the close connection between reading and speaking and also foster interest in more extended reading.

Oral reading is important throughout the elementary school because it reveals the individual child's need for teacher help. The child's

---

11. Dorris May Lee and Roach Van Allen, *Learning to Read Through Experience,* 2nd edition (New York: Appleton-Century-Crofts, 1963).

chances for success in school and in life will be greatly enhanced if he pronounces words clearly and correctly and speaks with good voice quality and normal pitch. Listening to the child read or speak gives the teacher the clues she needs to help him achieve better speech.

Reading

Reading, as the skill through which children pursue much of their education, is closely related to all the language arts.

Reading expands the child's vocabulary and gives him new words to enrich his speaking and writing.

It is difficult to overestimate the importance of reading, or the pleasure it can bring to children.

Reading provides the child with models of sentence structure and grammatical form which help establish his standards for good language expression in speaking and writing. Oral reading provides him with practice in using these sentences and grammatical forms correctly so that they become habitual.

Reading enriches the child's reservoir of ideas upon which he can draw for conversation, letters or written reports. Stories may be reorganized into scenes and scripts for puppet shows, informal dramatization or more formal plays.

Literary reading may stimulate in the child an increasingly sensitive perception of his world and thus lead to various forms of creative expression including original written composition.

Written Language

Written language activities are facilitated by the child's fluency in speech. If some person skilled in handwriting will serve as his amanuensis, he can actually compose poems, stories and letters before he can read. Later his reading ability will contribute to his written language ability, but his own original composition uninfluenced by primer models has a quality of uniqueness.

Writing helps to develop the child's ability to recognize and use words and sentences. Writing necessitates close attention to the characteristics of letters and words and thus contributes to learning handwriting and spelling and creates willingness to learn them. Writing reinforces the child's vocabulary and frequently requires additions to his vocabulary in order to express his ideas.

Phonetic skills useful in speaking and reading also are useful to the child in writing a word. The word analysis the child enploys in learning to spell also has a transfer value to reading.

Work in vocabulary development, word meanings, word analysis and the use of the dictionary aid the child in reading as well as in expressing himself in written form.

Reports are frequently written on material read. Material composed by children and recorded by them or their teacher often is used as simple reading material in recording progress made in science or social studies.

Language Arts Inseparable

The various language arts are truly inseparable. One component cannot be thought of alone. The *word* is the common denominator in

Some children will use language more fluently and with more pleasure if puppets are used effectively in the language arts program.

listening, speaking, reading and written language. First the child hears and then begins to understand the speech of others. As these experiences are repeated and extended, he babbles and begins to imitate the sounds he hears. Finally, he differentiates his speech sounds and develops the language of expression. As his comprehension and expression develop, he learns the relationship between real experiences and the symbols of oral and written language. Later he encounters systematically arranged letters and words, associates them with experiences, and thus learns to read.

In this developmental continuum, his teacher may encourage him to compose or actually write his own stories[12] *before* he uses a preprimer or primer. The reading of what others have written follows extensive experimentation with his own written language.

In and out of school, the child meets situations requiring the use of the language arts. The more vital and stimulating these situations the more progress he will make toward mastery. We say "toward mastery" advisedly because actual mastery is probably never fully attained by anyone in any language or any component of the language arts. As long as a person lives, he can improve his powers of concentrated listening, the effectiveness and quality of his speech, and his competence in oral and written expression.

The challenge to the elementary school teacher is to provide experiences which will release children to express themselves orally in conversation, discussion, dramatic play and dramatization. Out of the richness and vitality of experience provided by the total program and by conscious direction of attention to the beauty and power of good speech and writing, children can acquire competence in effective communication while developing uniqueness and spontaneity of expression.

Language Arts and Other Curricular Areas

Since language is the means by which ideas are shared, it is basic to all living and learning. It is impossible to conceive of a society in which people work and live together without the facilitating medium of communication. It is equally impossible to think of any activity in the classroom that does not require and also afford opportunity to practice the arts of communication. The language arts have no intrinsic content. Language is used in talking or writing about man's relationship to man, man's relationship to his physical environment and the multitude of systems and institutions—domestic, economic, political, social, educational, religious, vocational, aesthetic—that man has devised to control and promote these relationships.

Language and thinking have a close relationship. In the schools of a democracy, the first concern of the teacher is to help children to learn to think. Teachers guide the learning experiences so children will find themselves in problem-centered situations with needs, desires, and questions which stimulate them to think. To solve problems, children must

---

12. *Ibid.*

be able to recognize them and to state them clearly; they must be able to gather and summarize pertinent information about their problem, weigh the significance of their facts and draw tentative conclusions. They must be able to test conclusions tentatively accepted and finally act on the basis of their best thinking.

Whether thinking can exist without language is doubtful. Evidence indicates that thinking is done in words. At least it is certain that to share an act of thought it is necessary to clothe the ideas in precise words which convey meaning to the listener. Many variations are told of the story of the little girl who was admonished to think before she spoke. "But," she protested, "how can I tell what I think until I hear what I say?" The idea contained in the story is essentially sound; words do help clarify thought.

Language Arts in the Social Studies

No richer opportunity for language development can be found in the school curriculum than that afforded by a dynamic social studies program.

Many descriptive curriculum units reveal the pathway followed by children exploring a culture, a significant era in history, or the development of an industry.

Courses of study usually recommend *The Westward Movement of the United States* for intensive study in the fifth grade.[13] This is a particularly desirable placement for the great American epic. Boys and girls of ten and eleven crave adventure. They can identify with the simple life of the settlers of Kentucky, the pioneers who opened up the territory west to the Mississippi, and the covered wagon trains crossing the plains to the Pacific. This is their story, their great tradition! They want to get inside the experience and become one with it.

What does such a study do for the development of children in language arts?

Dramatic Play

Oral language development is stimulated by exciting episodes made to order for dramatic play—life at Boonesborough—hunting in nearby woods, bringing water from streams, tending fields outside the fort,

---

13. See Lavonne A. Hanna, Gladys L. Potter and Neva Hagaman, *Unit Teaching in the Elementary School* revised edition (New York: Holt, Rinehart and Winston, 1963), pp. 468-499.

washing clothes, caring for infants, cooking, eating, guarding the fort. All of the things the pioneers did can be relived in play. Making candles, spinning, going on the long hunt, trapping, Boone's capture by the Shawnees, Indian attack on Boonesborough, Indian life, the Wilderness Road, building a cabin on the Ohio can be exciting episodes in dramatic play. The dramatic incidents are limitless. Day after day the play continues with an accompaniment of the language of the hardy Americans who conquered a continent.

Use of Reference Material

The play is meaningful and fun only if the players have command of accurate facts. What was Boonesborough like? How did the people live? Why did the pioneers move west? Why was Independence an important "jumping off" place? How did the pioneers travel west? What did the pioneers take with them? How were the pioneers organized? How were the wagons organized for the trail? How long did it take to travel along the different routes? What were the hardships encountered? Who were the people the pioneers met in the West? What kind of country did they travel over? What were the main stopping places?

Finding the answers to these questions so the play would be more authentic involved the children in extensive reading of textbooks, library references, charts and graphs. They shared information found in books, they validated questionable information, they increased their vocabulary, they participated in discussion periods to plan and evaluate work to be done or accomplished. In their dramatic play, they wrote letters to folk in Independence. They wrote and told "tall tales." They kept a diary of the trip. They took notes for reports. They recorded locations on maps. They learned folk songs and made up some songs of their own.

Space does not permit recording all the language experiences these children had, much less all the learning experiences. They sewed costumes, made guns, constructed covered wagons, painted, experimented, tried out the industrial arts processes. All these activities went on in the give-and-take of a miniature classroom democracy. Reference materials were rich and numerous. Important as this study was in specific learnings for children, its primary justification is the contribution it makes toward establishing a clear understanding of American ideas and ideals and of present day life in America. This understanding is gradually established through constantly contrasting the simplicity of life in pioneer days with the complexity of life in the modern machine age.

Children learn in Science by observing and listening, then asking significant questions.

Language Arts in Science

In the effective teaching of science, emphasis is on observing, reading, measurement and critical thinking. In science the observer is a "reader" of the phenomena and events of the environment. His reading from books should *follow* and not *precede* experimental verification. The aim of the teacher is to acquaint pupils with the complexities of scientific phenomena. The more the child understands the meaning of these the more easily can he interpret the printed symbols that designate them.

The Los Angeles County Course of Study[14] records a science experience of first grade children triggered by a child's question: "What makes the water in our fish bowl green?" The teacher saw in the child's

14. A Guide to Curriculum Development and Course of Study for Elementary Schools of Los Angeles County (Los Angeles: Office of the County Superintendent of Schools, 1965), pp. 331-333.

question the opportunity to deepen the group's understanding of inter-action and interdependence as she guided them in their search for data to answer the question.

The hypotheses advanced where characteristic of six-year-olds:

One child thought the fish ate plants and that some of the green from the plants squirted out of the fishes' mouths, causing the water to be green. Another child thought the sun melted the plants, while others thought the green water could have been caused by the fish food, the pebbles, rocks, or a little metal frog in the fish bowl or possibly by something in the air.

Imagine the vitality of this oral language period with the teacher creating a classroom climate where it was safe to advance "guesses" and where the teacher "accepted and attached significance to ideas."

The children interviewed people, looked at pictures in books, listened to significant parts read by the teacher. They learned about the "characteristics of fresh water fish, about their habitat, and the fact that algae caused the water to be green. They looked at algae projected by a microprojector." The children discovered that there are many sources of information, pictures, people, books and that wonderful equipment could open new worlds for them.

"But what caused the algae to grow?" was the next question. How could they find out? They could experiment. They decided to:

1. Clean out the fish bowl
2. Add only the fish to the clean water
3. Add one thing at a time to the fish bowl
4. Study the green water and plants
5. Put fish bowl in different places in room.

The amount of planning and discussion that this ambitious project required stretched language capacity to the utmost. Certain children assumed responsibility for tasks related to the project. One girl visited the museum with her parents and saw a display of algae. She painted a picture of the algae which she shared with her classmates.

In the course of their experiences the children arrived at generalizations as follows:

1. Fish live in water
2. Water has oxygen in it
3. Fish get oxygen from water

4. Plants give off oxygen
5. Sunlight affects the growth of plants
6. A great amount of sunlight was involved in making a great amount of algae
7. Rocks provide a place for fish to hide from the sun
8. Snails help keep the fish bowl clear

Science understandings were deepened for these young children; they increased their understanding of interaction and interdependence among living and nonliving things. They grew in using methods of observation, inquiry and experimentation. They incorporated new information into their frameworks. They arrived at sound conclusions based on ability to "read" the phenomena of their environment.

From the point of view of language arts, they discussed a problem of interest to them and planned ways to find out cause and effect for themselves. They acquired new vocabulary. They found it necessary to use some measurements concerning the effect of various lengths of time in the sunlight on the growth of the algae. They found satisfaction in expressing their conclusions in the most precise language they had at their command. Because they were unable to use the skills of reading and writing, they used the scientific methods of observation, inquiry, problem-solving; these are the methods of the scientist although at his level of sophistication he must read what other scientists have discovered and publish his findings.

Language Arts and Mathematics

Mathematics is a special product of man's ingenuity to abstract the property of number from objects and to communicate basic mathematical concepts. Much that has been previously noted about the relation of language arts to science is equally applicable to mathematics.

Today's children are learning to think in terms of basic mathematical concepts through a curriculum which offers continuous opportunities to use concrete models and experiences. Numerals, symbols of operation and relationships, mathematical sentences, graphs, rules have meaning for children when they are learned in a sequence based on gradually broadening and deepening understanding. Children learn by making mathematical discoveries for themselves and developing their own ways of attacking mathematical problems.

Since correctness and precision are characteristics of all effective usage of language, these qualities cannot be applied in higher degree than to the language of mathematics.

Planning the School Schedule

If the time spent in school is to be most productive of learning, the school program must be characterized by careful planning in order to make the most effective use of every day during these important years of a child's school life. The various activities included in the curriculum must be organized and carried out in ways that encourage the highest level of living and learning.

The language arts benefit when children are involved in planning the days activities.

In planning the schedule of activities, a teacher must consider all of the subjects required by law or by the governing authority of the local school district. Since communication between and among educators is fostered by powerful professional associations, by the circulation of many professional books and periodicals, and by nationwide use of the same textbooks, most educational programs bear a strong resemblance to one another. Restrictions usually refer to subjects to be taught and do not extend to how the teacher will organize for instruction in the classroom. No doubt some teachers feel more comfortable with one type of organization while others seem to believe another is more efficient.

Whatever arrangement of the daily program is made, the language arts will be best served if the elementary school day affords:

1. Time for planning and discussion
2. Time to solve problems
3. Time to acquire knowledge and skills
4. Time to enjoy the aesthetic
5. Time to create
6. Time to play, rest, and secure nutrition.

The language arts become an integral part of the entire day regardless of the subject taught or the particular organizational pattern followed.

Time for Planning and Discussion

Children need opportunity to talk over plans for the day, to discuss work that needs to be done and materials needed for doing it, to determine the part each child is to play in planned activities, and to evaluate what has been accomplished in previous work periods.

The teacher uses these periods to keep oral language standards high, to be sure that time is being efficiently used, to develop new interests, to develop new vocabulary and to stimulate higher levels of thinking.

Time to Solve Problems

All life situations are full of questions. Learning to make wise decisions is of supreme value to the individual. Problem-solving is a kind of learning which must begin early in the educative process and continue as a lifelong endeavor. Problem-solving is a daily experience which develops judgment, thoughtfulness and initiative.

A group of eight-year-olds made a study trip to the harbor and saw the fireboat respond to an alarm. When they returned to school many questions were asked about how a fire in the hold of a boat is put out. The problem was clearly stated and written by the teacher on the chalkboard. Several children suggested ways the fire might be put out. These methods were all carefully listed by the teacher for further consideration. Apparently there were differences of opinion, but no evidence was advanced to substantiate any of the children's ideas. The teacher asked: How could we find out? Again a variety of suggestions was offered—another trip to the harbor to interview the captain of the fireboat and a visit to the library to seek information were accepted as feasible suggestions. Then the teacher said that she would perform an experiment which might help them to find the solution. The teacher thus helped the children to find still another way to solve their problems.

A glass beaker became the hold of the boat; an inch length of a burning candle in the bottom of the beaker became the fire in the boat. By pouring a mild acid over baking soda in a retort equipped with rubber cork and tube, the teacher was able to direct a stream of carbon dioxide into the "hold." The experiment was repeated several times by the children with the same result. All the time questioning and thinking went on.

Said one child, "You made a gas in which fire won't burn." Said another, "It takes oxygen for fire to burn. You pushed the oxygen out of the beaker with another gas." For the eight-year-olds this was a sufficient explanation.

The teacher occupies a significant role in problem-solving when guiding and encouraging children to a solution. The opinions offered by the children are all accepted to be tested in various ways—having firsthand experiences, reading authoritative material, interviewing qualified persons, observations, and carrying on experimentation. Children see the importance of clear thinking and clear expression of ideas and are led to extend their knowledge through reading and through discussion with knowledgeable persons.

Time to Acquire Knowledge and Skill

Children learn subject matter in relation to their experiences. Skills must be acquired in reading, oral and written expression including handwriting and spelling. Other skills in the use of numbers, tools, paint, clay, the singing voice must also be acquired.

An effective teacher takes time to give
individual help to children.

Because of the wide range of differences in individual capacities,
these skills are most efficiently acquired individually or in very small
groups where teacher guidance can be largely individual. Rarely do all
the children in a group require instruction in the same specific skill.
Handing out duplicated exercises in language to every child in a class is
time-wasting and merits being called "busy work."

Whatever time is provided for skills should be utilized as a teaching
period for the teacher as well as a work period for the children. When
each child is progressing at his own rate, the teacher has opportunity to
give individual guidance. The teacher wishes to develop the child's initiative and so she encourages him to go ahead with his own tasks in his

own way but helps him when he needs help. The teacher wants to help the child develop a sense of responsibility and so encourages him to accept the obligation of completing his task. The teacher wants to help the child to grow in accuracy and so encourages him to check his work. Finally, the teacher wants to help each child develop judgment and habits of analytical thinking, and so helps him to appraise his work, to see where he needs to improve and to decide whether he is ready for the next step. These activities are at the heart of effective teaching and are best achieved in a face-to-face relationship. The more individual guidance the teacher can provide the more effective will be the results. This is the unanswerable argument for teachable-size classes in the elementary school.

Time to Enjoy the Aesthetic

Children need daily contact with beauty in order to develop the appreciation that comes from frequent and pleasurable experiences. Each day should bring its quota of memorable contacts with art, music, literature and nature. All of these contacts involve the language arts.

The impressions children receive from these experiences stimulate an emotional response which in turn suggests creative expressions. Children will find a variety of individually satisfying ways to express themselves creatively.

Authentic reproductions of paintings, recordings of beautiful poems, stories, music, are available to supplement the teacher's artistic gifts. No environment is so meager that it will not yield rocks, driftwood, shells, flowers or mosses which can be arranged artistically for enjoyment.

Time to Create

If the child's time in school is filled with vital experiences and children are given opportunity for firsthand contact with their environment through study trips, creative expression is most likely to emerge. Learning and creative expression come as children strive to re-create their experiences. Many children will strive to re-create their experiences in patterns of beautiful words; others may choose other media. The teacher sets the stage and protects the child so he can give his own interpretations and express his own unique feelings. A child must feel comfortable in a classroom to be free enough to express his honest self. Every creative artist is highly sensitive to criticism of his product. Most teachers recognize this feeling and strive to help parents and children in the group to know that this is "holy ground" to be treated with under-standing and reverence.

Time for Play, Rest and Nutrition

Childhood is the period of significant physical growth. Human happi-ness and social usefulness depend upon sound bodies. The school must safeguard the child's physical well-being and provide him with a whole-some rhythm of rest and activity.

The school that serves children best permits a maximum of freedom to move about, to use their large muscles, to choose from a variety of strenuous and less strenuous activities.

Children need additional nutrition during the school day for effective school work. You cannot teach hungry children. Sound nutritional practices established in childhood, however, are the basis for important lifelong habits.

The Daily Schedule

Providing time each day for the foregoing activities is more impor-tant than the number of minutes allocated to a given subject or the sequence in which the experiences are ordered. The best daily schedule is probably one made every day by the teacher and the children in terms of the learning needs of the group. In any event, whatever sched-ule is arranged, the teacher should consider it only as a flexible guide to a well-balanced school day.

A teacher of a second grade class found the following daily schedule useful in providing a balanced program for seven-year-old children.

Daily Program for Second-Year Children

8:30—8:45	The children hang up coats, check in library books, talk with the teacher, help in getting room ready for the day's work or play outdoors.
8:45—9:45	Planning period. Opportunity to ask questions, to solve individual problems, to determine individual and group purposes and to focus attention upon new needs as revealed during the play and work periods of the previous day.
	Work period in social studies and science.
	Discussion and evaluation period.

9:45—10:00	Midmorning lunch
10:00—10:50	Aesthetic experiences
10:50—11:00	Recess
11:00—11:30	Music—singing songs, playing with rhythm instruments, listening to music, creating music
11:30—12:05	Supervised lunch period
12:05—12:35	Rest period
12:35—1:35	Development of skills in language arts and numbers
1:35—2:00	Outdoor play
2:00—2:30	Literature
2:30	Dismissal

Although the program seems to show only an hour and a half devoted to the language arts, listening, and speaking, reading and written language permeated all the activities with these young children.

A teacher of a fifth grade finds a comfortable organization in the following schedule.

Daily Program for Fifth Grade Children

9:00	Informal greetings, routine matters, flag salute, current happenings of personal interest which individual children wish to share
9:15	Integrated curriculum unit
10:25	Midmorning lunch
10:40	Health and physical education
11:10	Language arts
12:00	Lunch, rest, playground activities
1:00	Mathematics
1:40	Music
2:00	Rest and recreation
2:10	Reading activities
3:00	Rest and recreation
3:10	Unscheduled time
4:00	Dismissal

This schedule provides for two fifty-minute periods daily devoted to language arts activities per se but again many language arts skills are used in the study of the integrated curriculum unit. Children plan and discuss work, prepare and give individual and committee reports, arrange bulletin boards and the like.

This particular teacher is enthusiastic about the period listed as "unscheduled time." During this period individuals or small groups have an opportunity to pursue their own interests. An abundance of suitable books, pictures, maps, tools and other material must be available for reporting, illustrating and experimenting. The teacher who has a broad background of experience and an inquiring mind will be most successful in guiding the various interests in art, crafts, literature, science, international relations, music, drama, and puppetry that may emerge. Probably the best teaching will be done at such a time when the impetus for learning comes wholly from the children.

The Weekly Program

The teacher must give thought to the scheduling of activities that do not occur daily. These include orchestra and glee club practice, study trips, school newspaper, school council, auditorium periods, gardening activities, safety patrol, library periods, special classes, health examinations. All these can provide valuable learning opportunities if well planned and carried forward at a high level.

Plans for use of facilities or equipment used jointly with other groups will do much to avoid confusion. The full use of the auditorium or multipurpose room, audio-visual equipment and other materials should be carefully scheduled. If children participate as much as possible in planning and in setting up learning situations in which special equipment and materials are used, they will have valuable experience in group discussion and decision making on highly practical problems.

Whatever weekly plans are made, the teacher's regular daily schedule is important and must be sufficiently flexible so no activity suffers unduly because of absence of children for other activities. Any plan must be flexible to be useful; variations from the plan are inevitable but the teacher's watchfulness will prevent any significant activity from suffering because of scheduling.

The Yearly Program

The course of study provides the basic yearly program but usually these publications contain more suggestions than any group of children could encompass during a school year. The teacher who knows the particular group of children is the professional person best qualified to study the recommendations in their entirety and select those most suitable for the needs of the group.

Informal testing of children reveals material they may already know and helps the teacher determine the particular learning experiences requiring emphasis. Efforts to diagnose individual pupil's needs early in the school year will justify the expenditure of the teacher's time in revealing the crucial needs upon which the individual's progress depends.

Planning for Language Arts Instruction

At all levels of the elementary school, the teacher must make provision in the daily, weekly and yearly schedule for developmental experiences in all components of the language arts: listening, speaking, reading and written language. School systems frequently provide courses of study, teachers' guides to language arts instruction or textbooks which determine the grade placement of specific learnings.

In general, the following topics are included and have application at all maturity levels:

Listening

Throughout the child's school years, he should be helped to realize the numerous benefits that come to a good listener. He will be able to learn many interesting things, follow directions accurately, avoid many unpleasant situations and have more fun with his friends if he knows what is going on about him.

As he grows older, listening leads to a genuine interchange of ideas in conversation and discussion. Many opportunities arise to test how well children listen by discussions following newscasts or a talk presented on radio or television.

Speaking

Many teachers distinguish between two types of speaking activities: oral language and creative oral expression.

Oral Language

Functional language is used in sharing experiences, conversing, making introductions, conferring and interviewing, using the telephone, and participating in meetings. Oral language is functional when it is used to communicate information and express opinions. The development of effective practical expression is a continuing need through the school.

Progress will vary with individual children so grade level placement of specific skills is meaningless. In working with the children, the teacher can develop standards for oral language appropriate to the level of maturity of the particular group.

Creative Oral Expression

Oral expression can be creative as a child is free to express his thoughts and feelings in his unique fashion.

Creative language grows out of a child's reaction to his out-of-school experiences and to planned experiences in school. The teacher provides many opportunities for rich, sensory experiences—seeing, hearing, smelling, tasting, feeling—and for observing changes and distinguishing characteristics. Children are encouraged to express experiences, conversation, discussion, dramatic play, dramatization, story telling and reporting. It differs from functional oral language because of the feeling element injected by the speaker. He calls upon his own background of experience to which he has reacted emotionally and expresses himself in patterns of words that share his feelings with the listener. Such spontaneous oral language occurs only in a classroom climate where the child feels safe to be his honest self.

Reading

Learning to read is a major purpose of the primary school child. Reading to learn becomes the purpose of the child in the middle grades. Reading is truly the path to many vicarious experiences. The path can be a rough and thorny one, however, unless the teacher recognizes the readiness, the needs and the capacities of each pupil and adapts instruction and materials to the individual child. Small flexible groups or individualized instruction makes such adaptation feasible. Attempting to teach a large group of children as though they were all alike dooms the teacher to feelings of inadequacy and frustration and his pupils to experiences of failure.

The emphasis should always be on the child rather than on materials to be covered and skills to be learned. It is not important that every child in a grade read the same books or acquire the same skills. What is important is that the child succeed at every step in the process so that every day means growth in power for him regardless of what other children may accomplish.

Many teachers wisely seek the cooperation of others in extending children's reading experience. A study trip to the public library opens new "treasures for the taking" to many children. Children's librarians are experts in fitting "the right book to the right child." Many public libraries provide story hours after school or on days when school is not in session.

One way to evaluate the reading program of a school is by the number of children who have library cards and the extent to which these are used.

The cooperation of parents will be needed in order to take children to the library when distances are too great for children to walk or where other conditions necessitate adult guidance. Parents are greatly interested in children's reading and are eager for suggestions from the teacher or librarian concerning gift books suitable for particular children. Parents' interest in children's reading is so great that Nancy Larrick's guide to children's reading has been a "best seller" and a third edition is now available as a paper back.[15]

Written Language

Written language includes functional written expression, creative written expression, handwriting and spelling.

Functional Written Expression

Reporting, class newspaper, records, letter writing may be classified as forms of functional writing. Their major aim is to present information for a specific purpose. They will be useful at all levels of maturity and will improve as the school provides vital experiences in which they are put to use. As children mature, they learn to keep records of social studies activities, science observations and experiments, meeting of school councils and the like. They learn the art of taking succinct notes for later reference. They learn to outline. Grammar and punctuation become increasingly important to guarantee accuracy and precision. Words continue to be fascinating means of conveying more and more complex ideas.

---

15. Nancy Larrick, *A Parent's Guide to Children's Reading,* 3rd edition (New York: Doubleday & Company and Pocket Books, 1969).

Holidays can provide the motivation and stimulation for children to add to their writing vocabularies words which are already in their speaking and understanding vocabularies.

Creative Written Expression

Schools are striving increasingly to release the creative potential in every form and particularly in written composition. Teachers attempt to maintain a relaxed, flexible supportive classroom atmosphere in which children are encouraged to write. Experiences are provided which offer children something to write about: discussions, conversations, pictures, music, films and filmstrips, study trips connected with social studies or science, listening to stories or poems, sharing original writing with others, producing original plays. Criticism is never negative lest the wells of inspiration be dried up at their source.

Handwriting

No writing is effective unless it conveys ideas to others in a legible form. Individuality in style and form is permissible but not to the point where it interferes with legibility.

Instruction in handwriting usually is given to the entire group of children and followed with individual evaluation and help.

Handwriting is a physical skill that improves with increased muscular and eye-hand coordination and practice. It is a courtesy to write legibly for those who read handwriting, so enough practice must be provided to insure this minimum standard.

In certain cultures, writing is considered a fine art. The royal road to self-realization may be via calligraphy. In our utilitarian culture, the calligrapher is not classified as an artist but many children develop feelings of self-worth because of praise received for the excellence of their handwriting. Most teachers stress correct form, ease of production and legibility of the product as acceptable goals.

Spelling

Writing is not socially acceptable unless words are spelled correctly. In contrast to the casual attitude people take toward handwriting, deviations from standards in spelling are not tolerated.

Awareness of the importance of spelling words correctly grows as children use words in writing and never as a result of learning to spell long lists of unrelated words orally or in written form.

Children usually are encouraged to keep a file or notebook of the words they use most frequently for ready reference. Picture dictionaries are useful with young children and small dictionaries with carefully selected lists of words provide early instruction in the employment of this invaluable tool of the scholar.

The ultimate test of a child's competence in spelling is not his daily grade on a list of spelling words but his correct and facile use of a correct spelling vocabulary in all his written expression.

Summary

The language arts are truly inseparable, and while one may receive more emphasis at one point in the school day than another, it must be recognized that one seldom speaks unless someone listens, and that most writing is meant to be read. Facility in one aspect of language suggests a similar level of ability in others—a child seldom reads or writes better than he speaks. Thus, it appears to be a mistake to compartmentalize the facets of the language arts, to ignore the opportunities for developing several skills during one portion of the school day. Flexibility in scheduling allows the teacher and the children an important degree of freedom as they work and learn together. Language in all its aspects, flourishes in a rich permissive classroom environment and tends to shrivel and diminish under rigid rules and harsh discipline. As teachers work together and as individual teachers plan with groups of children, they will make sure that none of the language skills will be neglected, but they will also be aware of the need for a degree of autonomy, for some "room to breathe," even in today's overcrowded curriulum.

EXTENDING YOUR LEARNING

1. Examine at least three language arts curriculum guides. Be prepared to write an analysis of, or discuss, the following issues:
   a. What is the evidence of articulation from grade to grade? Do goals and objectives appear to be consistent and sequential?
   b. Who wrote the guide? What is the evidence that classroom teachers were, or were not involved in preparing the guide?
   c. The author of this chapter makes a strong plea for an *integrated* or correlated approach to teaching the language arts. Is there evidence of such an "interrelationship" in the guides you've surveyed?
2. Examine two or three language arts textbooks. The following "guide-points" may help to focus your examination and a written or oral analysis of your findings.
   a. Is the emphasis primarily on *written* language (writing letters, reports, etc.) or is there evidence that the linguists have been heard, and oral language (speaking and listening) is given the emphasis it deserves, considering its utility in out-of-school life.
   b. Are the language arts treated as facets of a unitary developmental process— or as separate entities? What is the justification for the separate subjects approach? the "integrated" approach?
   c. Is help provided for the teacher who wants to vary his approach, and to adjust his program to better meet the needs of the children in his class?
3. Construct dioramas, or prepare diagrams, showing a functional yet creative approach to classroom design. Try this, assuming you are teaching in a self-contained classroom and also assume you have team-teaching responsibilities for teaching writing, spelling, reading and "language" (grammar and usage).
4. List the materials (projectors, tape recorder, etc.) which you would consider important for a primary classroom; an intermediate classroom.
5. There is no chapter in this text dealing with the implications of a rich and varied literature program for teaching the language arts. How do *you* think an

effective literature program would enrich and contribute to the goals of a language arts program, as suggested in this chapter, or in one of the guides surveyed?

BIBLIOGRAPHY

Anderson, Paul S. *Language Skills in Elementary Education*. New York: The Macmillan Company, 1964. Chapter I, pp. 1-44.

Applegate, Mauree. *Easy in English*. New York: Harper & Row, Publishers, 1960.

Bond, Guy L. and Eva Bond Wagner. *Teaching the Child to Read* (fourth edition). New York: The Macmillan Company, 1966.

Burns, Paul C., Betty L. Broman, and Alberta L. Lowe Wantling. *The Language Arts in Childhood Education* (second edition). Chicago: Rand McNally and Company, 1971.

Burrows, Alvina T., Doris C. Jackson, and Dorothy C. Saunders. *They All Want to Write*. New York: Holt, Rinehart and Winston, Inc., 1964.

Dallman, Martha. *Teaching the Language Arts in the Elementary School*. Dubuque, Iowa: Wm. C. Brown Company Publishers, 1967.

Dawson, Mildred A. and Frieda A. Dingee, *Children Learn the Language Arts*. Minneapolis: Burgess Publishing Co., 1966.

Fitzgerald, James A. and Patricia G. Fitzgerald. *Teaching Reading and the Language Arts*. Milwaukee: The Bruce Publishing Co., 1965.

Frazier, Alexander (editor). *New Directions in Elementary English*. Champaign, Ill.: National Council of the Teachers of English, 1967.

Goldstein, Miriam B. *The Teaching of Language in Our Schools*. New York: The Macmillan Company, 1966.

Goodmand, Kenneth S. (editor). *The Psycho-linguistic Nature of the Reading Process*. Detroit: Wayne State University Press, 1968. Papers presented at a symposium at Wayne State University, 1965.

Greene, Harry A. and Walter T. Petty. *Developing Language Skills in the Elementary School*. Boston: Allyn and Bacon, Inc., 1967.

Heilman, Arthur W. *Principles and Practices of Teaching Reading*. Columbus, Ohio: Charles E. Merrill Books, Inc., 1967.

Lee, Dorris M. and Roach Van Allen. *Learning to Read Through Experience*. New York: Appleton, Century, Crofts, 1963.

Logan, Lillian M. and Virgil Logan. *A Dynamic Approach to Language Arts*. New York: McGraw-Hill Book Company, Inc., 1967.

May, Frank B. *Teaching Language as Communication to Children*. Columbus, Ohio: Charles E. Merrill Company, 1967.

Moffett, James A. *Student-Centered Language Arts Curriculum, Grade K-6, A Handbook for Teachers*. Boston: Houghton Mifflin Company, 1968.

Mussen, Paul Henry, John Janeway Conger and Jerome Kagan. *Child Development and Personality* (third edition). New York: Harper & Row, Publishers, 1969. Part I-II, pp. 281-604.

Oral Language and Reading. Papers collected from the 1967 spring institutes on the elementary language arts. Edited by James Walden. Champaign, Ill.: National Council of Teachers of English, 1969.

Petty, Walter T. (editor). *Issues and Problems in the Elementary Language Arts*. Boston: Allyn and Bacon, Inc., 1968.

Smith, James A. *Creative Teaching of Language Arts in the Elementary School.* Boston: Allyn and Bacon, Inc., 1967.

Smith, James A. *Creative Teaching of Reading and Literature in the Elementary School.* Boston: Allyn and Bacon, Inc., 1967.

Sowards, G. Wesley and Mary-Margaret Scobey. *The Changing Curriculum and the Elementary Teacher.* Belmont, Calif.: Wadsworth Publishing Company, Inc., 1968. Chapter 6-7, pp. 121-191.

Strang, Ruth. *Diagnostic Teaching of Reading.* New York: McGraw Hill Book Company, 1969.

Strang, Ruth, Constance M. McCullough, and Arthur Traxler. *The Improvement of Reading* (fourth edition). Columbus, Ohio: Charles E. Merrill Books, Inc., 1964.

Strickland, Ruth. *The Language Arts in Elementary School* (third edition). Boston: D.C. Heath & Company, 1969.

Tidyman, Willard and others. *Teaching the Language Arts* (third edition). New York: McGraw-Hill Book Company, 1969.

Tiedt, Iris and Sidney W. Tiedt. *Contemporary English in the Elementary School.* Englewood Cliffs, N.J.: Prentice-Hall, Inc., 1967.

Focus

A quotation from a letter from the author of this chapter to the editor brings into focus rather clearly the reasons for revising a chapter on "Creative Drama."

"The concept of theatre games is new since the first edition and a paragraph or two treats that activity. "Drama" seems to be taking over for "Dramatics" in the terminology so I have gone along with that trend. The bibliography has some 8 new books in it . . . . The Courtney, Hodgson and Richards, Slade and Way are all new and all important works—and all from across the Atlantic." The reader may be surprised to find so much happening—even the name has been changed—in such a few years!

One wonders if the glowing reports concerning the relaxed atmosphere, the smiles, the obvious joy in learning which seem to pervade the British infant schools stem from the same roots which are responsible for several of the most significant references on creative drama coming from Britain. Americans have been told before that they are too self-conscious, and tend to take themselves too seriously! The educational implications of this have been all too obvious since the post World War II drive for improvements in science and mathematics curricula.

Beresford Menagh shares with Helen Heffernan a belief in the value of every human being. He writes that "All human beings are potentially creative." Further, he believes that a *utility* centered life, a *utility* centered school curriculum does not represent the full life, or the curriculum which will help one live a rewarding life. A school program which trains one to do a job and no more is ill equipping its "products" (pupils) to function effectively in today's complex world.

Creative drama, the author writes, can be an invaluable aid in helping children understand first, *themselves,* and, as a result *others.* Creative drama can also be an effective vehicle for helping pupils communicate more effectively with each other. It is more than a tool however, and can do much more than "enrich" the program in literature or social studies!

Menagh very effectively counters most, if not all, of the "I can't"arguments. He discusses space requirements, teacher preparation, and suggests some easy, pleasant beginning steps which should not embarrass the teacher or the pupil.

Understanding ourselves and others has never been more important than it is today. A successful program in creative drama can contribute to such understanding and can help each of us become a more creative and effective human being.

H. Beresford Menagh *chapter three*

creative drama and improvisation

Introduction

"Dramatic education is at the basis of all education that is child centered. It is the way in which the life process develops and, without it, man is merely one of the upper primates."[1]

A group of forty men and women were silently clawing at the air in front of them as they walked slowly around a large meeting room. One person alone in the middle of the room occasionally made suggestions.

"Feel that air," she said. "Really feel it."

The people fingered the invisible substance, pinching it between thumb and forefinger or rolling it in their hands.

"Now," said the lady in the middle, "every few steps take you into a new enclosure. You go through a wall into a cubicle the person in front of you has just left. The air in there is different. It has a different feel. The floor in there is different. Feel the difference."

The people responded openly. Some obviously stepped over a threshold, lifting the feet high from the floor. Some pushed against an unseen barrier. Some swayed on the unsure new ground, almost losing their balance. Facial expressions showed a wide variety of responses as the people imagined a wide variety of sensations. The leader suggested

---

1. Richard Courtney, *Play, Drama and Thought: the Intellectual Background to Dramatic Education* (London: Cassell and Company Ltd., 1968), p. 57.

other activities and the people paired off to toss imaginary objects back and forth, objects which seemed to change in nature even as the people handled them. They experimented with mirror action in which one person would move and his partner would imitate him immediately as if mirroring the movement.

This was not an exercise in group therapy for persons with psychological or sociological problems. It was a demonstration of improvisation and theatre games for the Central Atlantic Regional Educational Laboratory staged recently near Washington, D.C. The leader was Viola Spolin, well-known for her use of theatre games and improvisation to develop creativity and ability in communication.[2]

In another meeting room in another city, thirty top executives were divided into groups of five, each gathered about its own table. Conversations were animated in one group, passive in another. In one group a man directed pointed criticism at another while a third came to the latter's defense. A member of one group was obviously suffering the disregard of his fellows while he tried hard to be accepted. In another group one man ignored the approaches of his fellows as he tried to remain aloof from the proceedings. Later, under the direction of a leader, the executives examined their experience and drew conclusions about interpersonal relationships under varying circumstances.

This was an experiment in role-playing staged by a management consulting firm for the American Society of Association Executives at one of its leadership seminars and critiques held in New York.[3]

In yet a third situation a group of children were imagining they were hungry goats as they tried to learn how the three Billy Goats Gruff felt before they outwitted the troll. Imaginatively they picked and tasted some dry, prickly tumble weed and their faces showed their disgust. Bits of imagined bark, a hard stone, and a stick similarly caused registers of disapproval. Various elements of the story were experienced as the children prepared thus for the reading of the story.

The children were in a classroom at a Navaho school high on the

---

2. This occurred during a one-day demonstration in 1967 as part of a six-week workshop in innovative educational techniques. For the Spolin approach to improvisation see, Viola Spolin, *Improvisation for the Theatre* (Evanston, Illinois: Northwestern University Press, 1963). See also John Reed Hodgson and Ernest Richards, *Improvisation: Discovery and Creativity in Drama* (London: Methuen and Co. Ltd., 1966).

3. The program was designed by Lawrence-Leiter and Company of Kansas City in 1968. For a general work on problems of interpersonal relations and leadership which could suggest many uses for role-playing, see, Bernard M. Bass, *Leadership, Psychology, and Organizational Behavior* (New York: Harper and Brothers, 1960).

continental divide in New Mexico. The leader was a teacher helping his charges through an experience in creative drama as part of their language learning.[4]

The immediate and specific objectives of the three leaders in these situations were different but the ultimate objectives were essentially the same. Of particular importance were the experiences enjoyed by the participants for in all three situations they were fundamentally similar. The theatre games leader was demonstrating an educational technique for developing personal creativity. The role-playing leader was helping executives develop awareness of problems in interpersonal relations. The creative drama leader was helping children become better equipped in language arts. All participants in each situation, however, engaged in the same kind of activity. They exercised their imaginations, they created individual character and action in a group activity, and they put their personal tools of body or voice to work innovatively in an imagined situation. In each situation the ultimate objective was to help people become better equipped as human beings.

Education for Utility

Becoming fully equipped as human beings and achieving a complete measure of human worth is not easy in a technologically oriented society. There are many tendencies in such a society that militate against it, not the least of which is one to make education utilitarian, that is, make it serve as training for a job. Almost anyone who is asked why he should get an education will probably reply that an education is necessary for getting a job. A Harris Survey shows almost three out of four, or 74 per cent of parents believe the primary purpose of going to college is "to get a good job."[5] Newspapers contain items about the problems of young men and women who do not complete high school and consequently fail to obtain employment. Federal, state and local governments exhibit concern about the apparent relationship between unemployment and lack of education. Programs are proposed and instituted in which people are helped not only to complete high school but to obtain a higher education and in some cases even to engage in graduate work. It is taken as almost axiomatic that the more education a

4. This occurred in the writer's classroom at the United States Indian Service School, Crownpoint, New Mexico, 1952.
5. Louis Harris, "College Goal Splits Parents, Children," *Los Angeles Times* (March 18, 1965).

person has the greater are his job opportunities. Thus it appears to many that the function of education in our American society is to prepare people for making a living.

Because of this common conception of the function of education, students in colleges and universities can be heard complaining about spending time, even "wasting" time, on a course of study not directly related to their particular job-goals. Students preparing to teach are perhaps less prone than others to complain about such courses because they generally accept the idea that the more they know about themselves, their relationship to others and their relationship to their universe the better equipped they are for teaching growing human beings. But there is hardly a student who has not heard another student complain, "What do I need with botany in mechanical engineering?" or "What do I need with physics when I'm going to be a teacher of American literature?" or "What good is a course in speech for an agronomist?" For these students, the criterion of merit in any educational pursuit seems to be utility.

Pressures of Technology

Utilitarianism received a strong impetus following the successful launching of Sputnik almost a decade and a half ago. Clamors were heard across America for greater emphasis on mathematics and science in education. One respected scientist became better known in some circles for his views of technological education than for his achievements in physical science. A well-known military officer became a regular writer in newspaper columns about a no-nonsense approach to education. A superintendent of public instruction in one of the large states was elected with a platform that emphasized the "3-R's" and no "frills." Even Dean Harold Benjamin's charming satire, *The Sabre Tooth Curriculum,* well known to all educators as a call for modernization of educational method and content, became to some a call for utility in education, that is, for specific job training. A dramatic result of this upheaval in educational thought was seen in California where, five years after Sputnik, the State Legislature passed the "Fisher Bill" which called for a major revision of credential requirements and empowered the State Board of Education to draw up the regulations necessary to implement the bill. Had the legislative measure been put into effect as originally intended by the State Board, the various arts would have been eliminated as subjects for a teaching credential in California.[6]

Human Needs

In spite of the utilitarian tendency in educational thought, that is, the tendency to assume human education has the practical function of preparation for making a living, making a home and raising a family in a technologically oriented society, one ancient, worldwide truth still holds. Any animal makes a living, gives birth to and rears its offspring, obtains shelter, and even explores its universe. It is true that human beings have made some remarkable refinements in these basic pursuits but the unknown man who died in his cave 5,000 years ago after making a living with spear and ax made no less or no greater an impression on human progress than the man who passed away this year after making his living with an electronic computer—or the gray wolf who perished alone in the snows of the Yukon after a successful life with fang and claw. All three received educations that were practical for their societies and all three may have had a proportionately narrow or broad understanding of themselves, their relationship to their fellow-creatures and their relationship to their universe. Education for making a living, for making a home and raising a family is a part but only a part of the story—the part which may be called animal, which is carried on in every lair, den, cave and burrow on every hill and in every valley on the face of the earth. Education that is concerned with what a child needs as he grows, that enables the child to continue his growth even after he reaches physical maturity, that helps him achieve an appreciable degree of human worth—this kind of education is the other part of the story. Meeting these needs is a function of education with which every teacher must be concerned.

The needs of a growing human being are many. He has physical needs; he has to do and play. He has mental needs; he must find out what and how and why. His social needs must be met with an understanding of his relation to the group, the community, and the world. His spiritual needs demand development of his personal spirit, his personality and individuality. Finally he has emotional needs; he must learn to release and control his emotions and develop his "feelings."

---

6. The California situation is summarized in Lee Korf's, "Annual Report of Southern California District AETA," (Washington: American Educational Theatre Association, July 24, 1963, mimeographed).

Everyone in education is concerned with these needs. Although some specialists may emphasize one or more of them, none may forget any of them for teachers teach human beings, not animals. A teacher therefore must do more than prepare a person to make a living; he must meet human needs.

Some of the attributes of man that truly set him off from the animal—that give some indication of his worth as a human being—are his imagination, his ability to create, his sense of beauty, his sense of the aesthetic, and his appreciation of form. These are attributes that must be developed if human beings are to achieve some stature, some measure of dignity and of worth. These attributes are expressed in that area of human endeavor generally called the creative arts. Sensitivity to the arts therefore constitutes a uniquely human ability, one which all human beings need to develop.[7]

Reasons for the Arts

There are two major reasons for developing understanding of and sensitivity to the arts. First, the arts are important to human beings because they are ways of arriving at truth. The artist's insight is keener than that of ordinary people; his response to life is more keenly felt and more keenly expressed. This is one of the things, after all, that makes him an artist. He feels or senses the essence or meaning of things whether that meaning be found in a simple emotion stimulated by a silent sunflower whose blossom always seeks the sun, or in a more complex emotion stimulated by compassion for the human predicament of people caught in war. Having gained an insight into a truth lying in an event, situation, or thing, the artist is moved to move others; to transfer the insight he has gained, the truth he has known, to other human beings; to present them with a view of life; to move them to experiencing a truth about themselves, about their relationship to their fellow men, or their relationship to their universe or their deity.

A Way to Learn Truth

As a result of experiencing this revelation of truth, people become better people because they become more understanding people. This is true whether they are moved to pity with Arthur Miller by the effect of

---

7. Throughout this discussion, "arts" refers to the aesthetic or creative arts rather than what are commonly called the practical arts.

false goals on a man or stimulated to laughter with Molière by the foibles of man. It is true whether they are moved by a Renaissance painter to celebrate the magnificence of man or stimulated by a contemporary "pop" artist to sneer at the silliness of man. The arts help people to recognize the intense and continuing value of the human being who can be anything from the exalted figure of the Greek tragedians to the pointless creature of the contemporary absurdists. Because the arts help human beings understand themselves, discover truths about themselves and gain an insight into the nature of their lives, it is important that human beings develop a sensitivity to the arts. Of all the arts, the art of theatre deals exclusively with man and although this art has often been the instrument of the most trivial entertainment, it is nevertheless a universal means of understanding man. The understanding of man is one of the greatest needs facing any child in school, any student in college, or any human being in the world. Truths about the nature of man must be sought and the need to seek and discover these truths must be felt by all children in school. The need exists; it is incumbent on teachers first to develop in children a feeling of the need and then to help them meet the need. Truths about the nature of the human being, his relation to his fellows and to his universe may be discovered through the arts.

A Way to Communicate

The second major reason for developing understanding of and sensitivity to the arts is that the arts are the most universal means of communication among people. There are many things that interfere with communication. Inexactness is probably the most obvious block. Consider the simple concept of "bigness" and compare what the word "big" conveys to the child looking through a window, the biologist looking through a microscope or the astronomer looking through a telescope. Consider the even greater problem in communicating exactly the much more complicated meanings of "love," "hate," or "frustration." It is easily seen why inexactness often results in the confusion or embarrassment of one or all parties involved in the communication.

Another block to communication is ineptness. Many motion pictures, television programs, stage plays, novels, poems, and comic strips have based their laughter-provoking premises on man's clumsiness in attempting to express himself. In a more serious vein, a real problem faces the parent who must discipline his child while somehow still conveying his feeling of love for the child. Consider the predicament of the teacher who must condemn the work of a child while somehow conveying the idea that the child himself is not condemned. The breakdown in communication that occurs at these times due to the ineptness of the transmitter of the communication, the receiver, or both, is a situation familiar to almost everyone.

Misinterpretation of a word or act is another hindrance to communication that nations as well as people go to great lengths to avoid. The ancient joke about the man with a wink in one eye having his malady taken to mean something other than a muscular problem has its counterpart in daily existence. The "Darling!" uttered by a movie star ought not to be misinterpreted as genuine personal endearment. Many an election has been lost by a candidate who misinterpreted opinion polls and many an examination has been failed by a student who misinterpreted instructions.

Overcoming Subjectivity

Finally, and above all, the subjectivity of man constantly hinders communication, that is, man constantly tends to see events in terms of his own experience. The "Oriental mind" was for generations inscrutable to many Occidentals simply because the Occidental placed Oriental thought and behavior in an Occidental frame. "He will react the way I react and behave the way I behave" is an error in assumption made by man throughout his history. Man tends to put things in his own terms. One of the difficult jobs facing a teacher is finding out not just what he must teach but whom he must teach. This is a never-ending quest because the "who" changes with every pupil the teacher has throughout his teaching career. This is one reason that a good teacher can teach the same subject on the same grade level year after year with vigor and excitement: with every class he meets a new challenge to overcome his own subjectivity, to understand new people, to find out who they are, to meet them on their home ground, and to help them move out to uncover new ground. This is what makes teaching young people one of the most demanding, most responsible and most exciting professions in the world. This is what makes teaching an art as well as a science. Unless a teacher can overcome some of his own subjectivity and learn who his pupils are, his communication will be inadequate and he can expect little more than surface learning to occur.

It is clear that there are many hindrances to communication and that words alone are frequently an impoverished means of conveying meaning. The artist, on the other hand, can show understanding, meaning, feeling and emotion that cannot be communicated in any other way. The produced play, for instance, through character and action, can form a bridge between the subjectivity of the playwright and that of the viewer; between the subjectivity of the actor or the designer and that of the audience. The costumer or the director may be incapable of communicating in words precisely their feelings, but through the play they communicate their special comment on joy or sorrow, on beauty or sordidness, on hope or despair, without hesitation and without fear of being misunderstood.

In addition to being a bridge between the subjectivity of the artist and that of the audience, the arts are a bridge between one observer's subjectivity and that of another observer. Seated in a theatre, for instance, may be a thousand or more people, all strangers to one another. As the play progresses they laugh in common, are apprehensive in common, share emotions in common and share a common understanding. When the play is over they are no longer strangers. They have been united in a common bond more real and more pervasive than any oath they might take together or any conversation they might hold. Their individual fears, prejudices, loves, hates and many of the other things that create the subjectivity of human beings have been bridged, if only temporarily, by art. That this is so has been demonstrated time and again by strangers in the lobby of a theatre who are willing to exchange smiles or even words after a play but who avoid any such evidence of human recognition and understanding before the play. These bridges between the subjectivity of people are greatly needed and can be built by learning to understand and appreciate the arts.

Those are some of the things that make the arts, and especially the social art of theatre, important to the growing, learning young person. He can come closer to knowing truth, he can communicate more readily and he can achieve some degree of his potential worth as a human being. If he can do these things he need have no worry about the specific job in which he will make his living. He will have no problem whatever his place in life in being happy, productive and vital. As he makes his home and his living, he will realize above all some measure of his worth as a human being.

The Nature of Creative Drama

Granted the importance of theatre art in meeting needs of growing young people, the question is one of where and how to start. All human beings are potentially creative. Indeed, studies have shown that every child is endowed with those sensibilities that characterize the artist.[8] He has sensitivity, imagination and a willingness, even a desire, to express his feelings and his responses to life openly and imaginatively. All too often his creative urge may be stifled by the requirements of a technological society oriented to utilitarianism. Whenever a child stops being creative, it is held, one can be certain it is because outside influences have inhibited his development.[9] One of the teacher's jobs, to put it simply, is to develop not inhibit the child's creativity, sensitivity and imagination. The child needs skills, most certainly, but he also needs imagination if he is to use those skills for human ends. He needs to express himself creatively and he needs to improvise imaginatively with those skills and with himself, that is, with his own native tools, his body and his voice.

The process of developing the child's ability to express himself creatively in a group situation, improvising imaginatively with his body and his voice, is known variously as creative dramatics, creative drama, child drama, playmaking, or, with older children and adults, improvisation.

The fundamental purpose of creative drama, then, is essentially that of education in general: to foster the growth and development of the child. It does this specifically by helping him to develop his individual spirit within the group while at the same time developing cooperation with the group, and by helping him develop self-realization, imagination and creativity. Through creative dramatics the child therefore is enabled to improve social attitudes and relationships, achieve greater confidence and emotional stability, become increasingly aware of his environment, improve vocal and bodily expression, and develop independent thinking and personal creativity. Of special concern to the teacher of language arts is the way in which creative drama helps guide children naturally towards reading readiness, word study, the appreciation of poetry and

8. Victor E. D'Amico, *Creative Teaching in Art* (New York: International Textbook Company, 1953). Compare Courtney's statement, "The essential characteristic of man is his creative imagination," in Richard Courtney, *op. cit.,* p. 7.
9. Viktor Lowenfeld, *Creative and Mental Growth* (New York: The Macmillan Company, 1947), pp. 1-4.

the understanding of literature and its relation to creative story-telling and choric interpretation.[10]

Requirements of Creative Drama

The requirements of creative drama are few, consisting only of a group of children with a qualified leader and a space in which to function. There is no need for a script or for the technical aids so frequently associated with theatre production—no scenery, lighting, costumes or make-up. The only physical environment required is a space such as almost any classroom can provide with the tables and chairs pushed back. These tables or desks and chairs may, of course, be used from time to time. There is no audience but that possibly provided by the participants themselves waiting for their turn to create and evaluating the work of their classmates. The absence of an audience indicates one of the differences between creative dramatics and theatrical display. "Theatrical," as Stark Young makes clear in his excellent discussion of the nature of theatre, pertains to the theatre and to performance.[11] Indeed, it is held by some that it is for the sake of an audience that theatre exists.[12] Unlike children's theatre, then, creative drama is a participant-centered experience and an audience is to be avoided. Children's theatre, on the other hand, is designed for a child audience and generally uses adult performers. It is a fully sophisticated theatre art utilizing all the techniques of the art to create a finished, polished performance for an audience of children. Although children's theatre is an important part of a child's education, comparable to visiting an art gallery, it lies in an area outside the scope of this chapter.[13]

The requirement of a qualified leader is most important if the dramatic activity of the children is to be truly creative. The fundamentals of creative leadership are those of any good teacher. The creative leader must have imagination: he must be aware, resourceful, able to recognize potentiality in simplicity, and able to awaken the imagination of others.

---

10. See Mabel Wright Henry, editor, *Creative Experiences in Oral Language* (Champaign, Illinois: National Council of Teachers of English, 1967).
11. Stark Young, *The Theatre* (New York: Hill and Wang, 1954), p. 49.
12. Theodore W. Hatlen, *Orientation to the Theatre* (New York: Appleton-Century-Crofts, 1962), p. 269.
13. For an excellent presentation of creating theatre with children in a more formal way in education, see Richard Courtney, *Teaching Drama: A Handbook for Teachers in Schools* (London: Cassell and Company Ltd., 1965). For the preparation of children for creating theatre for an audience see Richard Crosscup, *Children and Dramatics* (New York: Charles Scribner's Sons, 1966).

He must have spirit: he must be enthusiastic and able to fire the spirits of others. He must have the quality of greatness: he must be willing to teach by example, to enter into the spirit of the child's activity with genuine enjoyment, and yet be able to guide.[14] Certain attributes of the good teacher can be emphasized as especially important for the creative dramatics leader. In addition to being understanding and creative, the leader must be discriminating and able to help the unselective child to select so that form can be developed from the formless. The role of the leader has been further described as that of one who provides the proper stimulation for creative thinking.[15] Specifically, the leader must have four basic capabilities.

1. He must know how to set the stage, so to speak, for the creative act, that is, he must provide a suitable climate and mood and prepare the child emotionally and intellectually to exercise his imagination in order to create character and motivated action. This frequently includes preparing the parents as well as the children so they will not only be interested but will also provide encouragement. The teacher must motivate the child to understand a situation, feeling, or event and, once understanding it, to be enthusiastic about demonstrating it. He might ask the children, for instance, to remember with closed eyes a place they associate with some pleasant event, to recall the various sensual responses associated with the place and event and to relive those responses in their imagination. When the situations are discussed and the children are enthusiastic about demonstrating their feelings, they are then ready to create dramatically.

2. The leader must be equipped to provide the idea or stimulus for dramatic creativity. This may be a situation, event or object uncovered in a "show-and-tell" experience shared by either the child or the teacher; a selection of music or poetry; a true or fictional story; a current or historic event; or an idea uncovered in the preparation for the creative dramatics experience.

3. The leader must provide the opportunity for free response, must encourage that response, and be able to guide it and develop it into form. This requires on the part of the leader not only a strong interest in theatre but a sound understanding of character and action, their

14. Geraldine Brain Siks, *Creative Dramatics* (New York: Harper and Brothers, 1958), pp. 122-140.
15. Burdette S. Fitzgerald, *World Tales for Creative Dramatics and Storytelling* (Englewood Cliffs, New Jersey: Prentice-Hall, Inc., 1962), p. 1.

interrelationship, and the means of creating them. It follows that the successful leader of creative drama must have a sound working knowledge of the art of theatre.

4. The leader must be able to guide the children in evaluation. Through careful questioning, for instance, he must guide the children to distinguish between the believable and the unbelievable in a creation of character or action, to recognize honesty and completeness in expression, and must encourage the children to experiment, to venture, to develop and expand their imaginations, and to improve their skill in the use of their native dramatic tools, their bodies and their voices.

The Functions of Creative Drama

Educators generally ascribe two legitimate, basic functions to creative drama: that of an art in itself to be taught alongside any other art such as music,[16] and that of a tool or method either for teaching other subject areas or for correcting personal or social aberrations. The first function, that of generally meeting human needs through the art experience, has been discussed above. The function of creative drama as a method for treating problems in personal or social adjustment lies in the realm of psychodrama and sociodrama, both highly specialized fields that lie outside the scope of the present discussion. A third function, that of recreation disassociated from education, has been attributed to creative drama in the past but has been rightly discredited by Winifred Ward and all who have come after her.[17] Although there may be a few places in the United States where the attitude still prevails that creative drama is a useless though harmless way of keeping children occupied during leisure time, such an attitude is fast disappearing. There is, in addition, a growing awareness of the meaning of recreation in modern educational thought, a meaning more closely associated than in the past with the concept of re-creating. It is not unusual today to find close cooperation between workers in recreation programs and those in creative drama.

As a teaching tool used in other areas, creative drama has been suc-

---

16. This philosophy is more prevalent in England than in the United States but is now growing in this country. See Peter Slade, *Child Drama* (London: University of London Press, 1954), Peter Slade, *Child Drama and its Value in Education* (Bromley, Kent: Stacey Publications, 1967), and Brian Way, *Development Through Drama* (London: Longmans, 1967).

17. Winifred Ward, *Playmaking with Children* (New York: Appleton-Century-Crofts, Inc., 1957), p. 16.

cessfully integrated in the elementary school program in many cities not only in language arts but in such areas as nature study, science, and social studies. In all these areas of study, there are five broad, common objectives in using the art:

1. To highlight material studied in a given unit.
2. To intensify the child's experience in the area studied.
3. To stimulate further investigation and study.
4. To develop the ability to integrate subject matter.
5. To increase the desire for learning.

Creative Drama and Nature Study

In nature study, for instance, natural phenomena are made a part of the child's experience through dramatization. Events determined by or accompanying the change of seasons, for instance, thus are made real and meaningful to the child because through his personal creation he makes them part of his personal experience. He may create the story of Mike and Esther, two robins, who have trouble building their nest in the Spring. They search for the right materials, carefully shape the nest in the right kind of tree, and invent a song as they rhythmically flap their wings. Seeds grow, flowers open their petals to the sun, spiders spin their webs, eggs hatch and dangers appear and are overcome in the struggle for life. Finally, clouds blow up, wind bends the trees, leaves fall, seeds are scattered in their own special way, the rain comes down in torrents and the birds give up their home to fly to the South.

Creative Drama in Social Studies

Creative drama is used successfully in many schools to help the child understand the nature of the events, activities or situations studied in a given unit and to understand the feelings, the choices, the lives, and the human predicament of the people involved in historic and current events, in the trades and professions, in government, industry and agriculture, and as an aid to understanding and comparing the various cultures.

Creative Drama and the Language Arts

Creative drama is readily used as a tool in conjunction with the language arts for the two arts are closely related. In this connection it has two major values. First, words can be brought to life and their meanings intensified by means of the kinesthetic sense when verbal symbols and mental images are physically portrayed. Thus reading, listening, speaking, and less directly, writing, can be motivated and understanding and appreciation enhanced. The second value, one less obvious but perhaps even more important than the first, involves the nature of language as an art. Creative drama can be used to develop an understanding and appreciation of the fundamental qualities of the art of language, written or spoken as poetry or prose. These qualities, common to all the arts under various names, are unity, emphasis, coherence, balance, rhythm, and mood.[18]

Qualities of Art in Language Arts

1. Unity is adherence to the subject; the relating of all parts to the whole. In any properly constructed paragraph there is a central topic and everything in the paragraph must deal with or contribute to that central topic. In like manner in any dramatic entity there is a central idea or concept and unassociated, irrelevant, or disconnected bits of expression must be avoided. In addition, unity demands the sufficient and proper development of a concept within a unit. Inadequate expression of an emotion or idea in a dramatic entity violates the same principle as inadequate development or support of an idea in a unit of written or spoken composition.

2. Emphasis is the expression of the kernel, the core, the heart and soul of a concept and can be achieved by four general means:

    a. Rearrangement: the positioning in time and space so a specified part is more easily recognizable.

    b. Proportion: the apparent subordination of the less important to the more important.

    c. Intensification: the use of contrast, unexpectedness, movement, or vibrancy to achieve a compelling, dynamic, climactic, or "dramatic" effect.

    d. Repetition: the recurrence of a line, sound, form, rhythm, movement, color, mood, or other fundamental to make that element insistent or apparent.

3. Coherence is the logical and probable relationship of one part to another part within the whole. In order to maintain coherence, every

---

18. Unity, coherence, emphasis, selectivity, proportion, rearrangement, intensification, and mood are suggested as "principles" underlying all art by Alexander Dean in his classic, *Fundamentals of Play Directing* (New York: Holt, Rinehart and Winston, 1941), pp. 5-9.

student of composition avoids such hindrances as misplaced modifiers and dangling participles. A form of coherence in dramatic art known as motivation is highly important. One action must be logically related to another or must evolve from it and an action performed by a character must "grow out of" that character, that is, the action must be motivated by the nature of the character. A more technical application of coherence is the maintaining of logical relationships among sound, sight and sense—what is said and done must suit the meaning of the situation.

4. Balance is an equality in weighting of two or more parts and may be considered as a special kind of proportion. In English composition, parallelism is an example of one use of balance. The dramatic artist is concerned with balance between opposing forces in a conflict, the relationship of one character to another, the relative strengths of the protagonist and the antagonist, the balance of vocal and physical characteristics of the various actors, and the weighting of the visual aspects of a dramatic entity.

5. Rhythm is periodicity or pulsation, the more or less regular recurrence of emphasis. In dramatic art it is sometimes further defined by attributing to it a quality of producing "a conscious or subconscious feeling of organization and progression."[19] Some even suggest that this progression has direction, leading to the final aim of the artist.[20] In music, various types of rhythm are well defined and can be named and specifically described. In poetry, some rhythmic units and devices are well defined and given names such as the iambus, rhyme, and certain kinds of consonance, while other forms of rhythm can be described only generally by such terms as "flippant" or "ponderous." In dramatic art, rhythm occurs in many forms, some exceedingly complex, but unfortunately specific definitions are almost completely lacking. Rhythm is important in dramatic art and in the development of sensitivity and creativity in children, however, so its various manifestations and uses in dramatic art are described following.

Kinds of Rhythm

Rhythm in drama is most easily noted in poetic dialogue where the recurrence of certain accents, sounds and inflections establishes the

19. H.D. Albright, William P. Halstead and Lee Mitchell, *Principles of Theatre Art* (Cambridge, Massachusetts: Houghton Mifflin Company, 1955), p. 431.
20. Richard Boleslavsky, *Acting: the First Six Lessons* (New York: Theatre Arts Books, 1949), p. 112.

rhythm of spoken language. The rhythm of such poetry, however, is so arranged that it suits the sense, mood or emotional content of the action. In the following excerpt from a speech by Dromio in *The Comedy of Errors,* Shakespeare created a rhythm that gives a flippant, light, tripping effect by using a great many short vowels, a great many consonants, especially the "stop" consonant sounds of "k," "t," "p," and "b," very few long vowels, and very few of the "glide" consonants such as "l" and "r." In addition, the phrasing is short and abrupt, agreeing with the short and sharply defined thought units.

> The capon burns, the pig falls from the spit;
> The clock hath strucken twelve upon the bell—
> My mistress made it one upon my cheek;
> She is so hot because the meat is cold;
> The meat is cold because you come not home;

The metric pattern that Shakespeare used in this speech is iambic pentameter, the same as that used by Marlowe in the following lines from *Doctor Faustus.* Now, however, the rhythm is ponderous, giving an effect of great sweep and dignity. The words and phrases are longer, there are more long vowels, more use of the gliding consonants of "l" and "r," and longer, larger and more impressive cadences to make the rhythm suit the emotional content and meaning of the action.

> Monarch of hell, under whose black survey
> Great potentates do kneel in awful fear,
> Upon whose altars thousand souls do lie,
> How am I vexèd with these villains' charms!

Closely related to poetic dialogue is poetic prose, an outstanding example of which appears in Singe's *Riders to the Sea.* In Maurya's prophetic lament just before the body of her last son is brought in, the individual accents of words and phrases rise to a series of climaxes, each one of which is followed by a three-beat cadence. Not only do the individual beats of syllables work together to form larger or heavier beats, but these small groups work together to form still larger beats of thought or emotion groupings. The tragic rhythm so created, linked to the tragic content of the dialogue and the action, can be detected even in a silent reading of Maurya's speeches but it must be remembered that Singe wrote the play not to be read silently but to be spoken aloud and acted. To the rhythm found in reading the words on the printed page, therefore, must be added the rhythm created by the human voice and that created by bodily movement, all coordinated to create the unified, coherent rhythms of dramatic dialogue.

Rhythm is an essential attribute of dramatic action as well as of dialogue and is achieved through the proper utilization of climaxes in a scene. A scene may begin with relatively low emotional content and gradually increase in intensity to a climax. This climax constitutes a beat or pulsation of dramatic action and these emotional beats are arranged to create a rhythmic pattern suiting the dramatic content of the scene. A play is a series of actions all making up the one, major, unified action. Each minor action has its own beat, that is, its own dramatic climax. An action begins, builds to a climax and is completed, transformed, or stopped by the beginning of a new action. The new action then builds to its climax and gives way to another new action. The line of these pulsations, their relationship to one another, their frequency, intensity, and arrangement create a rhythmic pattern which illuminates the action and gives it movement.

A typical example of this kind of rhythm can be found in a television "Western" play. A poker game is in progress at a table in a saloon. An argument develops between two of the men and builds in intensity. This action is stopped by a third man who demands that the cards be dealt. As the cards are dealt, everyone is suspicious of the dealer and the action of dealing builds to a climax. This action is ended when one man hits the dealer on the head with a bottle whereupon a new action, that of a rough-and-tumble fight, ensues and builds to its climax. This entire scene is ended abruptly with a pistol shot as the United States marshal enters and starts a whole new action.

An alternation in thoughts expressed through both dialogue and movement creates a rhythm which in turn conveys mood and meaning in a dramatic action. The long opening speech of the character, Rose, in Harold Pinter's little play, "The Room," alternates between inconsequential references to household trivia and somewhat fearful references to a dark, basement apartment in what is otherwise a static scene. Yet these changes in thought, illuminated by appropriate changes in the voice and bodily movement of the character, create an erratic but pronounced rhythm that in turn creates an intense and foreboding mood, building suspense almost immediately and creating a sense of tension progression.

Other kinds and uses of rhythm found in dramatic art are sometimes simple, sometimes complex, and almost numberless. Musical and dance dramas use the rhythms of music side by side with dramatic rhythms, the one supplementing and clarifying the other. Specific music rhythms can be combined with dramatic action as in *West Side Story* where the syncopated rhythm effects are intrinsic to the meaning of the play. Metrical dialogue is sometimes used for emphasis or to give a mechanical effect as in some expressionistic dramas. The art of drama, being highly complex, affords a tremendous variety of rhythms but it is also an art that is highly representative of human life and therefore cannot bear rhythms that are made too obvious.

6. Mood is the essence of an object or event in terms of a generalized human feeling. It is a product of both content and form, deriving from the particular ways in which unity, emphasis, coherence, balance, and rhythm are used in the art object, from symbols and from the spectator's approach to the object or event. If a selection of poetry or of music with tripping rhythms and small, bright contrasts is used to stimulate the creative activity of a group of children, for instance, one can expect the light, merry mood so created to influence their activity and it is to be expected that the resulting physical movements will be quick and light. The creating of mood is an important process in children's creative drama.

The Processes of Creative Drama

The processes of creative drama, like those of any art, are interwoven and in actual practice can hardly be separated. For obvious reasons, however, they are described separately here and in increasing order of complexity, but it is to be remembered that not all processes will be found in any one creative drama experience nor would a series of "lessons" necessarily be built on the ascending order of complexity such as that to be given. The experience described at the beginning of this chapter involving the Navaho children, though an early one for them, involved the enactment of a complete story with concomitant exploration of rudiments of character portrayal, while only a beginning was made in developing some skill with basic sense perception and rhythm appreciation. Specifically, the processes are those found in five kinds of activities or experiences: theatre games and dramatic play, rhythmic experiences, sense perception, mood development, and story creation.

Theatre Games

The men and women engaging in strange actions described at the beginning of this chapter were undergoing some loosening-up exercises in creativity. They played games not with an object such as a ball nor with rules such as pertain in a ball game, but with their own imaginations and ingenuity. This kind of game is called a theatre game because it has to do with performance by the human being using only his own native instruments, the body and the voice, in a creative way. The object of theatre games is to help free the body, the voice and the imagination.

In the early stages there may be self-consciousness and embarrassment because people tend to be shy in responding to an imaginative world. A good leader, however, gets everyone absorbed in the work at hand, joins in himself, and the participants rapidly gain self-confidence and a sense of security. Physical loosening-up exercises generally precede the games followed closely by games to develop awareness of what is done with the body in terms of such things as space, weight and speed. The voice is exercised with attention to kinds and qualities of sounds and the agility of the mouth. Concentration is emphasized in the games or exercises with a carefully planned program to develop awareness of the senses. The players look to observe detail, listen to qualities and meanings in sound, touch to feel size, shape and texture, smell kinds and qualities, taste flavors and intensities and act and react with combinations of these. After a good degree of concentration is achieved the players find they can observe with insight and experience, develop new ideas from old and find that they are building extensive, useful imaginations. The games are repeated with variations as warming up exercises prior to more formal work in improvisation or dramatization.

Dramatic Play

Known to many people as make-believe, dramatic play is an experience common to almost all young children. The child invents an imaginary playmate or imagines himself an astronaut, teacher, rabbit, or railroad engine and creates a suitable environment for the role in which he has cast himself. One six-year-old invented a character he called "George" who lived in the drain of the wash basin and made gurgling sounds as the water went down. For more than a year George was responsible for other sounds about the house and from time to time would come out to play with the child. Then the family moved and when they heard a strange sound in the new house, the parents suggested it was made by George. The child disagreed and in one breath showed that he, like all normal children, recognized the difference between imagination and reality, playing and being, that he could be quite objective about his creations and further, that he could creatively explain the discard of an imaginative object when the natural process of maturation had made that particular creation no longer necessary. The child said simply, "Aw, George isn't real and anyhow, he just lived at the old house." In such dramatic play the child gives expression to a basic creative urge, an urge that is sometimes stifled, unfortunately, by unknowing or unsympathetic adults. By creating a character for himself and inventing situations in which that character can operate, the child learns about his environment and prepares to cope with it. He develops his imagination, gains skill in the use of his body and voice, and improves his ability in problem solving.

Stimuli for Dramatic Play

Motivation for guided dramatic play is found in poetry, music, riddles, stories, class trips, holidays, special events, or just the day-in and day-out routines of school and home life. In turn, properly guided dramatic play motivates attitudes that help get jobs done. It does not substitute phantasy for reality and shield the child from facing and coping with life situations. Instead it helps him prepare for experiences he must meet by developing in him positive, creative attitudes toward those experiences. Thus, for example, he is prepared for making trips, performing social amenities, accepting a new arrival at school or at home, visiting the doctor or dentist, or understanding and observing rules.

Throughout these dramatic play experiences, the involvement of the child's emotion is important. It is not enough for him to assume a character and engage in some action; he must find excitement, perhaps, or suspense, happiness or sadness. Feelings must be involved. Without the involvement of feelings an action by itself is a physical and sometimes an intellectual exercise, valuable enough in itself, but not necessarily creative in terms of dramatic art. If a child says simply, "I'm a bird," and perfunctorily waves his arms up and down, he may reap some physical benefits but hardly any creative ones such as might obtain were he to experience the joy of one of the four-and-twenty blackbirds released from a pie. Action motivated by the feelings of the character differentiates creative dramatic play from other forms of play such as the ordinary singing game. The creative dramatics leader helps the child understand the character, the situation in which the character finds himself and the feelings involved, and encourages him to express through action whatever emotion the situation invokes; in other words the leader helps the child to motivate the action.

Rhythmic Experiences

Of all the underlying attributes of art, rhythm is probably the one most easily recognized by children and is certainly one to which they readily respond. The development of a sense of rhythm is important for the child's understanding and appreciation of and participation in the arts. Creative rhythmic experiences are designed specifically to develop physical, intellectual, and emotional responses to rhythm. In younger children, simpler rhythms are used to develop and coordinate the larger muscles. With older children, more complex rhythms are introduced and greater skill is developed in the control and use of the smaller muscles.

Like dramatic play, rhythmic experiences are made creative experiences when character and motivation are introduced. There are certain values in simple walking, marching or skipping exercises, generally performed in a circle with a musical accompaniment, but with no motivation other than the request of the teacher. These exercises take on creative values, however, when the children assume the identities of characters motivated by feelings and when their action suits the nature of their characters. Thus the children become members of a United States Olympic team, perhaps, joyfully marching beneath their flag past the reviewing stand on their way to receive a trophy. They might be old men, hot and tired, hobbling along with canes, determined to go the full length of the parade before sitting down and resting. They might be dolphins leaping with excitement as they respond to the applause of children along the shore. Similar dramatic situations involving emotion may be invented for other standard rhythmic exercises: mowing the yard when the grass is easy to cut and when it is tall and tough; throwing snowballs from a snow-fort—and getting hit by a soft, wet one; climbing a steep ladder to rescue a frightened kitten caught high in a tree; swimming away from Captain Hook's ship in cold, rough water to reach the shore where weiners wait to be roasted over a big bonfire.

Older children are challenged by more complex situations. A mechanized factory suggests many starting points for experiences with rhythm that have virtually no limit to their complexity. A trip to a soft-drink bottling plant, a large bakery, or almost any factory will reveal many rhythmic operations of varying complexities which can be personified by the children. Variety and excitement can be introduced when one part misbehaves or when the whole operation speeds up until the machine flies apart or a switch is thrown and the machine grinds slowly to a halt. Sound effects to accompany the various operations can be made with stamping feet, clapping hands, snapping fingers or clucking tongues, or properly selected music can be used to provide background, establish tempo, and create a desired mood. Such experiences require considerable concentration even for adults, and are excellent for developing rhythm appreciation. A wide variety of creative rhythmic experiences are suggested in publications available in most libraries and the leader of creative drama should explore the potentials of such experiences.[21]

Sense Perception

Response to environment depends on awareness of that environment and awareness in turn is determined in a large measure by the senses of touch, taste, sight, smell, and hearing. It follows, then, that the development of skill in sense perception and skill in showing response to sense stimuli is an important process in creative drama training. The development of sense perception and expression is generally concomitant with the development of other skills in creative drama, especially with younger children, and is motivated by the feelings or emotions. It is not difficult, however, to associate the emotions with sense stimuli as many sensations can be roughly classified on the emotional bases of either pleasant or unpleasant. Thus there may be a pleasant smell, a bad taste, an ugly sight, a friendly touch, or a horrible sound.

A frequent starting point for work in sense perception is an actual experience of the children which might be provided by a trip to the zoo, for instance, or by a number of objects brought to the classroom

---

21. See especially Gladys Andrews, *Creative Rhythmic Movement* (Englewood Cliffs, New Jersey: Prentice-Hall, Inc., 1952).

by them or the teacher. Adequate preparation is made during such an experience for the subsequent recall of the sensory impressions. When the stimulus is removed, that is, when the trip is over or the objects have been taken away, the children are encouraged to relive the sensory experiences and to react visibly to reach remembered impression. Other sources for sensory experiences can be found in poetry, stories, music, objects in the classroom, or the children's own hands, hair, or clothing. Exercises in reacting to sensory stimuli that might be derived from actual life experiences include the following:

Touch: You are eating candy and some sticks to your hands. You are stroking a kitten and come across a burr.

Taste: You are drinking sweet lemonade and start nibbling on a bitter lemon seed.

Sight: You see a beautiful butterfly going from flower to flower and there is a sudden flash of lightning.

Smell: You enter a kitchen where cookies are baking and some milk boils over on the stove.

Hearing: You hear wind in the trees at night and a branch falls to the ground with a crash.

Almost any good text in acting will suggest other exercises to increase sensory awareness and response though such exercises may have to be adapted to suit the needs and experiences of a particular age group.[22]

Mood Development

Closely related to the development of sensory perception and response is the creation of moods. A brightly burning, crackling fire causes certain sensory responses—one sees a number of shades of orange and yellow in various shapes and hears certain explosive sounds in various degrees of loudness—but the sensory responses alone do not adequately convey the essence or meaning of the fire. The essence is obtained by interpreting the information acquired by the senses in terms of feelings. The direction or nature of these feelings will vary depending on other accompanying intellectual or emotional stimuli and on the past experience of the viewer. Thus the same fire might create a

---

22. See for instance, Samuel Selden, *First Steps in Acting* (New York: Appleton-Century-Crofts, Inc., 1947), pp. 237-58.

warm, friendly, sleepy mood in one person, a merry, lively mood in another, and an apprehensive, even fearful mood in yet another. The overt response of the first person might be to lie down and go to sleep, of the second to jump up and dance, and of the third to cry and run away.

The fact that given stimuli produce varying moods makes a demand on the creative drama leader and at the same time provides him with an opportunity. The leader must adequately prepare the children for a creative experience by providing suitable stimuli for a given desired mood. If, for instance, a selection of poetry with a prevailing mood of mystery is used to provide the idea for a creative drama experience, it is desirable to establish a sense or feeling of the mysterious to key the children to the mood of the poem. This can be achieved by both sensory and intellectual means. The appearance of the classroom can be changed to make it darker, perhaps, or decorations and exhibits can be introduced. Sound stimuli can be added by means of carefully selected music or appropriate, strange sounds. An appeal to the sense of smell can be made by using one or more unusual perfumes such as are available in a great variety of room deodorants. Even strange flavors can be introduced in the form of mild spices such as thyme, oregano, or rosemary, though younger children are less willing to experiment with unknown tastes than older ones. Whatever sensory appeal is used, the purpose is to stimulate interest and help create the appropriate mood. Anything inappropriate to the central mood and idea of the poem is avoided. Intellectually, the children are prepared by questions designed to stimulate and channel thought and to help them interpret their sensory responses in terms of the appropriate mood.

Ways of Introducing Complex Experiences

Specific exercises in creating mood can be used to introduce more complex experiences in creative drama or they can be evolved from simpler experiments or from work with sense perception. Each of the relatively static situations in the list which follows suggests a particular mood and involves a number of creative processes for its realization. To these can be added a great many more situations whose number and variety are limited only by the imagination. As children become experienced in creative drama and come to understand the nature of mood, they will have many suggestions of their own for situations that illustrate a specific mood and will delight in creating that mood with the situations they themselves have invented.

1. In a game of hide-and-seek, the person looking for you is just coming up to where you are hiding.
2. The school bus has just left without you.
3. You have just won a race.
4. The candy bar you worked hard to earn has fallen in the mud.
5. A dolphin is doing tricks just for you.

More complex and dynamic mood situations provide the beginnings of story creation. To any of the foregoing situations, for example, might be added a subsequent action that sustains the mood, breaks it, or changes it to another, contrasting mood. With older children, further variety is introduced in these or other situations by experimenting with mood effects on a number of disparate characters. In other complex situations, a musical selection, poem, story, or descriptive paragraph selected for its mood content may require that the children create character and character-motivated action for full realization of the mood. Dramatic play which tends toward establishing a definite mood might well evolve into a complete story with character, action, conflict, and resolution. An example of such play might be "picnic fun" in which the prevailing and sustained mood is one of joy and excitement with a contrast in mood provided at the end. There would be preparation for the picnic, getting to the site, activities at the picnic, and then a rush for shelter because of a sudden rainstorm.

Story Creation

The most obvious and frequent source of stories for creative enactment is the children's own reading, whether it be that prescribed by the course of study in language arts or other subject areas or that come across in collateral materials or simply in free reading. A closely allied and frequently used source is a story read or told, preferably the latter, by the creative drama leader. Not all stories, however, are suitable for dramatization. The following criteria are useful as a guide in making a selection.

1. Characters, whether human or not, should be clearly defined, logically motivated, and should be active rather than passive. Younger children are capable of creating characters with relatively simple motivations while more complex characters are challenging to other children.

Whether simple or complex the characters, particularly the main ones, should have interesting though not necessarily pleasing traits, and should be distinct from one another. Generally the nature of the character is determined in a story as in life—by what the character does and why he does it. Other clues are what he says and why he says it; how he responds to others and how they respond to him; and how he behaves in front of others and how he behaves when others are not around.

2. Conflict expressed through action is the key to drama in any story. The main character must want something, must go after it, must face opposition, and must act to overcome that opposition. The action should be organized in a well-defined plot that advances in a relatively straight line from attack, to major climax or crisis, to resolution.[23] If an otherwise good story lacks sufficiently clear organization for a particular age-group, or if one or more subplots obscure the main plot, the story can be adapted and retold. Adequate preparation by the leader is necessary, however, for such retelling.

3. The setting for the action should be interestingly and clearly described. Not only should there be adequate details about the place of the action but such elements as the time of day and the time of year, the weather, and the country should be included. As the action moves from place to place, new settings should be clearly indicated.

4. The language should evoke mental images with strong sensory and emotional appeal. While long descriptive passages should be avoided, descriptive modifiers of substantives and verbs are desirable. Good language is most likely to be found in good literature.

5. The central idea, subject, mood, or theme should suit the age group and the occasion. In dramatic art, the theme is a statement in a sentence of the author's point of view or insight into life as demonstrated by the action in a given work and may be strong in some dramatic stories and weak in others. In a fable by Aesop, the theme is expressed as a moral which the story demonstrates and which is an important element in the story. In some excellent stories that are quite suitable for dramatization, the theme may be weak, unimportant, or even trite. The central idea or subject, sometimes called the literary theme, may sometimes prove a more helpful guide than dramatic theme in selecting a story for creative dramatization.

---

23. The leader of creative dramatics should become familiar with dramatic structure. See especially Kenneth Thorpe Rowe, *Write That Play* (New York: Funk and Wagnalls Company, 1939).

Sources of Story Ideas

Not all of the foregoing elements will be fully developed in all stories suitable for dramatization. Although all elements should be present, their complete development in the printed story is hardly desirable as this would leave little motivation for the children to exercise their own creativity. Before the child can create, however, he must find adequate answers to the questions of who, what, why, where, and when and he must be stimulated to find more answers and to translate those answers into action. A story in which all elements are fully developed might benefit children more as literature on the printed page than as creative drama on the classroom floor when few of the purposes of creative drama are served.

Stories for dramatizing can be found in narrative poems. Non-narrative poetry demands greater exercise of the imagination in developing plot and lyrical poetry may provide only a mood or feeling as a starting point for story development. News and current and historic events provide action and sometimes character for a story but motivation, feelings, and some sense of intimacy with and understanding of the characters generally has to be developed and a sense of conflict introduced to make the story suspenseful and dramatic.

Music, like lyric poetry, can set a mood as a starting point for story creation. "Programmatic" music is generally more valuable for this purpose than "absolute" music. Some music almost tells a story and some has become traditionally associated with a particular story. The creative dramatics leader guards against any tendency to force children into creating a story that fits preconceived or traditional notions of the program of a particular musical selection. Dukas' "The Sorcerer's Apprentice" does not conjur up in all children a vision of a Walt Disney cartoon character commanding a broom to carry water, although once the children have seen the motion picture *Fantasia* they will likely visualize Mickey Mouse whenever they hear the selection. Some music, like Ravel's "Bolero," sets a very strong mood but with very little and very slow development and may prove discouraging rather than encouraging to the imagination of young children.

Pictures, whether illustrations or individual paintings, are a rich source of story ideas. The pictures should be large enough for all to see clearly and are best if in color. Action pictures with strong mood content provide opportunities for the children to exercise their imaginations as they find answers to Who? What? and Why? Older, more experienced children may find challenges and excitement in developing a story from the stimulation provided by a nonobjective painting but more realistic paintings provide a more productive basis for creative drama with young children.

Approaches to Dramatizing Stories

Whether a complete story is told to the children or the children develop their own story from, perhaps, a mood suggested by a fragment of music, the approach to dramatizing the story is essentially the same. Characters must be created—characters who feel and do. A character, even a fully developed one in a story that is told, does not live and breathe until the child creates him with his own imagination, his own feelings, and his own body and voice. The creative drama leader therefore leads the child first to understand the character, then to create the feelings of the character, then to act as the character motivated by those feelings. Similarly the story does not come to life dramatically until it is created by the children through their own feelings and actions. In this connection there need be no concern about a possible problem of the child's "being" the character or of his actually living the part. He "tries on" the character through his imagination—experimenting, appraising, rejecting, keeping, evaluating, and trying again. He does not become a tree bending to the wind, a conductor taking tickets, a gnome dancing in the moonlight or any other character or thing; rather he becomes what Martha Graham describes as "the miracle that is a human being, motivated, disciplined, concentrated."[24]

The child, then, does not become anything but rather creates the thoughts, creates the feelings, and creates the actions of the character, making them a part of his own experience. Having created character, with each child trying each character, perhaps, the children then proceed to create the individual segments of action that make up the play. A play is composed of a series of actions each one having its own point or meaning and the leader must have these actions and their meaning clearly in mind before beginning work with the children. The action units or "scenes" are developed one by one and new scenes added as the children find motivation for them, or dropped if there is no need for them. The function of the creative drama leader throughout this

24. Martha Graham, "A Modern Dancer's Primer for Action," *Dance: A Basic Educational Technique*, editor, Frederick Rand Rogers (New York: The Macmillan Company, 1941), p. 178.

process is not that of the traditional theatre director but rather that of an inspiring guide who stimulates the children to do their own thinking, their own exploring, their own creating, and their own evaluating as he leads them toward a planned goal.

Dialogue is introduced when it can be properly motivated by the feelings of the characters. Generally a scene is developed first without dialogue, speech being added when it can be properly motivated by the feelings of the characters and the requirements of the scene. There is good reason for this. When a child reads a story or hears one, he readily translates words into action in his imagination, hence words easily become a substitute for action. When a scene is developed without dialogue, the meaning of the scene therefore has to be made clear by means of action and action alone, which is the very soul of drama. In addition, when the child does not have the crutch of words, particularly someone else's words, to depend upon, he is likely to realize more fully the nature and feelings of his character and likely to develop more fully the portrayal of that character.

After each characterization is attempted, each action performed, each scene played, and the whole play developed, there is a period of evaluation by the children themselves, guided by the leader, to find how something might be better done. Then there is the replaying to put the suggestions to work and to find improvement. This evaluation occurs after rather than during a bit of playing so as not to interrupt the creative process in action. The child creating the smallest Billy Goat Gruff may not be a Rembrandt, a Stravinsky, or an Olivier. He is nonetheless an artist at the moment, unknown and little, using his insight into life, using his imagination, concentrating, creating, communicating, and achieving some measure of his worth as a human being.

EXTENDING YOUR LEARNING

1. Some educators believe specialization has made education so splintered that children cannot grasp relationships between various bits of learning. How might the concept expressed by Richard Courtney at the beginning of this chapter be used in unifying school curricula?
2. What is your position with respect to formal drama in the elementary school? Should children memorize parts, create scenery and costumes, perform before an audience? What is the difference between creative drama and formal drama or theatre? Which in the elementary school should receive major emphasis? Does this vary according to level?
3. Examine a unit for language arts or develop one yourself and list the opportunities within this unit for enrichment through creative drama.

4. Select three or four trade (here defined as non-textbook) books written for children of either primary or intermediate grade. Which characters might children portray with ease and enjoyment? Which incidents from the books would be interesting and appropriate to create with the children? Select one book which portrays a way of life or a group of characters rather far removed from that which is familiar and commonplace to the children you will probably teach. What might children learn through assuming such an unfamiliar role?

5. For your future use compile an annotated bibliography of poems with strong rhythmic appeal, of poems suggesting a pronounced mood, and of poems suggesting strong sensory impressions. Select a half-dozen poems and stories that would not be useful for creative drama and say why they are inappropriate.

6. List ten distinct moods—use more than one word in the description if necessary. For each mood list the five senses and suggest at least three specific items for each of the senses that would help enhance the given mood. Be specific in listing a particular piece of music, a particular taste sensation, etc.

7. Select a poem, a piece of music, a painting, a piece of sculpture, a colorful scarf or other suggestive object. Each selection must have a definite mood. State the mood in terms of human feelings. Gather objects which enhance or reinforce that mood for each selection by means of appeals to the five senses. Describe an action with characters and setting which might grow out of the mood.

8. Work with a friend regularly for a week on the exercises in concentration of the senses described on pp. 50-57 of *Improvisation* by Hodgson and Richards or in another text. Try some of the beginning acting exercises in Selden's *First Steps in Acting,* the improvisation exercises in Spolin's *Improvisation for the Theatre* or the rhythm exercises in Andrews' *Creative Rhythmic Movement.* Keep a notebook on your personal progress. How does this work relate to your teaching language arts?

BIBLIOGRAPHY

Albright, H.D., Halstead, William P., and Mitchell, Lee, *Principles of Theatre Art.* Cambridge, Massachusetts: Houghton Mifflin Company, 1955.

Andrews, Gladys, *Creative Rhythmic Movement.* Englewood Cliffs: Prentice-Hall, Inc., 1952.

Bass, Bernard M., *Leadership, Psychology, and Organizational Behavior.* New York: Harper and Brothers, 1960.

Boleslavsky, Richard, *Acting: The First Six Lessons.* New York: Theatre Arts Books, 1949.

Courtney, Richard, *Play, Drama and Thought: The Intellectual Background to Dramatic Education.* London: Cassell and Company Ltd., 1968.

_____,*Teaching Drama: A Handbook for Teachers in Schools.* London: Cassell and Company Ltd., 1965.

Crosscup, Richard, *Children and Dramatics.* New York: Charles Scribner's Sons, 1966.

D'Amico, Victor E., *Creative Teaching in Art.* New York: International Textbook Co., 1953.

Dean, Alexander, *Fundamentals of Play Directing.* New York: Holt, Rinehart and Winston, 1941.

Fitzgerald, Burdett S., *World Tales for Creative Dramatics and Storytelling.* Englewood Cliffs: Prentice-Hall, Inc., 1962.

Graham, Martha, "A Modern Dancer's Primer for Action," *Dance: A Basic Educational Technique*, ed., Frederick Rand Rogers. New York: The Macmillan Co., 1941.

Hatlen, Theodore W., *Orientation to the Theatre*. New York: Appleton-Century-Crofts, 1962.

Henry, Mabel Wright, ed., *Creative Experiences in Oral Language*. Champagne, Illinois: National Council of Teachers of English, 1967.

Hodgson, John Reed and Richards, Ernest, *Improvisation: Discovery and Creativity in Drama*. London: Methuen and Company, Ltd., 1966.

Lowenfeld, Viktor, *Creative and Mental Growth*. New York: The Macmillan Company, 1947.

Rowe, Kenneth Thorpe, *Write That Play*. New York: Funk and Wagnalls Company, 1939.

Selden, Samuel, *First Steps in Acting*. New York: Appleton-Century-Crofts, Inc., 1947.

Siks, Geraldine Brain, *Creative Dramatics*. New York: Harper and Brothers, 1958.

Slade, Peter, *Child Drama*. London: University of London Press, 1954.

_____, *Child Drama and Its Value in Education*. Bromley, Kent: Stacey Publications, 1967.

Spolin, Viola, *Improvisation for the Theatre*. Evanston, Illinois: Northwestern University Press, 1963.

Ward, Winifred, *Playmaking with Children*. New York: Appleton-Century-Crofts, Inc., 1957.

Way, Brian, *Development Through Drama*. London: Longmans, 1967.

Young, Stark, *The Theatre*. New York: Hill and Wang, 1954.

Focus

How important is listening? Consider the amount a child learns before he learns to read. Keep a record of the waking minutes of a typical day spent listening, speaking, reading and writing. The answer is evident. Listening is the primary vehicle for learning in an individual's most formative years. It remains extremely important, in terms of time spent and information processed, throughout life.

The listener is subject to demands from the speaker which the writer cannot make on the reader. The speaker determines the rate at which listening must occur if a majority of the information presented is to be processed. It is possible to re-read, to "regress" for purposes of verifying something or to enjoy a well-written passage again. The listener is denied these privileges. In many respects, listening represents a more difficult set of skills to acquire and use effectively than are those related to reading. A multitude of factors, not all within the listener's control, can interfere with or contribute to effective listening—the physical setting within which listening is to occur, the physical condition of the listener and his affective response to speaker and topic, to mention just four. Listening is not easy!

The model provided by Ralph Kellogg is particularly helpful in clarifying what listening includes, and how it occurs. It is, obviously, a more complex process than had been assumed in the period when research in listening was just beginning. Because it is complex; because it is important in terms of learning and interpersonal relationships, it, like speaking, deserves more attention in the elementary school than it typically receives. A child who has been helped to understand when marginal listening is appropriate and adequate and when critical listening skills must be applied will certainly operate more effectively in today's media-filled, noisy world than will a child who hasn't had such guidance. Kellogg notes that few systematic listening programs have been developed, and yet it seems clear that the 'incidental' approach used for so many years has been and is inadequate. Identification of listening as an important area of the elementary curriculum is of recent origin—the author indicates that the first research in listening was reported in 1917. Much remains to be done—"listening" refers to an extremely significant and complex group of skills which determine, in large measure, the degree of academic and social success a person will achieve. Work in this area is deserving of an elementary teacher's best efforts.

Ralph E. Kellogg —————————————————— *chapter four*

listening

Children in the elementary schools of today will become the adults of their communities and nations one and two decades in the future. What will their world be like? What knowledges, attitudes, skills and values will they need for their personal welfare and the collective benefit of the society they will help shape and in which they will live? How will they acquire the competencies necessary to prepare themselves for their future roles? These and other similar questions continue to be asked by the lay public and educators alike as they critically analyze the present school program and plan for its improvement. A brief look into the future to discern continuing trends of development is necessary for a perspective of the role of listening instruction in the elementary curricular program.

The Knowledge Explosion

It is obvious to even the uncritical observer that there has been an accelerated rate of technological change in the past decade. Many scholars indicate that this rate of change will increase even more rapidly in the future. A major force in this change is the unprecedented explosion of knowledge. Application of new knowledge causes technological change which, in turn, helps generate additional new knowledge. A prediction that the elementary age child of today will have available in his lifetime at least twice the amount of information compared with that available to his parents is conservative indeed. The explosion of knowledge and rapid technological change will provide opportunities and problems of greatly increased complexity for the child as he becomes the adult of tomorrow.

Listening: A Vital Link to Knowledge

One future problem will be how all this new knowledge will be learned, communicated, and utilized. In taking advantage of the opportunities and accepting responsibilities for the problems ahead, critical thinking and effective communication of such thinking through all communication media will be necessary. Currently in evidence is the increased utilization of the mass media of television with international television already a technical reality. The linking of persons in their homes to relatives and friends across the nation through direct dial telephone is but a stage of development from which international phone communication by an increasingly large number of persons will be forthcoming. The organization of library sources of knowledge via computer-linked data phone television systems holds promise of nearly instantaneous request and reception of information.

Whatever simple or complex communication systems are devised to transmit information and knowledge, their final link will continue to be the mind of the individual person, child or adult. The vehicle of the mind which the individual will use most in incorporating new information will be language. Language is processed in the mind largely through listening and speaking. The acquisition of knowledge through effective listening will continue to be a high priority need for the citizen of the future.

Value Formation Through Critical Listening

The knowledge explosion, in and of itself, has no positive or negative value. Expansion of knowledge and rapid technological change are presently causing and will continue to cause thoughtful persons to question their effect upon the formation of values in the individual. Will the child—adult of tomorrow—develop his values based upon the individual critical analysis and judgment in the knowledge explosion? Will he recognize such common propaganda tricks of "name calling," "glittering generality," "transfer," "testimonial," "plain folks," "card stacking," and "band wagon" which may be used in attempts to sway his thinking and opinion relative to social, political, and economic issues? Values will be influenced in the mental processing of information transmitted through various communication systems. The final link of any system will continue to be the mind and thought processes of the individual involving the use of language. The need for the adult of tomorrow to be able to assimilate, analyze, synthesize, and evaluate great amounts of information through language and to relate this to a value system will be greater than ever before. An increased quantity and quality of thinking through listening to language cannot be escaped by the elementary child as he progresses through life. The individual and collective cost of evasion will be too great.

Listening; Time Involvement

Another way in which the importance of listening might be considered is in terms of the amount of time spent in listening in comparison with the other language skills. Rankin, in an early study in 1926, found that a selected group of representative United States citizens spent about 45 per cent of their language communication time in listening, 30 per cent in speaking, 16 per cent in reading, and 9 per cent in writing.[1] Wilt found that elementary teachers believed that children were spending a major part of their day reading and that learning to read was the most important skill to be learned. Her timed tabulation of activities of school children in their elementary classrooms revealed quite divergent information however: 57.5 per cent of the classroom activity time was spent in listening.[2]

Casual observation in the elementary classrooms of this nation will reveal that speaking-listening is the major mode of instruction. Mathematically one can see that in the speaking-listening process in classroom instruction a greater amount of time will be spent in listening. If children were organized into teams of two each with one child speaking while the other child listened and vice versa, the percentage in time in speaking and listening each would approximate 50 per cent for each child. When groups of children larger than two are involved in oral

1. Paul T. Rankin, *The Measurement of the Ability to Understand Spoken Language* (Doctoral Dissertation; Ann Arbor, Michigan: University of Michigan, 1926). *Dissertation Abstracts* 12 (1952): 897.
2. Miriam E. Wilt, *A Study of Teacher Awareness of Listening as a Factor in Elementary Education* (Doctoral Dissertation; State College, Pennsylvania: Penn State College, 1949). Summary: *Journal of Educational Research* 43 (April, 1950): 626-36.

language communication, or when the teacher is talking to the total class or subgroups of the class, the percentage of time involved in listening by the individual child necessarily will become greater than time spent in speaking. The importance of listening in terms of quantity of time spent in classrooms and in life generally seems easily apparent. Rankin's and Wilt's investigations are illustrative of other studies which validate this seemingly simple but often unconsidered fact.

Listening Facilitates Social Adaptation

The relationship of listening to social adaptation in our culture is interesting to consider. Early in the history of the United States literacy was considered to be very important. Public schools were established to provide opportunities for the development of universal literacy. Literacy was commonly meant to mean competence in reading and writing. Effectiveness in social conversation and public speaking was also recognized as an attribute of the "literate" person. This tradition remains within our culture today. Typically listening skill has not been made explicit as a part of "literacy"; however, its importance is fundamental to the other skills. Barbara states, "In our particular culture, people judge your character, your intellectual capacity, your social standing by the way you talk and listen."[3]

Four major reasons for the development of effective listening ability have been cited:

1. The explosion of knowledge requiring the processing of greater amounts of information through listening.
2. The need for critical thinking in the development of values through language listening.
3. The relatively high percentage of time spent in listening as compared with the other intake of thought in language through reading.
4. The facilitation of personal and social adaptation through becoming more "literate" through listening.

Status of Listening Instruction in the Elementary School

Once the importance of effective listening has been accepted the question naturally arises, "What are we doing now?" "What is the current status of listening instruction in the elementary schools?" Ander-

---

3. Dominick A. Barbara, "Healthy and Neurotic Aspects of Listening," Bulletin: *Auxiliary Council to the Association for the Advancement of Psychoanalysis* (New York), p. 2.

son states that "except in isolated instances, virtually the only instruction in listening that children and young people receive in the schools is the quite useless admonition of 'pay attention' and to 'listen carefully.' Listening, at all educational levels, has been the forgotten language art for generations."[4] The writer has been recently engaged in one of the twenty-seven research projects funded by the U.S. Office of Education in studying first grade reading and language arts methodologies.[5] Fifty teachers in San Diego County, California, selected because of their teaching competency utilizing the traditional method language arts program and the experience approach language arts program, included little direct instruction in listening skill development. These teachers are judged to be typical of the best elementary teachers across the nation.

A simple test will give face validity evidence of the lack of extensive direct instruction in listening skills. The reader might ask himself or any elementary teacher whom he knows three questions:

1. Did you receive any direct instruction in the improvement of your listening skills while in elementary school or at any level of education?
2. How many elementary teachers do you know or have you heard about who provide systematic instruction for their students in the development of listening ability?
3. What materials of instruction are currently available for use in elementary classrooms to help the teacher provide listening skill instruction?

At a time when critical listening ability is increasing in importance, common practice in elementary schools still includes little conscious systematic or sustained concern for helping children improve their listening.

A Theory of Listening

When someone says, "He listens well!" what is really meant? Clearly an explanation of such a statement would vary from individual to individual depending upon his concept of "listening" and the nature of the listening process. At one level "listening" can be described as the physi-

---

4. Harold A. Anderson, "Needed Research in Listening," *Elementary English* 29 (April, 1954): 215-224.
5. "A Comparative Study of Two First Grade Language Arts Programs," Research Project Funded by the U.S. Office of Education. Submitted by the San Diego County Department of Education (May 28, 1964).

ological reception of physical pulsation or vibration through the auditory nerve system. Usually such vibrations are transmitted through the air and received initially through the ears. This definition implies no linkage of the vibration with thought processes or meaning and leaves the source of vibration completely open. At this level of "listening" the *acuity* of the ears and related parts of the auditory nerve mechanism of the individual is all that is required. At another level "listening" can be described as the process of receiving the sounds of other human beings' oral language through the auditory nerve system and distinguishing likenesses and differences among the various units of sounds. This narrows the definition to language but still implies no relationships to the proc-

PERCEPTION LEVEL I	
	Scope of Input
	Total physical world capable of transmission visually or auditorally
Hearing	Requirement of Individual
	Auditory and Visual acuity
Seeing	Reaction Level of Individual
	Physical reception, no comprehension or interpretation
PERCEPTION LEVEL II	
	Scope of Input
	Total World of Spoken or Written Language
Listening	Requirement of Individual
	Auditory and Visual Discrimination
Observing	Reaction Level of Individual
	Recognition of likenesses and differences of phonemes and graphemes (sound and visual language units)
PERCEPTION LEVEL III	
	Scope of Input
	Total World of Spoken and Written Language
Auditing	Requirement of Individual
	Auditory and Visual Comprehension
Reading	Reaction Level of Individual
	Comprehension and interpretation of language symbols

FIGURE 5.1. Relationship of levels of visual and auditory perception in "reading" and "listening."

ess of thinking and interpretation. At this level of "listening" *auditory discrimination* is required of the listener. A third definition of "listening" is that it is the process of hearing, recognizing, and interpreting spoken symbols. This last definition is given by Brown as a definition of "auding."[6] Auding might be conceived as *auditory comprehension* of language signals or symbols. This term has been used to differentiate more precisely the relationship of "listening" to spoken language and its interpretation in the thinking process of the individual. Russell has used a simple formula to show the relationship of these different interpretations and their comparison to a similar sequence of meaning in reading: Seeing; observing; Reading—Hearing; listening; Auding.[7] A more detailed analysis of these relationships is shown in Figure 5.1.

It becomes apparent that the term "listening" is an overall generic term in general popular usage which has different levels of meaning and interpretation. For purposes of this chapter the reader is asked to retain the term listening to mean all three levels indicated in Figure 1. It should be remembered that focus on improvement of children's listening competence at Level III is the major concern of the language arts program.

A further differentiation of levels of listening can be made at perception Level III: Comprehension and interpretation of language symbols. One method by which this can be accomplished is through the use of Bloom's Taxonomy.[8] Six general levels of thought processes are delineated in the taxonomy: Knowledge, Comprehension, Application, Analysis, Synthesis, and Evaluation. Using this model of thought levels, one can readily think of a different purpose or level for listening to a conversation or formal oral presentation relating to each of the given thought levels. A specific example of listening comprehension levels using this model follows.

Assume that the following information was being presented orally. The listener might be required to comprehend at each of the six different levels. A question will be asked after the selection to illustrate each level of comprehension.

6. Don Pardee Brown, "Auding as the Primary Language Ability" (Doctoral Dissertation; Stanford, California: Stanford University, 1954) Abstract: *Dissertation Abstracts* 14(1954): 2281-2282.
7. David H. Russell and Elizabeth F. Russell, *Listening Aids Through the Grades* (New York: Teachers College, Columbia University, Bureau of Publications, 1959), p. 3.
8. Benjamin S. Bloom, editor, *Taxonomy of Educational Objectives,* Handbook I: *Cognitive Domain* (New York: Longmans, Green and Co., 1956).

Land animals have a harsh living environment such as polar regions, jungles, and deserts. Creatures of the seas have life much easier. Water temperatures in the tropics seldom exceed eighty-five degrees. Waters at the poles usually are not colder than thirty degrees.

Question 1—Knowledge Level: Recall of Specific Facts Presented

Tropical waters usually do not go above _____ degrees in temperature?

Question 2—Comprehension Level: Simple Interpretation of Facts Presented

The ranges of temperature from tropic to polar waters is approximately _____ degrees?

Question 3—Application Level: Application of Ideas Presented to a Different Specific Situation

Land animals of the desert region must be more adaptable to temperature extremes than sea animals. Explain.

Question 4—Analysis Level: Analysis of Relationships of Component Parts of Ideas Presented

The water mass of the world stabilizes temperature extremes of the world's land masses. True or false? Why?

Question 5—Synthesis Level: Restructuring of Component Parts to Form a Concept or Generalization Not Given in the Presentation.

If you could change the temperature of the land and seas of the earth to be most ideal for all existing life what would you do?

a. Make no changes.
b. Decrease land temperature range 50 degrees.
c. Increase water temperature range 20 degrees. Why?

Question 6—Evaluation Level: Judgment of Ideas Presented Against Ideas or Values of the Listener

How would you compare the quality of life on other planets with life on earth knowing the extreme temperature ranges of most other planets?

Basic Premises of a Comprehensive Theory

This model of the cognitive domain ranges far beyond the level of listening comprehension practiced by most persons. The components of the listening theory presented thus far suggest a basic premise of the over-all theory.

Basic Premise A

Listening is a complex process, taking place at many levels ranging from simple reception of vibrations through abstract levels of thinking. In its most meaningful sense, listening must be closely linked with all levels of thought processes.

When one considers the four language skills of listening, speaking, reading, and writing in terms of their development within an individual during his early years and throughout his life the fundamental importance of listening becomes obvious. If one were to consider crying, gooing, cooing, etc., as speaking, it might be technically correct to say that a baby speaks before he listens. But when one thinks of these four skill areas within the framework of the language system of the particular culture, one realizes that the infant listens to the language for a considerable length of time before he speaks the language. A background of much experience in hearing oral symbols and relating them to objects and actions previously experienced is necessary for the child to learn to speak, to read, and to write. The first language symbolization of experience takes place through listening. Understanding this process is central to all other thinking and practice in language arts instruction.

The infant or young child touches, sees, hears, and in most every sensory way possible, experiences his mother. After much repetition of listening to the sound of "mama" as he experiences his mother he gradually begins to understand that the spoken sound of "mama" symbolizes or represents his mother. In this manner he is introduced to the first oral language word of his culture through listening. He reinforces this understanding through speaking by saying "mama." Whatever meaning the word "mama" has when he hears or speaks it will be related directly to the kinds of experiences he has built up in the interaction between him and his mother. From this seemingly simple but very complex intellectual beginning he rapidly builds his own oral language within the scope and limitations of the experiential and linguistic environment of his family and neighborhood. The linguistic environment initially is experienced totally through listening and speaking. Reading and writing will be introduced normally at a later stage of development. Through this process, meaningful experience builds upon prior meaningful experience and is communicated through language symbols building upon language symbols. This process is lifelong and cumulative. A step-by-step progression of this developmental process with concepts central to each step is illustrated in Figures 5.2 through 5.6.

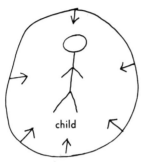

The young child experiences his environment through his various sensory systems.

FIGURE 5.2. Environment experienced through senses.

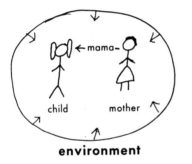

The child hears specific elements of the environment symbolized in language.

FIGURE 5.3. Auditory symbolic intake process.

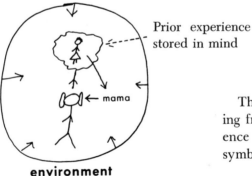

Prior experience stored in mind

The child takes meaning from his prior experience to the oral language symbols he hears.

FIGURE 5.4. Reconstruction of experience process.

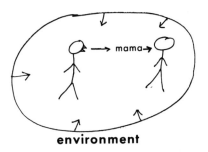

The child speaks about prior experiences using the oral language symbols which he has heard.

FIGURE 5.5. Auditory symbolic output process.

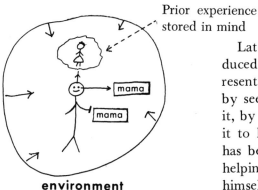

Prior experience stored in mind

Later the child is introduced to the graphic representation of the sound by seeing someone write it, by someone's showing it to him after it already has been written and by helping him write it for himself.

FIGURE 5.6. Visual symbolic intake and output process.

Additional basic premises to the listening theory arise from these ideas:

Basic Premise B

Language is symbolization of experience and has meaning only in relationship to prior experience.

Basic Premise C

Language communication through listening-speaking takes place through a common background of experience which each person using the language brings to the oral sounds of the language.

Basic Premise D

Language meanings may be similar between individuals but in the final analysis are individual in nature because each person is unique, with unique experiences.

Basic Premise E

Experience symbolized in oral language is taken in the mind of the individual through listening, reconstructed by relating the oral symbol to past experience and projected from the mind of the individual in language through speaking or writing.

A developmental hierarchy is typically followed by most children in their natural development of language from early infancy through the elementary school years. This hierarchy is illustrated in Figure 5.7.

Refinement of language usage comes last.

Writing follows as a means of self-expression.

Reading comes next with the normal child.

Speaking develops early in life.

Listening is the first step toward maturity.

EXPERIENCE is the foundation of all language development.

FIGURE 5.7. The relationship of experience and listening to the other language arts skills in the typical instructional program.

There is little research evidence to indicate at what stages of development children's reading vocabulary surpasses their oral language usage vocabulary. It has been observed that usually in the upper elementary and junior high years most children's reading vocabulary extends beyond the oral language vocabulary which they use in common social discourse. This phenomenon might cause one to question the fundamental importance of listening as a foundation to the skills of reading and writing in later stages of development. The writer is not aware of any definitive research explaining this phenomenon; however, the following hypothesis is presented: Reading and writing involve an "internal dialogue" of speaking silently to oneself and listening to oneself. In this connection a person reading silently is speaking to himself about the words on the page and then mentally listens to himself speaking. A similar process occurs in writing, that is, the writer says the words and internally listens to them as he writes. Thus a reader may encounter a new word foreign to his present listening vocabulary. He can pronounce the word only to the extent that he can relate it to the sound system of the language, hence internal listening within the mind becomes involved. The reader may gain an approximate meaning of the word from the context of the sentence and the paragraph in which he finds it. The meaning of the words in the context will have their roots in the prior listening experiences of the reader. Pronouncing a new word is related to sound, therefore is based upon prior listening; understanding a new word in reading rests upon its relationship to other words whose initial meaning first was symbolized through the listening process.

From these ideas two basic premises of the listening theory emerge:

Basic Premise F
Listening is the process which provides the basic foundation upon which all other language skills develop. Comprehension of meaning in Speaking, Reading, and Writing rests upon the base of comprehension in Listening.

Basic Premise G
A person "listens" as he utilizes the other language skills by carrying on an internal mental dialogue as he speaks, reads, and writes.

The theory of listening presented here reflects a range of levels from auditory acuity of sound vibrations through comprehension and interpretation of abstract concepts symbolized in language. The focus of listening instruction beginning in the elementary school and continuing throughout life should be in the direction of improving the meaningful interpretation of higher level concepts symbolized in language.

Goals of the Listening Instruction Program

That listening is a distinctly separate mental process from reading but related to it, has been reasonably well substantiated. Many research studies have investigated the relationship between listening and reading abilities. There is strong but not conclusive evidence that instruction in listening skills will positively influence achievement in reading. The relationship of the design of the listening skills' instructional program to the skills of reading seems to be important to the degree of transfer from listening instruction to reading achievement.

Most persons knowledgeable in the research relating to the skills involved in the language arts and teachers who put language arts instructional programs into effect are aware of the interrelationships of the skills of listening, reading, writing, and speaking. Because of this, a crucial question faces the person developing the design of instructional programs in listening. Should instruction in listening have as its major goal the provision of the foundation support for achievement of more effective reading or should instruction in listening be taught primarily because it is important that all persons learn to listen more effectively regardless of whether or not this affects reading? Generally speaking, it is known that many things can be taught to children in the elementary school which were once thought impossible if appropriate instructional processes are used and enough time is provided. The criterion of efficiency becomes important here: the most learning with the least amount of instructional time. In this framework the teacher should help children improve their listening skills because this is a worthy goal in itself but should always attempt to help children transfer such skills into the reading process whenever possible.

A Synthesis of Listening Skills

A list of the skills of listening, in the final analysis, is a product of an arbitrary decision of the one making the list. Undoubtedly there will be scientific validation of the existence of listening skills in future investigations and research. At present little inquiry along this dimension of listening has been made. Most skills of listening which are given in courses of study, professional journals, and textbooks therefore are the result of best thinking on a logical basis, rather than an empirically determined basis. Perhaps this should not discourage the practicing teacher too much, however, since the same observation would apply to many of the skills of reading which are included in teachers' manuals and student materials which have been and are being used across the nation to teach reading. We do not know everything about how children learn and think, yet we continue to help them to learn and to stimulate them to think.

The lists of listening skills presented here are the writer's synthesis of those indicated in the professional literature. They are drawn largely from the work of Wright[9] and Lundsteen.[10] Illustrative examples or explanations follow the statement of each skill to facilitate greater understanding. The reader is directed to note the relationship of these skills to thinking processes as previously indicated in Bloom's Taxonomy.

Listening to Get Information

Skills requiring attention and following directions

Maintaining attention through a difficult speech

This skill is largely one of mental concentration upon the speaker and what he is trying to say, regardless of the manner of presentation.

Anticipating a speaker's ideas

This skill grows from the maintenance of attention. It involves thinking with the person who is speaking. It may include anticipating the next word, phrase, or thought which the speaker might use or projecting an idea or conclusion far ahead of what the speaker is saying at the moment. Usually the first kind of anticipation is done in small group conversation and the second in listening to longer formal presentations.

Following verbal directions given in a sequence

Directions here might range from simple "Do this" and then "Do that" at the preschool or kindergarten level to an involved complex operation in a particular specialty field at the graduate level.

Repeating messages given verbally

Recall of exact detail and sequence after a period of time delay is necessary.

Skills used in detecting speech organization

Discovering the main ideas

Many test items utilized in standardized achievement and intelligence tests which give a short paragraph, and ask the student to select the main idea illustrate this skill.

9. Evan L. Wright, *The Construction of a Test of Listening Comprehension for the Second, Third, and Fourth Grades* (Doctoral Dissertation; St. Louis, Missouri: Washington University, 1957). Abstract: *Dissertation Abstracts* 17 (1957): 2226-2227.

10. Sara W. Lundsteen, *Teaching Abilities in Critical Listening in the Fifth and Sixth Grades* (Doctoral Dissertation; Berkeley: University of California, 1963).

Determining the plan of organization

The process involved in this skill might be called mental outlining. Discovering the several "main ideas" of a speech and their sequence is required.

Recognizing illustrative examples

Example: Which statements (1, 2, 3, or 4) help prove statement A.

A. An animal is sometimes easy to tell from other animals because one part of its body is very strange or unusual.
   1. Some rabbits have tails that look like powder puffs.
   2. The dog has hair on his back.
   3. The cat has sharp teeth.
   4. The tiger has claws.

In a speech, illustrative examples are used to support main ideas.

Critical Listening

Skills requiring analysis and synthesis of information

Relating heard material to own experiences

In this skill the listener thinks about what he knows and its likeness to and difference from his previous experience.

Making use of contextual clues to determine unknown meanings

Example: A. Nancy was playing with a knife. She wasn't careful, and she lacerated her finger.
   1. She bruised her finger.
   2. She hurt her finger.
   3. She cut her finger.

Discerning between fact and opinion

Example: Are these facts or opinions?
   1. Many trees have red leaves in springtime.
   2. Birds are happier than animals.
   3. St. Louis is the friendliest city in the world.
   4. The stars are far away from us.

Recognizing that which is relevant

This skill is similar but more complex than the recognition of illustrative examples. Examples to illustrate a main point or an idea are subordinate to the idea being presented. Relevancy involves degrees of relationship between ideas which may not necessarily be illustrative of each other.

Example: The struggle in Viet Nam is an illustrative example of armed military conflict. The Viet Nam conflict may be relevant to a theoretical discussion of the possible causes of nuclear war but not an illustrative example of it.

Making logical inferences from what is heard
Example: Billy loved to eat. He ate too much every chance he got, especially when sweet things were around. One afternoon, the bakery man gave him a small cherry pie. What do you think Billy did?

1. He sat down and started eating.
2. Billy decided to take the pie home for supper.
3. He ate one bite and threw the rest away.
4. He gobbled up the whole pie.

Keeping an open mind before forming opinions
This skill is more linked to the emotional attitude of the listener than most of the other skills. Mentally it may involve any or all of the other listening skills and withholding the formation of an opinion until those speaking have had opportunity to present all their information.

Skills relating to the analysis and judgment of propaganda
Many of the other skills of listening are involved here. The recognition and identification of certain generalized methods of persuasion used in propaganda should be learned by any competent listener. Some of these included name calling, glittering generalities, transfer, testimonial, card stacking, side tracking, band wagon, bad words, and glad words.

The Kellogg Listening Model

The sections of this chapter thus far have attempted to provide some background information related to the phenomenon of listening, its importance, its relationship to other language skills, and some of the specific listening skills. Since the time of the first edition the author has been aware that a systematic comprehensive theory of listening which could be easily applied in everyday practice or in teaching listening in the classroom had not been formulated. Since writing the first edition, serious thought has been given to formulating such a working listening model. Given all the ideas of the first sections as general information, the Kellogg Listening Model presented here represents the best thinking and practice the author can suggest at this time. Hopefully improvements will be made upon this model by the author and others as further thinking takes place regarding listening instruction in the future.

The Kellogg Listening Model has been presented to teacher groups, executives, hospital personnel, administrators and others with practice sessions in its application. Response of these personnel generally has been quite positive. The model is formulated in such a way that it can be remembered without notes or other materials, thus easily applied should one wish to do so. Secondly it seems to have "made sense" to most persons who have been exposed to it. Third it seems to have generic application, that is, it can be applied to different and varied content of ideas expressed in oral form. At this point no systematic research has been undertaken to verify the effects of the use of the model. Subjective response has been positive. Readers are encouraged to apply the model to their own listening habits and to use it in classroom instruction and judge its relevance for themselves.

The model is organized in such a way that a person has to remember no more than four things at one time in thinking about it or explaining it. So let us begin. It has been suggested previously that there are three perception levels: acuity, discrimination, and comprehension. These levels are utilized in this model and are shown in Figure 5.8. Listening acuity means that the ear mechanism must be functioning to allow the sound waves to reach the brain. *Level I: Acuity,* is necessary for listening to take place on *Level II: Discrimination.* At Level II the ear and mind must be able to discriminate likenesses and differences in sound, nuance, pitch, rhythm and volume. Discrimination of likenesses and differences in sound at Level II is necessary for listening at *Level III: Comprehension.* Listening comprehension means that the mind not only hears the likenesses and differences in sound but attaches meaning and understanding to those sound differences based upon previous experience with similar sounds. Thus we have three levels of listening. Immediately the question comes to mind, what kinds of sound might one listen to which need to be incorporated in the model. Three different categories of sound are shown in Figure 5.9. These categories are; *sounds of nature, sounds of man-made objects,* and *sounds of man's language.* To test the model at this point ask yourself the question, "Are there any sounds which you can think of or have heard which would not fit in one of these three categories?" Thus far in presentation of the model, no sound has been presented by anyone which could not fit into these categories. Occasionally questions arise regarding into which category a given sound might be placed. For example, where would the sound of one's stomach growling fit? If the definition is made that sounds of nature are those sounds which are nonman related but relate only to the physical or animal world then it would fit as a sound of a man-made object.

By placing Figure 5.9 on top of Figure 5.8 we have the basic framework of the listening model as shown in Figure 5.10. The model then consists of three levels of listening involving three different categories of sound. The reader is requested to select an example of a sound of nature and follow it from Level I: Acuity, through Level III: Comprehension. For example one might think of the sound of a bird chirping. In order to listen the ear must have the acuity to arrest the sound of the bird. After hearing the sound the listener might be able to distinguish some likenesses and differences in the sound. Does the bird sound the same at all times? Does it sound differently from another kind of bird? If it sounds differently from another bird the listener is immediately at Level III, comprehending the meaning of the difference of sound. Or perhaps the sounds of a single bird at one time cause the listener to know that it is agitated, fearful, happy, a young bird, or mature bird, etc. In similar fashion the reader could select the sound of a man made object and follow it through the three levels of listening, such as the sound of an airplane. At this point it can be noted that the levels of listening are hierarchal, that is, they build upon each other, and that achievement at Level I is necessary for achievement at Level II and this for achievement at Level III.

In the column of listening to man's language the following example drawn from an actual incident may help the reader's understanding. Two boys were talking and at the stage of argument. One boy had used the word "chalk" in a sentence. The other boy maintained that it didn't make any sense. The second boy had heard the word as "shock" rather than "chalk." In this example the second boy had listening acuity but did not correctly discriminate the differences in the initial "sh" and "ch" sounds and therefore comprehended incorrectly.

It is in the third column; listening to man's language, that a great amount of time is consumed by most persons who live and associate with other human beings. The cell of the model dealing with discrimination of man's language is where much instruction in "phonetics" takes

The Kellogg Listening Model

III	Comprehension
II	Discrimination
I	Acuity

FIGURE 5.8. Levels of listening.

The Kellogg Listening Model

Nature	Man Made Objects	Man's Language

FIGURE 5.9. Categories of sound.

place in the primary grades of school. Helping children to listen in this cell is important in the school program but not the major purpose of utilization of this listening model. It is in the upper right cell of the model; Comprehending man's language, that we now turn our attention. How does one comprehend man's language through listening? How could a listener train himself to become a better listener through more effective comprehension? How could a teacher teach children listening comprehension? It is in this cell that the thinking processes can be merged with listening. In the final analysis listening is not complete without thinking.

The Kellogg Listening Model

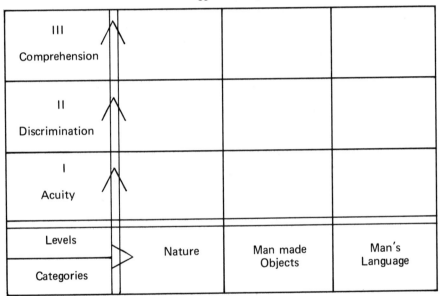

FIGURE 5.10.

The reader is now asked to visualize four levels of comprehension within the comprehension of man's language cell. If we call the sounds of man's language that we hear "data" these levels are: Data Recall, Data Analysis, Data Synthesis, and Data Applications. These four levels again are hierarchal. Data recall is necessary for data analysis, synthesis, and application, etc. These levels are shown in Figure 5.11. The mental operations involved in each of the levels of comprehension are shown in the middle column. Data recall requires memory, data analysis requires deductive thinking, data synthesis requires inductive thinking and data application requires both deductive and inductive thinking.

The Kellogg Listening Model

Comprehension Levels	Mental Operation Levels	Question Levels
4. Application	Deductive and Inductive	So How
3. Synthesis	Inductive	So What
2. Analysis	Deductive	Why How
1. Recall Data	Memory Recall	What, When, Where, Who

FIGURE 5.11. Comprehension of man's language.

At this point the reader may be thinking, "This all appears logical but what do I do when I am listening to be sure that I listen (comprehend man's language) at each of these four levels?" The third column showing levels of questions provides the answer and is that portion of the model which the listener must hold in his mind (remember) while he listens in order to apply the model. After one has listened to a conversation, speech, broadcast, etc. he can ask himself questions at each of the levels. At the data recall level he would ask questions of a What, When, Where, and Who nature. What was said, when did it happen, where did it happen and who was involved or who said it? All of these questions require the listener to remember or recall what was presented in the oral language model. At the data analysis level the listener would ask himself questions of a Why and/or How nature. Why did that happen, why did that person take that action, how did this happen, how did this fact relate to that other idea which was presented? These kinds of questions require the listener to analyze, disect, think through the relationships of the ideas which were presented. At the data synthesis level the listener might ask himself the questions; "So what is the main idea, so what does all of this mean?" These kinds of questions require him to synthesize or distill, or draw out the significant or important ideas which were presented.

At the data application level of comprehension, of man's language, the listener would ask himself these kinds of questions. "So how can I apply that main idea to a new situation? So how can I apply that idea to me?" These kinds of questions require the listener to analyze the likenesses and differences of a different situation with the one presented and to see the relationships involved, thus both deductive and inductive thinking are required.

In applying The Kellogg Listening Model then, a listener needs to mentally ask himself questions at four levels *as* he is listening or *after* he has listened. These questions are Who, What, When, Where; Why and/or How; So What, and So How.

Application of The Kellogg Listening Model

The Kellogg Listening Model has been and can be applied in helping adults improve their listening abilities. Each reader, if he so desires, can improve his listening behavior through use of the model. This claim is made on such a universal basis because in the experience of the author, very few persons have a conscious strategy which they employ when listening. This question has been asked of many persons. Thus far the only conscious strategy which any person has indicated to the author which he uses in listening is that of concentrating upon the speaker. This is a very important first step and necessary in any strategy of listening. However, it does not give any direction for how the listener might mentally process the data which has been heard. The Kellogg Listening Model can be explained step by step to children and practice given for them to use it. A teacher may also, without explanation, apply the model to a class discussion after stories or other materials have been read to children, by simply asking questions proceeding up the hierarchy of comprehension from data recall to data application.

Even preschool and kindergarten children can respond to different levels of questions if they have had sufficient experience background to relate to that which is heard. The model is equally applicable at the graduate level of instruction. The nature and levels of sophistication of the content and the specificity of the questions can be modified to fit the level of the listeners.

Some teachers have initially responded to the idea of a structured model of listening by saying that this would tend to put children in a straight jacket of thinking. It should be understood that the kinds of analysis, synthesis, and application made by different children or adults will vary greatly depending upon background of experience and levels of sophistication. The model does not suggest that all persons should hear a presentation and arrive with exactly the same conclusion by applying the model. This would deny what is known about language communication processes. In response to the concern that this is only one model, the author has suggested to others that they develop one or more different models which are also useful and can be easily remembered and applied. It is hoped that in the future several different models might be developed for individual or classroom use. Until that time the author poses these questions to the reader: Have you ever been exposed to a conscious strategy of listening? Do you know a conscious strategy of listening and have it incorporated into your behavior? Can this listening model serve as a tool for you to improve your listening? Is it not better to know one listening tool and be able to apply it effectively personally and in teaching, than to have either no tool, or a vague, undifferentiated tool which is not consciously applied? Until the reader is able to develop a better tool and apply it he is challenged to understand and use this one.

Role of the Elementary Teacher in Listening Instruction

A program in any curricular area should give consideration to several specific components of instruction: time, place, method, content, students, instructional materials including teaching materials or pupil materials, and evaluation. One could analyze the various listening programs today in terms of how each of these components of instruction has been considered in its program design. Currently the writer knows of no listening skills instructional program which has considered all of these components in any systematic fashion for even one entire year of the elementary school. Several researchers have developed a series of lessons usually for a portion of a year at one grade level. Currently there is no commercially available listening skill instructional program which systematically moves from developmental level to developmental level or grade level to grade level. In addition to this lack of assistance for the teacher, teacher training institutions traditionally have included little if any emphasis upon teaching listening skills.

Both of these phenomena are understandable when one realizes that the first research on listening appreared in 1917 and that in 1961 Duker's extensive bibliography on professional articles and studies in listening included only 725 items. In contrast, it has been estimated that 2,700 studies on reading were produced between 1881 and 1945. Until such time as the research into listening has provided a more solid basis of knowledge for pre-service training and the design of instructional programs, there will not be widespread instruction in listening skills. What then is the elementary teacher to do until more favorable conditions exist? Five general suggestions are presented. The teacher might:

1. Engage himself in a long-term project of learning more about effective listening and improving his own listening abilities. Concentration on improving one specific skill at a time, then moving to another skill is recommended. "Are You Listening" by Nichols and Stevens[11] and "The Art of Listening" by Barbara[12] are excellent general references for the adult who wishes to begin a program of self-improvement. This may seem like a strange first suggestion. It is based upon the following rationale: If the teacher becomes involved in developing his own listening ability, he will begin to understand the many thought processes and techniques which are involved in effective listening and thereby be in a better position to assist children. The self-improvement resulting for the teacher will cause him to recognize the benefits of improved listening ability and therefore probably become more persistent in helping students he teaches to improve their listening. In the process of becoming a more effective listener, the prospective or practicing teacher will obtain more knowledge of the world around him and become more aware of other individuals within his environment.

2. Apply the concept in Basic Premise F in preparing students for listening, speaking, reading, and writing by providing as much direct

---

11. Ralph G. Nichols and Leonard A. Stevens, *Are You Listening?* (New York: McGraw-Hill Book Company, Inc., 1957).

12. Dominick A. Barbara, *The Art of Listening* (Springfield, Illinois: Charles G. Thomas, 1958).

experience as possible relating to the concepts which students are expected to learn in any content area. Having students listen or read without adequate related experiential background will only frustrate them and waste instructional time from meaningful learning. In short, the teacher should not expect the listening and reading process to bring about learning unless these processes are cast within the experiences of the learners. Listening and reading can only help the learner enrich, elaborate, extend, summarize, synthesize, analyze, etc., the basic experiences which he brings to the language symbols involved in the listening and-or reading process.

3. Prepare a diagnostic and achievement check sheet of listening skills appropriate to a student grade level. Use it as a basis for instruction in the various skills. Drawing children's attention to the importance of listening, the specific skills involved and providing definite opportunities for their development will give them more help with the evolution of their listening skills than many elementary children will ever receive.

4. Obtain a copy of Russell's "Listening Aids Through the Grades."[13] This paperback publication, listing 190 listening activities for children in the elementary school, gives specific examples of classroom activities which can be utilized to teach listening skills. These might be selected on the basis of the organization of listening skills which have been devised in the diagnostic and achievement listening check sheet. Search of other course of study documents in language arts for additional specific suggestions of classroom activities will provide additional assistance.

5. Plan directed lessons in teaching language listening comprehension utilizing The Kellogg Listening Model. Practice utilizing the model in your own listening behavior prior to such lessons in order to more fully understand how each of the four comprehension levels provides the foundation for the next level of comprehension. Select stories to read to the class which best illustrate how the model works in the initial introduction of it to the class.

Conclusion

An attempt has been made to point out the importance of effective listening in the world of tomorrow and to indicate the rather bleak reality of the limited listening instruction currently provided in the

---

13. David H. Russell and Elizabeth F. Russell, *Listening Aids Through the Grades* (New York: Teachers College, Columbia University, Bureau of Publications, 1959).

elementary school. The need for the development of a theory of listening has been cited by writers in the professional literature. A comprehensive theory providing background of the relationship of listening to the other language areas of speaking, reading and writing has been formulated and presented. Cast within this theory, The Kellogg Listening Model has been explicated with a challenge to the reader to apply the model to his own listening behavior or formulate a better model. Specific skills of listening have been cited should the reader wish to utilize these for teaching purposes rather than The Kellogg Listening Model. Finally some first steps of study and activity have been suggested for the beginning teacher or teacher who is initially delving into the personally and professionally challenging study of the listening process.

EXTENDING YOUR LEARNING

1. Illustrate by two specific examples each of the basic premises indicated in the theory of listening presented in this chapter.
2. Explain The Kellogg Listening Model to a group of friends in such a manner that they can understand it. Provide for a practice application of the model by having them listen to a story, then pose questions at each of the four language comprehension levels.
3. Develop a diagnostic and achievement listening skill chart utilizing either the skills of listening or The Kellogg Listening Model and describe procedures by which it might be utilized at a specific grade level.
4. With a group of classmates or friends collectively develop or research a series of teaching activities which could be used to help students develop each of the listening skills indicated in the skills of listening section or select stories which might be used in application of The Kellogg Listening Model.
5. Study a suitable reference on propaganda analysis. Listen for and record examples of different propaganda techniques which are heard during the period of one week.

BIBLIOGRAPHY

Alameda County School Department, Materials on programs in oral communication. 244 West Winton Avenue, Hayward, California.

Anderson, Harold A. "Needed Research in Listening," *Elementary English*, 29:215-224, April, 1954.

Barbara, Dominick A. *The Art of Listening*. Springfield, Ill.: Charles C. Thomas, 1958.

_____. *Health and Neurotic Aspects of Listening*. Bulletin, Auxiliary Council to the Association for the Advancement of Psychoanalysis, New York.

Beery, Althea. "Interrelationships Between Listening and the Other Language Arts," *Elementary English*, 31:164-172, March, 1954.

Bloom, Benjamin S. (ed.). *Taxonomy of Educational Objectives*. Handbook I: *Cognitive Domain*. New York: Longmans, Green and Co., 1956.

Brown, Don Pardee. *Auding as the Primary Language Ability*. Doctoral dissertation; Stanford, Cal.: Stanford University, 1954. Abstract: *Dissertation Abstracts, 14*:2281-2282, 1954.

"A Comparative Study of Two First Grade Language Arts Programs," Research Project Funded by the U.S. Office of Education. Submitted by the San Diego County Department of Education, May 28, 1964.

Duker, Sam. "Goals of Teaching Listening Skills in the Elementary School," *Elementary English, 38*:170-174, March, 1961.

———. *Listening Bibliography*. New York: Scarecrow Press, 1964.

Lundsteen, Sara W. *Teaching Abilities in Critical Listening in the Fifth and Sixth Grades*. Doctoral dissertation; Berkeley: University of California, 1963.

Nichols, Ralph G., and Leonard A. Stevens. *Are You Listening?* New York: McGraw-Hill Book Company, Inc., 1957.

Rankin, Paul T. *The Measurement of the Ability to Understand Spoken Language*. Doctoral dissertation; Ann Arbor, Mich.: University of Michigan, 1926. *Dissertation Abstracts, 12*:897, 1952.

Russell, David H., and Elizabeth F. Russell. *Listening Aids Through the Grades*. New York: Teachers College, Columbia University, Bureau of Publications, 1959.

Wilt, Miriam E. *A Study of Teacher Awareness of Listening as a Factor in Elementary Education*. Doctoral dissertation; State College, Pa.: Penn State College, 1949. Summary: *Journal of Educational Research, 43*:626-636, April, 1950.

Witty, Paul A., and Robert A. Sizemore. "Studies in Listening," *Elementary English, 35*:538-552 (December, 1958); *36*:59-70 (January, 1959); *36*:297-301 (May, 1959).

Wright, Evan L. *The Construction of a Test of Listening Comprehension for the Second, Third, and Fourth Grades*. Doctoral dissertation; St. Louis, Mo.: Washington University, 1957. Abstract: *Dissertation Abstracts, 17*:2226-2227, 1957.

Focus

Structural linguists, perhaps in order to stress the importance *of* speech, occasionally defined language *as* speech. This is an oversimplification, but it is certainly true that man's development of writing systems have followed and were patterned after the phonological systems he has already developed. It's been estimated that from 75 per cent to 90 per cent of our language use is in the "oral" area—speaking and listening. Oral language *is* important, and the school's responsibility in this area can hardly be overestimated.

In discussing the child's acquisition of language, Frost noted that the infant quickly discovers that he can "modify his immediate world" by vocalizing—cooing or crying. By the time the child enters school, even if the term "school" refers to nursery school or kindergarten, he has acquired a large speaking vocabulary. The exact size of this vocabulary, even for the so called "average" child, has not been determined; note the variation between the findings of M.D. Smith (1926) and M.K. Smith (1941) reported in Chapter One. The speaking vocabulary of the "typical" five or six year old is at least two thousand words, and probably a great deal larger. The young child also has effective if not complete control over the phonological system of his language. He knows how to use pitch, stress, and pause to reinforce or hide meaning. Jean Berko* and Carol Chomsky** report that the young child's grasp of the morphological system of his language is generally good, although there are large and significant gaps. In other words, a school beginner is not a beginner with language, although much remains to be done.

Robert Bloom points out that language growth should be considered a continuous process. Development of facility in using the oral facets of language is of considerable importance. The classroom program in oral language has been, for too long, relatively unstructured and, perhaps, haphazard. Bloom argues for clearly stated objectives, a place on the daily schedule for directed experiences in speaking, and for continuous evaluation, by teachers and pupils, toward established goals. The elementary teacher's responsibility is great in every facet of the language arts, but because oral language is so very important throughout life, a teacher's responsibility in this area can hardly be overstressed.

---

*Jean Berko, "The Child's Learning of English Morphology," *Word* 14 (1958): 159-177.
**Carol Chomsky, *The Acquisition of Syntax in Children from Two to Ten* (Cambridge, Massachusetts: The M.I.T. Press, 1969).

Robert M. Bloom

chapter five

a program
for oral english

Oral English in the school curriculum has risen to a place of great importance. The demand for more effective communication has reached down into the earliest years of childhood and has extended itself with an explosive impact into almost every aspect of higher education. The word "dialogue" alone has taken on a new significance and reflects the eminence that oral communication has attained wherever there is any possibility of conflict or misunderstanding.

"In this setting," the authors of an interesting article on communication skills point out, "the humane and crucial task for the schools is to increase the ability of people to talk together as a primary way of understanding one another. As teachers, we should make the development of effective oral communication our classroom goal for the seventies."[1]

But long before the child experiences his first hours in school his speech pattern has started to take shape. His ability to gather meaning and his ability to communicate are closely related and in most cases both have developed together. His earliest training in speech commenced when the names which his elders attached to the common objects of his environment became familiar to him and he began as part of his basic speech experiments to imitate the sounds they repeated.

1. Morton Botel and John Dawkens, "Tune in on Oral Communication," *Instructor* (April, 1970), p. 56.

While he was still a toddler he acquired a really substantial supply of words that were associated with his daily experiences, words that he understood and was able to pronounce fairly intelligibly. He learned to react to simple directives, such as *sit, stand, come, stay, walk, wait,* or *up,* and to make his own characteristic responses to those commands. At this point he began to substitute verbal replies for non-verbal, oral articulation for gestures and emotional outbursts. His language education, in other words, had begun to "take."

As he continued to mature he became involved in deeper interests and more complex activities which brought an even wider vocabulary grasp and usage. Every new sensory adventure was a source of new understandings and added subsequently to his index of descriptive words. A coaxing curiosity drove him to explore further, to make associations, to enrich his concepts, to ask questions. With careful guidance he could be led to narrate his impressions of what he had seen or heard, and can often do so in creditable fashion. Some of the words might have been repeated over and over, some fumbled and mispronounced, some stammered; but the important thing is that in the gush of related ideas there emerged a genuine pattern—and this word-pattern was a significant landmark in his linguistic achievement.

It is well to remember that by the time the child is ready for pre-primary schooling he has expanded his ability to communicate orally from one-word statements to simple sentences. He has built up an extensive speaking vocabulary. He can give a running account of what has caused him emotional distress or a detailed description of something interesting which he has encountered. Consequently, his education in oral expression is well advanced.

Language development is not an orderly process that takes place in parallel sequences among children of the same age levels. Like physical and intellectual growth it is quite complex in its rate and its scale of progress. It depends upon so many factors that few children develop according to an expected schedule of mastery. Therefore, in order to shape his curriculum, the teacher is obliged to capitalize on the attainments of each of his pupils. He must understand the various elements influencing language growth and he must cut his pattern around them.

In the fulfillment of linguistic goals the following principles seem most pertinent, and should be considered in the setting up of a program:

1. *Some growth in language proficiency takes place constantly.* The rate may not be equal among children, but as each adds a fund of new concepts through experiences of different kinds there is bound to be an increase in vocabulary. The same situation occurs in the refinements of speaking. Some children without effort make remarkable gains in pronunciation and in the expression of ideas while others lag behind. With help however many of the latter pupils can move ahead to close the gap.

2. *There is a difference in the pattern of maturity.* Progress in development centers first upon the natural endowment of the child and next upon the amount of meaningful experiences which make an impression upon the child. The pupil who is the product of a middle-class home where the parents are intelligent and capable and provide a warm and wholesome relationship is one who is most likely to mature at an early age. A child of less fortunate background and experience may take longer in arriving at an acceptable point for formal schooling.

3. *The rate of growth is dependent upon a variety of conditions.* There are different phases of maturity which must be accounted for in the aggregate development of language among children. Any number of conditions can retard or accelerate the growth of language proficiency. When children are first entered into kindergarten their parents are often asked to fill out registration forms which supply the teachers with important information. In some ways they will give clues as to why one child is withdrawn and inarticulate while another seems independent, outgoing and sophisticated. These forms in many school systems contain a list of communicable diseases common to childhood. There is usually another list or questionnaire to be filled out which provides a history of illness other than the contagious type, operations, accidents, outbreaks of allergies, and the like. When completed, the information may be invaluable to the teacher particularly in relation to speech. There are many factors, physical or psychological, which may impede the growth of speech during the early childhood years. One example would be a siege of illness during which the child might be bed-ridden or confined without much companionship. A physical defect such as a cleft palate or a hare lip, unless corrected by surgery, could make a child reluctant to call attention to himself by talking. Physical fears, family friction, or feelings of inferiority could deprive a child of normal linguistic development. Other reasons for set-backs could include such conditions as periods of unusual insecurity, glandular changes, under-

nourishment, rapid physical growth, or a temporary deficiency in hearing. Any one of these could be an episode which is long-lasting or brief but which might nevertheless be an obstacle in the path of steady progress.

4. *Individual differences offer a challenge to the teacher.* It is essential for teachers to realize that as far as their capabilities and inclinations are concerned children are not shaped in the same mold. Teachers must accept the child who is reserved and often unwilling to communicate as well as the pupil who chatters on tirelessly. Between the two types there may be no distinction in intelligence; but in family background, in the kind of upbringing, in interaction among members of the family, in health, sensitivity and breadth of experience there could be a world of difference. The teacher must analyze the influences that have been brought to bear upon each child and take them into account in establishing a program of speech improvement. Both teacher and child stand to gain from such careful analysis.

Development of Speech in the Pre-Primary Years

For the pre-primary pupil the basic means of expression is oral. To a great extent, through the apparatus of speech, he reveals his thinking processes, his desires and his fantasies. He discloses as well the depth and breadth of his sensory perceptions—what he has learned by seeing, hearing, feeling, smelling and tasting. In many cases the older members of his family have advanced his readiness for formal training by providing him with calculated opportunities for learning. They have supplied him with the names of many objects in his little universe and have patiently coaxed him to point out the objects and repeat the sounds of their names until he mastered them. They have taught him little songs and poems to widen the scope of his vocabulary and his imagination. They have given him toys, simple puzzles, games and coloring books to develop his visual discrimination, his ability to manipulate, and his skill at identification.

The immediate problem for the pre-kindergarten or the kindergarten teacher is to analyze the extent of the pupil's language growth. This may be done through observation—by watching him, by listening to his conversation, by asking questions, and by recording his vocabulary. This analysis may be accomplished with the help of a tape recorder or by listing in a notebook words he uses most frequently. Once the teacher has a clear view of the child's capabilities he can then plan a program tailor-made for progress.

In what ways can the pre-primary teacher prepare the child for the more difficult forms of language that are to be taught in the grades? Unless he already possesses a wide vocabulary background the more abstract concepts that the pupil encounters in school will be indeed baffling and unintelligible. The teaching trend however has already been established. Parents have contributed to the child's word power by exposing him to experiences from which he has derived most of his concepts. But what has been casual and occasional at home must now become more direct and structured; what has been informal teaching now becomes formal with the aid of strong motivation.

The following suggestions can be useful in organizing a program for the improvement of oral skills.

1. *The use of manipulative devices.* Four and five year old youngsters enjoy using the large and small toys or building blocks of different shapes which contribute to their motor coordination. Molding clay, play dough and plasticine are favorite materials to be kneaded and squeezed into provocative shapes. There is an extensive array of articles like these available for early childhood education. The materials can motivate the child to build or to balance, or to produce forms which enlarge the scope of his imagination. The finished products also provide endless opportunities for enriching the vocabulary through discussion and story-telling.

2. *Interchange of ideas.* In both the pre-kindergarten (or nursery class as it is sometimes called) and in kindergarten the knowledgeable teacher arranges for times when the pupils can unburden themselves of any thoughts they have in mind, any information, any items of news which they consider of interest to the group and perhaps worth discussing. No matter how abrupt, disjointed and often irrelevant the flow of discussion seems to be among the children seated around the teacher, what counts is the teacher's strategies in spurring as many pupils as possible to participate and in arousing their zeal for vivid expression.

The ritual of shared experiences, if consistently repeated, should aim at the following desirable targets:

a. Recognition of courtesy standards: one child speaking at a time without interruptions; an established order of speakers; avoidance of monopolizing the discussion.

b. Ability to regulate the voice—moderating it if too loud, making it more audible if too soft.

c. Acceptance of desirable social attitudes—interest in other children's remarks and willingness to swap ideas.

d. Enrichment of vocabulary.

e. Ability to think in an orderly manner.

f. Improvement of speaking skills: ability to speak in complete and clear-cut sentences; consciousness of pronunciation and enunciation.

3. *Field trips.* Short, timely walks in the neighborhood of the school, or bus rides to places of interest to youngsters can extend the opportunity to learn something about their environment. These movements outside the school walls are made more meaningful by preliminary discussion to stir the children's curiosity and to focus their attention specifically upon things they are to observe. Immediately after the trip a lively review of what the pupils have seen helps to strengthen their concepts and contributes further to their ability to express themselves.

4. *Additional methods for developing oral expression.* Children have a natural instinct for dramatization and this inclination may be used in many ways to motivate speech. Below is a list of activities teachers may attempt:

a. Recite rhymes and perform finger plays.

b. Initiate imitative rhythms.

c. Have the pupils record informal conversations on the tape recorder. Play the recordings back and have the children listen.

d. Use hand or stick puppets as a device for telling personal experiences, dramatizing favorite stories or nursery rhymes.

e. Use rhythms to dramatize experiences. Have the pupils tell where they have been and what they have seen.

f. Use toy telephones to carry on conversations.

These devices and others which an enterprising teacher is willing to try are of great value in lengthening the strides towards oral proficiency. Their objectives can be reached with imaginative planning and with repeated trials.

Goals of Oral Language in the Primary Years

The primary teacher treats oral communication as a concomitant skill to match with reading or with written communication. All three skills are assimilated quite rapidly, although not always at the same pace. Even though the "sentence sense" is fairly well advanced among primary grade children, concentration upon the sentence becomes more important. The sentence is emphasized almost from the beginning in reading. In writing the teacher develops his stories on experience charts in the form of sentences as well. By the time the pupil enters the first grade he has already begun to use various structural forms. The natural tendency is to speak in longer sentences and to develop the sentences with well-defined elements.

Some children have not as yet reached the point of readiness where they are able to speak with any amount of ease and fluency. For most of these pupils it is necessary to go beyond the usual procedures. The teacher can encourage them to join into activities which will motivate them to speak more freely. He should then watch for evidence which shows when the children are more comfortable in exchange of ideas with their classmates.

In their everyday interests young children are egocentric and are likely to be concerned with objects and situations which are personal and immediate. These elements should be taken into consideration at first when the teacher is preparing oral activities for his class. If the teacher is alert to provide his pupils with opportunities for expression, their stock of ideas continues to grow and their vocabulary expands. The children are able to engage in discussions involving concepts that are somewhat abstract and an organization of thought that is more sophisticated.

Progress depends upon the establishment of standards and goals. Children should be guided into an awareness of the wisdom of rules and objectives for reports and discussion and they should be able to evaluate their own progress in terms of these values. In fact, they can be encouraged as a part of their class procedure to devise their own rules and aims. Once those have been established and accepted the class is more likely to act in conformity with their guidelines.

The following graded list of objectives may be incorporated into a program for oral language on the primary level.

Grade One

Principal Goals

1. Implementation of vocabulary in as many ways as possible with words relating to the pupils' experiences.

2. Emphasis upon the ability to think more clearly and logically. Children learn to keep the elements of their topics cohesive and relevant.
3. Expansion of children's interests. Encouragement to report briefly on outside activities, books read, sporting events, hobbies, etc.
4. Improvement of the ability and the desire to share ideas.
5. Increased consciousness of sentence structure. Reduction of the tendency to ramble and to speak in "run-on" sentences.
6. Elimination of speech defects.
7. Increased awareness of discussion techniques and courtesies.
8. Improvement in the organization of ideas.

Essential Skills to Emphasize

1. Speaking in a voice audible to the audience.
2. Selecting topics that are interesting to an audience and timely in their contents.
3. Observing rules of courtesy in discussion and recitation.
4. Using a wide choice of descriptive words.
5. Developing a brief report or story in a logical sequence.
6. Pronouncing and enunciating words distinctly.

Functional Activities

1. Directed discussion derived from various situations:
   a. Ideas gained from experiences in school.
   b. Stories and poems read in class.
   c. School topics, such as science, health, art or mathematics.
   d. Films, filmstrips, tape recordings, phonograph records.
   e. Role-playing with characters demonstrating simple rules of courtesy.
   f. Lessons or episodes in character education.
2. Sharing knowledge in narrative form:
   a. Telling stories about experiences which occurred at home or elsewhere.
   b. "Making up" original stories.
   c. Re-creating stories heard or stories read in children's books.
3. Making reports to a group:
   a. Giving accounts of simple research on timely topics of interest to the class.
   b. Relating to the whole class the results of group activity.

4. Recitation in class.
   a. Answering questions in clear-cut sentences.
   b. Manifesting by example the rules of courtesy.
   c. Asking for information.
   d. Asking for permission to leave the room, to take materials, to share other children's materials, etc.

Grade Two

Principal Goals

1. Continuation of the objectives pursued in Grade One.
2. Accumulation of an additional stock of vocabulary words.
3. Oral improvement made an all-day activity.
4. Advancement of the ability to organize more complex thoughts.

Essential Skills to Emphasize

1. Review of skills learned in Grade One.
2. Improving pronunciation of more difficult words.
3. Enunciating digraphs, such as *sh, th, wh.*
4. Modulating the voice according to the text and the mood of the talk.
5. Sticking to the point in discussion.
6. Additional rules of courtesy to be observed.
7. Using simple introductions—parent to teacher, parent to friend, etc.
8. Answering the telephone and taking a message.
9. Engaging in more extended conversations.

Functional Activities

1. Activities of Grade One continued with further refinements.
2. Role-playing situations:
   a. Telephone conversations with emphasis on courtesy, modulation of voice and choice of words.
   b. Situations involving introductions.
   c. Dramatizations using school topics as centers of conception.
3. Simple book reviews.
4. Story-telling programs for entertainment or for assemblies.

Grade Three

Principal Goals

1. Extension of experiences and concepts.
2. Further enrichment and refinement of vocabulary.

3. Improvement of clarity and fluency in speech.
4. Provision of ample situations for the exchange of ideas.
5. Emphasis placed on the importance of self-evaluation.

Essential Skills to Emphasize

1. Review of skills previously learned.
2. Enunciating with care the initial and final consonant sounds in words.
3. Giving correct pronunciation of words used in conversation and informal classwork.
4. Using sentence variation, including more frequent experiments with the compound and complex sentences.
5. Developing interesting beginning sentences and ending sentences.
6. Explaining ideas and facts in more extended detail.
7. Giving directions that are accurate and clear.
8. Using additional common rules of social courtesy.

Functional Activities

1. Continue activities of Grade Two, advancing from simpler to more complicated situations.
2. Discussion of possibilities and planning in class for group enterprises.
3. Practice with role-playing situations in order to help some pupils to become more articulate.
4. Class club meeting with different types of introduction included, such as the introduction of officers or speakers.
5. Telephone conversations involving the taking of messages.
6. Dramatization of well-known scenes from stories which the pupils have read.

The aims and procedures outlined above may be considered as a core of essentials. Further refinements and modifications are advisable however and could increase the capabilities of the pupils. A rich assortment of activities could make the primary years memorable for most youngsters. But a structured program is needed to help the child change in his oral behavior. From a creature who is self-centered, hesitant of speech and inexperienced with groups, he can be guided into becoming one who is urbane, articulate, socially responsible and highly effective in the expression of ideas.

Individual Differences Among Children

Whether he is dealing with oral expression or with any other topic scheduled for instructional purposes the teacher must consider certain frames of reference in developing his curriculum. A most important aspect is the provision for individual differences among the pupils. In the planning of an overall program these differences must be taken into account. A discussion of the major distinctions might help to clarify the reasons for their involvement in program-making.

1. *The Intellectual Capacity of Pupils.* The great range of learning ability displayed by the children in the classroom offers a special instructional challenge. The teacher must not only recognize the dissimilarity of pupils in intellectual power but he should know the techniques which are most effective in helping each towards highest achievement.

It is essential first of all that children proceed at the pace best suited to their abilities. Those who are relatively more able need the least direction, attain mastery of skills with little drill or repetition, and arrive at abstract relationships with ease. The "slower" child, however, requires careful guidance in proceeding from step to step. His understanding is broadened by means of concepts which are derived through concrete experiences. The significance of these ideas is fixed in his mind by frequent discussion and explanation. He needs much more practice than the gifted child in building his skills and more time to work out the means of reaching the simplest goals. His vocabulary is likely to be limited and is maintained and increased only with patient treadmill repetition. The gifted pupil, on the other hand, has a flair for values and perceptions which enables him to grasp ideas with speed. It is possible that here and there a bright child may be reserved and hesitant of speech, but he is more likely to be quite articulate and can bound ahead in his achievement of oral competence.

2. *Emotional Conditions Affecting Pupils.* In establishing a program for oral training attention must be given also to emotional differences among children. That language development can be obstructed by emotional instability is a principle underscored with wide-spread investigation. The image of the withdrawn child who isolates himself from his classmates and who remains mute and diffident is a common one in educational experience. The aggressive child, the rebellious child, the pupil who is ordinarily quiet and reserved but who occasionally bursts into an explosive temper tantrum—these are often found to have serious

language deficiencies. Sometimes an episode in the life of a child may provide a temporary set-back in language growth—perhaps the advent of a new baby who supplants the pupil as the center of attention, or anxiety over parental disapproval, or hospitalization of a parent with its accompanying depression of insecurity and fear of possible death. The least a teacher can do when confronted by children burdened with emotional problems is to provide understanding and extend help in overcoming the language impediments and social inadequacies. This assistance should take a practical form which is to include measures for restoring a sense of security and through this feeling of security renewed self-confidence.

3. *Socio-Economic Status.* One of the foremost factors affecting educational policy is the socio-economic background of the pupil. The term "middle-class" on the one hand has a certain identity for the sake of curriculum development and on the other hand such expressions as "disadvantaged," "underprivileged" or "culturally different" are used rather loosely for directing policies in educational planning involving children of rural or urban slum areas. A whole new literature has developed around the social forces motivating the two groups. Study after study has been made in a search for methods to reduce the gap between the two classes and in particular to eliminate the apathy and the failure-orientation which are often bench-marks of the culturally different.

The informed teacher in urban centers should be aware of the dislocation and the ferment caused by the steady movement of a vast population from neglected rural or semi-rural areas to the dark and squalid city slums. They must recognize the verbal deficiencies brought about by the double disaster of broken home and blighted background. They must take into account the frequent shifting within the city from one district to another, from one apartment to another, and from one school to another, all of which results in appalling consequences in education.

For those who make up the great middle class there is a marked conformity to values which tend to enrich social and educational behavior. The children live in a more stable environment, and in a very high percentage of cases both parents are present to guide them. In contrast, the youngsters from culturally deprived homes exist in families that are quite often fatherless and under conditions that are all but chaotic.

A characteristic of the poverty-stricken home, especially one with a large family, is the lack of warmth and "togetherness" in communication. At mealtimes and at bedtime this situation is most noticeable. In middle-class families these are usually the occasions for discussion and interaction between adults and children. But among those of the lower income brackets this bond of interaction is almost unknown. Each child comes into the kitchen to take what is prepared for him by mother or else goes to the refrigerator to "fix" himself a meal with whatever is available. Mother is often too busy with her youngest child or children to sit at the table with the others or even to urge the older ones to sit together. The opportunity for extensive conversation is lost. At bedtime too the same situation exists. The youngsters often go to bed individually at their own convenience rather than follow a regular schedule or established time. The quiet moment when bedtime stories are read or imaginative tales are spun is almost non-existent.

Conversation between grownups and children in middle-class homes is a natural part of daily living. The parents are generally quite fluent in speech and communicate so freely that the children learn with little effort. When the child is very young the adults will urge him to repeat words and correct him if he pronounces any incorrectly or if he is in error when attaching a name to the wrong object. This personal attention continues even when the child is old enough to learn about the environment beyond his immediate surroundings. He is taken to the park, to the zoo, to the beach, and is exposed to different objects there. His parents give him picture books and discuss the contents with him. The child's language is thus increased progressively by the expansion of his horizon and by the interplay of questions and responses relating to all he has seen, heard and done.

In the homes of culturally different children the adults often use a crude and limited language and the answers to questions are likely to be in monosyllables if they are answered at all. The child is seldom given the chance for enriched experience beyond the confines of his neighborhood. The instability of his family life affects his language growth to such an extent that when there is emotional tension within the family circle the child often attempts to escape the disturbance by closing himself inside a wall of silence, blocking off as much communication as possible.

It is easy to understand why a gap soon opens between the child who is deprived and the one who is privileged. The child who is reared in a solid middle-class home soon begins to use words as precision tools of thought. He learns early in life to express his wants, his emotions and his intentions clearly and effectively. He begins to discriminate in his concepts by comparing, differentiating and abstracting aspects of his environment as well as describing his feelings and his thought. The extent of vocabulary between the disadvantaged and the more affluent pupils betrays the result of background conditions. In general, children from poverty-stricken homes are deficient in words that deal with abstract ideas—words for class names, categories and subtle comparisons. In their experience with adults they learn language which is terse and grammatically different, when contrasted with middle-class "standard" grammar. The disadvantaged child, it might be said, begins school poorly prepared for the language tasks of the primary grades and unskilled in handling prolonged speech sequences. These are handicaps which the oral language program must be geared to overcome.

To summarize the objectives of speech in the pre-primary and primary grades the outline below provides a list of principal expectations demanded of children if they are to assert themselves with outstanding performance.

1. Pre-Primary Goals
    a. To develop an adequate fund of words
    b. To provide opportunities in discussion to share ideas
    c. To increase skill in expressing ideas in sentence patterns
    d. To foster an awareness of environment
    e. To encourage favorable social attitudes in group situations
    f. To learn stock expressions of courtesy
2. Primary Goals
    a. To enlarge the scope of a speaking vocabulary
    b. To encourage frequent formal discussion
    c. To provide occasions for simple reports and story-telling
    d. To promote progress in using clear-cut sentences
    e. To stimulate organization of thought in logical sequence
    f. To increase sensitivity to environment
    g. To extend concepts and expressions of courtesy
    h. To initiate discrimination of usage

Development of Speech with Minority Groups

The relentless influx of certain minority groups into the major cities has made the teaching of oral English in urban schools more complex and exciting. For the children involved the sudden shift into a confusing and often hostile environment renders the problem an overwhelming one. Everything is strange—schools, teachers, procedures, class-mates—and all require special skills of adjustment. The power to understand quickly is not always within the resources of the newcomers. The code-words which they already know and use have been developed within the framework of their homes and in the communities where they lived. This vocabulary is frequently a part of a local dialect with many idioms which are unfamiliar to teachers who are acclimated mainly to standard English. When the migrant family settles in a big city and children are admitted to school they are subjected in the classroom to a fusillade of new sounds. Not only must they assume the burden of comprehending them but they must learn to react to them with the proper response. Many of the children make a satisfactory adjustment and soon communicate without problems. But for some youngsters this is quite an undertaking. They have the option of "tuning out," of remaining inarticulate and being considered "slow"; or else they can make a safe accommodation and confine most of their dialog to monosyllables.

Needless to say, these children require deeper understanding on the part of their teachers. It is imperative for the teachers to learn as much as possible about the cultural and communicative background of their pupils. They must realize that children are more likely to be influenced in their speech habits by their peers than by authority figures in the schools.

The teacher's handling of speech training at all times must be extra sensitive. When he hears a black child say, "He *aksed* me for my pencil," his first reaction would be to "correct" him. But what strategy should he use? Should he stop and teach him the dominant pronunciation? Should he develop a spontaneous lesson on the consonant shift? Should he overlook his pronunciation for future private assistance? Or should he accept his pronunciation as a relevant and legitimate part of a speech pattern? An agonizing decision must be made. In oral language programs for children of minority groups, however, perhaps the last two choices are the most practical. Yet in the final analysis the most rational approach depends upon the make-up of the pupil.

A certain pattern may be detected in the behavior of migrant and immigrant youngsters that is meaningful in the teaching of oral communication. It is recognized that children as an aftermath of migration from a familiar area to an unfamiliar one are affected in various degrees. One stage of this maladjustment has been called the "mourning process."[2] This mood is brought on by a feeling of separation from people they loved and with whom they had found security. The most noticeable symptom is that of an apparent regression. The children seem less mature, sometimes withdrawn, sometimes clingy, but more often unheeding and playful. Their day in school is marked by distraction, by an inability to follow directions, by bursts of over-activity alternating with periods of day-dreaming. In the process of moving the families are often disorganized and lose whatever cohesiveness they had which contributed to the stability of the youngsters. Caught in this domestic quagmire the children are sometimes impelled to "act out" their sense of loss in fear and anger.

What is needed to help them overcome their frustrations is a knowledgeable effort to set up lines of effective communication. The teacher performs a service to the pupils by trying to reach them, to guide them in modifying feelings that block a change in their learning behavior— whether those feelings are manifested in shyness, hostility or a sense of disenchantment. He can start by meshing his explanations in class to their level of understanding. Once he has gained their acceptance he can encourage them to develop confidence in their own potential. This is an essential step before they are ready to speak with any degree of fluency. Then they can be led to express their thoughts beyond a reliance on monosyllables and curt phrases into a complete sentence structure.

It must be expected that many underprivileged children are likely to communicate in what has been called a "restricted" vernacular. The speech patterns of these children tend to be loosely structured, confined almost exclusively to simple or "run-on" sentences. The continuity is frequently fractured or interrupted with what could be called social interrogatives, such as, "You know that big book, huh?—the one on the desk?" An excessive dependence on a limited stock of words is also to be expected as well as resort to non-standard English. A common example is: "He gon' come by soon."

To add to the syndrome of circumstances, there appears to be evidence that among culturally different children an inferior auditory discrimination exists which retards their oral development still further. In order to overcome this handicap teachers have created an intensive

---

2. Outlined in a speech by Dr. Raquel Cohen at a meeting of teachers of English as a Second Language (Boston, December, 1969).

program for improving listening skills. Sometimes they tape a series of exercises and have the pupils repeat the words or sentences they hear. Whenever possible they train the children individually to concentrate on sounds—a great variety of sounds—and to reproduce them as accurately as they can. Once the pupils tune in it is amazing how quickly their interest lights up. They become more sensitive to fine shades of articulation and are eager to mimic the sounds.

Is there a possibility that the children of disadvantaged native minorities may expand their meager supply of words and colloquialisms independently into a really enriched vocabulary? The outlook is strong that as many new concepts, new terminologies and new experiences are assimilated a genuine change will take place. Kenneth S. Goodman supports this view in a most interesting and trenchant article. He says that schools can help children as they experiment with new language to handle unfamiliar concepts and situations. He makes his most striking point that pupils in adapting to linguistic change go through several phases. First, there is a recognition of "alternate forms" of language. Then there is experimentation with a *choice* in the alternate systems of expression, and finally comes an accommodation to the standard form and a gradual abandonment of the old forms.[3]

Professor Goodman's theory appears quite sound and should be regarded as a basis for action. Plans for effective linguistic change among inner city pupils would be made more profitable if teachers as a part of their language program would adopt Goodman's suggestions. They would expose their pupils to the standard forms in as many ways as possible but would guide them, not pressure them, into gradual acceptance.

Structures for Teaching English as a Second Language

Now that our nation has reverted to its traditional role as a magnet for immigrants coming from all parts of the world the responsibility of the school for providing facility in the English language has increased enormously. Especially where multi-lingual situations exist, where children have come from many lands, the teaching problem can be extremely frustrating.

Some school systems have attacked the problem by setting up "tran-

---

3. Kenneth S. Goodman, "Let's Dump the Uptight Model in English," *Elementary School Journal* (October, 1969), pp. 1-13.

sition" classes. These are all-day classes in which teachers with special training try to give the youngsters a solid footing in new language skills. They accomplish this through small non-graded groups where pupils are matched as closely as possible according to their levels of attainment in English. Such factors as age, size or previous grade placement have little bearing upon their placement in these groups. The teaching is individualized as much as possible and the emphasis is upon vocabulary building and rituals of conversation. The principal effort is to get the pupils into the mainstream of learning as soon as they have gained enough English language power. Once they have reached a functional level they are discharged to continue their education in regular classes.

Where comparatively small numbers of immigrant children are involved an alternative to the transition class is even more common. When the children are enrolled at school they are admitted into regular classes but are *released part-time* on a daily schedule or at frequent intervals during the weeks to work with a teacher of English as a Second Language. In these coaching sessions the basic pattern used is the aural-oral method re-inforced with an abundance of recognizable pictures or small replicas of common objects. The method is similar to the way conversational French or Spanish is taught in any beginner's course. The first step is the mastery of a stock of labels or identifications which are repeated in brief sentences, such as, "This a book," or "Is this your seat?" As the pupils progress the teacher strengthens retention by reserving a part of each lesson for review. The lessons as a whole however must not become stereotyped or mechanical; there is abundant opportunity for variation and renewed interest through simple dramatics, choral speaking and music. The children could make up simple little poems, and even supply the tunes, to initiate a feeling of comradeship among them. This is an example:

> I speak English, Hans speaks Dutch.
> We can't talk together much.
> But both of us should learn one way
> To say the things we want to say.

Development of Speech in the Intermediate Level

Educators are aware of many new and conflicting factors affecting the course of spoken language today—the impact of television for instance, the pressures of our technological society, an increasing emphasis upon the desirability of higher education, the steady expansion of employment in the service industries, the attrition of good speech habits in many homes and in the streets. They find the situation so fluid that it demands a constant re-examination of teaching practices. They know that the school itself to be effective must serve both as a laboratory and as a clinic for speech improvement.

This chapter has underscored the theme that formal training in oral language cannot begin too soon. The question is, what measures at each level of schooling will produce the best results? As the pupils advance from the primary to the intermediate grades, it is clear that the skills to be taught are so many and so varied that success depends upon an exacting program. Many teachers remember when the only program offered was an occasional on-the-spot training—an incidental lesson in language usage or speech correction after an oral report or a group discussion. It was thought that because this type of lesson served a highly functional purpose it was a most efficient instrument for teaching. Incidental instruction is still a useful device and it still has its place where on-the-spot correction must be made. But the tide has turned. Teachers have become more sensitive to the need for extensive oral development. They have come to the conclusion that sporadic drill is not enough; that the principles of speech and of speaking must be taught year after year and throughout the year as consistently and thoroughly as mathematics.

In support of an enriched program for the elementary school pupil, Martha Dallmann has said that "much additional development is needed to meet the demands that the school and society in general make of him and those that society makes of the adult."[4]

From a different point-of-view, Carrie Rasmussen remarked that it is "the opportunity and challenge of school to promote on the part of the children both active interest and increasing skill in the use of discussion."[5]

Margaret Painter years ago reached the conclusion that "one of the fundamental premises in effective oral training is that casual or incidental procedure is uncertain and inadequate."[6]

---

4. Martha Dallmann, *Teaching the Language Arts in the Elementary School* (Dubuque, Iowa: Wm. C. Brown Company Publishers), p. 35.
5. Carrie Rasmussen, "The Role of Speech in the Elementary School," *Elementary English* (January, 1952), pp. 6-14.
6. Margaret Painter, "Oral Emphasis in the English Class," *English Journal* 36 (September, 1947): 348-354.

About the same time Lauren L. Brink pointed out that there should be not only a consistent building up of basic speaking habits but that there should be generous time allowance granted to the student to find material, to organize, and to practice. He emphasized the importance of careful preparation by the pupil before delivering the talk through planning, outlining and reviewing the contents in several practice sessions until "the presentation of ideas is smooth and clear."[7] To meet the objectives under this procedure, he says, the teacher's task is two-fold: (1) He works with his pupils individually to check on skills, and (2) he works with the class as a whole on what has been said.

If the needs of speech in terms of today's curriculum requirements on the intermediate level could be satisfied inside the limits of the language arts period there would be no problem at all; but unfortunately the time allotted for formal speech work is generally too brief. We can keep in mind however the fact that oral English is not confined to language arts alone. Almost every subject is rich in the possibilities for improvement of speaking, and oral activities should be used in conjunction with or as an outgrowth of topical areas within those subjects wherever practicable. A sensible argument has been given that the "terms 'course' and 'period' usually are not associated with speech work nor are any other such terms that denote regular time set aside for 'training.' Rather, speech is involved in areas defined as *experience units* in the self-contained classroom. The urgency of need determines the prominence that speech skills will attain in the daily program."[8]

Experience units provide one answer to the teacher's problem as to how she can fit her oral language into a crowded schedule. They are a logical extension of the "show-and-tell" situations, the "sharing" times and the role-playing which are devices so common in the primary grades—in fact, a combination of all three in a more sophisticated way. A vital part of the task is to design those situations which lead children to practice the essential skills with imagination and spirit. For most teachers it takes little ingenuity to conceive of ideal settings. The major subjects in particular arrange themselves without difficulty into topical study units or "centers of interest" (as they are sometimes called) which yield abundant opportunity for development and expression.

---

7. Lauren L. Brink, "Extemporaneous Speaking in the English Class," *English Journal* (November, 1947), pp. 474-477.

8. Naomi C. Chase, "Speech in the Elementary School," *Elementary English* (March, 1953), pp. 137-141.

Even in the initial steps of these units (the part that is sometimes called the planning session), swift strides may be made towards achieving confidence and fluency. This is the phase where the youngsters are called upon to exchange ideas on how and in what form to present the knowledge they would get through their research. During the discussion that is carried on in the classroom or privately the children are rewarded with the satisfaction of seeing actual designs and objectives taking shape. If nothing else, the degree of spontaneity involved often arouses a powerful rivalry among them, drawing them out and making them express themselves. But what is most important is that their contributions to the discussion, no matter how insignificant, yields for them a favorable emotional consequence, a feeling of unusual achievement.

Next come the developmental steps of the unit. These also feature oral activities; but instead of the speaking being impromptu as it was in the exploratory phase, the oral work is now "prepared." The aim of communication here is to convey in a suitable and logical form the results of the children's findings in research work. The child may be activated into doing his work on his own initiative or under the teacher's direction, according to his ability. He learns how to limit his topic; then he cultivates his knowledge through the examination of source material in the form of reference books, text books, dictionaries, tables, charts, pictures, and other equipment. Having gathered his information he undertakes the problem of organizing it (preferably in outline form), and sharing it first with his team mates and then with the class. In some cases a simple report is all that is necessary. But he may also want to present his knowledge in ways that are even more interesting. He may proffer his information through a chalkboard demonstration, or an explanation of an exhibit, or an interview. He may cooperate with others to organize a panel discussion or a group meeting. He may choose to treat his information in some form of dramatization—a narrative, a playlet, a pageant, or the like. But no matter what form he selects, that type will offer a perfect platform for proficiency in speaking. On his part, the teacher could fit any one of those devices into his current schedule of goals, whether he is stressing enunciation or modulation of voice or building the vocabulary. Then the teaching of oral techniques which he is attempting can go along uninterrupted.

Advantages of Grouping

In the elementary grades and beyond most pupils are ready to undertake the practice of oral skills which grow increasingly more complex. For one thing, they are likely to experiment with a great variety of forms; and for another, their contributions become longer and more detailed. As a matter of fact, if the children in an average class were to try performing all in one day, as they often did in the primary grades, one could imagine what would happen to the last few speakers—what a restless and indifferent audience they would meet. But that is not all. As far as the teachers are concerned the worst hazard any one of them may face is a "let-down" which occurs when several pupils all keyed up to speak are forced to postpone their efforts. Often the mood or spirit which predominated seems ended then and there. When the lesson is resumed the children find it hard to retrieve that "first fine careless rapture." The factors of emotional readiness and interest curve which are involved are too important to be overlooked.

To avoid disappointment teachers have been using plans which limit the number of speakers each period. A favorite device is to organize committees for special purposes or to divide the class into groups whose talks are based upon similar research topics. With this procedure, since the oral work would not be too prolonged, the evils of boredom and interruption can be eliminated and the attitude of the pupils would be more favorable.

Grouping may serve an infinite number of purposes. In each division activities are often centered around a single problem or theme, and as long as this limitation exists conditions are set up for the pupils to engage in a specialized cooperative venture. The children can interchange the sources of their information or they can develop ideas together. They can consolidate their efforts in other ways too, such as establishing the goals to be reached or planning the methods of carrying out their assignments. Through all this it is important for teachers to remind themselves that groups must be kept quite fluid. They should last only until their objectives are carried out and then if need be they should be reorganized for further activity or disbanded altogether. When groups are formed again, however, pupils pool their talents and interests with other partners. In this way they learn to accept the challenge and stress of team participation.

To children who are reserved or of timid disposition grouping can be very helpful. For some of them it is an almost insurmountable ordeal to stand up before a large audience, but when they are surrounded by a small set of their classmates they are likely to be more relaxed and have more confidence in their own powers. The effect of physical nearness alone establishes an atmosphere of intimacy which helps them overcome their fears. Pupils like these offer an urgent challenge in the learning process, since the conscientious teacher would consider it a failure on his own part if he did not bring up a battery of techniques to help them. Once he has discovered who they are he can make arrangements to combat their deficiencies with individual instruction or with training in very small groups. Then with patience, resourcefulness and encouragement he can go far towards giving them incentives to conquer their insecurities.

For one thing, he may try a simple arrangement like bunching the children together and working with them in a more secluded part of the classroom. An illusion of privacy may be brought about if necessary by having the rest of the class assigned to work which will divert their attention from the remedial activity at hand. To help occasionally in coaching it is a good idea also to use some of the children who are advanced in oral accomplishment. When the actual reports or oral compositions are given the helpers could then be supportive by sitting in as listeners and thereby increasing the size of an acceptable audience. In fact, the pupils who receive special training should be accustomed as soon as possible to larger and larger audiences. The ultimate aim is to integrate them with the class as a whole and in this way to avoid any possible distinction which might label them as being inferior.

How would the teacher himself benefit by grouping in oral composition? The dividends for him are rich and gratifying. First of all, the division of a class into groups establishes a logical pattern in which he can teach a well-rounded lesson. With fewer speakers to account for on each occasion he is relieved of anxious clock-watching. He need not hurry the steps in the teaching plan. He will find leisure for a preliminary discussion either to arouse enthusiasm or to "set the stage" as it were. There can be sufficient time allowed for audience participation in the form of pupil evaluation. All the speakers can perform, give their talks or make their reports, the listeners can contribute their comments, and time will still be left over for the teacher to supplement the children's comments with those of his own. In effective teaching none of these elements can be omitted.

The fact that the group is limited gives the teacher another advantage which is of importance. It offers him a chance to study the needs of each child more in detail than would otherwise be possible. His observations can be recorded on a chart or in a notebook or he could capture the pupil's voice and contribution on a tape recorder. When the unit is complete the findings could be analyzed and could then be incorporated into future plans for individual training.

Education for Leadership in Group Participation

The basic purposes of oral language are the expression of ideas and the sharing of information but it must be recognized that communication has another role as well. The use of oral expression in the maintenance of social relationships is a function that is integrated with other services of speech. In fact, the whole adventure into discussion and debate is an effort to apply through group interaction the concepts of personal rights and courtesies. If the ends of democracy in the classroom are to be served, children should be conditioned towards learning these courtesies.

Not only should they be encouraged to master the principles of order in conducting meetings but they should experience something more— they should be guided into displaying initiative through leadership roles within their own groups. Whenever a group or sub-group presents an oral demonstration of some kind it is common to have a pupil selected to act in a leadership capacity. He may be called chairman, announcer, leader, moderator or "teacher," whichever title is most suitable to the activity. The teacher himself encourages the pupils to take on responsibility for the direction of the group. He advises them on how to conduct themselves, perhaps showing them by example what to do. Then he withdraws into the background as soon as possible, passing the initiative on to the class and engaging himself mainly with note-taking.

As far as the children are concerned, the change of position puts a different focus upon the picture. With the guidance of the group placed in their own hands they themselves become the principal centers of interest. The situation serves as an incentive for courteous attention and lively competition.

In the teaching of oral expression the functions of the chairman have often been misunderstood. Chairmanship need not be a perfunctory and unchallenging activity. Under proper direction it can be made into something vital, assertive and stimulating. Most children seem to accept the importance of this office without any persuasion. They see in the chairman's role a means of gratifying their own desires for leadership, and there is a healthy psychology in giving as many as would like a chance to show their skill.

If the pupils are willing to undertake the responsibilities of chairmanship, why not place their enthusiasm on a competitive basis? Why not rate them as carefully as are the scheduled speakers or performers in the group? Then at least they will have a basis for measuring their achievement. Chairmanship will no longer be considered a side-product of oral communication. It will rank as a highly significant element in itself.

One form of activity in which the chairman may play an especially vital part is the oral report. In this area he learns how essential good introductions are in placing the speakers at their ease and in arousing interest in their topics. He can learn in his remarks to eliminate mechanical repetition and to find with the simplest turn of expression a fresh approach to his introductory statements. Before long pupils can be made aware of the extensive combinations for introduction at their command and will take pride in displaying their creative skills. No matter how trivial it may seem, that little "extra something" which the chairman uses to flavor his comments is a tribute to his teacher's effectiveness.

Organization of Pupil Criticism

There is no more valuable learning experience to be gained by any class than in the earnest and thoughtful assessment of a speaker, even if on an informal basis. Since evaluation gives life and work its clearest meaning and deepest satisfaction, it is an ideal situation when the audience is sensitive to the merits of each talk or oral performance and at the same time is able to judge its shortcomings with discriminating intelligence. Every child needs to assess his progress in terms of understanding. But critical appreciation does not come from intuitive judgment only. The youngsters must have some specific standards for guidance, otherwise they will notice the trivial points and overlook the basic qualities that measure the effectiveness of a speech.

But what are some of the practical goals upon which teachers may depend for standards of evaluation? What steps may be recommended to increase pupil awareness of these goals? How may pupils apply these standards in order to improve their accomplishment?

First, children should have a gradual introduction to criticism. At the beginning of each year as soon as oral work gets under way only one or two points should be emphasized. Questions referring to good introductory and good ending sentences, for instance, might be placed on a chart or on the chalkboard—such questions as: *Did the speaker arouse the interest of the audience?* or, *Did he have a strong, clear purpose?* The audience could take note of them and use them for guidance in their critical evaluations, limiting themselves to those main points alone. As the class gains in mastery, these could be supplemented with others, one or two at a time. Later on, a great deal can be accomplished easily with a separate assignment for each pupil in the group. One student, for example, may volunteer to center his critical discussion after each talk upon the speaker's choice of vocabulary. He can be taught to listen for forceful verbs, colorful adjectives, or especially effective phrases which the speakers used. He can likewise center attention on limited vocabulary which is usually indicated by stereotyped expressions and words repeated over and over. Another child may be assigned to criticize techniques used by the speakers to arouse interest in their compositions, and so on. Each of the fundamental points can be reviewed until the children know them perfectly.

As long as they are given the privilege of making remarks about each report, pupils should learn one crucial lesson about criticism; and that is, that criticism need not be offensive. Teachers can suggest to them the importance of avoiding unnecessary bluntness and severity. It can be part of their social training to discover the favorable aspects of each talk as well as the undesirable features and to give as often as possible a balanced value judgment. The child's acceptance of this objective may be regarded in fact as a mark of his maturity.

Basic Elements in Evaluation of Oral Expression

To uphold the standards of evaluation for most types of oral expression teachers have depended upon the basic elements listed below. Others may be derived in the course of teaching experience to supplement these until there exists a sound comprehensive catalogue of critical points.

1. Evaluation of the beginning sentences whose function it is to arouse the interest and "set the stage." The introduction must be brief but vigorous enough to maintain a certain excitement or motivating force for the rest of the composition.

2. Emphasis upon the ending sentences as a means of "rounding out" the composition or forming a sort of "picture frame" effect.
3. Evaluation of the structural development—that is, the details of the story fitted into a logical pattern and forming a definite objective.
4. Discussion of sentences used—whether grammatical or rhetorical errors were included.
5. Attention focused upon the use of a colorful vocabulary or distinctive words and phrases which add vigor and originality to the composition.
6. Analysis of details involved—whether there has been the most effective use of description, suspense, or what is known as "climactic ladder-scaling."
7. Discussion of the speaker's vocal mannerisms—his enunciation, pronunciation, use of conversational tone and habits of modulation.
8. Criticism of his physical mannerisms—aimed at elimination of awkwardness or rigidity, and establishing habits that lead to ease and poise in speaking.
9. Consideration of the title—its suitability and its value in promoting attention to the narrative.
10. Evaluation of the interest pattern itself and methods used to maintain the attention of the group throughout the talk.

A Route to Explore

A model for an experience unit was one which was "staged" in a sixth grade class to correlate science and oral language. This unit resulted from an extensive learning experience in which the class explored the composition of and the possibilities for survival in outer space—such things as the effect of time, distance, weightlessness, orbital speed, re-entry, and other data.

Built into the unit was a general objective—an appreciation of the problems involved in man's invasion of outer space during a journey to the moon and subsequent return to earth. The more specific goals related to the following: (1) establishing reasons for outer space conquest—the why's of the unit, (2) classifying knowledge of outer space and the moon, (3) defining the relationships between earth and moon, and (4) conceiving the effect of lunar exploration upon man.

The students brought to the classroom an array of magazine articles and clippings from newspapers which they made available to the entire group for study. The clippings were catalogued and arranged on a bulletin board under separate headings. Pictures and posters of missiles, moon craters and moon rocks were collected and added to the display.

As the study progressed maps and charts of the solar system, both professional and student-made, were posted on appropriate spaces along the wall. Charts with a growing vocabulary list were placed strategically enough to command the attention of the pupils. Before long, a table in the "science corner" was gradually covered with related items—styrofoam mock-ups of earth and moon, cardboard models of space capsules and three-stage rockets, cut-outs of space suits and astronauts, and a diorama of a landing party on the surface of the moon.

The final activity, which featured oral English, had the benefit of a powerful motivating force. There was a dramatization in which a script called for three scenes: (1) the count-down and take-off, (2) the landing on the moon and (3) the return to earth. In preparing for the presentation the committee requested help in lettering transparencies for an overhead projector which they planned to use for an illustrated lecture on physical conditions in outer space and problems which scientists and astronauts must overcome. They also taped a narrative with sound effects to correlate with the take-off, the journey through space and eery arrival on the edge of a lunar crater. They even reproduced the surface of the moon through a pupil-made slide.

When the program was ready the pupils found they had collected a formidable array of materials. Each item complemented the others in creating a powerful illusion. The introduction was made, the lectures were given, the astronauts in their space suits crowded into their paper capsules, the room was plunged into darkness and the capsule shone in the glare of the slide projector. The reels on the tape recorder started spinning and the sound of the "count-down" lured the audience into complete absorption.

Partly through the accumulated materials and partly through the devices used in the lecture and dramatization and in the pupil-directed discussion and criticisms which followed, a significant lesson took place. In this way it is possible for oral composition to take on a new dimension.

Discussion of Current Issues in the Classroom

This chapter has dealt mostly with organized procedures for developing oral proficiency, but there is a trend in oral education that defies a structural framework—one that is free-wheeling and spontaneous and beginning to assume a significant place in the area of speech. In the upper levels, corresponding to grades five and six, the elementary class-room has become a stage for the give-and-take of free discussion. The lives of pupils have been affected by so many current problems that the issues alone act as incentives for discourse and debate. The news media, television documentaries, leaflets distributed through the neighbor-hood, posters displayed in public places, allusions made by elders or by other children at home—all have contributed to opinions which the youngsters for the most part are willing to express. The list of topics is flexible and constantly expansive so that there is a liberal choice of subjects for discussion. The teacher needs only a little background to initiate the talks but once the discussion has started his role is mainly that of a referee. He requires a certain amount of adroitness in prevent-ing digression or in discouraging some youngsters from monopolizing the conversation. A great test of his skill is in his ability to encourage each of his pupils to participate as much as possible, to recognize the special interests of the youngsters and whenever the situation warrants to call upon them as experts. He must encourage the use of critical ideas as a means of expanding the mind. He must also have the knack of maintaining the vigor and the excitement of controversy.

Topics for discussion should be suggested by the youngsters them-selves. They can be discovered in situations that are local, national or global. Points of contention, for example, can be found in such far-ranging problems as environmental pollution, American military in-volvement on a global scale, universal conscription, drug abuse, the minimum voting age, ways of coping with crime, the conscientious objector, and so on.

If they are directed skillfully pupils develop an ardor for research in newspapers and magazines or will listen more carefully to news broad-casts for material to use in their discussions. They will become familiar with the terminology needed to express themselves and, if challenged persistently, will develop persuasive logic and fluency to sustain their arguments.

The rewards of free discussion as a part of an oral English program are not in dexterity of contention but in an expanded vocabulary, a clarity of expression, and a mature understanding of issues common to our society.

Summary

Since recent trends emphasize the necessity of an intensive program in the teaching of oral communication, teachers should understand the specific problems involved and experiment with the steps which lead to favorable development. The goals of oral communication should be realized one step at a time, with considerable practice devoted to each technique. Training in the principles of speaking and speech must continue throughout the year and at every opportunity.

Teachers should recognize that oral language is not to be taught within a limited scope but should be tied in with all major subject areas. A most provocative setting for oral expression is the experience unit. It induces research work, it encourages a variety of speaking situations, and it provides a natural atmosphere for oral composition.

One advantage of the experience unit is that it allows for the division of a class into small groups for special assignments. This arrangement is a vital factor in several ways. First, it evokes a feeling of informality which makes the lesson in oral English more alluring. Second, it offers more security and helps pupils overcome a fear of speaking before an audience. Third, the small number of children involved in each group gives the teacher a greater chance to individualize his instruction. Finally, it provides a chance for more efficient corrective measures.

Grouping in oral English stimulates development in areas concerned with growth of character and personality as well. Modern techniques of discussion place a spotlight on the role of the chairman or group leader. Where the class is divided into small groups the post of chairman is changed quite often, and each child may have a chance to undertake the responsibilities of leadership. Special training in the techniques of chairmanship is therefore quite profitable.

The variety of expression which oral English assumes presents each group with a challenge in the way of organization, in methods of introduction and, wherever speaking deficiencies occur, in the use of corrective measures. To meet this challenge teachers and pupils alike may develop a permanent set of standards, using each time points of criticism applicable to the project on which they are working. These rules are to be emphasized and discussed until the pupils are sensitive to their requirements, and teaching should be continued until mastery is achieved.

The high road to excellence is reached only through the patient attainment of goals; and skill in oral communication too is derived from careful planning, from the steady application of knowledge, and from a program that is bold, consistent and inspiring.

EXTENDING YOUR LEARNING

1. Keep a list of your speaking activities during the day. How much time was spent in informal conversation? giving directions? participating in a serious discussion? directing a discussion or making a "speech"? In what other types of activities did you engage?
2. Listen to a four year old, an eight year old, and a ten year old. What *types* of sentences did they use? Note the *length* of their sentences and the children's ability to vary their speech patterns to fit their audiences and the occasion.
3. It has been said that "children seldom write better than they speak." Look over the *written* work of the eight and ten year old whose speech you carefully observed. Is this claim supported or refuted—at least for these children?
4. Examine several language arts textbooks. How much emphasis is placed upon oral language development? What types of activities are suggested?
5. For the same reasons, study several curriculum guides. What similarities and what differences do you find for suggested activities?
6. Read some of the classic textbooks on culturally different children by Reissman, Passow, Deutsch and Saltzman. Note the devastating effects which language deficiencies have upon learning.
7. Tape some impromptu "talk" by immigrant or culturally different children. In what ways do their dialects vary from standard expression? What program would you initiate to help these pupils?
8. Make a list of controversial topics of concern to the public at the present time. Which of these topics would you consider interesting for discussion in an intermediate classroom? Why would you select these and reject the others?

BIBLIOGRAPHY

Abercrombie, D., "Conversation and Spoken Prose," *English Language Teacher*, October 1963, pages 10-16.

Bloom, Benjamin S., Davis, Allison, and Hess, Robert, *Compensatory Education for Cultural Deprivation*, New York: Holt, Rhinehart and Winston, Inc., 1965.

Botel, Morton and Dawkins, John, "Tune in on Oral Communication," *Instructor*, April 1970, p. 56.

Brink, Lauren L., "Extemporaneous Speaking in the English Class," *English Journal*, November 1947, pp. 474-477.

Bromwich, Rose M., "Developing the Language of Young Disadvantaged Children," *Education Digest*, September 1968, pp. 19-22.

Buck, M., "Helping Children Develop Speaking Abilities," *Education*, April 1960, p. 451.

Burks, Ann T. and Guilford, Polly D., "Wakullah County Oral Language Project," *Elementary English*, December 1969, p. 606.

Carpenter, H.M., "Study Skills: Oral Reporting," *Instructor*, May 1965, pp. 13-14.

Chase, Naomi N., "Speech in the Elementary School," *Elementary English*, March 1953, pp. 137-141.

Dale, Edgar, "Understanding the Vocabulary Development of the Disadvantaged Child," *Elementary English*, November 1965, pp. 778-786.

Dallmann, Martha E., "Reports Vitalize Social Studies," *Grade Teacher,* February 1961, p. 44.

————, *Teaching the Language Arts in the Elementary School,* Dubuque, Iowa: William C. Brown Co., 1966.

Davis, D., "Let's Reach for Speech," *Education,* October 1959, p. 745.

Dawson, Mildred A., *Teaching Language in the Grades,* New York: World Book Company, 1950.

Eastman, M., "Talk Up!" *Grade Teacher,* September 1961, pp. 136-142.

Gallegos, B. B., "Toward Better Speech," *Elementary School Journal,* April 1962, pp. 375-379.

Goodman, Kenneth, "Let's Dump the Uptight Model in English," *Elementary School Journal,* October 1969, pp. 1-13.

Hartman, M., "Way to Good Speech for All," *Ohio School Journal,* November 1963, pp. 24-25.

Hintze, H.K., "Speech Improvement: An Overview," *Elementary School Journal,* November, pp. 91-96.

Hopkins, T.A., "The Spoken Word," *Education,* November 1963, pp. 166-169.

Hunter, E., "The Importance of Children's Oral Language," *Grade Teacher,* April 1964, p. 51.

Laufer, H., "Show-and-Tell in the Kindergarten," *National Education Association Journal,* October 1963, p. 63.

Lindberg, Lucille, "Oral Language or Else," *Elementary English,* November 1965, pp. 760-761.

Manolakes, G., "Oral Language and Learning," *Elementary English,* November 1963, pp. 731-734.

Marquard, Richard L., "Language Development—A Proposal for Improvement," *Elementary English,* December 1968, pp. 1077-1079.

Sister Mary Florentine, "Speech Habits for Five-Year Olds," *National Catholic Education Association Bulletin,* August 1963, pp. 531-534.

Sister Mary Nora, "Oral Composition: An Essential Competence in the Language Arts," *National Catholic Education Association Bulletin,* August 1960, pp. 364-366.

May, Frank, "The Effects of Environment in Oral Language Development," Part I—*Elementary English,* October 1966, pp. 587-595.

————, Part II— *Elementary English,* November 1966, pp. 720-739.

Millsap, L., "Oral Reporting," *Elementary English,* February 1965, pp. 197-200.

Munkres, A., and others, "Helping Children in Oral Communication," *Teachers College,* 1959.

Painter, M., "Oral Emphasis in the English Class," *English Journal,* March 1953, pp. 137-141.

Rasmussen, Carrie, "The Role of Speech in the Elementary School," *Elementary English,* January 1952, pp. 6-14.

Stewart, W.A., "Foreign Language Teaching Methods in Quasi-Foreign Language Situations," *Non-Standard Speech and Teaching of English,* Washington, D.C., Center of Applied Linguistics, 1965.

————, "Urban Negro Speech: Sociolinguistic Factors Affecting English Teaching," in R. Shuy (ed.), *Social Dialects and Language Learning,* National Council of Teachers of English, Champaign, Ill., 1964.

Van Riper, Charles and Butler, Katherine, *Speech in the Elementary Classroom,* New York: Harper and Brothers, 1955.

Whipp, Leslie, "The Child as Language Teacher," *Elementary English,* April 1969, pp. 466-470.

Focus

In reviewing each chapter, for purposes of preparing these introductions, the editor has been impressed by every author's belief that the area in which he is writing is of crucial importance, deserving of a teacher's best efforts, and difficult and complex, both from a teaching and learning point of view! Ferris' first paragraph is not intended to discourage the teacher of writing. It is simply his intent to sharpen the reader's perceptions regarding the complexity of the writing task, and to remind teachers of the many influences which affect children's ability to put on paper that which is sincere, genuinely expressive and "correct" when judged by most criteria of form.

If one doubts the claim that writing is not easy, to do *or* to teach *others* to do, he need only refer to his own personal experience, and to the limited amount of writing required by most elementary teachers. The editor, as a college teacher, has had the surprising response to a poetry writing assignment (in a Language Arts methods class) that this was the *first* time such an assignment had been given. The class was composed of college juniors and seniors, and the response came not from one student but from several. Do teachers avoid making more than routine letter writing assignments (thank-you notes following a field trip) because *good* writing is difficult to stimulate, because the mechanics become "messy" (children finish at different times, need varying amounts of help with spelling or other mechanics) or because they are puzzled about evaluation? Does one tell a child his product is "good" because to do other-wise is to stifle? If this is the teacher's standard approach, from where does the child gain a set of criteria by which to judge his own writing or that of others?

Time for writing presents another set of issues; if one writes, or asks children to write "when the muse strikes" (the first snowfall, the first crocus) writing will occur infrequently, and how can one predict that the first red maple leaf of the fall will be equally stimulating to each pupil? On the other hand, if writing is required regularly, if time in the daily program is set aside for writing the chances of each pupil being motivated are even less!

These are a few of the reasons Donald Ferris believes that teaching writing isn't easy. These are a few of the issues he discusses, in an objective and practical manner, in this chapter.

Donald R. Ferris

chapter six

teaching children to write

If you have ever tried to teach children to write, you know, together with thousands of other elementary teachers, that it is not an easy task. If you have not tried, be prepared for a difficult, frustrating and often exasperating experience. You may question the wisdom of such frankness about the difficulties you will encounter. On the other hand, it is not the intent to discourage you from teaching children to write; nor should you expect nothing but failure as you teach. Successes will come and they will be sweet; the purpose of mentioning the difficulties is to prepare you for the frustrations you will inevitably meet. Having been duly warned, let us look at the nature of language and its written form for some clues to the causes of some of the difficulties to which we've referred.

The Nature of Language and Writing

Linguists tell us that speech is the real language. By this, they mean that in the history of cultures spoken communication precedes the development of a written language. This is true not only in the history of a culture but it is also true in the developmental history of an individual. The young child's language development follows a general pattern: he learns to listen to language and understand it before he learns to express ideas through spoken language; he expresses ideas in spoken language before he learns the written language of his culture (if his culture has a written language). Children acquire these language skills at different ages but in the same sequence.

Speech serves as the medium of idea exchange among human beings. "Language is a purely human and non-instinctive method of communicating ideas, emotions, and desires by means of a system of voluntarily produced symbols."[1]

Children learn to create patterns of sound symbols which communicate their ideas to others. Sapir's definition of language notes that it is an exclusively human method of communication. The capacity for human language is based upon man's unique brain. The human brain with its sensitivity to happenings in the surrounding environment enables human beings to communicate their unique perceptions of the environment more or less accurately to each other through the medium of language. The symbols of language are used to represent the reality one perceives. Spoken language is an abstraction of the world of reality. Speech represents reality through sound symbols. Written language, on the other hand, is even further removed from reality. Writing is a symbolization of a symbolization. Written language is a system of scratches and squiggles (graphemes) which stand for the sound elements in human speech. Written language stands for speech which is a rough representation of reality.

In teaching children to write it is essential that the teacher remember the relationship between spoken and written language. Spoken language precedes writing and establishes patterns for it. A child who can create a clear spoken sentence has a skill that is necessary in learning how to write. It might be said that all that remains to be learned are the mechanics and conventions of the language: handwriting, spelling, punctuation, capitalization and conventional forms. This is in no way to minimize the number or difficulty of the skills which remain to be learned. The point is that the child already knows the structure of the language well enough to be able to formulate sentences that are recognizable and understandable to another native speaker. It is also true that the child's written language will usually reflect his habitual level of usage. If the child says "He don't," he will probably write it. Any attempts to have the child write at a higher level of usage than he speaks is unrealistic. This does not, however, argue for a postponement

---

1. Edward Sapir, *Language: An Introduction to the Study of Speech* (New York: Harcourt, Brace and World, 1921).

of teaching a child to write until he "cleans up his speech." The habit of proofreading what one has written should be taught as soon as the child reaches the stage in his writing where he is accepting some independence—even if it is only checking to see if he has copied something from the chalkboard correctly. This habit of proofreading will not assure that everything the child writes will be cast at an appropriate level of language; however if he reads what he has written it does help him to detect and eliminate garbled sentences. More will be said about techniques for teaching proofreading later in this chapter.

Types of Writing

The terminology related to teaching children to write is confused and confusing. Chiefly, it suffers from being too rigidly dichotomized: there is practical and personal writing; creative and noncreative writing; prose and poetry; utilitarian and imaginative writing; original and stereotyped writing. It is difficult to talk of teaching children using any of these dichotomies. Obviously the categories of prose and poetry overlap with the creative and noncreative categories; it is possible for a piece of utilitarian writing such as a personal letter to be written creatively. Similarly, it is obvious that something written in the form of a poem— let us say in iambic pentameter—may be hackneyed and trite.

The inadequacy of any of the pairs of terms mentioned to describe children's writing accurately lies in their failure to recognize the nature of writing. There are three facts which should be recognized: (1) writing is a *process* which yields a *product;* (2) writing has a *purpose* or a *function* and (3) writing can be evaluated to determine its *quality*—how adequately it fulfills its purpose and to what extent it possesses the literary qualities desired.

Writing as a Process and a Product

Writing as a process involves the application of skills in translating spoken language or thoughts into the conventions of "language written" so that it is intelligible to the reader. (The dyadic nature of the language arts presumes that a writer will have readers just as a speaker will have listeners. Perhaps it ought to be thought as equally strange for a writer to write without a thought for a reader as it is for a man to talk to himself.) Writing one's ideas requires handwriting which is minimally legible, spelling that is at least partially phonetic, a vocabulary adequate to the ideas to be expressed and some skills of organization of the ideas so that they are intelligible to the reader. These skills having been exercised a *product* results, which we may or may not be able to categorize formally as an essay, a short story, a novel, a poem, a friendly letter, a business letter or one of the other kinds of writing which can be classified by form, length, or as fiction or nonfiction.

The Purpose or Function of Writing

The product which results from the writing process will appear in a certain form according to the purpose for which the writing was being done. It is the function of a friendly letter to communicate ideas from one person to another who is beyond the range of voice contact. Before a writer chooses to write a friendly letter, he must have the intent or purpose of communicating with the other person. He probably chooses the form for communicating which is customary and adequate for his purpose. (He may invent a new form which more adequately suits the task he has set for his communication; this might be evaluated as possessing originality. This illustrates the evaluative aspect of writing which is further discussed later.)

Evaluating the Qualities and Adequacy of Writing

Both the process and product of writing can be evaluated. One who would evaluate the process of writing must settle for the subjective introspective evidence of the writer. This makes the evaluation of the mental process of the author less dependable albeit no less interesting. The task of evaluating whether the writer's mental processes were "creative" is difficult to imagine.

The product of the writer is a more tangible thing to evaluate; for example, if the quality of originality in writing is defined as being related to how frequently a particular idea occurs among a number of written products, it is possible to rate writing products as being more or less original.

Even though the qualities of original writing may be listed, the task of evaluating the writing of a particular student is still difficult. Through a survey of several professional publications during the period from 1929 to 1959 Carlson suggests seventeen possible qualities which might be found in original writing and suggests that there probably are many more. The qualities which Carlson found are listed following and will not be discussed in detail. The reader is referred to Carlson's excellent article for a more complete explanation of the qualities.

"(1) novelty or freshness, (2) individuality, (3) a personal quality revealing the self, (4) emotion or feeling, (5) "becomingness," related to identification, (6) imagination, (7) a recombination or restructuring quality, (8) an abstractive element consisting of finding the essence, (9) immediacy, (10) dynamic vitality, (11) curiosity, (12) reservoir of experiential data, (13) perceptive sensitivity, (14) flexibility or versatility, (15) symbolism, (16) coherent unity, and (17) an expressive—communicative element."[2]

An impressive list! Some of the qualities probably are not immediately meaningful and not directly applicable to elementary school children's writing. Carlson simplified her findings on originality for use in a study of original stories of fourth, fifth, and sixth grade children. She defined an original story as "a form of narrative or descriptive composition which is novel, non-imitative, and one which appears with statistical infrequency."[3]

Writing as a Process

Learning to write is a long and complicated process. Because it is a process—which is to say that it moves from step to more complicated step—it builds upon past experiences and learning. It is an emerging ability. The earliest experiences a child has in translating his spoken words into written symbols builds upon his ability to use the patterns of his native language. He can never write anything which he cannot think or speak. The development of thinking, oral language and written language are simultaneous. Just as learning to express thoughts in words is dependent upon listening to the language and learning its patterns, so readiness for learning to write is based upon the development of spoken language to a level necessary to learning to write. The development of oral language has been discussed in Chapter 4 and will not be further discussed here except to point out that readiness for written language is developed through some facility with oral language.

Before a child can write independently he must learn to write the symbols which, when arranged and spaced correctly, create the written

2. Ruth Kearney Carlson, "Seventeen Qualities of Original Writing," *Elementary English* XXXVIII (December, 1961): 576-579.
3. Ruth Kearney Carlson, "Recent Research in Originality," *Elementary English* XXXX (October, 1963): 30-31.

equivalent of his spoken language. To put it more conventionally, he must learn handwriting, spelling, punctuation and capitalization. The basic dilemma in teaching children to write with exactness and beauty is that they learn to do this only through opportunities to write without having perfectly formed letters, correctly spelled and capitalized words, and correctly placed punctuation. Handwriting, spelling, capitalization and punctuation, although difficult and complicated to teach, are easier to teach than the selection and arrangement of the words in thought units which are called sentences. As the child's thinking becomes more complex and he develops rich concepts, he learns words which then may become part of his writing vocabulary. Because all of the language arts are interrelated, the source of the child's new written vocabulary is the people with whom he talks and the books that he reads.

The Transition from Oral to Written Communication

The goal of the school in teaching writing is to produce individuals who are independent writers: individuals who can handle the personal and social demands for writing in their lives. More will be said of these specific functions and purposes later. When the child enters school, he will be using oral communication at a more or less adequate level. Some children will be facile in their use of spoken language; others will reflect contact with less stimulating language learning environments. Knowing that readiness for learning to write is based upon a child's development of oral communication skills, the wise teacher will not expect each child to be ready to learn to write at the same time. For the child whose speaking skills are less well developed, the teacher will provide opportunities for listening to stories read or told by him.

Some children will already know that writing is "talk put down on paper." Others will have to learn this. The teacher should create opportunities to write children's sentences on the chalkboard. Through this, children learn not only that spoken language can be translated into written language, but also are introduced to such conventions as capitalizing the first word of a sentence. (The term *sentence* should be used.) They are introduced to the convention that words are made from letters, that writing in our language goes from left to right, and that the end of a sentence is indicated by a "stop sign" or a question mark.

After the children have learned that what they say can be written, the teacher should encourage them to dictate sentences which are then written on the chalkboard or on sheets of paper large enough to be seen by the children involved in the activity. As the teacher does this, the conventions of written communication should be pointed out—the capital letter with which the sentence begins and the terminal punctuation which indicates the end of a thought unit.

An effective and much-used device for recording children's language is the experience chart. An experience chart is written on a large sheet of paper so that it can be seen by all children participating in the activity. The chart is used to record the children's statements about some experience they have had together with the teacher. It might be used to record facts or impressions the children have received from a visit to the firehouse, the bakery, or some other community resource. Writing an experience chart is a good activity to use with a whole class. Although some of the more verbally skilled children will be the ones who clamor to get their sentences written, even the less able child can participate in the writing because he has had the same experience. Through the use of the experience chart the children can discuss alternative ways of expressing their ideas and thereby get some idea of the flexibility of language.

As with any instructional device, the experience chart can be overused. The teacher should use it when the children's interest is high and the purpose for writing is understood by them. When the children have learned enough handwriting, they can copy the teacher's writing. Through this copying they get a feeling of independence in their writing.

Dictating to the teacher followed by copying is the first step in the child's gaining of independence in writing. As his skill in handwriting, spelling, punctuation and capitalization grow, he becomes increasingly independent in his writing. The teacher should encourage each child to become an independent writer as rapidly as he can, but should avoid the risk of the child's perceiving the teacher's refusal to help him with spelling or punctuation as punishment. If the teacher realizes that the child is eager to become independent in his writing, help can be given when it is needed without fear of its retarding the child's growth. In cases where a child is capable of becoming independent but prefers to depend upon the teacher for emotional security, the teacher can encourage the child in such a way that he is rewarded by his accomplishment. If children are given purposeful tasks commensurate with their skills, little difficulty will be encountered in getting them to write.

Developing Skills in the Writing Process

After the child gains some skills in writing and is becoming more and more independent, his continued development requires that he learn increasingly complex skills in spelling, mechanics (punctuation and capitalization) as well as enlarge the size of his vocabulary and his ability to write clear paragraphs which do not contain trite, overused phrases.

Punctuation Skills

Learning to use marks of punctuation often poses a major problem to the pupil and teacher. Perhaps one reason why this is so is that the teacher does not capitalize upon pointing out the similarities between punctuation in written language and the intonation, pauses and other conventions used in communicating meaning in oral communication. The marks of punctuation correspond roughly to signals to the reader which assure that what the writer intended to communicate is communicated. The period indicates the end of a thought. Both the semicolon and the colon, while not full stops, are heavier stops than provided by the comma. The comma in written communication corresponds roughly to pauses in spoken language.

The importance of punctuation to meaning in written communication is obvious in the following sentence: That that is is not that that is not. As the words are read, their meaning is probably not immediately apparent. When a comma is inserted between the first and second "is," the meaning of the sentence (far from a profound observation) is understood. If one were to hear this sentence spoken, the rising inflection on the first *is,* followed by a short pause, less emphasis upon the second *is,* a rising inflection on *not,* carry the major burden of the speaker's thought. This example illustrates the problem the writer faces; he must communicate his meaning with far fewer signals to the reader than are available to a listener. In their study of spoken language the linguists are interested in kinesics (the study of all the nonverbal signals that a speaker gives which helps a listener to understand the message being communicated). Gestures, facial expression, and bodily attitude are examples of kinesics which give signals to the hearer of the intent of the speaker's words. This further illustrates the linguist's statement mentioned earlier that writing is a symbolization of a symbolization. The function of punctuation, then, is the prevention of ambiguity in what the reader perceives as the writer's message.

Teaching of the function of punctuation in written language should not be postponed until the child has become somewhat independent in his writing. From the time he enters school and the teacher begins to read to him, an excellent opportunity exists to teach the function. As the teacher reads, the full stop indicated by a period at the end of the sentence can be indicated. The pause suggested by the comma can be shown. It is not suggested, of course, that the primary function of the teacher's reading to the child is to teach him punctuation. In reading to children "the story's the thing" and the danger of making a pleasurable experience like storyreading a deadly, dull punctuation-learning exercise is to be avoided. The practice of using reading to alert children to the existence of punctuation marks and their function further illustrates the interrelationship of all the language arts.

Rule Versus Style

The extent to which punctuation usage is dictated by strict inflexible rule or by the style, even whim, of the writer is a moot point. Spokesmen for all positions between the two extremes can be found. Perhaps a reasonable compromise between the two positions is suggested in G.V. Carey's delightful little book, *Mind the Stop*. He suggests that punctuation should be "governed two-thirds by rule and one-third by personal taste."[4] Although this position probably does not allow for as much flexibility as demanded by certain present day writers, it probably is about one-third more flexible in its position than that of many teachers. Not to be unfair to the teachers in question, likely it is also true that the two-thirds of the punctuation skills that can be learned by rule are those to be learned in the elementary grades. The one-third personal taste that Carey speaks of in the use of punctuation can probably best be exercised by the individual who is well on the way to developing his own literary style.

What are the punctuation uses that ought to be taught in the elementary school? Professor Furness at the University of Wyoming has suggested what a teacher should know if the pupil is to be helped to overcome the seven most common errors in punctuation.[5]

---

4. G.V.Carey, *Mind the Stop: A Brief Guide to Punctuation with a Note on Proof Correction* (Cambridge University Press, 1958), p. 1.
5. Edna Lue Furness, "Pupils, Pedagogues, and Punctuation," *Elementary English* (March, 1960), pp. 187-89.

Errors	Possible Causes	Suggested Teaching Procedures
1. omission of period at end of sentence	a. carelessness b. indifference c. poor observation d. haste	1. Have pupil read aloud his sentences and ask him to note that he drops his voice and pauses at the end of the statement. 2. Tell him that this drop pause is a stop and that in writing the period represents this stop.
2. omission of period after abbreviation	a. carelessness b. insufficient practice c. lack of "abbreviation consciousness"	1. Show the difference between a word and an abbreviation. 2. Explain that some words are abbreviated and that others are not.
3. failure to use a colon	a. intellectual, immaturity b. lack of sensitivity to emotional overtones of written material	1. Show that the colon is a mark of anticipation, directing attention to what follows. 2. Explain that the colon is a contrast to the semicolon, which is a stop, almost a period.
4. omission of question mark after a question	a. carelessness b. indifference	1. Teach the following concept: Use a question mark when there is a quick rise in voice and then drop back to the basic level.
5. failure to set off a non-restrictive clause by a comma	a. lack of appreciation of a suspension of thought b. lack of observation	1. Show how the relative and its clause can be removed without destroying the sentence. 2. Call attention to the fact that the non-restrictive clause furnishes additional information. 3. Help pupils see a *that* clause as subject or object is an integral part of the sentence and hence is not pointed by a comma. 4. Call attention to the misreading which may occur in a *for* sentence; e.g., The day seemed long (,) for the class was tired. 5. Use colored chalk to make the commas stand out. 6. Cover the relative and its clause and ask the class to read the sentence.

Errors	Possible Causes	Suggested Teaching Procedures
6. failure to set off a series by commas	a. carelessness b. lack of writing experience c. lack of attention to details d. misunderstanding of the concept of *series*	1. Write on the board the example: *long, hot, sultry afternoons.* 2. Show that *long, hot, sultry afternoons* really stands for *long* and *hot* and *sultry* afternoons. 3. Explain that there are commas between long-hot-sultry because each stands in the same relation to the noun *afternoons.* 4. Write on the board: old rock garden. Explain that *old* modifies *rock garden* rather than *garden.* 5. Explain that in *old, rock garden* the comma throws the emphasis upon *rock.*

7. lack of commas setting off an appositive	a. failure to understand the relation of the insertion to the sentence proper	1. Place on the board several sentences and several appositives. Ask the pupils to choose the proper appositive for each sentence.
		    a. Mary Jones, ____, is an intelligent girl.
		    b. Denver, ____, is in Colorado.
		    a. The Queen City of the Plain
		    b. Miss America of 1970
		2. Let the class discover for themselves that the appositive is separated from the rest of the sentence by one comma when the appositive comes last in the sentence.
		3. Show that, when the appositive is removed from the sentence, a complete thought remains.
		4. Cover up the appositive and ask the class to read the sentence.
		5. Show the difference in meaning between
		    a. his brother John arrives (implies he has only one brother)
		    b. his sister, Dorothy, arrives (implies he has more than one sister)
		6. Use colored chalk to make the appositive stand out.

PEANUTS®　　　　　**By Charles M. Schulz**

Suggestions for Grade Placement

The suggested teaching procedures listed will not solve all the teacher's problems with teaching punctuation in writing; neither does it suggest the many other uses of punctuation marks in clear, correct writing. The following list suggests the grade placement for the major uses for punctuation marks which children should learn in the elementary school.

Grade one
　a. Period at the end of a sentence which tells something
　b. Period after numbers in any list

Grade two
　a. Items listed for grade one
　b. Question mark at the close of a question
　c. Comma after salutation of a friendly note or letter
　d. Comma after closing of a friendly note or letter
　e. Comma between the day of the month and the year
　f. Comma between name of city and state

Grade three
　a. Items listed for grades one and two
　b. Period after abbreviations
　c. Period after an initial
　d. Use of an apostrophe in common contractions such as isn't, aren't, don't
　e. Commas in a list

Grade four
　a. All items listed for previous grades
　b. Apostrophe to show possession

    c. Hyphen separating parts of a word divided at end of a line

    d. Period following a command

    e. Exclamation point at the end of a word or group of words that makes an exclamation

    f. Comma setting off an appositive

    g. Colon after the salutation of a business letter

    h. Quotation marks before and after a direct quotation

    i. Comma between explanatory words and a quotation

    j. Period after outline Roman number

Grade five

    a. All items listed for previous grades

    b. Colon in writing time

    c. Comma to indicate changed word order

    d. Quotation marks around the title of a booklet, pamphlet, the chapter of a book, and the title of a poem or story

    e. Underlining the title of a book

Grade six

    a. All items listed for previous grades

    b. Comma to set off nouns in direct address

    c. Hyphen in compound numbers

    d. Colon to set off a list

    e. Comma in sentences to aid in making meaning clear[6]

The first item in each list following that for grade one indicates that all items listed for previous grades should be taught. This statement suggests that learning to use punctuation marks in each of the situations listed is not acquired simply by one presentation by the teacher; each punctuation use must be repeated until it is mastered. Although this is not suggested by the list, it is also true that more advanced children should be taught those skills they need when they need them, and that teaching not be postponed because "they aren't supposed to get that until third grade."

Capitalization Skills

Compared to punctuation skills, those relating to the use of capital letters are neither as numerous nor as discretionary. Many elementary school children make the error of using capitals where they are not

6. Harry A. Greene and Walter T. Petty, *Developing Language Skills in the Elementary Schools* (Boston: Allyn and Bacon, Inc., 1963), p. 124.

needed. The problem in teaching the use of capitals is as much teaching when not to use them as it is teaching when to use them. Greene and Petty suggest the following grade placement of capitalization skills:

Grade one
a. The first word of a sentence
b. The child's first and last names
c. The name of the teacher, school, town, street
d. The word I

Grade two
a. Items listed for grade one
b. The date
c. First and important words of titles of books the children read
d. Proper names used in children's writings
e. Titles of compositions
f. Names of titles; "Mr.," "Mrs.," "Miss"

Grade three
a. Items listed for grades one and two
b. Proper names: month, day, common holidays
c. First and important words in titles of books, stories, poems
d. First word of salutation of informal note, as "Dear"
e. First word of closing of informal note, as "Yours"

Grade four
a. All that is listed for preceding grades
b. Names of cities and states in general
c. Names of organizations to which children belong, as Boy Scouts, Grade Four, etc.
d. Mother, Father, when used in place of the name
e. Local geographical names

Grade five
a. All that is outlined for previous grades
b. Names of streets
c. Names of all places and persons, countries, oceans, etc.
d. Capitalization used in outlining
e. Titles when used with names, such as President Lincoln
f. Commercial trade names

Grade six   a. All that is outlined for preceding grades
                  b. Names of the Deity and the Bible
                  c. First word of a quoted sentence
                  d. Proper adjectives, showing race, nationality, etc.
                  e. Abbreviations of proper nouns and titles[7]

Written Vocabulary Development and Word Selection

As soon as a child begins to read and write he has four definable vocabularies:[8] (1) the recognition vocabulary, (2) the reading vocabulary, (3) the writing vocabulary, and (4) the speaking vocabulary. A study of children's recognition vocabulary by Smith indicates that a first grade child's vocabulary may be as large as 24,000 words; since this study was done in 1940 it is highly probable that replications of such a study would show that children's vocabularies have grown through the influence of travel and the mass media.[9]

The recognition vocabulary is the largest of the four, however, and the child does not use all the words in his recognition vacabulary in his writing. The reading vocabulary is likely to be larger than the writing vocabulary and the speaking vocabulary is the smallest of all. Since in the beginning the child is likely to write as he talks, the need for vocabulary development in writing can be seen.

The growth and enrichment of vocabulary, as well as the content and context of his speaking and writing, derives from the child's experiences. The child acquires new vocabulary as the need occurs to communicate his experiences to others. The teacher who is aware of the dynamics of vocabulary development will provide both the new experiences and the opportunity to communicate to others the descriptions of the experiences and the child's reactions to them.

Vocabulary Development Techniques

The following list suggests a number of techniques which may be used by the teacher to develop vocabulary:

---

7. *Ibid.*, p. 125-26.

8. Charlton Laird, *The Miracle of Language* (Greenwich: Fawcett Publications, Inc., 1957), pp. 226-27.

9. Mary Katherine Smith, "Measurement of the Size of General English Vocabulary Through the Elementary Grades and High School," *Genetic Psychology Monographs* 24 (November, 1941): 311-45.

1. Informal conversation and discussion, stopping to give attention to words when the situation and the interest make it advisable.
2. Reading aloud to children material which they can understand and enjoy and which enriches and supplements their own reading as well as adds to their appreciation of their cultural heritage.
3. Reading textbook material with the children when it is difficult—reading and talking, talking and reading—to make vague and unfamiliar ideas clear ones through association and application to the children's own experience.
4. Taking field trips to gain firsthand experience. Both careful planning and follow-up activities are essential for the complete experience.
5. Using film and other types of auditory and visual aids which fit the study and add to its values.
6. Expressing new meaning graphically through various art mediums.
7. Dramatizing words very simply, as in the old game of charades or through more elaborate play.
8. Encouraging children to keep individual records of new vocabulary.
9. Keeping group records of the new vocabulary found in various experiences.
10. Giving attention to shades of meaning, to colorful words, to action words, to words that are especially vivid and effective.
11. Encouraging children to discover meaning from context and perhaps to check their meaning with the dictionary, at times, to determine their success in deducing meaning.
12. Working various types of exercises which meet the need of the group or individual; there are many kinds:
    a. Working with prefixes and suffixes
    b. Searching for synonyms and antonyms
    c. Checking in a list all words of like derivation
    d. Completing sentences by adding suitable words or word groups
    e. Matching words and definitions
    f. Fitting words into categories; animals, things to eat or drink, words describing people, words dealing with measuring. Keeping lists of these in the classroom to help with writing
    g. Word-meaning tests

       rapid   happy   slow   fast   race
13. Carrying on dictionary activities

14. Reading, reading, reading. The more the children read, the more meanings they learn.

Reading things one is interested in

Reading easy things for fun

Reading anything and everything that adds to the value of the things one is doing or studying

Reading to build new interests

Reading newspapers, magazines, books, catalogs—anything that adds interest to living[10]

The techniques listed are broadly suggestive of activities which may be used by a skillful teacher; the skillful teacher is still more important than the techniques in teaching children to acquire and use words. The importance of the teacher is well-stated by Applegate:

> "A teacher cannot give children a feeling for words unless she has it herself. But she can get a feeling as her children get it. The door is open to even the most colorless teacher; but to the colorful, not only is the door open, but the windows are up and the sun is shining through. You may be weak in your arithmetic teaching, be a poor writer, and be a worse musician; but, if you can give your children a feeling for words, you have changed their lives and given them genii which will serve them all their days and lead them into new and strange experiences."[11]

Writing: Function and Purpose

Writing is a process which follows the patterns of spoken language, the conventions of spelling, punctuation and capitalization and utilizes forms which are familiar to the reader. The product yielded by the writing process more or less adequately fulfills the function or purpose for which it was created. The degree to which the product is adequate is determined by the clarity of the purpose for which it was created and by the skills possessed by the writer. Both skills and purpose are important to the adequacy of the final product. There must be a purpose for the writer's writing and there must be sufficient skill to achieve the purpose. It is the intent in this section to discuss the possible functions and purposes for the child's writing.

---

10. Ruth G. Strickland, *The Language Arts in the Elementary School* (Boston: D.C. Heath and Company, 1957), pp. 237-38.

11. Mauree Applegate, *Helping Children Write* (Evanston: Row, Peterson and Company, 1954), p. 132.

Teachers' and Children's Goals for Writing

In the teacher- and textbook-centered classroom the child's needs for writing are given little attention. The emphasis is placed upon the child's learning the skills necessary to writing with little attention to providing meaningful opportunities for him to exercise and develop his skills in writing through purposeful writing experiences. The child's purpose in this classroom situation is satisfying the teacher. The teacher sets the tasks and the child is rewarded for following the teacher's directions. In this situation, the child's motivation for writing is extrinsic, that is, the purposes for writing originate with the teacher, not with himself. Intrinsic motivation is more effective in teaching children to write. With intrinsic motivation the teacher is still the director of learning; the classroom environment is structured by him so that many meaningful opportunities for writing are provided for children. Children see writing as fulfilling their personal needs rather than following the teacher's directions. The wise teacher realizes that self-motivated activities in writing are also effective in teaching the skills of writing. When children write real letters that will be mailed to real people, the need to spell correctly, to write neatly and to punctuate correctly is clear. The letter the child has written has purpose and function: the purpose is to communicate ideas to the person to whom he is writing; the letter form serves this function.

Providing Purposes for Writing

As the child gains increasing independence in his written communication, the number of situations in which he can find purposes for writing rapidly increases. While the following list from the Florida curriculum is perhaps most appropriate for the intermediate and upper elementary grades, many of the situations can be adapted to the skills of children in the lower grades.

1. Situations requiring letters
   a. Social notes of thanks, sympathy, invitation, etc.
   b. Business letters, orders for materials, preparations for a trip, or requests for information
   c. Friendly letters to pen pals or foreign friends
   d. Gift tags and greeting cards
2. Situations needing a record
   a. Plans made
   b. Class activities, events, sports, excursions, or science discoveries

   c. Minutes for clubs

   d. Room histories, diaries, or logs

3. Situations requiring filling out forms

   a. Registration slips, examination blanks, applications for admission to Red Cross swimming classes, checks, and receipts

   b. Telegrams or cablegrams

4. Situations requiring

   a. Reports by individuals or groups

   b. Panel discussions

   c. Directions and recipes

   d. Lists of materials—properties needed for a play or similar activity

   e. Dictation or copying of information or directions

   f. Bibliographies

5. Situations needing publicity

   a. Advertisements, notices, or announcements

   b. Articles for school or local newspaper

   c. Headlines for newspaper articles

   d. Legends for bulletin boards and exhibits

   e. Room duties to be posted

6. Situations stimulating

   a. Original arithmetic problems

   b. Riddles, puzzles, jokes

   c. Word pictures of people and places

   d. Editorials, news stories

   e. Stunts, skits, plays

   f. Song dramatizations, original choral readings

   g. Poems, stories, myths, fables[1][2]

The Importance of Intrinsic Motivation

Before a child begins to write, he must see the writing as being important to him; he must be motivated to write. The chief task of the teacher is to provide the motivation for the child's writing. This is true for the writing which has been called utilitarian or practical writing—the writing of reports, letters and memoranda—as for personal or imaginative writing of diaries, poetry, or creative prose. The division of writing into the categories of utilitarian and imaginative is arbitrary. It is hoped that all writing children do will be personal and imaginative. While a business letter is primarily utilitarian, most people have received a letter

---

12. Florida Department of Education, *Experiencing the Language Arts, Bulletin No. 34* (Tallahassee: State Department of Education, 1948), p. 137.

written for the purpose of soliciting a subscription to a magazine or even for collecting an overdue bill which, while patently utilitarian, is engaging and "creative" in its appeal. The apparent conflict between imaginative (creative) writing and practical (utilitarian) writing is well resolved by Tidyman and Butterfield:

> Some authorities and teachers regard creative work as the basis of the language program; others regard it as a valuable supplement—another kind of activity. If by creative work is meant expressing one's own thought and feeling, then certainly all work should be creative. If, on the other hand, creative work refers to a kind of expression that is highly imaginative, emphasizing feeling, and emotions, employing many figures of speech and striving for especially vivid words and phrases, then creative work seems to take its place as a distinct activity. Creative work in the latter sense provides an emotional outlet, stimulates the imagination, broadens the vocabulary, and, through efforts at production, lays a basis for the enjoyment of imaginative literature. It has value for children, but a particular value for the child with a gift for literary expression. [13]

Consistent Encouragement of Creative Expression

The position taken in this chapter is that all children's written work should be creative within the limitations imposed by the purpose and the form of the writing. This emphasis upon creative expression is valuable for all children and is particularly valuable for the few children who have literary talent. This position does recognize, however, that some kinds of writing better lend themselves to creative expression. The following examination of the functions and purposes of children's writing therefore has been divided into two sections: (1) utilitarian writing which discusses the primarily formal (utilizing a particular form) such as the business letter and other primarily nonimaginative forms and (2) the creative, which discusses the writing of personal, imaginative, self-expressive literary forms, such as poetry.

Utilitarian Writing

The term utilitarian writing in no sense suggests that creative or imaginative writing is not purposeful or useful. Utilitarian writing serves social ends primarily, although not exclusively: a letter to a friend, a business letter, a report to other class members, an article for the classroom newspaper. Because utilitarian writing must clearly communicate

---

13. Willard F. Tidyman and Marguerite Butterfield, *Teaching the Language Arts*, second edition (New York: McGraw-Hill Book Co., Inc., 1959), pp. 26-27.

the ideas the writer wishes to convey, it offers the teacher opportunities to teach the importance of correct spelling, punctuation and capitalization. In the writing of letters, notes to parents, invitations and the like, the child sees the writing as being purposeful and is motivated to see that the punctuation serves to clarify meaning, the spelling is correct, the handwriting legible and the sentences are complete even if recopying is necessary to assure that his message is understood by the receiver.

Moffett suggests two basic purposes or functions for realistic writing which are appropriate to grades one through six: "writing down" which involves note-taking and transcribing and "writing up" which refers to the preparation of final copy, usually for publication, which is based upon talk or notes.

In "writing down," records are made of (1) outer sights and sounds and (2) inner thoughts and feelings. From human speech comes three kinds of "writing down": (1) sensory recording, (2) taking dictation, and (3) the keeping of calendars and writing letters.[14]

Moffett's "writing down" and "writing up" are quite similar to what is called utilitarian writing in this chapter. The descriptions of imaginative and creative writing corresponds to what Moffett calls "writing out." Both terminologies refer to the creative processing of experience which results in a personalistic form of writing.

Friendly or Social Letters

Many situations requiring the writing of friendly letters or social notes are presented in the typical classroom and many more can be created by the skillful teacher. The following are just a few of the purposeful activities:

Writing get-well notes or informative letters about classroom projects to classmates who are ill.

Invitations to parents to attend open house, plays, work exhibit, culminating activity in a unit of study, lunch, etc.

Notes requesting parent's permission to bring supplies for a science experiment or demonstration.

Notes requesting permission to bring pets to school for the annual "Pet Parade."

14. James Moffett, *A Student-Centered Language Curriculum, Grades K-13: A Handbook for Teachers* (Boston: Houghton-Mifflin Company, 1968), pp. 117-274.

Letters to relatives, friends or pen pals. Names and addresses of pen pals in other states and nations can be obtained from the following sources:

The Christian Science Monitor
Boston, Massachusetts

The Junior Red Cross
Washington, D.C.

The International Friendship League
40 Mt. Vernon Street
Boston, Massachusetts
(fifty cents an address)

Parker Pen Company
Janesville, Wisconsin

Foreign Correspondence Bureau
P.O. Box 150
Newton, Kansas

Student Letter Exchange
Waseca, Minnesota
(twenty-five cents an address)

Dyer's Pen-Pal Service Organization
R.F.D. 3
Seguin, Texas

Letters to radio, television or motion picture celebrities and professional athletes expressing appreciation and perhaps requesting photographs.

Thank-you notes for gifts received or favors done.

Writing to Santa Claus.

Letter of congratulation to a friend who has recieved some honor or won some prize.

Letters to magazines or newspapers expressing an opinion on some topic or thanking the editor for the content.

Almost all of the letters suggested may be written by children in any elementary school grade with varying amounts of help from the teacher. The situations utilized by the teacher will be determined more by the children's interest than perhaps any other factor. Since friendly letters and social notes are essentially intimate and personal communications composed in private, some artificiality is interjected when, in the early grades, friendly letters are composed by the whole class and then copied by each child. Whatever artificiality is interjected in the situation is perhaps justified by the fact that children are introduced to friendly letter writing in a whole class situation and learn from the teacher that it is a satisfying and important activity which more and more assumes its personal and intimate nature when children become increasingly independent through the development of their writing skills. Especially to be stressed by the teacher is the writing of letters and notes of thanks for gifts and services, expressing congratulations, and other social forms which some children may not learn about outside of school.

Given a situation in which the child sees the purpose for writing a friendly letter, the teacher next has to teach the form and content of the letter. The form of the friendly letter is perhaps best introduced through a large classroom chart showing each of the parts labeled: heading, greeting, message, closing, and signature. With this chart on display the teacher can then read a real letter pointing out its parts which correspond to the chart. The chart should be left on display in the classroom until all the children have mastered the form of the friendly letter.

Teaching the content of a friendly letter is more difficult than teaching the form. One way that this might be done is to use the message of the friendly letter mentioned as an example of an interesting letter. After the teacher has read the letter the children discuss the qualities that make it interesting. For contrast, a less interesting letter might be read and the two compared. The letter that the teacher chooses as a model of content for a good friendly letter should contain the following characteristics: (1) it should be informal and conversational in tone, (2) it should relate personal information about the writer and his activities in which the writer feels the reader would be interested, (3) it should help to clarify and communicate the writer's message through correct spelling, punctuation, capitalization and sentence structure, (4) it should invite the reader's response through inquiries about his activities in which the writer is interested.

After the initial teaching (and reteaching to some or all children, if necessary) of the form and content of the friendly letter, the teacher should provide many meaningful situations such as those suggested in which the children may develop their skills in writing many different kinds of friendly letters and social notes.

Business Letters

Teaching children to write business letters has a built-in bonus for the teacher: after they have learned the correct form and appropriate content, the children may write for some of the many free instructional materials available. Writing these letters is purposeful and interesting to the children and the free materials they receive provide the stimulus for further utilitarian writing of reports using the materials. Since writing business letters requesting free materials is one of the best ways to provide meaningful practice, a few sources of the addresses of many industries which provide this service are listed below:

Free and Inexpensive Learning Materials, published by the Division of Surveys and Field Services, George Peabody College for Teachers, Nashville, Tennessee, 37203. This paperbound book of about 275 pages is published biennially and is well-indexed by subjects and topics likely to be studied in schools.

The Superintendent of Documents in Washington, D.C., upon request, will place your name on the mailing list for free mailings of the many kinds of documents published by the federal government. Some of the government publications may be obtained without cost by writing to your congressman or senators.

Other sources of free and inexpensive material are:

Weisinger, Mort. *One Thousand and One Things You Can Get Free,* (#6), 75¢, Bantam Books, 666 5th Avenue, New York, New York, 10015.

O'Hara, F.J. *Over Two Thousand Publications Yours for the Asking,* 95¢, Signet Book, Q 3691, New American Library, Incorporated, 1301 Avenue of the Americas, New York, New York, 10019.

Having first introduced the form and content for the friendly letter, a discussion of the similarities and differences between the friendly letter and the business letter may be led by the teacher. The inside address, the more formal greeting, the terse businesslike tone of the message and the formal closing will probably be the characteristics of the business letter which the children will notice as being different from the friendly letter.

It would be desirable to display a chart in the classroom showing the form of the business letter until it has been thoroughly learned by all children.

In addition to writing for free materials from the sources mentioned, many other situations occur or can be created by the teacher to provide meaningful opportunities for children to write business letters.

Letters written requesting visits to community resources such as the fire station, post office, airport, beaches, and state parks, television or radio stations, museums, railroad or bus stations, bakery, poultry or fish hatchery, nursery or greenhouse, soft drink bottling plant, dairy, municipal water treatment plant, municipal, state and federal government agencies.

Letters to members of the community who have extensive knowledge of some subject requesting that they speak to the class or give a demonstration.

The key ideas to be remembered in teaching children to write both business and friendly letters are that the purpose for writing should come from a situation which is meaningful and important to the child and that the letters should be prepared according to standards which insure that the letter's message is understood by the recipient. Implicit is the assumption that the letter will actually be mailed. Attention to these details in teaching will help toward the child's acquisition of the important skills and rewards of letter writing.

Creative or Imaginative Writing

The writer's purpose in creative writing is different from that in utilitarian or practical writing. While it is true, particularly in the friendly letter, that utilitarian writing may have some personal creative elements, the purpose for the writing is to communicate a message with little attention to its personal or literary qualities. Utilitarian writing is centered upon the task to be accomplished; creative writing, on the other hand, focuses more upon the individual's unique perception of the world in which he lives and the expression of this perception through the sensitive, original uses of written language. Creative writing seeks more to express the writer's affective or emotional reactions to his experience while utilitarian writing centers more upon the cognitive or intellectual aspects of experience. It should be noted, however, that no consensus exists among the authorities on what constitutes creative writing.

Techniques for Motivating Creative Prose Writing

Assuming that the teacher has created the free, open and supportive classroom atmosphere in which a child's creativity can develop and flourish, techniques for releasing the child's unique personal and original responses through writing must be provided. The techniques in the following list have been used by teachers at all levels in the elementary school. Because of the variation found among children in a typical elementary school grade, the techniques are not arranged according to grade. The teacher is encouraged to experiment with the techniques according to the level of skill and interest of the children in his class. He may wish to modify the techniques to fit the unique characteristics of his class.

1. Make one envelope for each of the five parts of the story:
   a. Main character
   b. Character trait
   c. Scene or setting
   d. The problem
   e. What happens

   Have the pupils suggest what will be written on the slips to go into each envelope. The slips in the first enevelope will have on them suggestions for the main character in the story the children will write. The slips in the second envelope will have suggestions for the character trait of the main character. For example, the child may draw from the first envelope a slip with "a child of ten" printed on it; this would be the main character for his story. A slip would be drawn from each envelope to get the component parts of his story.

2. The teacher reads the beginning of a story and the children write the ending to the story.

3. Make a "Poetry or Story Box" from a cardboard box and paint it with tempera. Whenever a story or poem is written by a child during his free time, he drops it into the box.

4. Have a "Quiet Hour" every week when everyone, including the teacher, does some sort of creative activity—writes, paints, draws, sews, models.

5. A series of short motion picture films called the "Finish the Story Series" are available for use in teaching creative writing. These films are available for purchase from:

   Eastin Pictures Company
   707 Putnam Building
   Davenport, Iowa

   Show the film *The Hunter and the Forest—A Story Without Words* as motivation for writing. This film has the sounds of nature, but includes no speech.

6. The teacher may write on the blackboard several descriptive phrases which concern some experience the children have had. For instance, six or eight phrases such as "rugged lineman," "jump pass" may be written on the board. The children are then asked what subject that reminds them of, and are asked to write a story using those phrases on the board.

7. The whole class makes a beginning for a story and each member of the class writes his or her own ending.

8. Ask the children to write about trips and reactions to trips they have taken. The teacher should ask some motivating questions before the children begin.

9. Listen to classical music and have the children write their reactions to the music.

10. Have the children list topics that have inspired them to write poetry such as:

   a. The First Snow
   b. Some Signs of Spring
   c. Some Smells I Like

11. Show the children a picture, preferably in color, and ask them to close their eyes, imagine they are in the picture, and write the things which they smell, see, and feel while they are in the picture.

12. Have the children write their reactions to a situation which the teacher suggests. For example, have them complete the following sentences with their own reactions:

   a. Once I was very frightened when. . .
   b. The most beautiful sight I have seen was. . .
   c. If I had $10,000, I would. . .

13. If the teacher is alert, she can overhear children talking about the things in which they are interested. Then, during the creative writing period, the teacher may suggest topics of interest upon which certain children may write.

14. Suggest that the children write about the things which are on their minds before they go to sleep.

15. Ask the children to write their associations with certain emotionally-colored words such as "cozy." This exercise helps them to recall sense experiences which will help them in other creative writing.

16. As an exercise in recalling sense experiences, suggest that the children make a list of all the things they would see, hear, smell and feel at:

   a. The circus
   b. A baseball game
   c. A hike in the woods
   d. The beach

17. As a first experience in story writing, the teacher writes the beginning sentence of a story on the chalkboard. The class chooses

among the sentences suggested by class members and a story is completed. The children might copy the story as a writing exercise.

18. Show the children a picture such as a boat sinking with the survivors in a life raft. After a brief discussion, have the children write a short story telling where the ship was going, how it was sunk, and what happens to the survivors.

19. Read the children a setting to a certain story. Ask them to write a story that might have taken place in that setting. For example, a jungle setting would probably lead to a story about wild animals.

20. Read an adventure story to the children. After having discussed the personalities of the characters, have them pick their favorite character and write a story of an adventure which this character, because of his personality, would probably have.

21. The teacher writes five or six words on the chalkboard. These words would be used to build the plot of the story. For example, log cabin, girl, old man, dog, baby. These words are to be used by the children as the framework for the story with them building the plot.

22. Write six or eight descriptive phrases on the chalkboard. After discussing the associations the children have with these phrases, ask them to write a story using as many of the related, descriptive phrases as they can.

23. Show the class one or more large colored pictures depicting some action. After discussion of the pictures and noting of details, the children are asked to write a paragraph describing what happened either fifteen minutes earlier or fifteen minutes later.

24. The teacher may make a statement of an imaginary situation such as, "What if, when you woke up in the morning, you looked into the mirror and saw it wasn't you?" The children are instructed to write an explanation of the situation.

25. After the completion of a basal reader unit on legends, folklore or tall-tales, these stories are reviewed and the children are told that they may make up a story of their own.

26. The experiences from which children write creatively come through their senses—sight, touch, taste, hearing. To develop a child's sensitivity to sensory experiences the following techniques can be used:
    a. Have the children close their eyes. The teacher passes some object around the room. The children are asked to write *how* it feels rather than *what* it feels like.

    b. Have the children sit with their eyes closed for one minute with the instructions that after that period of time they will write everything they felt, heard and smelled.

27. The teacher tells the story of the god, Neptune. The children write stories about the effect that this god might have on the sea.

28. After reading stories about Paul Bunyan, the children may write stories of other adventures that he might have had.

29. The children and/or the teacher make puppets. Stories or plays about the adventures the puppets might have are written by the children.

30. Have the children write stories about what they would do if they were teacher.

31. Forms which look like Rorschach ink blots may be made by dropping tempera or colored ink into the pre-creased center fold of a sheet of glossy paper. The sheet is then refolded along the center crease making a design as the ink or paint is forced out of the crease onto the paper. Multicolored blots can be made by adding more colors after each preceding color on the sheet is dry. When the ink or paint is dry, the sheets can be pressed flat with a warm iron and mounted with rubber cement on illustration board or other heavy backing. These inkblots can be displayed on a chalkboard tray as motivation for creative writing. Each child will write a different story. (A spray coating of clear plastic from a pressurized can will help to protect the inkblots from soil.)

32. Use the shapes of objects, people or animals discovered in clouds as the subjects for stories.

33. Objects whose source and function are unknown to the children are displayed. The children write stories about the source or function of the objects or about the people who might own or use the objects.

34. Objects such as an old kerosene lantern or other things such as wearing apparel, a book, etc. are displayed. The children write stories in which they assume that they are the object, telling about things they have seen, adventures they have had or people they have known.

35. Have a sealed box or bag containing various objects which the children can shake and feel. The children then write stories about what is in the box or who might have owned the objects.

36. When children get ideas for topics to write about, they write them on cards which are deposited in a box. When children have free time and wish to write, they draw a card from the box to get a topic to write about.

37. The class is divided into groups and each group is given a sack containing various costumes, props, and equipment. The children write a play in which they create characters according to these costumes and props. These plays can then be presented to the class.

38. A picture from a book or newspaper is magnified and copied using an opaque projector. The children write a story about the picture.

39. Use a sequence of three or four pictures as a stimulus for writing a story. To create new pictures, a picture from another unrelated sequence can be substituted for one or more of the pictures.

40. After playing music from *Carnival of the Animals* children can write descriptions of real or imaginary animals suggested to them by the music.

41. Have the children each take two animals and combine their characteristics to make an imaginary animal. Write about the characteristics of the new animal.

42. Have the children write stories about what would have happened to Jack, in Jack and the Beanstalk if he hadn't had an ax when the giant was climbing down the beanstalk. Storie_ can be written about situations in other well-known stories such as Red Riding Hood.

43. After studying units in reading such as fairy tales or adventures the children write stories of the same type.

44. Have children write stories about the adventures of such well-known characters as Tom Sawyer as if they were alive today.

45. Have the children listen to unknown sound recorded on tape. They then write a story or poem about what the sound made them think of.

46. Display a picture about Halloween (or some other holiday), together with some words the children might use in a story about the picture.

47. Mount pictures with rubber cement inside manila folders. On the inside of the folders facing the picture, print, with a felt-tip pen, words which can be used in a story about the picture. These folders can be located in the classroom so that children have access to them for an independent activity. For the older children the pictures should be increasingly ambiguous, that is, they should be differently interpreted by different children.

48. The child is told to imagine that he is a person three inches tall. He is to write about what would happen if a physical law, such as gravity, were suddenly no longer in effect.

49. The child writes about what he would do if he found himself locked in the house alone, without television.

50. Have each child write down ideas for activities to do by himself; with two other people; with four other people.

51. The children are asked to describe something they would like to invent.

52. Each child is asked to select some invention and write a humorous or fanciful story about the conditions which led to its invention.

53. The teacher may suggest that the child write an imaginary conversation between the sun and the moon. To give the children some ideas for this, certain facts about the two bodies such as relative size, distance between and the presence of man-made satellites may be mentioned.

54. Play a record to create a mood and background for story writing. Suggested records: The Moldau by Smetana, "On the Trail" from the Grand Canyon Suite by Grofe, Stravinski's Firebird Suite, A Night on Bald Mountain by Mussorgsky.

55. After reading the story of "Pegasus, the Wingéd Horse," ask the children: "What would you do and where would you go if you could have Pegasus for a day?"

The following techniques are suggested by Baker and Rose:

1. Imagine that you are a star creature and make a visit to this world we know. Tell of your surprises.

2. Imagine that you have a space ship that can take you to another planet. Tell of your experiences.

3. Imagine that you have an animal that can talk. Tell of your experiences with this animal.

4. Imagine you have a pair of seven-league boots. Describe a day's adventure in time and space.

5. Imagine that you can put on a special pair of glasses and see a thousand years into the future. Describe a scene that you might witness.

6. Imagine that you are an inch high or three times your size. How would the dimensions of your present world seem to you?

7. Imagine that you can make yourself invisible by using magic fluid or by putting on a special garment. Describe your adventures.[15]

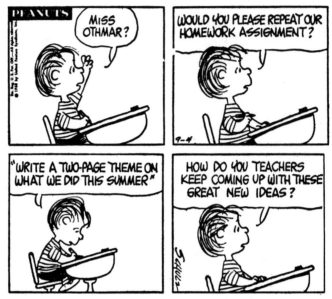

Children's Poetry Writing

The same classroom atmosphere which the teacher develops to encourage creative response in prose writing will encourage poetry writing. Writing poetry necessitates the use of a different form which better fits the ideas to be expressed and the particular language in which the ideas are to be expressed. Children can be introduced to the form and content of poetry through the teacher's reading poetry to them. The poetry selected should be drawn from experiences which are meaningful to the children. Through the teacher's reading, children gain an appreciation for poetry and upon this appreciation the teacher builds. Poems that children like can be discussed and the poetic uses of imagery discovered. As children's language develops, they will become increasingly able to express their ideas in imaginative, original and cre-

---

15. G. Derwood Baker and Elizabeth Rose, "Creative Writing in the Junior High School," *Educational Leadership* (May, 1957), pp. 478-482.

ative words. The developmental sequence in learning to write poetry is similar among all children, but the learning does not take place automatically; the teacher must guide each child's growth.

Guides to Performance Expectancies

While space does not permit a detailed discussion of teaching poetry writing, a helpful guide to subject matter and style expectancy is given by Walter:

1. First and second grades (ages 6 to 8)
   a. Subject matter: immediate experiences
   b. Style
      (1) Largely narrative
      (2) Little or no rhyme
2. Third and fourth grades (ages 8 to 10)
   a. Subject matter
      (1) Immediate experiences
      (2) Remembered experiences
   b. Style
      (1) Narrative enhanced by picture words
      (2) Simple analogies
      (3) Little rhyme
      (4) Occasional use of couplet and ballad stanza
3. Fifth and sixth grades (ages 10 to 12)
   a. Subject matter
      (1) Immediate experiences
      (2) Remembered experiences
      (3) Imagined experiences
      (4) Ideas about the natural world
   b. Style
      (1) Falling off of narrative
      (2) Expansion of picture-making quality
      (3) Conscious use of analogy and imagery
      (4) Use of simple verse forms and some rhyme
      (5) Originality of thought and phrasing
      (6) Sincerity of feeling but not depth of feeling
4. Junior high school (grades 7, 8, and 9; ages 12 to 16)
   a. Subject matter (change of approach)
      (1) Immediate, remembered, and imagined experiences

        (2) Emotional experiences; deepening of feeling

        (3) Ideas about the natural world

        (4) Ideas about the relationship of people

        (5) Ideas about self

        (6) Beginning of the subjective approach to experience

   b. Style

        (1) A groping for form and pattern, even in free verse

        (2) First use of the vocabulary of emotion

        (3) Occasional appearance of the longer poem

        (4) The attempt to make a complete statement of the idea[16]

Arnstein's book is also recommended as a guide for teaching children to write poetry.[17]

Hughes Mearns' classic book *Creative Power* is an excellent resource for the teacher of elementary school creative writing. Chapter XI "Poetry is When You Talk to Yourself," is a delightful reading experience filled with practical suggestions for teaching poetry.[18]

Carlson's recent article gives an interesting history of the publication of children's poems and suggests some techniques for teaching children to write poetry. An excellent up-to-date bibliography follows her article.[19]

Evaluating Children's Writing

Evaluating children's writing ought to include attention to all those educational values which are pursued in teaching them to write. Among these would certainly be included accuracy in spelling, punctuation, and capitalization and the use of correct forms in writing such as those for the friendly letter and the business letter. Outcomes such as these are relatively easy to assess; these are objectives which deal with correctness and the mechanical aspects of writing. Since these objectives are relatively easy to assess, the teacher is likely to give first attention to them.

---

16. Nina Willis Walter, *Let Them Write Poetry* (New York: Holt, Rinehart and Winston, 1962), pp. 83-84.

17. Flora J. Arnstein, *Poetry in the Elementary Classroom* (New York: Appleton-Century-Crofts, 1962).

18. Hughes Mearns, *Creative Power: The Education of Youth in the Creative Arts* (New York: Dover Publications, Inc., 1958), pp. 106-115.

19. Ruth Kearney Carlson, "The Sunset Is a Pretty Pink Dove—Children's Voices in Poetry," *Elementary English* XLVI (October, 1969): 748-757.

One facet of the teacher's role is usually thought of as that of "grader-of-papers." This role persists even in the face of the evidence that children learn the mechanics of writing more readily when they are made responsible for their own proofreading and corrections. In utilitarian writing in particular children should, from the very beginning, be taught to make first drafts, proofread and rewrite in order that the reader is able to understand the ideas the writer is attempting to communicate. Standards and form charts to which the child can refer in the classroom help to encourage independence and correctness. When the child first begins to write, the teacher will of course give more assistance and guidance, but his goal should be to encourage the child to become an increasingly independent writer. This goal is reached most rapidly when the child does not depend upon the teacher to make sure that his writing is correct. With all good intentions, a teacher may continue to grade or correct a child's papers without realizing that once the child has noted the grade he has received, no further attention is given to improving his writing. He is content to be "a C student."

The outcomes of the child's imaginative writing are less objectively assessed. The content of the writing is more personal and original. The assessment of literary merit and originality requires more subjective judgments. Because this is true, teachers are tempted to follow the pattern of correcting and grading the spelling and mechanics in imaginative writing just as they have in utilitarian writing. Often this results in discouraging the child. When his story is returned by the teacher with errors marked with red pencil he is not encouraged to expose his original ideas to further criticism in the future. He may choose the less threatening alternative of withdrawing into himself.

An alternative approach is one which emphasizes the personal, unique content of imaginative writing rather than correctness on first draft. The teacher should help the child to clarify his ideas and put them into more readable form; ideas which are imaginatively expressed should be pointed out and the child complimented for them. Correctness in writing is not unimportant, it is just less important than the ideas being expressed, and the clarity and beauty with which those ideas are expressed.

EXTENDING YOUR LEARNING

1. Read the article by Birdwhistell listed in the bibliography. Prepare a report and demonstration on *kinesics* for members of your class.

2. Examine the list on pages 153 and 154. In one column list those writing situations which require utilitarian writing; in another column list those which require imaginative writing. Place a check mark in either column beside those situations which might require both kinds of writing.
3. Find and compare some different definitions of creative writing. With which do you agree. Why?
4. Develop a list of qualities with examples which can be utilized in evaluating children's imaginative writing of prose and poetry. (See Walter, *Let Them Write Poetry*, Chapter 8.)
5. Using some of the techniques for motivating imaginative writing, collect samples of children's writing from several grades and compare them. You may wish to evaluate the samples using the list you developed in suggestion 4 above.
6. Using one of the sources of free and inexpensive materials listed on page 194 select and write on index cards several sources of materials on topics which the class you expect to be teaching will study some time during the school year. Plan to make the file box in which these cards are filed available to the children and encourage them to write business letters requesting these materials.

BIBLIOGRAPHY

Applegate, Mauree. *Helping Children Write*. Evanston: Row, Peterson and Company, 1954. 173 pp.

Arnstein, Flora J. *Poetry in the Elementary Classroom*. New York: Appleton-Century-Crofts, 1962.

Baker, G. Derwood, and Elizabeth Rose. "Creative Writing in the Junior High School," *Educational Leadership*, May, 1957, 478-482.

Birdwhistell, Ray L. "Background to Kinesics," *ETC: A Review of General Semantics*, XIII (Autumn, 1955), pp. 10-18.

Burrows, Alvina Treut, Doric C. Jackson, and Dorothy O. Saunders. *They All Want to Write—Written English in the Elementary School*. New York: Holt, Rinehart and Winston, 1964. Third Edition. 281 pp.

Carey, G.V. *Mind the Stop: A Brief Guide to Punctuation with a Note on Proof Correction*. Cambridge: University Press, 1958. 130 pp.

Carlson, Ruth Kearney. "Seventeen Qualities of Original Writing," *Elementary English*, XXXVIII, (December, 1961), 576-579.

——. "Recent Research in Originality," *Elementary English*, XXXX, (October, 1963), 30-31.

——. "The Sunset is a Pretty Pink Dove—Children's Voices in Poetry," *Elementary English*, XLVI, (October, 1969), 748-757.

Florida Department of Education. *Experiencing the Language Arts, Bulletin No. 34*. Tallahassee: State Department of Education, 1948.

Furness, Edna Lue. "Pupils, Pedagogues, and Punctuation," *Elementary English*, March, 1960, 187-189.

Greene, Harry A., and Walter T. Petty. *Developing Language Skills in the Elementary Schools*. Boston: Allyn and Bacon, Inc., 1963. 572 pp.

Laird, Charlton. *The Miracle of Language*. Greenwich: Fawcett Publications, Inc., 1957. 255 pp.

Mearns, Hughes. *Creative Power: The Education of Youth in the Creative Arts*. New York: Dover Publications, Inc., 1958. 272 pp.

Moffett, James. *A Student-Centered Language Curriculum, Grades K-13: A Handbook for Teachers*. Boston: Houghton-Mifflin Company, 1968. 503 pp.

Sapir, Edward. *Language: An Introduction to the Study of Speech.* New York: Harcourt, Brace and World, 1921.

Smith, Mary Katherine. "Measurement of the Size of General English Vocabulary through the Elementary Grades and High School," *Genetic Psychology Monographs,* 24:311-45, November, 1941.

Strickland, Ruth G. *The Language Arts in the Elementary School.* Boston: D.C. Heath and Company, 1957. 464 pp.

Tidyman, Willard F., and Marguerite Butterfield. *Teaching the Language Arts.* Second Edition. New York: McGraw-Hill Book Co., Inc., 1959. 403 pp.

Trauger, Wilmer K. *Language Arts in Elementary Schools.* New York: McGraw-Hill Book Company, 1963. 393 pp.

Walter, Nina Willis. *Let Them Write Poetry.* New York: Holt, Rinehart and Winston, 1962. 179 pp.

Focus

Writing an introduction to a chapter one has written is an interesting and challenging writing assignment!

Handwriting is understressed, under-valued and poorly taught. There's general agreement, among teachers and laymen as well, that achievement in this facet of the Language Arts is not adequate. The claim, supported by some research, that the quality of pupil's handwriting has not deteriorated, that it's no *worse* than it was a generation ago, seems to provide little justification for giving handwriting the limited attention it typically receives, in grades beyond the first and second, at least. The trend which supports *adding* to the elementary school curriculum (foreign language, creative dramatics,) without *subtracting* anything has made it very difficult for a teacher to find time to give children directed and specific help in handwriting. The problem is compounded if the teacher's handwriting isn't very good, if the help he received in his teacher education program was inadequate, and if he finds almost everything else he teaches more interesting and rewarding than handwriting.

The writer feels compelled to follow the pattern set by every other author, and insists that handwriting *is* important. The pencil and pen are not going to be replaced by the typewriter in the near future, at least. Problems due to miscalculations in decoding another's illegible scrawl are too numerous to need recounting here. The situation is too serious to be joked about, but that is the typical response.

What can be done? Can handwriting, both manuscript and cursive, be taught more efficiently? Is there some way of doing more, accomplishing more, in less time? Should typing be taught, as legibility insurance, in the elementary school? Individualized instruction takes time, much time, but is there another way of working with the left-handed child or the child with motor-perceptual handicaps?

In this chapter, the writer has raised these issues, and others—the trite and much debated issue of when should cursive writing be introduced is treated—and hopefully, the reader will acquire the understanding necessary for taking a position. The real objective is broader than this, however. If attitude change *can* result from reading, it is hoped that the reader will decide that helping children learn to write legibly and easily is not dull, uninteresting, or unworthy of a professional time and effort.

chapter seven

Pose Lamb

teaching and improving handwriting in elementary school

Despite the evidence regarding the serious commercial, industrial, professional and personal penalties exacted for illegible handwriting (letters that are never delivered, doubts concerning the identity of the donor of a gift because his card can't be read, etc., etc.,)[1] there appears to be little evidence of increased concern among teachers for improving handwriting instruction, either at preservice or in service levels. The writer has recently surveyed a number of the most widely used "methods texts" assigned to prospective teachers for use in preparing to teach the language arts. In one such text, two paragraphs were devoted to a discussion of handwriting. In another, three pages. In a third, the term wasn't even mentioned. After reviewing the research evidence and literature related to what he calls "The Present State of Handwriting," Lowell Horton writes, "Many writers have expressed concern over a deterioration of handwriting quality, and emphasis in present schools. Popular publications have emphasized the decline in handwriting legibility by relating some humorous and some tragic results of mistaken letter formations. Although it seems to be generally believed that handwriting instruction does not receive the attention it deserves, in view of the essential role it plays in contemporary society there are some studies available which suggest that children of today write at least as

---

1. Robert O Brien, "The Moving Finger Writes—But Who Can Read It?" *The Saturday Review* (July 18, 1959), p. 8.

well as children of earlier generations. There is some evidence of renewed interest in research in handwriting instruction."[2]

It seems reasonably clear that neither elementary school pupils nor their teachers are devoting the time or the energy to handwriting which was customary a generation or two ago. If, as Horton suggests, the quality of handwriting has not declined, one could assume that no one has really suffered because of the current deemphasis in elementary school curricula (if not in research). One could also assume, however, that with somewhat more attention, the development of programs illustrative of the findings of research in perceptual motor learning, and with more teachers who exhibit interest and competence in this area the quality of handwriting could be much better than it is. It's difficult to understand why we should take pride in the fact that we seem to be doing no worse than we used to!

Handwriting is important. There may be a time when the almost exclusive use of typewriters, dictaphones, tape recorders and the telephone will eliminate the need for applying pencil or pen to paper. That time has not yet arrived. Handwriting is an essential tool of communication, a means by which we record our feelings and ideas for others (or for our own future reference). If these ideas and expressed feelings are to communicate effectively, to produce the desired reaction or result, then they must be written legibly!

If legible handwriting is also pleasing to the eyes, this is an added bonus, as is the ability to write rapidly. If one has a great deal to say, there is an obvious advantage to being able to write quickly as well as legibly. Of the most commonly expressed goals or objectives of handwriting programs—legibility, ease, neatness, and speed—legibility must be termed the most important. Our goal as elementary teachers is to help children acquire a handwriting style which can be read easily without strain, so that the ideas expressed are quite clear to the reader. What is of most importance are the ideas expressed, not the handwriting style or speed with which these words are put on paper.

Children must nonetheless be helped, first to learn to write legibly, clearly and neatly, and to work consistently toward better handwriting throughout the elementary school period and beyond. It is an expected courtesy to those with whom one is communicating through writing to eliminate unnecessary flourishes and affectations, to make one letter

2. Lowell Horton, "The Second R: A Working Bibliography," *Elementary English* 46 (April, 1969): 426-430.

clearly distinguishable from the next, and to present what is written in a neat and easily interpreted form. To accept a sixth grader's poor handwriting as inevitable, to admit that one's own handwriting is a poor example for pupils to follow, seems to be an evasion of responsibility for teaching such an important tool of communication.

One purpose of this chapter is to help clarify the position of hand-writing instruction in the elementary school curriculum and to help provide some perspective from which to view handwriting so that its importance is neither underemphasized nor overemphasized. To claim, as some do, that teaching handwriting is unnecessary, that communication will soon be primarily through telephone, telegraph, tape recorder and the typewriter is somewhat analogous to claiming that teaching the basic addition facts is out of date, since pupils will refer to pocket computers for such mundane data in the future. While the telephone and the other means of communication referred to have obviated the need for some laborious writing, there clearly is still a need for teaching and reteaching the skill of communicating through the handwritten word.

How Is Handwriting Taught?

What is a typical handwriting program in today's elementary schools? How is the sometimes neglected, much-maligned second R taught—if at all? Two studies, with somewhat contradictory findings, will provide some data regarding the present status of handwriting instruction. Petty reports that 30 per cent of all school systems have no handwriting programs at all and 50 per cent of the school systems surveyed do not provide a separate handwriting period.[3] Findings reported in *New Horizons for Research in Handwriting*[4] are somewhat more reassuring. Herrick reports that 98 per cent of the teachers involved in a national survey and 95 per cent of those in the Wisconsin Survey he directed indicated that they did teach handwriting.

Herrick's findings further suggest that class periods for teaching handwriting are usually fifteen to twenty minutes in length regardless of grade level, but for the first four grades teachers usually planned five

3. Walter Petty, "Handwriting and Spelling: Their Current Status," *Elementary English* 41 (December, 1964): 839-844.
4. *New Horizons for Research in Handwriting*, edited by Virgil Herrick (Madison, Wisconsin: The University of Wisconsin Press, 1963).

periods a week; for grades five through eight, the number of periods per week was reduced to three. In direct contradiction to Petty's statement, Herrick reports:

> Schools favor a separate handwriting class period plus teaching handwriting in some meaningful context in all subject areas. Fifteen per cent of the responses indicated handwriting and spelling were taught together regularly.[5]

What factors are emphasized in the handwriting periods? Herrick's findings suggest that in the primary grades, correctness of letter formation, neatness of writing, size and uniformity of letters and spacing of letters and words receive major emphasis. In the fifth and sixth grades, speed receives more emphasis, and so does the alignment of words and sentences.[6]

Respondents representing 14 per cent of the schools participating in Herrick's survey reported that only cursive writing was taught; in 7 per cent of the schools, only manuscript writing was taught. Respondents in this national survey indicated that in 79 per cent of the schools, both manuscript and cursive writing were taught, with the transition from manuscript to cursive occurring in the second half of Grade Two or the first half of Grade Three.[7]

Grade Level Goals

The surveys reported in the preceding section provide a very brief overview of the content of typical handwriting programs, but it may be helpful to have more specific grade level goals or objectives detailed. The following are composite goals or objectives, and represent summaries of material included in several curriculum guides:

Kindergarten and First Grade

1. Children should exhibit familiarity (both through discussion and frequency of use) with writing as a form of communication. This suggests that the teacher will utilize labels, charts, and stories dictated by children to accompany pictures.

2. Children probably will learn to write their names and usually will master the basic shapes used in manuscript writing. Many will be able to

---

5. Herrick, *op. cit.,* p. 20.
6. Herrick, *op. cit.,* p. 21.
7. *Ibid.,* pp. 19-20.

write short notes, stories, invitations, holiday greetings, etc., and most will be able to copy these from the chalkboard.

3. By the last months of first grade most children have mastered the manuscript alphabet, upper and lower case letters. A few will not reach this stage until second grade.

4. Most pupils can correctly write the ten basic numerals.

Second and Third Grades

1. A majority of children have achieved mastery of the manuscript alphabet to the extent that they can write original stories, reports, etc. By the end of the second grade handwriting has become a truly functional tool for most children.

2. Children are becoming more skillful in spacing words and letters, and alignment of words and letters on a paper does not present the difficulties it once did. As a result papers are neater, more legible, and more attractive.

3. If the transition from manuscript to cursive writing is made in second or third grade, and it usually is, it is made gradually. While certain elements of joining letters, introduction of slant, etc., may be "taught" to an entire class for the purpose of saving time, it is not expected that children will make the transition with uniformity or with equal ease and ability.

4. Although children are making the transition from manuscript to cursive writing, skill in manuscript writing is maintained. Many children will continue to use the latter for independent writing activities because it is faster and easier for them.

5. Children are becoming increasingly aware of the significance of such details as punctuation, margins, paragraphs, etc.

6. Ball-point pens are introduced as writing instruments, this "introduction" frequently occurs in third grade.

Fourth, Fifth and Sixth Grades

1. Children are achieving mastery of cursive writing and developing individual writing styles.

2. Manuscript writing is still maintained for labeling, map work, charts, etc. Children are encouraged to retain this skill throughout the elementary school period.

3. Children are acquiring the objectivity necessary for self-evaluation of handwriting. Teachers have encouraged this in the primary grades, of

course, but more emphasis is placed upon self-help and individual responsibility for handwriting improvement in the intermediate and upper grades. Proofreading receives a great deal of emphasis.

4. A degree of mastery is achieved in fields related to handwriting such as punctuation, paragraphing, identification and placement of topic sentences, etc.

5. Pens (ball-points) are used with as much ease and fluency as pencils. Fountain pens may also be used.

Commercial Systems

Although there is little evidence that such an adjustment is made in the handwriting programs included in the surveys reported thus far, it appears that there is a genuine need to make more provisions for individual differences in handwriting programs.[8] The left-handed child, the poorly-coordinated child, the child with vision problems, generally receive less help than they deserve in learning to write legibly and easily. Undoubtedly some of the reasons for this inattention to individual differences relate to professional disinterest in teaching handwriting. Lack of interest reflects in teaching just as it does in learning. It is submitted that another reason is the general and almost complete reliance upon commercial handwriting systems which may tend to support, tacitly at least, a "lock-step" approach to handwriting instruction.

Herrick writes:

> The greatest single factor in determining the nature of the instructional program in a given school is the commercial system of handwriting instruction being used. This is perhaps more true for handwriting than any other area of the elementary school curriculum.[9]

Petty makes a similar statement, then adds:

> As many as sixteen commercial programs are in use, with another ten commercial systems being used which emphasize other facets of the language arts. These latter then, therefore, are classified as only partial handwriting programs. The various handwriting programs show considerable divergence in letter forms sequence in the introduction of letters and recommended teaching practices.[10]

Three of these systems will be discussed, primarily to illustrate the variation and the careful attention to articulation and sequential development built into these programs.

---

8. *Ibid.,* p. 20.
9. *Ibid.,* p. 27.
10. Petty, *op. cit.,* p. 841.

Handwriting With Write and See, produced under the direction of B.F. Skinner, with the assistance of Sue Ann Krakower. Chicago: Lyons and Carnahan, Inc., 1968.

This is a "programmed" series in which the pupil works with a special pen and writes on specially treated paper. His correct responses (properly formed letters) are immediately reinforced by the appearance of a grey rather than a yellow line. The following comment is included in the guide: *"Handwriting with Write and See* permits the individual child to work largely by himself, but important functions remain for the teacher. The books cannot teach correct posture, the proper use of a writing instrument, the normal order of working from upper left to lower right, or the order and direction in which the component strokes of a letter are constructed."[11] Materials are provided for making the transition in either Grade 2 or Grade 3. Capital letters are taught first, and letters are grouped and sequenced according to difficulty.

Writing space is reduced to one half each (manuscript) in Book 2. Lower case cursive letters are taught first, with strong emphasis on the connective strokes. Evaluation of slant, space, and size is emphasized in Book 3. In Book 4, uniformity of style and legibility are stressed. Evaluation and refinement of cursive writing, analysis of mistakes and some advanced perceptual work are emphasized in Books 5 and 6. Manuscript writing is reviewed.

You Can Write by Aubrey E. Haan and Bernadine C. Wierson. Boston: Allyn and Bacon, 1965.

The authors recommend instructional periods of about twenty minutes a day, five days a week in handwriting. Materials for making the transition from manuscript to cursive writing in Grade 2 or Grade 3 are provided, but the authors write: "The child is usually ready to make this change sometime in the third grade."[12] They further note that some children may wait until Grade 5 to change, and some children may never change! Letters are introduced in the order of their difficulty, the *i* and *e* first, then a group of "bubble" letters (o, a, and c). In making the transition from manuscript to cursive writing, children are introduced to the slant strokes first, then to connecting strokes. However, "joining" is taught very soon, for purposes of making handwriting functional.

---

11. Teachers edition, *Handwriting With Write and See,* p. 2.
12. Teachers edition, *You Can Write,* p. T-6.

MANUSCRIPT ALPHABET SHEET

Grade one

LOWER CASE LETTERS

UPPER CASE LETTERS

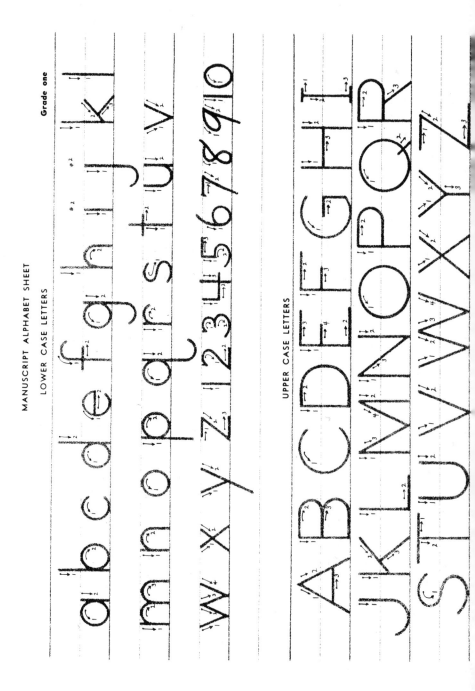

MANUSCRIPT ALPHABET SHEET

LOWER CASE LETTERS

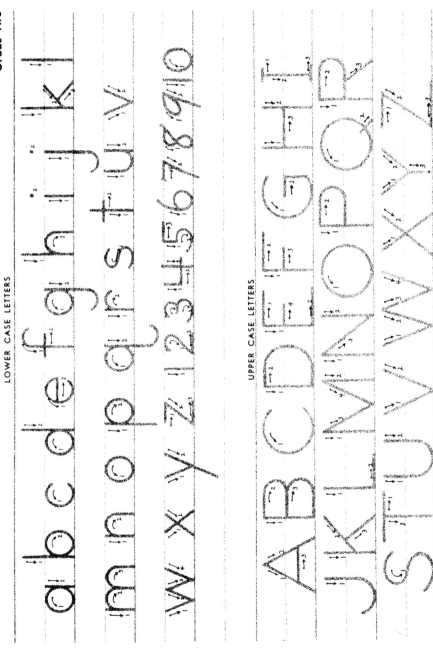

UPPER CASE LETTERS

Courtesy of Zaner-Bloser, Inc.

CURSIVE ALPHABET

Grade three

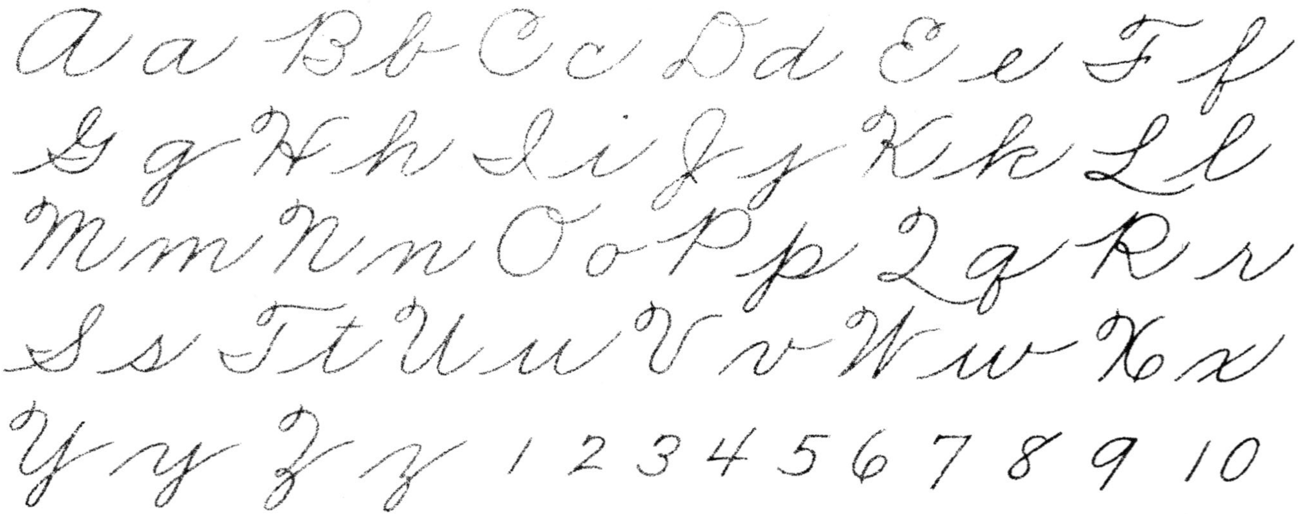

Aa Bb Cc Dd Ee Ff
Gg Hh Ii Jj Kk Ll
Mm Nn Oo Pp Qq Rr
Ss Tt Uu Vv Ww Xx
Yy Zz 1 2 3 4 5 6 7 8 9 10

MANUSCRIPT ALPHABET

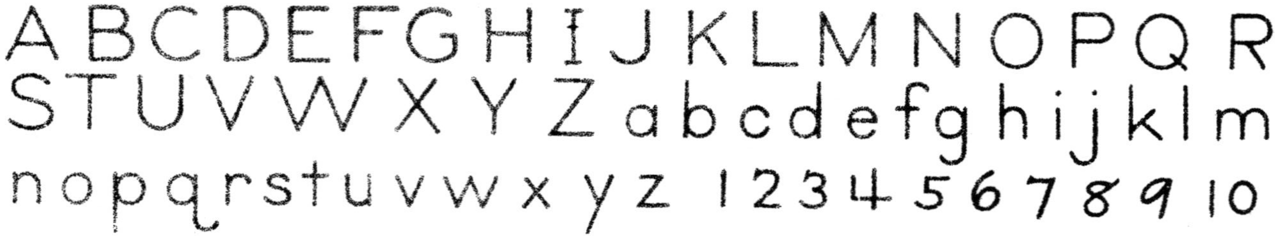

A B C D E F G H I J K L M N O P Q R
S T U V W X Y Z a b c d e f g h i j k l m
n o p q r s t u v w x y z 1 2 3 4 5 6 7 8 9 10

Courtesy of Zaner-Bloser, Inc.

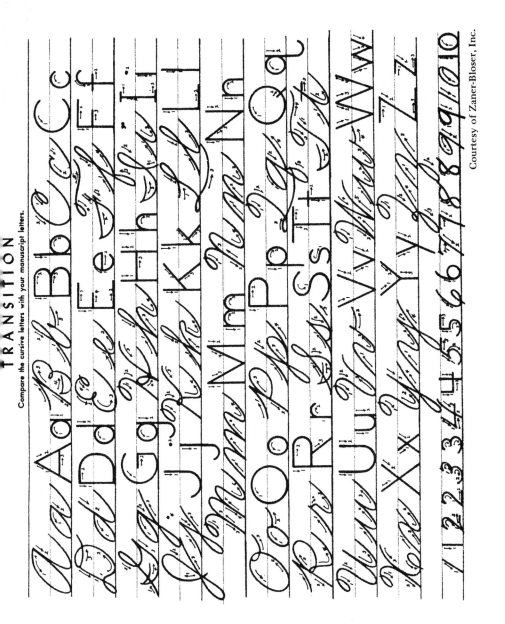

219

MANUSCRIPT ALPHABET

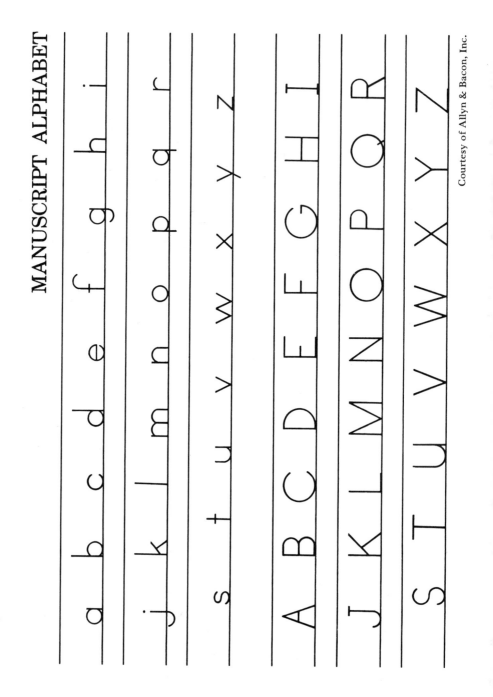

a b c d e f g h i

j k l m n o p q r

s t u v w x y z

A B C D E F G H I

J K L M N O P Q R

S T U V W X Y Z

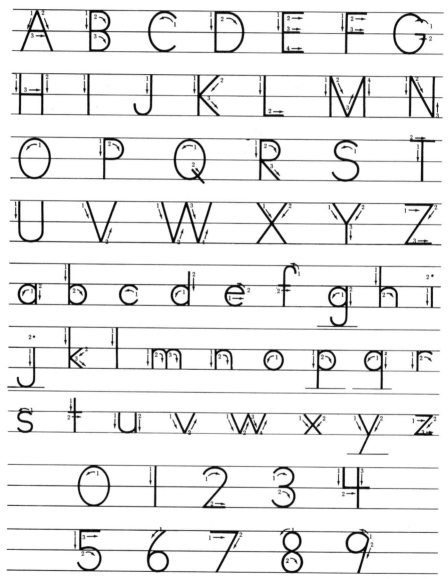

Courtesy of Lyons & Carnahan

The Cursive Alphabet

Courtesy of Lyons & Carnahan

A set of evaluation sheets accompany each work text. These are translucent sheets with correct models of letters and words written on them. Children can note their own errors by placing the evaluation sheet on top of their own writing.

Pictures of children, illustrating correct posture, pencil position, and paper angles (for left- and right-handed pupils) are included in the pupils texts.

Expressional Growth Through Handwriting by Clinton S. Hackney, Emma Harrison Myers and Parker Z. Bloser. Columbus, Ohio: Zaner Bloser Company, 1969.

The basic program consists of a series of "Handwriting Recorders": "Ready! Set! Go!" (Readiness—kindergarten) "Sound Off" (Grade 1—Manuscript) "Off We Go!" (Grade 2—Manuscript and transition editions available) "A New Universe" (Grade 3—Transition and Cursive Editions available) "Gliding Along" (Grade 4—Cursive) "Upward Thrust" (Grade 5—Cursive) Gaining Momentum (Grade 6—Cursive). There are also materials for Grades 7 and 8 (one book) and for adults who wish to improve their handwriting. Quantities of ancillary materials are available, including a new set of Evaluation Scales.

Pupils are taught that there are four basic strokes in manuscript writing: straight vertical, horizontal and slant lines and circles. Letters are presented in pairs or groups to show like and unlike parts. Slant and "joining" strokes are taught together in the transition process.

In contrasting the alphabets reproduced here, the reader will notice the differences in the lower case manuscript e's, the upper case manuscript I's, the cursive w's (upper and lower case) and the differences in the use of "loops" to begin y's and z's. It is clear that although the commercial systems have much in common with each other, they are *not* identical.

What is the value of using a commercial system, if any? There are several. One reason for adapting a commercial program is the low quality of most teachers' handwriting. Example is very important. Noble writes:

> Handwriting is an unpopular subject with teachers, probably because adult handwriting tends to be inferior to that of students in quality. Still, it is generally recognized that handwriting is primarily acquired through copying models and that the teacher's models are constantly with her students. It is the author's experience that peculiarities in the handwriting of a teacher are often found in her student's work as well.[13]

13. B. J. Kendrick Noble, "Handwriting Programs in Today's Schools," *Elementary English* 40: 511.

With a consistent, neat and legible model (from the publisher of the commercial program) available to pupils at all times, a teacher's poor example may be less damaging. The usual arguments favoring extensive reliance upon textbooks can be summoned to support the adoption and careful use of a commercial handwriting program: better and easier grade level articulation, preparation by "experts," the saving of teachers' time and energy, etc., etc.

The reader has already seen that in the case of handwriting textbooks the "experts" are in considerable disagreement and a teacher using one series rather than another might be somewhat hard-put-to identify specific advantages of the adopted series, as contrasted with those of a competitive series.

If a copybook-workbook series is selected the selection should be made by classroom teachers who will have to use the series, with the advice of and in concert with school system administrators.[14] Some publishers employ consultants who will provide in-service help for teachers in the form of workshops and lecture-demonstrations. Referring again to the significance of the teacher's example, such in-service help should be considered a valuable "plus" accompanying the newly adopted handwriting series. Teachers who use an adopted series will try, insofar as it is practical, to use the program in a manner which promotes each child's handwriting growth. This means supplementing lessons taken from the guide or manual with additional practice sessions and omitting some lessons which are unnecessary for reasonably bright, well-coordinated youngsters. It also means that the teacher and the children will be aware of the need for neat, legible handwriting *whenever* communication is the goal, not only during the handwriting period when the example of the copybook is clearly evident. Nor can the teacher excuse his own poor writing on the basis of the good example set by the handwriting series or the alphabet cards accompanying the series.

If handwriting series have caused some programs to become rigid and inflexible, it is not because of anything inherent in the series but because of the way too many teachers have used them. Wisely used, a carefully selected handwriting series can be a valuable tool, aiding the teacher in many ways.

---

14. For an example of how this process worked in one large school system see Jessie K. How, "Handwriting Is Important: Seattle Prepares a K-12 Program," *Elementary English* 41 (December, 1964): 851-853, 932.

In discussing the use of a handwriting series, the terms "cursive" and "manuscript" writing have been employed. These terms may require definition. Manuscript writing is similar to printing; cursive writing involves the connection of letters and frequently some "slant" to the writing. These two styles or methods of writing will be discussed in more detail in the following sections.

Why Manuscript Writing?

"Manuscript" writing, also called print-script and print handwriting, had its genesis in Great Britain in the early part of this century. Enstrom writes:

> Our present primary writing began in London, England in 1913 when a Mr. Edward Johnston gave a talk before a group of London teachers and outlined an "ideal program in writing." Mr. Johnston's chief interest was a study of the handwriting of ancient manuscripts and the current use of such writing for formal resolutions, diplomas, etc. Like men who develop a love and enthusiasm for a particular area he waxed eloquent with the desire that men immediately adapt his pet ideas. His fond hope was that his ancient Italic manuscript be taught in the schools of his day. Because of his ability to foresee primary grade difficulties, he recommended that these children begin by learning a simple Roman style and later move to the broad edge pen work he loved so well.[15]

Teachers tried and liked the "simple Roman style;" they liked it so well that the hoped-for move never took place! The name manuscript was given to this simple style—based then, as now, on circles, straight lines and combinations of these shapes—because it was imitative of the style used in ancient manuscripts. In spite of current efforts to change the name (note the title of the article by Enstrom) most primary teachers in the United States refer to this style as manuscript writing and it will be called manuscript writing throughout this chapter.

Johnston's "simple Roman style" came to the United States in the second decade of this century. Classes in the "new method" were taught at Columbia University's Teachers College. Miss Marjorie Wise, from England, taught such a course in 1922, calling the method "print-script." Teacher-educators in this country were almost immediately won over; manuscript writing became as popular in the United States as it had been in Great Britain. Although there are distinct differences in the alphabets devised by various commercial firms, some adaptation of

---

15. E.A. Enstrom, "Print Handwriting Today," *Elementary English* (December, 1964), p. 846.

the basic circle-straight line alphabet is used in the great majority of first grade classrooms in the United States today.[16]

Rationale For Manuscript Writing

A careful examination of the three manuscript alphabets included with the descriptions of the commercial programs should make clear several of the most important reasons for the widespread acceptance of manuscript writing as a "tool" particularly appropriate for young children.

1. There are only two basic shapes to master, the circle and the straight line. One publisher claims there are four, but three, the straight vertical, straight horizontal and slant, are obviously closely related. Every letter is one of these shapes or a combination of two or more. The shapes of the letters are not so difficult for immature hand and finger muscles to master.

2. A second reason for using manuscript writing with young children is related to combining the letters of an alphabet into words. Cursive writing, by its very name, suggests the joining of letters in a "running script" or a "course." Words formed of manuscript letters permit a child to pause, to stop, to rest, whether or not a word has been finished. This also contributes to ease and early success in communicating.

3. A comparison of any of the more widely used manuscript alphabets[17] with the print type used in the reading materials prepared for beginners will illustrate the third and perhaps the most compelling reason for teaching manuscript alphabet. The letters of most manuscript alphabets and the print used in most primary reading materials (trade banks, basal readers, newspapers and magazines) are so similar as to be almost indistinguishable. The upper case or capital M (M,M), W (W,W) and the lower case k (k,k) vary in the different systems, and may differ from the print in books; the a (a) in many textbooks is probably not the manuscript a (a) the children have learned to make.

---

16. Enstrom, *Ibid.,* p. 846, says the teaching of manuscript writing in the primary grades is practically universal in the United States.

17. The student will probably want to compare the beginning writing systems advocated by the commercial firms listed in the bibliography. The publishers' addresses are included, and it has been the writer's experience that these publishers are quite generous in supplying prospective (and in-service) teachers with information about their programs as well as an abundance of sample illustrative material.

These ordinarily are not difficult adjustments for children to make. Children who learn manuscript writing learn that what they write can be read, just as the charts made by the teacher and the preprimers can be read. Reading and writing, then, are seen as related processes. Although there certainly is more to writing and reading than translating oral language into and from print, it does seem probable that the beginning reading process is facilitated by the use of a writing system which is not entirely unrelated to reading. Both reading and writing would seem beneficial when children are helped to see the close relationship between the two.[18,19]

Although Herrick's findings offer conclusive evidence that the use of manuscript writing is far from universal (14 per cent of the respondents indicated that cursive writing was taught in the first grade, primarily because it seemed hard to justify teaching a skill which would be abandoned in a year or two), Horton's comment on the current status of manuscript writing seems appropriate here:

> Since the introduction of manuscript writing in this country in 1921, its acceptance has been rapid and nearly complete. This is especially true as we view the many other educational innovations which have enjoyed momentary attention but have later faded from the educational horizon. Most schools now begin with manuscript writing in the first grade with a tansition to cursive provided in the latter part of second or the first part of third grade. Much of the research in the twenties and thirties centered in a controversy between teaching manuscript and teaching cursive handwriting; recent entries deal with methods for making the transition, or in some cases whether a transition is desirable.[20]

How Do We Begin?

Assuming the wisdom of beginning with manuscript writing, the next question seems to be "how?" Several methods have been advocated and each appears to have merit.

Materials for Beginning Writing

The chalkboard is widely used in the beginning stages, almost universally for demonstration of correct letter formations by the teacher and

---

18. E.M. White, "Interrelating Reading and Writing in Kindergarten Through Grade Three," University of Chicago, Conference on Reading *Proceedings* 25 (1963): 123-126.

19. Dorris May Lee and Roach Van Allen, *Learning to Read Through Experience,* 2nd edition (New York: Appleton-Century-Crofts, Inc., 1963).

20. Horton, *op. cit.,* p. 426.

also for practice by children. The surface is large and the teacher can watch several children at once to check reversals, incorrectly formed letters, etc. However, several problems present themselves when the chalkboard is used. Children see poor examples written by beginners like themselves rather than models worth emulating. When mistakes are made before a group, much tact is required in order to correct a child's errors without embarrassing or unduly discouraging him.

Another problem is fatigue which can result when the child's arm must be raised to form each letter. If the reader has attempted chalkboard writing for any length of time, the fatigue problem has almost certainly presented itself. It can be more severe for the hands and arms of immature six-year-olds.

The left-handed child is likely to encounter problems similar to those of the left-handed diner placed between two right-handed people at the luncheon or dinner table. Spacing and placement at the chalkboard so each child has all the room he needs and so the left-handed child doesn't interfere with and isn't interfered with by right-handed children is very important.

If the chalkboard is used, lines (often painted on the board in more or less permanent fashion, sometimes in attractive colors) will help the child adjust the size of his letters, the spacing between letters and words and avoid slanting uphill or downhill. If lines aren't painted on the board, the teacher should use a chalkboard liner or a yardstick to provide guidelines which are very helpful to the beginner. It might be added that painted guidelines on the chalkboard are helpful to the teacher also, and often lines are provided at appropriate heights for children and others are designed for the teacher's use. If the chalkboard is used extensively by the children for drill or practice, the teacher should:

1. Attempt to provide guidance rather than criticism, to focus on correctly formed letters rather than mistakes, and to make suggestions tactfully and informally. It may be better if other members of the class are busy with other activities rather than at their seats, watching the group working at the chalkboard.
2. Make sure the group at the board is small enough so that each writer has enough room and so left-handed children are not penalized.
3. Provide guidelines to help the child gauge the size, shape, spacing and linear evenness of his writing.
4. Keep practice periods short, to avoid fatigue.

Because most of a child's writing will be done on paper and because holding a pencil is somewhat different from holding chalk, it hardly seems wise to limit even a beginner to writing on a chalkboard. Because the child can write large and can benefit from a teacher's direct supervision at the board (and this is difficult when an entire class of children are using paper and pencil and working individually at desks or tables) it seems that some practice at the chalkboard would be beneficial.

Large (18" X 24" or even 24" X 36" sheets) of newsprint are also used by many first grade teachers in introducing manuscript writing. Such sheets are either folded, to provide guidance for the height and relative size of letters, or lines are drawn for similar purpose.

Paper for beginning writers should be large, in keeping with our knowledge about the limited small muscle control of young children. Lines are widely spaced (*at least* ½" between lines) for first graders, and the spacing may be wider (1", 1½") for paper used in the earliest stages. It is to be expected that children will reduce the size of their writing after they progress through the stage in which *drawing* letters is a more accurate description of children's efforts than *writing*.

Large, thick crayons are often used as the first writing instruments. Beginner's pencils, large, thick, and with very soft lead, are tools with which the reader probably is already familiar. For some time teachers (and teacher educators) assumed that long, thick crayons, chalk or pencils were as essential for success in beginning writing as the large paper already discussed. Recent evidence, however, indicates that while extremely short, stubby pencils are not efficient instruments, the beginner's pencils are not as important as we once had thought. Length of the pencil and the point at which the pencil is grasped appear to be significant, but not the thickness of the pencil or crayon.[21]

Ball-point pens perhaps have a place in the writing program of the upper primary grades, but these are seldom used in beginning programs.[22,23]

Introduction of Letters

For some time, educators advocated the introduction of letters on the basis of common elements; all the "circle" letters were worked on

21. Paul C. Burns, *Improving Handwriting Instruction in Elementary Schools,* (Minneapolis, Minnesota: Burgess Publishing Co., 1962), p. 54.

22. Herrick, *op. cit.,* p. 28.

23. Rosemary Soltis, "Handwriting: The Middle R," *Elementary English* 40 (October, 1963): 605-607.

together; the letters which were basically "line" letters and those letters which varied or combined these basic shapes were taught last.

A study conducted by the Lewises, reported in 1964, focused on the *difficulty* levels of the various letters, lower case and capital. In other words, they ascertained which of the fifty-two (twenty-six capitals, twenty-six lower case) letters were hardest for the children to learn to make. The following table, reproduced by permission of the writers, summarizes their findings. The most difficult letters are listed first (Numbers 1 to 5 are the hardest, numbers 46 to 52 the easiest.)[24]

TABLE 7.1
Manuscript Letters in Order of Difficulty

1	q	14	U	27	K	40	F
2	g	15	M	28	W	41	P
3	p	16	S	29	A	42	E
4	y	17	b	30	N	43	X
5	j	18	e	31	C	44	I
6	m	19	r	32	f	45	v
7	k	20	z	33	J	46	i
8	u	21	n	34	W	47	D
9	a	22	S	35	h	48	H
10	G	23	Q	36	T	49	O
11	R	24	B	37	x	50	L
12	d	25	t	38	c	51	o
13	Y	26	z	39	V	52	l

As the reader can see the most difficult letters are those which might be called "descenders"—the q, g, p, y and j—and in the problem of relating the nondescending letters to the guideline the m is the most difficult. The easiest letters are those which are either straight lines or circles, without embellishment.

First grade boys appear to be more prone to errors than girls. As instruction continued throughout the year, girls showed greater progress. Left-handed children were slower beginning to write and continued to make more errors than right-handed children. Chronological age did not seem to make a significant difference, either in terms of readiness or rate of progress.

---

24. Edward R. Lewis and Hilda P. Lewis, "Which Manuscript Letters are Hard for First Graders?" *Elementary English* 41 (December, 1964): 855-858.

What Should Beginners Write?

The problem of content cannot be considered an either-or, black-or white issue. A wise teacher neither begins with meaningless shapes or even letters, the purpose of which eludes the pupil, nor expects the pupil to be able to record ideas simply because he has stated them. Trauger writes:

> Writing is a symbolization of speech and because speech, the primary form of language, is a symbolization of what the speaker had in mind to say, writing becomes a symbolization of a symbolization.
>
> Writing, being a derived form of language, is, therefore, communication twice removed from the original thought. It is not written speech; because of the contrasting natures of speech and writing, it cannot be. Much more happens in oral communication than can be shown with standard symbols on the written or printed page. These differences create problems for pupils; they also complicate the teacher's pedagogy.
>
> Written communication demands skill and pedagogy not required in speech. The child must learn the set of marks (graphemes) which his society uses to represent the elements of language. To make these marks and perform the act of writing he needs a degree of muscular coordination. Then he faces the complexities of spelling and the even greater difficulties of trying to represent, with written punctuation, the pauses, intonations, and kinesics* which he uses as eloquent signals in his speech. Also, there are the conventions of a printed page: spacing, letter and line alignment, and capitals.[25]

Obviously, then, the teacher of beginning manuscript writing must be concerned with something more than the experiential background of his pupils and the level of their spoken language. Just as *content* cannot be considered in isolation, neither can the *eye-hand coordination* of the child, or *his ability to successfully control his small muscles* in order to make his hands and fingers do what he wants and intends them to do.

It perhaps should be stated explicitly, although it certainly has already been implied, that each child in a kindergarten or first grade class will exhibit varying combinations of factors indicating readiness for handwriting or lack of it. A few children will remain at the stage at which they will write little more than their names and simple labels for pictures well into the second semester of the first grade. Almost any kindergarten teacher will testify to the fact that few children in kindergarten have the necessary motivation, general linguistic competence, and muscular coordination requisite for simple notes to parents, invita-

---

*The term kinesics is used by linquists to refer to gestures, facial expressions, etc., which deny, refute, or reinforce and support the words of a speaker.

25. Wilmer K. Trauger, *Language Arts in Elementary Schools* (New York: The McGraw-Hill Book Company, 1963), p. 59.

tions, and relatively complex stories to accompany paintings, drawings and other art work. To say "No handwriting" to a kindergarten teacher is educationally unsound, and betrays the same lack of understanding of individual differences, as would the edict that *every* child should be able to write at the conclusion of his kindergarten experiences.

The teacher of beginning writers and beginning writing will want to combine introduction of basic letter shapes, instruction in proper paper placement, guidance relative to posture, desk height, distance from the writing surface, etc., without doing violence to the ideas a child wants to express. There is a place in a beginning writing program for lessons in which the ideas are stressed, and for lessons in which the ideas are less important than learning to write certain letters and words correctly, neatly, and easily. In lessons of the first type, help will have to be given individually, there will be some dictation, with or without copying from the board, and the teacher may use the literature program, a field trip, or any other especially interesting experience as stimulus. In the second type of lesson, designed to improve children's handwriting competence, the teacher will rely upon the individual child's desire to strengthen his ability to communicate with others and his knowledge of the progress he has made since previous skill, drill or practice lessons to provide the necessary motivation. There is a fiction abroad which suggests that there can be no intrinsic motivation in a practice exercise in which gum, candy bars, or, at the very least, lavish teacher praise, must provide the spark which will cause a child to work upon improving a skill—especially so mundane a skill as handwriting. No teacher who has seen the pride in a child's demeanor as he exhibited to the teacher—or examined privately—an October paper and a much neater, more legible paper written just before Thanksgiving believes that a child gets no pleasure from demonstrated growth in handwriting.

How Long Should Manuscript Writing Skill Be Maintained?

It has been noted several times in this chapter that "typical" patterns of handwriting instruction provide for transfer, or transition, from manuscript to cursive writing in the second semester of second grade, or in the first semester of third grade, and the trend appears to be in the direction of making the change later, assuming that greater maturity will make the change easier, and that manuscript writing will be more functional if maintained somewhat longer. The reader will also recall that the publishers of most handwriting programs apparently prefer to leave the answer to the "when" question to the personnel of various school systems using the programs; they provide material for transition in both Grade 2 and Grade 3.

Patrick Groff has asked a different kind of question, consistently and eloquently. In two excellent articles he has suggested that the rationale for changing is a weak one indeed,[26] and also that manuscript writing, because of its greater legibility is actually preferred by "Big Business."[27] However, in more recent research conducted with Renaud, Groff has found that: "It appears that parents of both primary and intermediate grade school children favored the use of manuscript writing in grades one and two but would object to its continued use through grade six.[28] The parents indicated, however, that they believed manuscript writing was easier to read! Does this appear to reveal some inconsistencies? Perhaps, although the parents may have been expressing the hope that cursive writing might be made more legible!

E.A. Enstrom takes a position different form Groff's. After reviewing the characteristics of manuscript writing, Enstrom concludes: "These very features that make it possible for beginners to learn print also make print less desirable for adults to use as the chief writing tool."[29] Enstrom recommends beginning with a vertical manuscript, an easy transition to "slant print," which is retained throughout the elementary grades, and, finally, the joined, cursive writing style is taught. Few would argue with Enstrom's position that the development, the child's progress from stage to stage, is an individual matter, dependent upon various facets of perceptual and psychological "readiness." He quotes the results of a study he directed which indicated that 98.5 per cent of the teachers involved were successful in introducing cursive writing at or before mid year in second grade.[30] One might question whether or not one can speak of "class readiness," except in practical, pragmatic terms which recognize the difficulties involved in introducing a new and major learning task on an entirely individual basis. In another article,

26. Patrick Groff, "From Manuscript to Cursive—Why?" *Elementary School Journal* 61 (November, 1960): 97-101.

27. Patrick J. Groff, "Preference for Handwriting Style by Big Business," *Elementary English* 41 (December, 1964): 863-864, 868.

28. Albert J. Renaud and Patrick J. Groff, "Parents Opinions About Handwriting Styles," *Elementary English* 43 (December, 1966): 873-876.

29. E.A. Enstrom, "But How Soon Can We Really Write?" *Elementary English* 45 (March, 1968): 360-363, 382.

30. *Ibid.,* p. 362.

Enstrom writes: "Further, with proper teacher qualifications, it is easy to teach any phase of handwriting with a group approach, and reach ninety-five per cent of the group—then help individually the five per cent who fail. I have experimented successfully with this approach for many years, and know hundreds of teachers capable of doing the same thing with quality results."[31]

Two claims are frequently made for cursive writing. First, cursive writing is supposedly faster, and because a more individual style is encouraged by its use it is reported to be more acceptable than manuscript writing in signatures on checks, legal documents, etc. Evidence from the research relating to speed and legibility in manuscript and cursive writing is quite contradictory. The detailed summary of extensive handwriting research in the *Encyclopedia of Educational Research*[32] fails to lend support to making the transition to cursive writing on the basis of enhancing speed or encouraging individuality of style. Burns writes:

> The question of relative legibility and speed, between manuscript and cursive, has not been conclusively settled. At this time, there is not enough proof available to support the claim of exclusive superiority of either form beyond beginning instruction where manuscript is generally agreed to be better.[33]

Templin surveyed the handwriting of adults who had been taught by three methods—all manuscript, all cursive, and manuscript with a transition to cursive. Her findings indicate that:

1. Males continued to use manuscript writing throughout their adult lives. Thirty-six per cent of the males who had been taught cursive writing from Grade One had learned manuscript writing and preferred to use it socially and professionally.
2. Females used cursive writing to a much greater extent than males. Approximately one-third of the females who had been taught manuscript writing through Grade 6, learned cursive writing and preferred its use because manuscript writing is "too childish" or "not business-like enough."
3. Manuscript writing is generally more legible; "both the male and the female respondents from the all-manuscript population achieved a

31. E.A. Enstrom, "But How Shall We Teach Handwriting?" *Elementary English* 44 (February, 1967): 133-137.
32. T. Harris, "Handwriting," *Encyclopedia of Education Research,* edited by Chester W. Harris, 3rd edition (New York: The Macmillan Company, 1960), pp. 616-622.
33. Burns, *op. cit.,* p. 9.

higher mean legibility than did respondents from either of the other two handwriting populations included in this survey." The most significant finding:

4. " . . . . the transition from the manuscript to the cursive style of handwriting at any age or at any grade level tends to result in less legible adult handwriting."[3][4]

Templin's findings suggest that the one overriding reason for changing from manuscript to cursive writing—the only reason which merits very serious consideration—is the greater social acceptance or prestige of cursive writing. So long as manuscript writing is considered "too childish" and "not business-like enough," most elementary school faculties will probably feel compelled to teach cursive writing. It is not because cursive writing is faster, easier, or more legible, but because of the social stigma which has been attached to manuscript writing which creates the need to teach both manuscript and cursive writing.

When should the change from manuscript to cursive writing be made if, in fact, it should be made *at all?* There appears to be general agreement on only two issues: manuscript writing is more legible, in terms of both adult and child produced samples; and, *some* segments of society appear to expect a reasonably legible and efficient level of skill and performance in cursive writing as one of the "entrance requirements" for adulthood. A third generalization appears to be a bit naive, however, when one is confronted with the lack of convincing evidence regarding *what* constitutes handwriting readiness (at the transfer stage, at least) and the practical considerations involved in designing thirty different handwriting programs (within the stereotypically prescribed three to five weekly twenty minute periods) for thirty pupils. As noted, specific, behaviorally oriented, readiness signs are lacking, but teachers would do well to watch for the following in their pupils:

1. The pupil should be able to *read* cursive writing, and should exhibit strong interest in learning cursive writing.

2. The pupil will show signs of slanting his manuscript writing, and may join certain letters, rather than lifting pencil from paper after each letter is formed.

The fallacies in these generalizations are obvious. What level of reading skill should be expected (demonstrated) before instruction in cur-

---

34. Elaine Templin, "The Legibility of Adult Manuscript, Cursive, or Manuscript-Cursive Styles," *New Horizons for Research in Handwriting,* Herrick, editor, *op. cit.,* pp. 185-206.

sive writing is begun? What about the child who makes serious efforts to slant his writing and join letters, because of peer/sibling/parent/ teacher pressures (or some combination of these) in spite of only minimal perceptual-motor readiness!

It is clear that the teacher needs more specific guidelines, and, lacking these, Enstrom's position, suggesting that whole group instruction be supplemented by remedial work with individual pupils who need it seems to be the most practical method of solving the many problems which face a teacher during the "transfer" or "transition" stages of handwriting instruction.

Content In Cursive Writing

The teacher of cursive writing has several advantages over the teacher of manuscript writing. Children's interests are broader, their backgrounds of experiences are wider, and their vocabularies, (speaking, listening and/or understanding, and writing and/or spelling) are considerably larger. The choice of practice material is not nearly as limited as it typically is for beginners.

In the skill sessions leading to proficient cursive writing, it probably is wise to begin with words containing letters which are most similar to the manuscript letters which children already know how to make: lower case, a, e, d, g, h, i, l, m, n, o, p, q, t, u and y; upper case, B, C, K, L, O, P, R and U. Whether upper case or capital letters and lower case letters will be taught together or separately will probably be determined by the handwriting system adopted, but the emphasis should be on meaningful content and, in general, after the introductory phase, words, phrases and sentences will prove more interesting to children than prolonged drill on isolated letters or parts of letters. Spelling lists, group and individual, provide an excellent opportunity for meaningful practice and also afford a time-saving method of working on two important aspects of the language arts simultaneously.

After children have mastered the joining of letters, first those like manuscript letters which are easy to make, then those which are quite different or are difficult to master,[35] slant can be dealt with.* The

---

*Enstrom's suggested sequence will be recalled: vertical manuscript, "slant print," then cursive writing. The author takes the position that the child can provide clues regarding the join first or slant first issue. The teacher can surely *observe* and follow the lead provided by the child!

35. Burns, *op. cit.,* p. 24, lists the following as the most difficult cursive letters: Lower case: a, e, r, t, v, n, o and s—the r and s are quite different in their manuscript and cursive forms. Capital letters: I.

sequence of letters as well as slant can also be taught as suggested by the authors of the commercial system, but the foregoing sequence is commonly used. Slant is a somewhat individual matter, and provided backhand is avoided and the degree of slant in a child's writing is relatively even, the teacher should not attempt to dictate the degree of slant.

Prerequisites to Emphasis on Speed

Speed is one of the last aspects of cursive writing to receive attention. Before devoting instructional time to improving speed, the teacher may want to check for the following:

1. Does the child have mastery over the correct letter formation for the entire cursive alphabet? The relative size of letters often presents a problem, and this problem should be solved before there is any emphasis on speed. Improper formation of a "d" (it should not look like a "cl") and a "c" (a "c" shouldn't look like an "a," nor an "a" like a "c") should be corrected—these particular mistakes are among the most common.
2. Does the child recognize the need for improving his speed? If the child is continually "caught short" and doesn't finish work which he could reasonably be expected to finish, then, together with several other children with a similar problem, he could and should receive the teacher's help. To establish a rigid speed requirement (i.e., 50 words a minute by sixth grade) makes little sense for most children. In fact flexibility in speed—helping children adjust the speed with which they write in terms of the difficulty of the material—would seem to be much more important. We know one speed is inadequate for reading; so it is for handwriting.
3. Can speed be improved without sacrificing legibility and fluency? If not, it should be relegated to its proper position behind these more important goals.

Cursive Writing: A Summary

Because it is a skill which society at present expects children to acquire, cursive writing probably must be taught. Children should not be forced to use cursive writing before they have mastered manuscript writing. Two half-skills are not as useful as one skill thoroughly mastered. Children will vary in their readiness for cursive writing and should be allowed to begin and to progress in acquiring this skill at a rate appropriate for them, not one dictated by the teacher, a curriculum guide or a handwriting system. Manuscript writing will continue to receive some attention, so it will remain functional for children and teachers may want to use it for board work, as well as for charts, maps, and labels. It is quite important that children be able to *read* cursive writing, at least at a minimal level, before they learn to write it.

The Use of the Typewriter

With the increasing prominence of the typewriter in high schools and colleges as well as in business offices, its use in the elementary classrooms probably should be discussed. Limited research has been conducted on the feasibility of utilizing the typewriter in elementary school classrooms. Such research appears to indicate that children *can* learn to type at the fourth or fifth grade level.[36] With the present emphasis on "pushing down" subject matter and acceptance of the proposition that anything can be respectably taught at any level, we also seem to have a tacit, affirmative answer to the question, *should* elementary children be taught to type?

Questions Pertinent to the Teaching of Typing

The elementary school curriculum is already crowded. Ask any elementary teacher. Should we really attempt to teach typing, in addition to geometry, economics, cultural anthropology and the six or seven "basic" subjects, to eight, nine, and/or ten-year-olds? The decision to teach typing to intermediate or upper grade youngsters involves finding practical and theoretically sound solutions to a number of problems:

1. Where will typing be taught? The noise of even a few typewriters would seem to prohibit simultaneous instruction in reading, or any other subject, in the typical self-contained elementary classroom. Equipping each classroom with thirty or thirty-five typewriters would probably send taxes still higher. If a special typing room is furnished, would this give still more impetus to departmentalization in elementary schools?

---

36. Paul S. Anderson, *Language Skills in Elementary Education, op. cit.,* p. 99.

2. To whom should typing be taught? Should all children learn to type? Only the gifted? Those children whose handwriting is almost illegible? Only those children who appear to be college-bound, and who probably won't have an opportunity to take it later in junior high school or high school?
3. Who will teach typing? Can typical elementary classroom teachers teach typing? If not, do we teach typing by tapes, films, television, or should a specialist be hired—a high school typing teacher, perhaps?
4. How much time should be devoted to typing instruction? Should instruction in typing replace, at least in part, instruction in handwriting?

These questions cannot be answered until teachers and administrators have determined the importance of typing for elementary school youngsters. Children enjoy acquiring a new skill like typing. Boys who show little interest in writing neatly and legibly may be more interested in learning to use a machine that writes. Teachers would appreciate reading children's reports and stories which were typed rather than scrawled or scribbled. These appear to be immediate advantages to teaching typing to elementary youngsters; the long range advantage of typing ability in secondary school, college, or business need not be argued. Do we, however, teach something which will have somewhat limited current value, only something a pupil will need to know later?

Because this necessarily brief section devoted to typing has been somewhat pessimistic, has emphasized problems rather than advantages, it may be well to conclude with a quotation for a writer who takes quite a different position:

> I dare to suggest that "automated" (chiefly the typewriter at present, though we might well set our sights on a simplified note-taking machine, too) should be at least as prominent on the educational scene at all grade levels as are television automated learning devices and the like. All normal children should learn to type early in their school careers and make use of this skill constantly. Perhaps the typewriter and similar devices should largely replace handwriting for everything except brief notes and such things as bank checks. Then children could be taught to handwrite slowly, carefully and legibly, for speed needs would be met mechanically.
>
> The usual objection to typewriters for classrooms, their cost, does not impress me in this day of huge expenditures for educational hardware, much of it of unproved worth. If typewriters are desirable, as I believe they are, efficient ways to procure, use and maintain them can be found. Teachers of the mechanics of written communication who view handwriting in its proper contemporary perspective should be leaders in the move toward automated handwriting. There is much research to do here.

I hasten to add that pencils, and chalk-crayons are by no means obsolescent. Probably they never will be. Perhaps automating handwriting will result in more writing and therefore stimulate the sale of pencils, pens and crayons as much as radio stimulated the sale of phonograph records. Television did not kill radio, and as yet airplanes have not reduced the number of automobiles.[37]

We can surely agree that more research of a substantive nature, dealing with the purposes rather than the practicability of typing in the elementary school, is necessary before another curricular area or subject is added to an already crowded curriculum.*

Helping the Left-Handed Pupil

Left-handed children have had many problems to face as they progressed through school; furniture has been inappropriately designed for them, right-handed teachers have lacked both the knowledge of how to teach them to write legibly, (without hooking and smearing papers or hands) and a sympathetic attitude toward the peculiar problems of a left-handed person in a right-handed world. Fortunately this seems to be changing.[38] Teachers and parents are more permissive about left-handedness than they used to be, but ignorance of the best methods for helping left-handed children persists. The left-handed child must be helped to *see* what he's writing without the awkward "hooking" or the backhand so many develop.

Paper Placement

Enstrom,[39] among others, has several very specific recommendations about paper placement in particular, and feels that the mechanics have been too long neglected. He summarizes three recommended paper positions for *right*-handed children as follows:

---

*The reader may wish to examine *You Learn and Type,* a brochure which contains many specific suggestions for beginning programs and teaching typing in the elementary schools. In the brochure a seventy lesson program on 33 1/3 rpm records, is described in detail. The brochure may be obtained from the Gregg Densen, McGraw-Hill Book Co., Hightstown, New York, 08520.

37. Julian C. Stanley, "Proposals of Consultants for the Improvement of Research in Handwriting," *New Horizons for Research in Handwriting, op. cit.,* pp. 240-241.

38. Paul S. Anderson, *Language Skills in Elementary Education, op. cit.,* pp. 93-127.

39. E.A. Enstrom, "Paper Placement for Manuscript Writing, *Elementary English* 40 (May, 1963): 518-522, 552.

1. square placement, with the writer pulling the downstrokes directly toward him and producing a vertical writing that is similar to that found in reading books.

2. angled placement, with "straight" or vertical writing, parallel to the sides of the paper.

3. angled placement and slanted writing, similar to cursive writing.

The vertical placement (No. 1) is the most common, but arrangements must be made to assure visibility so the child's hand doesn't get in the way of the letter he's making. The angled placement (No. 2) makes the transition to cursive writing more difficult, since the child has been taught not to slant his writing even when the paper is slanted. The major disadvantage of No. 3 is the dissimilarity of the child's writing to the print he is trying to learn to read in books. Enstrom writes:

> The writer feels that all things considered, the square placement of the paper of the desk along with vertical manuscript is to be preferred at the beginning for right-handed writers.[40]

For left-handed writers, a *clockwise* paper placement is suggested, as well as a *sloped* desk. Left-handed children will probably benefit from using a lower desk top than that used by right-handed children.

In an article entitled "The Little Turn that Makes the Big Difference" Enstrom writes, summarizing research with left-handed pupils, "Pupils who gave the extra far turn (clockwise) to the paper not only added another important solution to the vision problem but also im-

---

40. E.A. Enstrom, "The Little Turn That Makes the Big Difference," *Elementary English*, 43:865-868; quotations from pp. 867, 868.

proved arm leverage to the point where both rate and quality were higher than the other suggested approaches—higher even than the norms set for average classroom writers." He continues: The chief understanding in solving the vision and leverage problems for teachers is that from the very beginning, regardless of method or style of writing taught, (a) the fingers must be back on the pencil, (b) the pupil should be placed in a desk that is below normal in height and (c) the paper must be turned clockwise extra far to further aid both vision and arm leverage. For the lefty this is "the little turn that makes a big difference!"

The incidence of left-handedness appears to be increasing, and the prospective teacher may expect to find not five or ten per cent but perhaps twenty per cent of the children in his classes preferring the left hand to the right. The reason is sociological rather than genetic. It is probable that few contemporary parents and fewer teachers are as rigid about using the right hand as was true in times past. The very term "sinister," with its unpleasant connotations, has its roots in the Latin term for "left;" "dextrous" and "dexterity" to the contrary are relatively complementary terms, deriving from Latin terms for "right."

Wisdom would seem to dictate some decision making, some planning, some examination of alternative proposals for guiding the left-handed pupil in handwriting, by individual teachers, and faculties, since their numbers are increasing and it is almost inevitable that the classroom teacher will have from two to five, or perhaps more, left-handed pupils every year who will require his special guidance. The writer must express the opinion that the left-handed pupil is fortunate if he encounters at least one left-handed teacher during the crucial period during which handwriting attitudes and habits are being formed.

The following suggestions are reprinted from a publisher's bulletin, with permission. The reader will note the variance with Enstrom's suggestions.

Suggestions for Helping
Left-Handed Children to Write

1. Paper placement.
   For manuscript writing, the paper should be placed slightly to the child's left with the lower edge of the paper parallel to the lower edge of the desk.

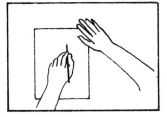

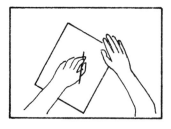

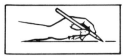

For cursive writing, the paper should be placed so that the child's arm forms a right angle with the lines on his paper.

2. Position at the desk.

   a. The child should be seated so that light does not cast shadows on his paper.

   b. He should hold his pencil above the sharpened portion so that he can see what he has written.

   c. He should keep his elbow fairly close to his body to prevent his curving his wrist.

   d. He should keep his hand below the line on which he is writing.

3. At the chalkboard.

The child should stand to the right of his writing. To prevent his curving his wrist, he should reach a little higher than a right-handed child reaches—but not above eye level.

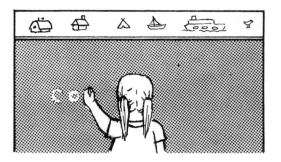

4. Left-handed children should be allowed to write with the slant that is most comfortable for them. Many will write vertically, or with a backhand slant, rather than with a forward slant.

5. If there are several left-handed children in one room, teachers may wish to seat them together so that children may observe and assist each other. If children are at tables, this arrangement will prevent bumping of elbows. Also, the teacher can quickly check the position of each of these students.

6. Be sure the desk is the right height. If a desk is too high, it is difficult for the child to keep his elbow close to his body.

The writers conclude:

The best time to prevent or correct poor habits is in the primary grades, but the intermediate teacher should not neglect giving instructions for both the left- and right-handed child. Incorrect habits can be corrected in the intermediate grades without harm if the corrections are made willingly by the student.[41]

Summary

The writer has taken a somewhat pessimistic position regarding the status of handwriting instruction in today's elementary schools. The handwriting curriculum is determined, in large measure, by the commercial program used, and most teachers would find it difficult to discuss the characteristics, strengths, and/or weaknesses of the system used, particularly as contrasted with other available programs. In language arts methods courses, prospective teachers are likely to find the text contains very little about handwriting, and it's probable that the instructor spends very little class time lecturing on or discussing the topic. Briefly, the current status of handwriting instruction bears little relationship to the importance of this communication tool. The telephone, dictaphone, telegraph and typewriter have not replaced the pen and pencil, yet, and are not likely to do so in the immediate future. It appears that more effective instruction is possible, without a significant increase in the time allotment (the ubiquitous twenty minutes, daily or thrice weekly). More effective instruction will result from greater professional interest in and attention to the issues involved, and although it would be naive to suggest that handwriting has no worthy competition for in-service (or pre-service) emphasis in courses, workshops, etc., it does not seem unreasonable to propose at least some attention be given to this topic. Furthermore, it could be hypothesized that even minimal efforts at upgrading handwriting instruction would yield more than minimal results. It seems rather strange to express satisfaction that we're probably doing no worse in this area than we used to! In what other facet of the curriculum do we take satisfaction in not losing ground?

---

41. Bulletin: "Helping the Left-Handed Child" (E.C. Seale and Co., Inc., 1965).

An intermediate position (between those favoring a "structural" and a "functional" approach) was taken, and the issues involved in making the transition from manuscript to cursive writing were discussed. It seems clear that regardless of when the change occurs, manuscript writing should not be abandoned. Children may be helped to make the transition in a group; as a total class, in fact, if Enstrom's suggestions are followed, but it will almost certainly be necessary to supplement this instruction with individual help given pupils who need it. Time allotments may be adjusted so that those pupils who need *less* time than the majority of the members of the class are not held back. One of the commercial systems described in this chapter has as its distinguishing characteristic programming, with the obvious advantages of immediate reinforcement and self pacing for the pupil. This may prove to be a partial solution to some of the problems raised related to handwriting instruction.

Typing in the elementary school was discussed with some objectivity, it is hoped. If the practical problems raised can be solved, typing may well prove to be a significant addition to the elementary school curriculum.

Some attention was given to the controversy surrounding the "best" approach to use with left-handed pupils. The conclusion reached was that teachers should in fact determine a practical, effective way of working with left-handed pupils, since the number of such pupils is increasing at a rapid rate.

If this chapter bears a "message" it is this: with only a little more concern for and attention to handwriting and better teacher preparation, we could be much more effective in this area of the curriculum which the writer does not consider uninteresting, mundane or obsolete. Handwriting deserves better treatment than it's getting.

EXTENDING YOUR LEARNING

1. Prepare a lesson plan, selecting an activity and adjusting the time limits of the lesson in terms of the age level(s) of the pupils:
   a. An introductory lesson in manuscript writing for a small group of mature kindergarten pupils or more typical first graders.
   b. A remedial lesson (manuscript) for a small group of second graders who are having difficulty differentiating between the 'b' and 'd,' the 'r' and 'n,' and 'c-b' and 'd.'
   c. An introductory lesson for an entire class beginning the transition from manuscript to cursive writing.
2. Select a panel to discuss the relative merits of changing to cursive writing in the second grade and/or waiting until third grade.

3. Develop, individually or in small groups, lists of criteria by which you would judge a child's manuscript and cursive writing. Then collect as many samples of children's handwriting as possible, and see whether or not your criteria are practical, easy to apply and actually discriminate.
4. Select one of the following topics for an oral or written report. Such reports should include a bibliography and should include presentations of the several issues involved as well as your own considered opinion.
   a. Should every elementary school child be taught to type?
   b. What should be considered in giving a grade in handwriting?
   c. Can handwriting be taught functionally, yet effectively, so the child will learn to write easily but will not develop the unfavorable attitudes toward handwriting that emphasis on drill sometimes promotes?
   d. Why is a teacher's handwriting so important? Is it possible for an adult to improve his handwriting significantly?
5. Prepare a brief evaluative comparison of two of the major handwriting systems. Include significant distinguishing characteristics, and a discussion of what appear to be the major strengths and weaknesses of each.
6. Using the sentence: "This is an example of my best manuscript (cursive) writing," write at least four times during the term (quarter, semester), and apply the criteria you developed. Make serious efforts to improve both your manuscript and cursive handwriting during the period you are enrolled in a language arts course and beyond.

BIBLIOGRAPHY

Andersen, Dan W., "Handwriting Research: Movement and Quality," *Elementary English*, 42:45-53, January, 1965.

Teaching Handwriting (What Research Says to the Teacher: #4) Washington, D.C., N.E.A., Dept. of Classroom Teachers, 1968.

Anderson, Paul S., *Language Skills in Elementary Education* (Chapter 3, "Handwriting") New York: The Macmillan Company, 1964.

Emerson, Caroline, "Remedial Handwriting," *Elementary English*, 43:756-758, November, 1966.

Encyclopedia of Educational Research, 4th Edition, Robert L. Ebel, Editor. New York: The Macmillan Co., 1969.

"Handwriting," pp. 570-577, Wayne W. Otto and Dan W. Andersen.

Enstrom, E.A., "But How Soon Can We *Really* Write?" *Elementary English* 45:360-363, March, 1968.

"How Shall We Teach Handwriting?," *Elementary English*, 44:133-137, February, 1967.

Enstrom, Doris, "In Print Handwriting, Preventing and Solving Reversal Problems," *Elementary English*, 46:759-764, October, 1969.

"Instructional Goals for Handwriting," *Elementary English*, 45:84-88, January, 1968.

"Reading—Handwriting Research," *The Reading Teacher*, 21:544-546, March, 1968.

Turner, Beatrice A., "An Analysis of the Effectiveness of a Program of Instruction Emphasizing the Perceptual Motor Nature of Learning in Handwriting," *Elementary English*, 47:61-69, January, 1970.

Turner, Beatrice A., "The Perceptual Motor Nature of Learning in Handwriting," *Elementary English*, 46:886-894, November, 1969.

Turner, Beatrice A., "Recommended Instructional Procedures in a Method Emphasizing the Perceptual Motor Nature of Learning in Handwriting," *Elementary English*, 46:1021-1030, December, 1969.

Groff, Patrick J., "From Manuscript to Cursive—Why?,"*Elementary School Journal*, 61:97-101, November, 1960.

Horton, Lowell, "The Second R: A Working Bibliography," *Elementary English*, 46:426-430, April, 1969.

Myers, Emma H., *The Whys and Hows of Teaching Handwriting*, Columbus, Ohio: The Zaner Bloser Company, 1963.

New Horizons for Research in Handwriting, Virgil E. Herrick, editor. Madison, Wisconsin: The University of Wisconsin Press, 1963.

Noble, J. Kendrick, "Handwriting Programs in Today's Schools," *Elementary English*, 40:506-512, 517, May 1963.

Plattar, Emma R., and Ellsworth S. Woestehoff, "The Relationship Between Reading Manuscript and Cursive Writing," *Elementary English*, 44:50-52, January, 1967.

Smith, James A., *Creative Teaching of the Language Arts in the Elementary School*, Boston: Allyn and Bacon, 1967 (Chapter 7, "Handwriting").

Renaud, Albert J., Jr., and Patrick Groff, "Parents Opinions about Handwriting Styles," *Elementary English*, 43:873-876, December, 1966.

Strickland, Ruth, The Language Arts in the Elementary School, 3rd Edition, Lexington, Mass.: D.C. Heath and Co., 1969 pp. 371-380.

Tidyman, Willard F., Charlene Weddell Smith and Marguerite Butterfield, *Teaching The Language Arts*, Third Edition, New York: The McGraw Hill Book Company, 1969 (Chapter 17, "Handwriting").

HANDWRITING PROGRAMS: COMMERCIAL SYSTEMS

The following are listed because they are so widely used. No bias toward these particular systems is implied. The student may want to review other systems which are available at the curriculum materials center of his teacher education institution.

Adventures in Handwriting, by Peterson Directed Handwriting. Grades 1-8, MacMillan, 1962. (MacMillan, 866 Third Avenue, New York, N.Y. 10022).

I Learn to Write, by Rosa Veal Ethelyn Davidson and Therese D. Norwick. Grades 1-8, Bobbs Merrill, 1968 (Bobbs Merrill—E.C. Seale Div., 4300 W. 62nd Street, Indianapolis, Ind., 46206).

Imaginary Line Handwriting Series, by Rebecca M. Townsend. Grades 1-8, Steck Vaughn, 1966.(Steck Vaughn, Box 2028, Austin, Texas, 78767).

Better Handwriting for You, by J. Kendrick Noble and the Handwriting Research Institute, Grades 1-3, 1966-1967. Noble and Noble Publishers, Inc., Subsidiary of Dell Publishing Co., Inc., 750 Third Avenue, New York, N.Y. 10017.

Better Handwriting for Everyone, By J. Kendrick Noble and the Handwriting Research Institute, Grades 1-8, Rev.; 1962. Noble and Noble Publishers, Inc., Subsidiary of Dell Publishing Co., Inc., 750 Third Avenue, New York, N.Y. 10017.

FILMS AND FILMSTRIPS

(Available for purchase or rent)

Filmstrips:

"Story of Writing" 26 frames; K-3; deals with the history of writing.
Filmstrips of the Month Club, Inc.
355 Lexington Avenue
New York, New York 10017

"The Story of Writing" 34 frames; 4-6, junior high, college, advanced. Also a history of writing.
Webster Publishing Co.
1154 Reco Avenue
St. Louis, Missouri

Filmstrips designed to complement and supplement the Zaner Bloser and Noble programs are available from the publishers. An l.p. record has been produced as part of the Noble program.

Films:

"Writing Through the Ages" 16 mm sound, black and white; 10 minutes; 4-6 history of writing as a means of communication.
Encyclopedia Brittanica Films
1150 Wilmette Avenue
Wilmette, Ill.

"Between the Lines" 16mm sound black and white, 20 minutes; 4-6; a history of writing from the invention of the alphabet to the present.
Modern Talking Pictures Service, Inc.
3 E. 45th Street
New York, New York 10022

Focus

If linguists have accomplished nothing else, they've succeeded in thoroughly frightening most elementary teachers! A linguist, and in this group Edith Trager Johnson is eminent, is a scientific student of language. Linguists approach language objectively, and they withhold value judgements, in most cases at least. Scholarly fields usually include a special vocabulary—common words (grammar) used in very specific ways or uncommon words (phoneme) developed to refer to new concepts. It may be the aura and the mystique which have surrounded linguistics, it may be that so few linguists have attempted to deal with the application of their findings, or it may be that one tends to be apprehensive about the very new, the unfamiliar, which has caused the general anxiety about linguistics which seems so prevalent among elementary teachers. It is probably a combination of these factors, along with general frustration resulting from the feeling that here is something *else,* new and important, which the teacher is expected to master.

Those linguists who have exhibited concern about the implications of their research for educational practice, and fortunately the author of this chapter is among these, have examined curricula in reading, in spelling, and in grammar/syntax. Because Edith Trager Johnson knows so very much about the phonological system of American English, her attention has been focused on spelling and phonological facets of reading. In this chapter, she suggests an approach to organizing the curriculum in spelling which is in part based on the frequency of sound-letter correspondences in our language. The result should be earlier independence in spelling and more thorough understanding of the phonological structure of our language.

The author has not taught in the elementary school. It was agreed that for this edition, as for the previous one, the editor would provide a "methods" supplement to her excellent chapter. While in basic agreement with the author about the need for some reorganization of the spelling program, and the value of understanding, thoroughly, sound-letter relationships, the editor repeats some of the questions educators have been asking interested linguists: questions related to function or utility, at the earliest levels, particularly, and questions about motivation.

This is a particularly challenging and significant chapter. It is worth the concentrated effort it demands of the reader. Linguistics is better understood than feared.

Edith Trager Johnson ———————————— *chapter eight*

the teaching of spelling:
a linguistic approach

Beginning with the publication of *Syntactic Structures* and continuing through his *Aspects of the Theory of Syntax* and beyond, Noam Chomsky and many other generative-transformational grammarians have built up an impressive body of literature dealing with the syntax of English and several other languages.

The still more recent developments in the field of linguistics have been in two directions. Some linguists have begun to work in the area of generative semantics which as yet seems to have little relevance to the teaching of spelling. The other direction in which linguistics has been turning is generative phonology. In that area, Chomsky and Halle's massive work on certain aspects of English phonology is the most important example, at this writing. Many references to English spelling are embedded there and, indeed, bear out the contentions of other earlier workers who pointed out that our orthography is quite regular and quite well-adapted to the morpho-phonemic alternations of the spoken language. One such reference is germane here.

> Notice, incidentally, how well the problem of representing the sound pattern of English is solved in this case by conventional orthography. [They give alternations like *divine-divinity, serene-serenity, profane-profanity,* with the first members of the pairs written *divIn, serEn, profAn.*] Corresponding to our device of capitalization of a graphic symbol, conventional orthography places the symbol *e* after the single consonant following this symbol. . . In this case, as in many other cases, English orthography turns out to be rather

251

close to the true phonological representation, given the nonlinguistic con-
straints that must be met by a spelling system, namely, that it utilize a
uni-dimensional linear representation instead of the linguistically appropriate
feature representation [i.e. the one used in their work] and that it limit itself
essentially to the letters of the Latin alphabet.[1]

Our traditional orthography, hereinafter referred to as TO, is generally regarded by linguists as an extra-linguistic system a secondary set of
symbols that represent the primary symbols, the phonological segments
often called phonemes. This has not prevented distinguished linguists
like Leonard Bloomfield,[2] Charles C. Fries and Robert A. Hall, Jr. from
devoting considerable attention to our spelling system and pointing out
that there is an enormous amount of regularity in it, along with its
irregularities.

Our system of writing is. . .alphabetic. This is proved by the simple fact
that we can write every English word by means of only twenty-six characters,
whereas a system of word-writing would demand many thousands.[2]

This chapter will be concerned primarily with TO and its relation to
the morpho-phonemes and phonemes of English. It will also treat. . .the
relevance of this, as seen by a linguist, to teaching American children to
read and to spell. First, however, there are things about the grammar of
the language and the format of the printed page to be considered.

Relationships of Semantics, Syntax, and Morphology

The study of meaning, classified as *semantics*, has made no systematic contribution to the teaching of reading. The teacher and student
both, however, make constant use of their knowledge of the different
meanings of words in order to select the appropriate one according to
the meanings of the other words and phrases in a sentence. It would be
sensible, although it is seldom done consistently in textbooks for beginning readers, to have words with interdependent meanings printed on
one or two lines, with a lot of space between the first group of such
words and each of the following groups.

---

1. Noam Chomsky and Morris Halle, *The Sound Pattern of English* (New York: Harper & Row,
1968), p. 184.
2. Leonard Bloomfield and Clarence L. Barnhart, *Let's Read* (Detroit: Wayne State University
Press, 1961), p. 25.

It follows that *syntax,* the study of the structure of phrases, clauses, and sentences, usually goes together with the semantics. If you have a noun phrase (say a determiner, followed by two adjectives and a noun) as the subject of a sentence, the rules of English syntax say that if the noun is "house" and the adjectives "adobe" and "enormous," and the determiner an indefinite article, then the noun phrase absolutely must be, in our usual prose style at any rate, "an enormous adobe house." It may not be, for instance, "a adobe enormous house" or any of the other theoretically possible permutations. The tie-in of syntax with semantics involves considerations like these: we can say "an enormous house" and we can say "an enormous molecule" in a sentence like "RNA has an enormous molecule compared to hydrogen." Obviously the referential meanings of "enormous' (the actual range of house-sizes against the range of sizes of molecules) differ by a very large order of magnitude. The linguistic meaning, however, is evidently something like "much larger than other members of a set."

Analysis of Phrase Structure

Syntax furthermore tells us a great deal more about the phrase structure of English, much of what we know intuitively about which words of a sentence belong together. The words in a noun phrase belong together, and so do the words in a verb phrase. Within the verb phrase the auxiliaries and main verb belong together, as do the words in the noun phrase that may follow, if the sentence contains an object or a complement. An adverbial clause like "when the time comes" hangs together, and in a primer for children it would be sensible to keep it all on one line, separated from contiguous words. Figure 8.1, shows the difference between such a book and one which, although for children, uses adult format.

Particular Uses of Phonology

There is at this point a tie-in with *phonology,* not with the vowels and consonants that the linguist calls segmental phonemes, but with the super-segmental phonemes of pitch, stress, and juncture that constitute the intonation patterns of English. The transformationalists' terms, Stress 1 and Stress 2, which generally correspond to the Smith-Trager primary and tertiary stresses, are awkard to write as numbers over syllables, e.g. $\overset{1\quad 2}{\text{operate}}$. The use of an acute accent for the loudest or

Zistel, Era. *Wintertime Cat.* New York: Holt, Rinehart, Winston, 1963	Hazen, Barbara Shook. *Rudolph* The Red-Nosed Reindeer. New York: Golden Press, 1958.

Page 1   Hello.
 	
     I am a cat.
 	
(2 lines on one page separated by white space, photograph of a cat)
	Once there was a reindeer named Rudolph, who lived at the North Pole, in Toyland.
	     Rudolph was younger and smaller than the other reindeer there. They all had proud, tall antlers. Rudolph's antlers were only tiny stubs.
	     Worst of all, Rudolph had a nose that was big and bright red. It was so red it glowed in the dark.
	
	(6 sentences on one page, colored illustrations)

Page 2   My name is
     Revey.
     What's yours?
(2 lines on one page separated by white space. Photograph pictures a cat.)
	Poor Rudolph! He wanted to be like the other reindeer in Toyland. Oh, to have a small, brown nose, instead of a big, bright red one!
	     The other reindeer made fun of Rudolph and called him names.
	     "Rudolph, the red-nosed reindeer," they teased over and over again until tears glistened on Rudolph's large red nose.
	(5 sentences on one page, colored illustration)

Page 3   I live
 	
     in a
 	
     house
 	
     in the
 	
     country. . .
(Incomplete sentence but complete thought with photograph of a cat)
	Sometimes the other reindeer made a circle around Rudolph and sang:
	     "Red-nose, red-nose,
	     A funny sight!
	     Big as an apple,
	     And twice as bright!"
	     They kicked snowballs with their tiny hoofs and covered Rudolph with a blanket of white fluffy snow.
	
	(2 long sentences, illustration)

Page 4   with some
     other cats.
(Completion of sentence from page 3 with photographs of cats)
	All the reindeer loved to play games. They played tree tag and snow slide and tumble bones.
	     But Rudolph was never asked to play. He stood behind a pine tree and watched. He was very lonely.
	(5 sentences with colored illustration)

FIGURE 8.1.

primary stress and of a grave accent for the next-loudest stresses seems simpler, e.g. óperate. While the Smith-Trager analysis cannot be formally taught to children, and can be taught in all its complexity only with difficulty to their teachers, it has implications. It does help the teacher to be aware explicity that the intonation patterns—the first thing each child learns about his language—the syntactic structure, and the semantics of a sentence reinforce each other. They each signal the subdivisions of a sentence. It would be helpful to the beginning reader to have stress marks on the loudest syllables of each phrase, with each phrase separated from the next by white space on the page. Here is a hypothetical example.

John James Jéffrey

Rùtherford the Thírd

wènt dówn   to the béach   each dáy.

Whenèver he wént   he toòk alòng his hámster.

Justified margins should be regarded as irrelevant, and the only consideration should be the correspondence of linguistic structure to the appearance of its graphemic representation on the printed page.

Considerations Related to Morphology

This leads us to *morphology,* to the uninflected words which take no grammatical endings, and to the inflected classes of words that do have grammatical suffixes. The uninflected word-classes generally acknowledged at the moment are these: interjection, *oh;* conjunction, *and, if;* determiner, *the, a, some;* intensifier, *very, extremely;* preposition, *with, between* and the sub-class of particles, *up, off* with their additional function of being in two-part verbs like *call up* and *put off;* modal, the nine auxiliaries *can, could, shall, should, will, would, may, might, must* which are followed directly by the basic form of the main verb.

The inflected classes are those ever-changing classes with referential meaning: noun, with possessive and/or plural forms *man, man's, men, men's;* personal pronoun, with subject, object, and two possessive forms, *I, me, my, mine;* verb, with its five forms, *eat, eats, ate, eating, eaten;* adjective and adverb, with their positive, comparative, and superlative forms, *fast, faster, fastest.*

The chief relevance to the teaching of reading or of reading instruction of these morphological facts of life would seem to be that the suffixes should never be separated from their stems by hyphens, and that an uninflected word should never be separated from the inflected word it accompanies, by being on different lines. In other words, "extremely" should never be printed with *extreme-* on one line and *-ly* on the next, nor should a sentence like "These pies must not be eaten" be broken up on the page at any point other than between *pies* and *must.*

Phonology and Its Relation to Reading Instruction

Leaving behind this brief treatment of the relevance of semantics, syntax and morphology to the teaching of reading, let us consider the very great relevance of phonology. The twenty-four consonant phonemes, the thirteen or fourteen vowel phonemes of English, and the spelling patterns used to represent them are of the utmost importance. (The writer says thirteen or fourteen vowel phonemes because for many West Coast speakers, and indeed others, there is no distinction whatever between *cot* and *caught, Lon* and *lawn, odd* and *awed.*)

Fries, in his last book,[3] felt it necessary to clarify the usage of the three terms *phonic, phonetic(s)* and *phonemic(s).* In this discussion, *phonic* will refer to the familiar methods of teaching children word attack and *phonetics* will mean only the science of speech sounds, with *phonetic* the appropriate adjective. *Phonemics* is the study of *phonemes,* the small number (12 and 65 are the known extremes for the languages of the world) of sounds in any one language that makes a difference in meaning. Most of the alphabets used in the world are attempts to represent *phonemic distinctions.* A *minimal pair* of words has words that differ by one phoneme only, e.g. *man/men, man/pan man/mad.*

In Figure 8.2, the twenty-four consonant phonemes are given. You may have seen them on a chart which used slightly different labels or different symbols, but there is general agreement on the fact there are these twenty-four distinctions for which we can find minimal pairs to prove that they make a difference in meaning.

---

3. Charles C. Fries, *Linguistics and Reading* (New York: Holt, Rinehart, and Winston, 1964), p. 134.

	LABIALS	DENTALS	PALATALS	VELARS	
STOPS	p	t	ch	k	vl.
and					(8)
AFFRICATES	b	d	j	g	vd.
FRICATIVES	f	th s	sh	——	vl. (8)
	v	dh z	zh		vd.
NASALS	m	n	——	ng	(3) vd.
RESONANTS	w	r,l	y	h	(5)
	Labio-dental Bi-labial	Apico-dental Apico-alveolar		Dorso-velar Glottal	(24)

FIGURE 8.2. English Consonant Phonemes.

The Consonant Sounds

A frequent answer to the question, "How many vowels are there in English? is "A, e, i, o, u, and sometimes y and w." Subtracting the five letters which unambiguously and always stand for vowel sounds, you have twenty-one that represent consonants. As you know by now, linguists are very stubborn about keeping letters and sounds apart. They also use the technical term *phoneme* for a speech sound in a given language. The statement that linguists, phoneticians, and other people concerned professionally with the phonological aspects of language might all make is this: English has twenty-four consonant phonemes, represented in the spelling system by the twenty-one consonant-letters, alone and in various combinations.

Questions Concerning the Consonant Phonemes

What are these twenty-four consonant phonemes, and how are they described? Whenever we classify a consonant sound, we ask three questions:

1. Where is the sound made?
2. How is the sound made?
3. Are the vocal cords vibrating?

Let us consider each question separately. When we ask where a sound is made, we want to know fairly accurately what the place of articulation is and which of the speech organs are involved. If the lips are involved, we call the sound a *labial*. If we want to be more technical and specify that both lips are involved we say, for instance, that /p, b, m/ are *bilabial*. Say the following words, in order to become aware that you are opening and closing your lips: peppermint, popular, babble, imbibing, mammoth, memory, pygmy, Bemelmans, pablum mobbing, moppet. Notice also that you are rounding your lips when you say /w/ in these words: willow-ware, wallowing, windshield wiper, wary, weary, whale. The phonemes /f, v/ are also labial sounds, *labiodental* to be exact, because the upper teeth touch the lower lip, as you will notice when you say these words: fife, fluffy, Vivian, revive, involvement, valve-fitter, fever, villify, favorite.

Here we have six sounds, then, which are made with the lips, and we can say that English /p b m w f v/ are all LABIALS.

In order to make almost all the rest of the English consonant sounds, we have to use some part of the tongue, the tip or *apex*, front or *blade*, back or *dorsum*. Some portion of the tongue touches or approaches the *teeth*, the *alveolar ridge* (the gums above the upper teeth), the roof of the mouth or *hard palate*, the soft palate or *velum*.

If the tongue is between the teeth, as is usually the case for both of the sounds spelled TH, we call the resulting sound an *interdental*. First try these words, all of which have the phoneme we write /th/ or /θ/, using the Greek letter *theta*: thin, thick, thwart, thimble, ether, athletic, path, wealth. Now say the following words, all of which have the other interdental sound which we write /dh/ or /ð/ with the barred-d borrowed from the Old English alphabet, where it represents the same sound: there, they, thus, then, either, bathe, soothe.

We may use the term DENTAL as a cover term for all the sounds made in the general area of the teeth, the two interdentals /th/ and /dh/, and the six sounds which are more precisely alveolars, made at or near the gum-ridge, /t d n s z l/. Say these words and observe the action of the tip of your tongue against the alveolar ridge: tattle-tale, dedicate, none, Nanny, sassy, zigzag, sissy, sizzle, Zasu, lily, lasso, lining, silly, Lizzie, teller, dollar, Sicily, knitting needle, Linda, lintel.

The eight sounds, then, that we can call DENTALS are /th dh t d s z n l/.

It is hard to generalize about the r-sound in the English-speaking world because it may be an alveolar tap for a Britisher who says "veddy, veddy," a truly retroflexed sound, made with the tongue curled back towards the roof of the mouth of a Midwestern American, or merely a continuation of the preceding vowel for an Easterner.

There are five phonemes, written /ch j sh zh y/ or /č ǰ š ž y/, which can be called PALATALS because the front part of the tongue, or blade, touches or approaches the hard palate in the course of the articulation of these sounds. Say the following words and observe that your tongue is near the hard palate, or roof of the mouth, when you make the consonant sounds: judging, Chichester, church, edge, shay chichi, azure, vision, yea, Jesuit, dying, Zsa Zsa.

Of the twenty-four consonant phonemes of English, there are four which can be called VELARS because they are made in the region of the velum, or soft palate. The sound we write /h/ involves no contact and very little friction, but the other three, written /k, g, ng/ or /k g ŋ/ do involve contact of the back part of the tongue, or dorsum, with the soft palate, or velum. Try to observe this as you say the consonants in these words: gag, giggle, khaki, cackle, kick, clock, keg, king, clinging, gang, ganging, groggy, Klieg, cocky, kicking, Gregory, conquer, quick, quahog, quacking, quaking, caking, gargoyle, gangling, Queequeg, crinkle, creaking, Gieseking.

A Summary of Consonant-Sound Articulation

So far we have talked about where along the speech tract the sounds are made—the sound that linguists analyze into the twenty-four consonant phonemes of English. Although many books have been written about the phonetic details of each of the phonemes in many regional and social dialects of English, much of what we, as English teachers, need to know about the place of articulation of the consonant-sounds can be summed up simply. There are four areas of the speech tract which are significant for English, namely labial, dental, palatal, and velar.

6 LABIALS: /p b m w f v / puppy, baby, mummy, wow, five
9 DENTALS: /th dh t d s z n l r/ thenceforth, Teddy, sizzle, nearly
5 PALATALS: /ch j sh zh y/ josh, church, azure, yea
4 VELARS: /h k g ng/ Hague, cake, gong

The Consonant Letters

The common orthographic representations of the twenty-four consonant phonemes of English are listed below. A hyphen preceding a grapheme indicates its occurrence in final position only; hyphens before and after indicate occurrence in medial position only. Parentheses indicate the environment of a grapheme. C represents "consonant" and V, "vowel." Some spellings which are "irregular" are omitted, although they occur in high-frequency words.

Consonant Grapho-Phonemics

/p/	p, pp, -pe
/b/	b, bb, -be
/t/	t, tt, -te, -(e)d
/d/	d, dd, -de, -(e)d
/k/	c(a,o,u,C), k(e,i), -ke, q(u), -cc, -ch, x
/g/	g(a,o,u,C) gu(ei) gg, -gue, -x-, gh-
/ch/	ch, -tch, -tu-
/j/	j, g(e,i,y), -dge, -ge
/f/	f, ff, -fe, ph, -gh
/v/	v, vv, -ve
/th/	th
/dh/	th, -the
/s/	s, ss, -se, c(e,i,y), -ce, sc-, -(e)s, x
/z/	z, zz, -ze, -se, -(e)s, x
/sh/	sh, ch, -che, -ti(on), -ssi(on), -ci-, -ce-
/zh/	-ge, -su-, -si-, -zu-, -si(on)

/m/	m, mm, -me, -mb, -mn
/n/	n, nn, -ne, gn, kn-
/ng/	ng, n(k,g,q)
/l/	l, ll, -le
/r/	r, rr, -re, wr-
/w/	w, wh, (q)u
/y/	y, u/ue, ew, iew
/h/	h

The Vowel Sounds

With vowels, there is no stopping the air or putting a speech organ in the way of the airstream to cause friction. There is only changing the shape of the oral cavity by moving the tongue to a position that we call *high* or *mid* or *low* and at the same time, *front* or *central* or *back*. The rounding of the lips also affects the quality of the vowel sound. In English all the front vowels are unrounded, all back vowels rounded.

Their arrangement is given in Figure 8.3.

The common TO representations of the fourteen vowel phonemes are given below.

Simple Nuclei

/i/	i (C), y(C)
/e/	e(C), ea(C)
/æ/	a(C)
/ə/	u(C), o, ou; unstressed a, e, i, o, u, y
/a/	o(C), a
/u/	oo, u
/ɔ/	aw au, o(r), al(C), (w)a(r)

Complex Nuclei

/iy/	e(C)e, ee, ea, e, ei, ie, (VC)y, (VC)ie
/ey/	a(C)e, ay, ai, ey, ei, ei(gh)
/ay/	i(C)e, (C)y, C(ye), C(ie), -igh, -ig(n), i(ld,nd)
/oy/	oy, oi
/aw/	ou, ow
/ow/	o(C)e, oa, o, oe, ow
/uw/	u(C)e, ue, ew, ui, ou, o, oo

Nuclei Before /r/ in Monosyllables

/ir/	ear, eer, ere
/er/	air, are
/ɔr/	or, ore, oar, (w)ar
/ur/	oor, ure
/ar/	ar
/ər/	ur, er, ir, (w)or(C), ear(C)

	SIMPLE		
	Front	Central	Back
High	/ i / pit	——	/ u / put
Mid	/ e / pet	/ ə / putt	——
Low	/ æ / pat	/ a / pot	/ ɔ / paw
	COMPLEX		
	Front	Central	Back
High	/ iy / Pete	——	/ uw / boot
Mid	/ ey / pate	——	/ ow / boat / oy / boy
Low	——	/ aw / bout / ay / bite	——

FIGURE 8.3.

Lists and charts like those illustrated are, of course, just restatements of information that has long been in the common domain. Figure 4 portrays what have been called grapho-phonemes, that is, the correspondences between the regular spelling patterns, the traditional names for the vowel sounds, and the phonemes, given in Smith-Trager transcription.

	LONG		SHORT	
Symbol				*Symbol*
/ ey /	taped, tape	A	tapped, tap	/ æ /
/ iy /	complete, Bede	E	abetted, bed	/ e /
/ ay /	ripen, ripe	I	ripple, rip	/ i /
/ ow /	moping, mope	O	mopping, mop	/ a,ɔ /
/ uw,yuw /	duly, rule cutest, cute	U	dull, dully cutter, cut	/ ə /
/ uw /	fool, kook	OO	full, cook	/ u /
/ oy /	boy, boil	OY	———	
/ aw /	now, noun	OU	———	

FIGURE 8.4. English vowel grapho-phonemes.

Analyses of the Grapho-Phonemes of English

The regular spelling patterns, which many linguists and teachers have long observed, have been systematically investigated by Dr. Paul R. Hanna at Stanford University under the sponsorship of the U.S. Office of Education. The project is called "Phoneme-Grapheme Relationships Basic to Cues for Improvement of Spelling" and has documented those relationships by computer analysis of the *Thorndike-Lorge Teachers' Word Book* and the *Merriam-Webster Collegiate Dictionary*.

An analysis of the grapho-phonemics of English also underlies Sir James Pitman's initial teaching alphabet, earlier called the Augmented Roman Alphabet. It is now called i/t/a and is beautifully worked out so that it can be used anywhere in the English-speaking world, as no purely phonetic notation could be. Not only is i/t/a independent of dialect variation, it is so designed that a four-year-old can use it with pleasure and profit and make the transition to TO with little trouble.[4]

---

4. Sir James Pitman, "The Future of the Teaching of Reading," presented at the Twenty-eighth Educational Conference by the Educational Records Bureau in the City of New York (October 30, 31, and November 1, 1963), pp. 1-5.

264 • THE TEACHING OF SPELLING

The i/t/a is not only superbly designed, but also successful, as has been demonstrated in hundreds of schools in Great Britain and in ever-growing numbers of schools in this country.

If, however, it is not possible to use i/t/a then the only sensible alternative is to teach the regularities of English spelling. Undoubtedly there are a small number of high-frequency irregularly-spelled words that must be taught as units. Those apart, the vast majority of words in the English lexicon are spelled regularly.

In fact, it seems that approximately eighty per cent of our lexicon is spelled regularly, although much of the remaining twenty per cent is, unfortunately, comprised of common words of high frequency. In Figures 8.5 and 8.6, there are typical regularly-spelled words for each of the six "short-long" pairs of vowel sounds (short A-long A, short E-long E, and similarly for I, O, U and OO). On both charts, the short-vowel words occupy the top half of the chart and the long-vowel words, the bottom half.

In 8.5, the columns are headed by consonant symbols between phonemic slant lines and they show words ending in the stops, affricates and /m, n/. In 8.6, there is the continuation of 8.5, with the columns headed by the symbols for the fricatives and /ng, l/.

Charts 8.7 and 8.8 give the same information more abstractly, showing only a word-ending for a group of words rather than a single word which typifies that group.

Omitted from both sets of charts are four consonants: the semivowels /w, y, h/ which combine with the simple vowels to make long vowels and diphthongs; also /r/ which is of a special nature because it so radically changes the phonetic nature of the preceding vowel.

To elaborate, in Figure 8.5, the regular spelling of each of the twelve vowel-sounds (all except /oy/ and /aw/) is indicated before the four voiceless and four voiced stops and two of the nasals, /p,t,ch,k/, /b,d,j,g/ and /m,n/. It is indicated by giving one of the many regularly-spelled words. In Figure 8.6, the spelling of those same twelve vowel sounds before /l/ and the other nasal, the four voiceless and four voiced fricatives, is indicated. That is, the six pairs /æ-ey/, /e-iy/, /i-ay/, /a,ɔ—ow/,/ə-uw, yuw/, and /u-uw/ are each represented by a sample word before /f, th, s, sh/, /v, dh, z, zh/ and /ng, l/. On both charts, the absence of a sample word indicates the absence of a regular spelling in monosyllables for that V + C sequence. There are in some cases two or even three regular spellings. There are also irregular spellings of many of the V+C sequences but they are not shown, of course, on this chart of

'Short'	/ p /	/ t /	/ ch /	/ k /	/ b /	/ d /	/ j /	/ g /	/ m /	/ n /
A	cap	cat	catch	pack	cab	cad	badge	gag	jam	pan
E	pep	pet	fetch	deck	web	wed	wedge	beg	hem	hen
I	rip	pit	pitch	pick	bib	bid	ridge	jig	him	win
O	pop	pot	botch	rock	rob	rod	lodge	log	prom	con
U	cup	but	hutch	luck	rub	dud	budge	jug	hum	fun
OO		foot		book		good				
'Long'										
A	ape	wait ate		cake	babe	maid shade	sage	vague	aim tame	pain lane
E	keep reap	meet heat	screech peach	leek peak	plebe	need bead	siege	league	beam	lean
I	pipe	night kite		like	bribe	ride			time	nine
O	hope soap	tote boat	poach	coke soak	robe	lode road	loge	vogue	home room	stone roan
U		newt mute		cuke	cube	lewd rude	huge	fugue	fume	hewn tune
OO	hoop	hoot	pooch		boob	food	stooge		broom	moon

FIGURE 8.5. Chart of regular spellings of words of one syllable ending in a consonant.

'Short'	/ f /	/ th /	/ s /	/ sh /	/ v /	/ dh /	/ z /	/ zh /	/ ng /	/ l /
A	Saff	path	pass	lash			jazz		pang	pal
E	Jeff	Seth	mess	mesh					length	dell
I	tiff	pith	hiss	fish			whizz		wing	will
O	doff	broth	boss	josh					gong long	doll
U	gruff		fuss	lush			buzz		sung	dull
OO	hoof									wool
'Long'										
A	safe waif	faith	case face		save	bathe	phase daze			male sail
E	leaf reef	heath teeth	cease fleece		leave	breathe	please sneeze			seal
I	life		slice		hive	blithe	rise size			file
O	loaf	loath both	coarse dose		loaves rove	clothe	pose doze			coal hole
U			puce use				muse fuze			yule
OO	proof	tooth	loose		groove	soothe	choose ooze			tool

FIGURE 8.6. Chart of regular English spellings.

266

'Short'	/ p	t	c	k	b	d	j	g	m	n /
A	ap	at	atch	ack	ab	ad	adge	ag	am	an
E	ep	et	etch	eck	eb	ed	edge	eg	em	en
I	ip	it	itch	ick	ib	id	idge	ig	im	in
O	op	ot	otch	ock	ob	od	odge	og	om	on
U	up	ut	utch	uck	ub	ud	udge	ug	um	un
OO		oot		ook		ood				
'Long'										
A	ape	ate		ake	abe	aid ade	age	ague	aim ame	ain ane
E	eep eap	eet eat	eech each	eek eak		eed ead		eague	eam	een ean
I	ipe	ight ite		ike	ibe	ide			ime	ine
O	ope oap	ote oat	oach	oke oak	obe	ode oad	oge	ogue	ome oam	one oan
U		ewt ute		uke	ube	ewd ude	uge	ugue	ume	ewn une
OO	oop	oot	ooch	ook	oob	ood	ooge		oom	oon

FIGURE 8.7. Chart of regular English spellings.

267

'Short'	/ f	th	s	sh	v	dh	z	zh	ng	l
A	aff	ath	,ass	ash	(ave)		azz		ang	al
E	eff	eth	ess	esh					eng	ell
I	iff	ith	iss	ish	(ive)		izz		ing	ill
O	off	oth	oss	osh					ong	oll
U	uff		uss	ush	(ove)		uzz		ung	ull
OO	oof									
'Long'										
A	aif afe	aith	ase ace		ave	athe		(beige)		
E	eef eaf	eeth eath	eese, – ce ease, – ce		eave	eethe eathe	eese, – ze ease, – ze			eel eal
I	ife		ice		ive	ithe	ise ize			ile
O	oaf	ooth oath	ose, – ce oase		ove oave	othe	ose oze			ole oal
U							use uze			we
OO	oof	ooth	oose		oove	oothe	oose ooze			ool

FIGURE 8.8. Chart of regular English spellings.

regular spellings. They are far less important than the facts of the regularities of English orthography and the other great regularities, i.e. before the suffixes *-es, -ed, -en, -ing, -y, -ish, -le, -er, -est* a consonant letter is left single to indicate a preceding long vowel and is doubled to indicate a short vowel.

That these basically simple correspondences between sound and symbol are not always taught has been the principal cause of the functional illiteracy from which so many Americans, adults and children continue to suffer.

Methods of Teaching Spelling*

Following the very thorough discussion of the basic linguistic principles involved in spelling the words of the English language,[5] it seems appropriate to devote some attention to the problems involved in organizing and facilitating a spelling program in elementary schools which will aid children in achieving independence in spelling and a favorable and responsible attitude toward spelling as an important communications tool.

Teachers, working together, and carefully surveying the materials available to them for help in selecting spelling lists, will determine the balance between lists based on linguistic principles and lists which are more functional in nature, but less helpful, perhaps, in terms of achieving pupil independence in spelling. This issue of balance in spelling programs is not the only problem facing teachers interested in effective spelling instruction. Other important problems are:

1. How much time should be devoted to spelling instruction?
2. How can an elementary teacher provide for adequate attention to the wide range of individual differences he will encounter in any group of pupils?
3. What method or methods of presentation and study are most effective for children in the elementary school?
4. What materials are most beneficial in a spelling program? How should a workbook or textbook be used, if at all? What types of audio-visual materials are most effective?

---

*This chapter supplement was prepared by the editor.

5. For interesting and significant discussions of the issues involved in the selection of words for a spelling list, see Richard E. Hodges and E. Hugh Rudorf, "Searching Linguistics for Cues for the Teaching of Spelling," *Elementary English* 42 (May, 1965): 527-533; Albert H. Yee, "The Generalization Controversy in Spelling Instruction," *Elementary English* 43 (February, 1966): 159-160.

Time Allotments for Spelling

The problem of determining the optimum amount of time to devote to spelling instruction is not of recent origin. In 1897 J.M. Rice published an article in the *Forum* dealing with this very issue.[6] Rice reported the results of a study he conducted, which indicated that more time was being devoted to spelling instruction than was justified on the basis of careful examination of pupils' test scores. Children who spent thirty minutes studying spelling appeared to show little superiority over pupils of equal ability who studied fifteen or twenty minutes a day. Petty writes:

> Early studies pointed out the faulty reasoning in expecting improved spelling ability to result from increasing the time devoted to spelling instruction, yet time allotments have recently been increased. In most instances not more than seventy-five minutes per week should be devoted to spelling instruction, and there is evidence that even less time accomplishes equal achievement. In most schools, spelling is taught five periods per week, principally because of the ease in the administration of such a program.[7]

Any discussion of time allotments for spelling instruction must concern itself with the *content* of that instructional period. If, in addition to giving attention to spelling, a teacher can also help to guide growth in handwriting and/or enrich children's vocabularies, this is certainly a desirable bonus. It seems obvious that much teaching and learning of spelling proceeds independent of the period of the day indentified as "spelling" or "language arts." Spelling instruction is going on when a fifth grader consults a dictionary to learn how a word is spelled and when a second grader experiments with several spellings of a word to *see* which one looks "right" to him. Nonetheless, there appears to be some value to devoting some class time to direct instruction related to the principles discussed earlier in this chapter, the identification and correction of spelling errors and the evaluation of pupils growth in spelling. Hugh Rudorf proposes the following objectives for a spelling program:

"The abilities we would be trying to develop would include:

1. The ability to discriminate between the phonemes of a language.
2. The ability to identify the graphemic options of each of the phonemes.

---

6. J.M. Rice, " The Futility of the Spelling Grind," *The Forum* 23 (1897): 169-172.
7. Walter T. Petty, "Handwriting and Spelling: Their Current Status," *Elementary English* 41 (December, 1964): 840.

3. The ability to identify syllables in oral speech.
4. The ability to recognize stress when present.
5. The ability to relate phonemes to their immediate environment.
6. The ability to recognize morphemes (meaningful units of phoneme combinations) such as roots, affixes, and inflections.
7. The ability to utilize certain principles of morphophonemics (how morphemes change in combination to form words; for example, the process of assimilation and synthesis).
8. The ability to relate meaning (as determined by syntax) to spelling (the homonym problem).[8]

It is appropriate to refer here to the problem of dealing adequately with individual differences, regardless of emphasis placed on "utility" versus "phonemic-graphemic regularity" as a basis for the selection of words. Most elementary classes enroll pupils of varying ability and competence in spelling as well as in other subject areas—a range of scores on standardized tests of academic achievement which equals or surpasses the grade level designation (at least three years in third grade, five years in fifth, etc.) is not at all unusual. If fifteen minutes a day, seventy-five minutes a week approaches the maximum time limits which can profitably be spent on spelling instruction, are these limits to be applied to children regardless of ability? Should the same amount of time be planned for the slow, the average, and the bright child?

Because spelling, like the other language arts, is not learned or taught in isolation, the question of how much time to devote to spelling instruction is a difficult one to answer. There is general agreement that incidental instruction, using every opportunity with the group and individual pupils to teach important spelling principles, is essential but by itself inadequate. If time is not scheduled for spelling instruction, this very important skill may be neglected. In deciding how much time to devote to spelling instruction, the teacher must consider the recommendations of state curriculum guides, local courses of study and typical practices in the school in which he teaches. He will also consider the children he is teaching—their strengths, their weaknesses, their attitudes toward spelling and his own ability to make provisions for these differences. An experienced teacher who is skillful in utilizing functional spelling situations—teaching spelling when and as it's needed—may wish

---

8. E. Hugh Rudorf, "Measurement of Spelling Ability," *Elementary English* 42 (December, 1965): 893.

to schedule fewer formal spelling periods. It may also be true that time allotments for spelling will vary from week to week. Some lists may be more difficult than others, or other activities may temporarily displace spelling as a subject of emphasis.

For all of the reasons listed, flexibility is essential. Only after a teacher has familiarized himself with the materials provided for spelling instruction, knows the specific state and local requirements, and above all knows the needs and interests of the children in his class can be answered the important but difficult question, how much time should I devote to spelling instruction?

Adjustment to Individual Differences

A teacher can arrange his spelling program to meet the several ability levels represented in his class in several ways:

1. Lists can be selected which are of varying lengths and/or difficulty levels. Brighter children, children with few spelling problems, can be given either more words to learn, words which are more difficult, or both.
2. Once a basic list has been mastered, children can use the time usually spent studying spelling for some other purpose.
3. Different methods can be used with children of different ability levels. Slow children may need much more direct teacher guidance than bright children or children who seem to learn to spell easily.

There are several advantages to the first method suggested. Differences in interests as well as differences in abilities can be taken into account when lists are varied. Much has been written and said in condemnation of the practice of giving the gifted child "busy work," or "more of the same," rather than challenging him at increasingly higher levels. Thus, it seems wise to use spelling lists of varying difficulty levels and to encourage children to learn to spell words which are foundational to subject areas other than the language arts. The social studies, science, and mathematics are rich sources for words which are of interest and will challenge superior spellers. Simply assigning more words does not appear to be as effective a method for challenging gifted children as helping them select words of somewhat higher difficulty level which are also relevant and interesting to individual children.

It should be noted that there is little evidence of agreement regarding the difficulty level of words among the several spelling series. A word which appears on the second grade list in one published series may appear on the third or even fourth grade list of a different series. Nevertheless, a bright child, with a minimum of teacher help, should be able to select or collate a list of words which is both more challenging and more interesting to him than the standard grade level list. Such lists are, with increasing frequency, being organized and patterned in a manner designed to help children discover and consistently apply the linguistic principles stressed by Professor Johnson. A "pattern" program may require a functional supplement, and of course the reverse is also true.

Study Beyond a Basic List

There are different points of view with reference to children being freed from further spelling work once a basic list has been mastered. It is certainly true that a few words comprise the major portion of the words most commonly written. Ruth Strickland summarized the research in this area as follows:

> The research of Ayres, Thorndike, and Horn provided the basis for many later and more extensive studies of adult writing vocabularies. The most important point to come from these studies was the revelation that a relatively small number of words and their repetitions—not over 3000—accounted for more than 95 percent of the total number of running words tabulated.
>
> Ten thousand words seems a fair estimate of the average person's lifetime writing needs. If children in the elementary school can master 2000 to 2500 basic words, learn how to build other words from them and learn to use a dictionary efficiently, they will be able to meet all their spelling needs.[9]

Once a child has mastered a basic list, why not free him for other learning tasks? There is certainly merit to this position, particularly in this era of the "knowledge explosion." However, limiting a child at a particular grade level to learning only those words on a publisher's adapted list hardly seems wise. Our language is a rich one, with from six hundred thousand to eight hundred thousand words—should not an alert, intelligent child have a chance to explore his language to whatever depth he likes? It appears we must refer again to individual differences. If a child has a very strong interest in math, science or history and is quite impatient with the routine of studying spelling words, then meeting minimal grade level requirements in spelling may be adequate. It is

---

9. Ruth G. Strickland, *The Language Arts in the Elementary School* (Boston: D.C. Heath, 1969), pp. 400-401.

surely wrong, however, to set unnatural limits for children who may well develop a real feeling for words—could perhaps develop some unusual abilities as writers—if their interest in language were encouraged. The availability of materials must be considered in discussing this problem. There are elementary schools without dictionaries, without supplementary spelling books and workbooks, indeed, without libraries! If classes are larger, and materials are limited, a teacher can hardly be blamed for feeling satisfied if grade level requirements are met. Other subject areas provide words, and there are surely other textbooks which can serve as supplementary spelling texts—sources for additional words. It is to be hoped that teachers will encourage interest in language and that facet of language we call "spelling" and that bright children won't be permitted to do the same assignment as everyone else and feel they have done enough when this is accomplished.[10]

Procedures With Children Who Have Difficulty
Learning to Spell

What about the other extreme—the child who is operating well below the level expected of him in spelling? Teachers have tried some of the following techniques and have found them effective:

1. the child chooses a shorter list than the majority of the class, a list he can reasonably be expected to master.
2. from a series other than that regularly used, the child selects a different list—he may work on this list during an independent study period, he may ask another child to help him or he may rely upon special "help sessions" with the teacher or his parents.
3. a child may join a group of children with similar problems and this group may use different words, different study techniques and methods than other classes.

The techniques used will vary from teacher to teacher and from school to school, but most teachers recognize that growth in the mastery of spelling principles requires some attention to the learner, his needs and interests, his strengths and weaknesses. Diagnosing spelling problems and developing a spelling program which takes into account both the structure of our language and the nature of the learner will result in effective mastery of our spelling system.

---

10. Paul Burns and Alberta Lowe, *Language Arts in Childhood Education,* (Chicago: Rand McNally & Co., 1966), pp. 274-275.

Spelling Methods

The two methods most commonly referred to are the "test-study" and the "study-test" method.

For upper grade children who operate at many levels in spelling, it appears to be best to check the pupils' knowledge of a given list prior to asking them to study the list. The "new" list is pronounced, corrected and children see immediately which words they know and which they don't know, which phoneme-grapheme relationships they understand and which they don't understand. They limit their study to mastering the words they don't know. Time, thus, is *not* wasted on "studying" words or patterns with which the child is already familiar.

Although there is some evidence to the contrary, the study-test method appears to be best for young children and for intermediate grade children with spelling problems. The child is given the opportunity to look at the new words, to write them, to locate familiar patterns, etc., before he is tested. Young children may be confused and some unfavorable attitudes toward spelling may result if they are asked to write an entire list of completely unfamiliar words.

Writing words is usually recommended as a study technique rather than oral spelling or "writing words in the air." Oral spelling leads to further sound-written symbol (phoneme-grapheme) confusion and it is certainly true that we have little need for spelling when we're speaking. The various spelling series suggest approved methods for studying a word, and most study routines are something like the following:

1. Look at the unfamiliar words, observe their configurations, known patterns, similarities to words already known, etc.
2. Write the unfamiliar words.
3. Check with a correct copy of the word.
4. If the word has been written correctly, use the same technique for the next word.
5. If the word was missed, apply appropriate word analysis techniques—phonetic analysis, structural analysis, etc.—as well as careful observation of the total word as presented.

Several word sources have already been suggested. It has been recommended that a child be permitted to adjust and select, to make the spelling list fit him, rather than trying to fit a list. If a basic list is to be mastered, it can be shortened, supplemented or altered in terms of group or individual abilities, needs and interests. It has already been suggested that lists be presented which will help a child discover many of the regular patterns in our language, perhaps supplemented by words which the child recognizes he needs to spell correctly.

In the primary grades, groups of children may keep a box, alphabetized and indexed, using 3 x 5 index cards to which they add words they are interested in learning to spell. This box also serves as a source for words needed in writing.

Intermediate and upper grade pupils may profit more by keeping individual lists—in a shorthand notebook, perhaps. Such a book should also be alphabetized for easy reference.

Teachers occasionally ask children to draw pictures illustrating these words, to write simple definitions or to use them in sentences. It should be kept in mind that establishing a single definition of a word may not be as beneficial to a child as exploring the many meanings of a word like "run."

Charts listing frequently used words—words related to a unit of work, perhaps, or to a subject of high interest to the children, are helpful in developing an awareness of the importance of spelling and, of course, for reference by children in preparing reports, writing stories and adding to their vocabularies.

Standards for Spelling

Children should accept responsibility for correct spelling whenever communication with someone else or a group is the objective. Proofreading is an important skill. It can be taught and learned. Teachers frequently criticize children for failing to check their work, but teachers have too frequently neglected to provide either the "check points" or the time necessary for proofreading. Even a primary grade teacher should help children determine the qualities essential for an acceptable letter or report (correct spelling is certainly one of the most important of these qualities) and should remind children occasionally that following the established criteria is a primary responsibility of a writer and a debt he owes to those with whom he wants to communicate.

It is also true, however, that the ideas expressed are generally more important than correctly spelled words. At least this is true when the object is self-expression and creativeness. Strict application of spelling rules may inhibit a child's creativity in the initial stages especially. Of course, if the poem is to be a part of a bulletin board display or is to be included in a class notebook or newspaper it will be read carefully, and perfected to the limits of the child's ability. Flexibility in applying standards of acceptable spelling is desirable, and probably *helps* a child's writing more than it *hinders* his spelling.

Materials for Spelling Instruction

Traditionally the hard-backed speller and the spelling workbook have been the most important if not the only spelling tools. These are frequently organized so that there is one activity for each day of the week—a pretest on Monday,* a phonics exercise on Tuesday, sentences using the words are written Wednesday (or sometimes a second test is administered) another word analysis skill exercise is provided on Thursday, and almost always the final test is given on Friday. A program of this sort requires little planning by the teacher, and perhaps meets the needs of the middle third of the class. Each child is required to learn, or to try to learn the same number of words, using the same methods. For reasons which should be clear to any careful observer of children, such a spelling program is, by itself, inadequate. It is frustrating to the child who has great difficulty with spelling, and boring to the child who spells with ease. Several methods for supplementing this type of program have already been suggested. Individually selected lists, group lists, and adjustments in the one list which a teacher may be expected to use should help to make the spelling program more interesting, more challenging and more effective. Several spelling series now include suggestions to the teacher for varying and supplementing the program.

Dictionaries of several types, at several levels, are an essential part of an effective spelling program. The same dictionary for each pupil can hardly be justified in classrooms where many different reading materials are available at many levels. Publishers have recently made available picture dictionaries, beginning dictionaries, and junior dictionaries, as well as dictionaries designed to help children progress from one dictionary level to the next. If proofreading and checking work prior to handing it in are to be encouraged, dictionaries should be easily available to

---

*It is somewhat difficult to see the purpose of the pretest since children proceed through all the other exercises whether all of the words were missed or none.

children.[11] Even a vast number of copies kept in the school library will hardly serve these purposes.

Teacher-made worksheets—crossword puzzles, fill-in-the-blank exercises, etc.—serve a very useful purpose. These can be devised to accompany individual lists or lists chosen by a small group. Pages or exercises from spelling workbooks can be used, and children can locate for themselves the exercises, puzzles, or tests they need if the sheets are filed according to the type of help they can provide—"initial consonants," "syllabication," etc.

One device which has proved extremely useful to teachers who want to individualize their spelling programs is the tape recorder. A teacher can record a particular list, pausing enough between the words pronounced easily to allow the child time for writing the word. Even the correct spelling can be pronounced, or the child can find his own correct copy of the list to see where he has made mistakes. A program has been described in which each child has his own tape on which he records his own list for testing purposes. The tapes are, of course, erased after each list has been mastered and can be used indefinitely.[12]

Charts and lists of words on the chalkboard or bulletin board should also be referred to in any discussion of spelling aids.

Commercially prepared games, "Scrabble," for example, or "Anagrams" may prove interesting to older children. Adaptations of some popular word games also are available for younger children.

Space does not permit a discussion of other aids for teaching and learning spelling—a resourceful teacher will find many ways and devices to enhance and vary what can be but should not be a dull, routine area of the elementary curriculum. Learning to spell can be a key to a useful and interesting facet of our language for teachers and pupils as well.

EXTENDING YOUR LEARNING

1. Of the fourteen vowel sounds, ten have regular spelling patterns. Look at the charts of regularly spelled words and Figure 4. Using the key words, how would you lead students to discover for themselves the regular use of final -e, and of single and double consonant letters, to indicate short and long A, E, I, O, and U?
2. Take two different desk dictionaries that have dissimilar pronunciation keys. On the chart, record the symbols that each one uses for the fourteen vowel sounds.

---

11. The entire April, 1964, issue of *Elementary English* is devoted to a discussion of elementary school dictionaries and their use.

12. Dorothy Johnson, "Spelling Self-Taught from Magnetic Tape," *Elementary School Journal* 63 (November, 1962): 78-82.

Chart of English Vowel Grapho-phonemes

Long	Phonemic Symbol	Dictionary	Short	Phonemic Symbol	Dictionary
A	/ey/		A	/ æ /	
E	/iy/		E	/ e /	
I	/ay/		I	/ i /	
O	/ow/		O	/a, ɔ/	
U	/uw,yuw/		U	/ ə /	
OO	/uw/		OO	/u /	
OY	/oy/		——		
OU	/aw/		——		

3. Survey two or three dictionaries[13],[14] designed for use in the elementary school. Are the systems of diacritical markings used the same or different? How are the following words "phonetically" described in each dictionary?

apple	acre
better	leisure
kitten	mighty
cotton	bloated
cutting	fusion

4. What is a "schwa"? (Consult the same dictionaries used to complete the first exercise.) Why does one dictionary use the schwa in a word like "up" /əp/ while another shows it as follows: ŭp? Would you or would you not encourage children to compare and contrast various dictionaries? Would this be enriching or confusing?

5. Consider the influence of dialect upon spelling. Can children correctly spell words containing sounds they neither use nor hear?
   In an area where *witch* and *which* are pronounced identically, you would not try to teach them to pronounce them differently. However, draw up a list of homonyms (like *witch*/*which*, for areas without /hw/) that the students must learn to *spell* differently.

6. If you are an Easterner who has three different vowel sounds in *merry*, *marry* and *Mary*, how will you teach the spelling of those three different families of words to Western children for whom they are homonyms as are *ferry*/*fairy*, *very*/*vary*, *Harry*/*hairy* and others?

7. If you are from the large area of the Southeast and Southwest where *pen* rhymes with *pin* and *gem* rhymes with *Jim*, you probably pronounce all words with short I or short E before /n/ and /m/, with the same vowel sound. How would you plan, without the help of a Professor Higgins to change your dialect, to teach Northern or Western children the spelling of such words?

8. If you are from the West Coast and pronounce such words as *cot* and *caught*, *odd* and *awed* alike, how will you help children from the same area learn the different spellings of the same sound?

9. What might be the cumulative effect of a phonetic alphabet like i/t/a on children's spelling? Several studies have dealt with this very problem; present the findings to your class in the form of an oral report or panel discussion.

13. G. and C. Merriam Webster, *Webster's Elementary Dictionary* (Springfield, Massachusetts: G. and C. Merriam Co., 1965).
14. Thorndike, Barnhart, *Beginning Dictionary* (Chicago: Scott, Foresman Company, 1964).

10. Survey several spelling series and note any phonetic inconsistencies in the lists— are *come* and *home* presented in the same lesson?
11. Develop a spelling lesson plan, consisting of no more than two typewritten pages based upon the development of one or two of the linguistic principles, discussed in section one of this chapter. List objectives, procedures, materials and evaluative techniques (consult Chapter 11).
12. If you are interested in teaching young children, develop a picture dictionary containing only pictured words with regular and consistent spellings.
13. The feature of /r/-lessness in the speech of a student, black or white, from any Atlantic coastal area from New England to Louisiana, may cause spelling problems. How will you deal with the fact that the following pairs of words, and many others, are and will remain homonyms: guard-god, sore-saw, par-Pa, court-caught, Carol-Cal, Paris-pass.
14. The feature of /l/-lessness is a less widespread problem but occurs in the speech of many Southeasterners and Southwesterners. How would you incorporate into your teaching the fact that the following pairs of words, and many others, are and will remain homonyms: toll, told-toe; help-hep; all-awe; tool-too, to, two; fault-fought.
15. The simplification of final clusters in Black English and that of others leads to even more problems than those in 13 and 14 because of the loss in pronunciation of the common endings *-es, -'s, -s', -ed.* Assume that the student understands the grammar and semantics involved and plan treating sets of homonyms like the following, as a grapho-phonemic problem. Pass-past-passed; fine-finedfind; Ben-bent-bend; poll-pole-polled-poled.

BIBLIOGRAPHY

Allen, Harold Boughton (ed.) Readings in *Applied English Linguistics*, second ed. New York: Appleton-Century-Crofts, 1964.

Bloomfield, Leonard. *Language.* New York: Holt, Rinehart and Winston, 1933.

Bloomfield, Leonard and Clarence Barnhart. *Let's Read: A Linguistic Approach.* Detroit: Wayne State University Press, 1961.

Brooks, Nelson. *Language and Language Learning.* Theory and Practice. New York: Harcourt, Brace & World, Inc., 1960, 238 pp.

Chomsky, Noam. *Syntactic Structures:* The Hague: Mouton and Co., 1957.

——. *Aspects of the Theory of Syntax.* Cambridge: The M.I.T. Press, 1965.

—— and Morris Halle. *The Sound Pattern of English.* New York: Harper & Row, 1968.

Fries, Charles G. *Teaching and Learning English as a Foreign Language.* London: Macmillan and Co., Ltd., 1957. 124 pp.

——. *Linguistics and Reading,* New York, Holt, 1964.

Gleason, Henry Allan, Jr. *Workbook in Descriptive Linguistics.* New York: Holt, Rinehart, and Winston, 1955.

——. *An Introduction to Descriptive Linguistics,* rev. ed. New York: Holt, Rinehart and Winston, 1961.

——. *Linguistics and English Grammar.* New York: Holt, Rinehart, and Winston, 1965.

Hall, Robert A., Jr. *Introductory Linguistics.* Philadelphia: Chilton Books, 1965.

——. *Sound and Spelling in English.* Philadelphia: Chilton Books, 1961.

Labov, William "Some Sources of Reading Problems for Negro Speakers of Non-standard English," *Teaching Black Children to Read*, ed. Baratz and Shuy. Washington, D.C.: Center for Applied Linguistics, 1969.

Lamb, Pose. "Linguistics and the Teaching of Spelling," Ch. 3, *Linguistics in Proper Perspective* Columbus, Ohio: Charles Merrill Publishing Co., 1967.

Langacker, Ronald W. *Language and Its Structure*. New York: Harcourt, Brace and World, 1968.

Lefevre, Carl. *Linguistics and The Teaching of Reading*. New York: McGraw-Hill, 1964.

Ohannessian, Sirarpi. *Interim Bibliography on the Teaching of English to Speakers of Other Languages*. Washington, D.C.: Center for Applied Linguistics, 1960. 53 pp.

Sapir, Edward. *Language: An Introduction to the Study of Speech*. New York: Harcourt, Brace and World, 1921.

Stageberg, Norman C. *An Introductory English Grammar*. New York: Holt, Rinehart and Winston, 1965.

Stevick, Earl. *Helping People Learn English*. New York: Abingdon Press, 1957.

Trager, Edith C. and Sara Cook Henderson. *Pronunciation Drills for The Learners of English: The P.D.'s*. Washington, D.C.: English Language Services, 800-18th St., N.W., reprinted 1964.

——. "The Systematics of English Spelling." Reprint Series in Language and Linguistics, No. 89. New York: Bobbs Merrill, 1964.

Trager, George Leonard, and Henry Lee Smith, Jr. *An Outline of English Structure*. (Studies in Linguistics, Occasional Papers, No. 3). Reprinted, Washington, D.C.: American Council of Learned Societies, 1957.

Waterman, John Thomas. *Perspectives in Linguistics*. Chicago: University of Chicago Press, 1963.

Focus

Linguistics; again. Dr. Hochstetler's particular field of interest is in grammar and usage, an area already identified as being of great interest to linguistic scholars.

Elementary teachers have some difficulty accepting the concept that a *descriptive* approach to language study is to be preferred to a *prescriptive* approach. If a child says "He don't" this is obviously "wrong" isn't it? Furthermore, elementary teachers are taught that learning is best defined as behavior change, and isn't movement toward "standard" English the direction in which we want the child's language behavior to change? What tends to be overlooked in this debate, which tends to become very emotional and unscientific, is that language change (social, regional and chronological) makes it very difficult to precisely determine what is standard. (A case in point: when did the reader last use or hear 'whom'?) This problem is discussed by the author, and the result, hopefully, will be a more tolerant, more enlightened and less emotional approach to language study and usage.

Several approaches to the study of grammar are identified and the most prevalent ones, in terms of classroom use, traditional, structural and transformational, are discussed in some detail. An interesting development has occurred since Dr. Hochstetler wrote the chapter for the first edition. During the early sixties one could observe an intellectual "battle" between the structuralists and the transformationalists, and the traditionalists, supposedly, represented an obsolete and useless position. The reader will note that efforts to change terminology (Form Class One instead of 'Noun') have been abandoned, for the most part, and most traditional vocabulary has been kept. Transformationalists as well as structuralists refer to sentence patterns, and the concept of "kernel" sentences is no longer so basic to transformational grammar.

The reader will note that there is little agreement regarding the number of basic sentence types. This is obvious when one reviews the newer elementary language arts texts as well. There is a trend toward identifying fewer types and *not* considering the verb *to be* as requiring entirely different treatment than other verbs.

Grammar, like handwriting, is seldom a teacher's "favorite" subject. It is hoped that some positive attitude change may result from reading and reacting to this chapter.

Ruth Hochstetler

chapter nine

facets of language – grammar and usage

Words, words, words! Our eyes, ears, and senses are bombarded with words. Some are pleasing; some are shocking; some are full of caring; some are filled with hate; some are telling facts; some are selling fiction, but all are being used for the purpose of communicating. Language is "the center of human experience." It is language that makes us human. It is language that helps us make sense out of our world.

If language becomes a living, fascinating part of a student's life, he begins to understand the limitless possibilities of language. When an individual becomes aware of just how it is that language helps him to replace and discover, to question and understand, to shift and change, and to shape and create, then he knows the wonders of language. If a teacher possesses the understanding and the feeling of the magnitude of language, he is likely to excite students in their study of language.[1]

The Importance of Language

Language is basic to a child's individual development as well as to his role as a participating member of social groups. Children grow in self-knowledge as they learn to use their language with effectiveness. Without understanding between and among people there can be little real

---

1. James E. Miller, Jr., "The Linguistic Imagination," *Elementary English* XLVII (April, 1970): 467-475.

empathy and there may be far too few who live harmoniously in a world where harmony is desperately needed.

Clear communication requires clear thinking and language is basic to this process. Language is involved with information, ideas and values. A person's feelings about his self depends upon his use of language, the response of others to his language and the feelings produced by the relationships which grow from his communication with others. Paul Roberts has stated that. . ."to understand your language is. . .to understand yourself, to get a notion of what it means to be a human being."[2]

There are many ways to define language. Commonly accepted are the following basic ideas about language. Most linguists agree that

1. Language is an arbitrary system.
2. Language is a human activity.
3. Language is based on convention.
4. Language is culturally transmitted.
5. Language is highly complicated.

James Bostain defines language as a social phenomenon, an activity that people engage in.[3] In *Curricula for the Seventies,* Frost and Rowland indicate that "language, broadly conceived, is the communicative vehicle for all human expression."[4] In his publication *Linguistics and Language Teaching,* John Hughes, a linguist, defines language as "the arbitrary system of vocal symbols by which thought is conveyed from one human being to another."[5] A rather complicated definition of language is one attributed to Dr. Owen Thomas of Indiana University. He states that language is "a set of sentences formulated from a set of elements, according to a set of operations, that obey a set of laws."[6] Professor Raven McDavid of the University of Chicago defines language as "the arrangement of meaningful words built up by derivational and inflectional suffixes, all pronounced by human beings in social con-

2. Paul Roberts, *English Sentences: Teachers' Manual* (New York: Harcourt, Brace & World, 1962), p. 6.

3. James C. Bostain, "The Dream World of English Grammar," *National Education Association Journal,* reprint (September, 1966).

4. Joe L. Frost and G. Thomas Rowland, *Curricula for the Seventies* (Boston: Houghton Mifflin Company, 1969), p. 232.

5. John P. Hughes, *Linguistics and Language Teaching* (New York: Random House, 1968), p. 143.

6. William A. Jenkins, "Let's Look at Language," in Andrew Schiller, et al., *Language and How to Use It* (Glenview, Illinois: Scott, Foresman and Co., 1969), p. xvii.

text."[7] Language is variously termed a skill, a medium, and a subject for study depending upon whether those discussing it are concerned with one particular aspect of language or another. Some of the foregoing statements are comprehensive; however, Mauree Applegate's aptly put phrase "to give children. . . a more personal vision of the world of words"[8] describes the challenge offered to elementary teachers.

Definition of Grammar

The focus of this chapter is on grammar and usage so that it seems desirable and necessary to define the two terms. A Random House Dictionary definition of grammar is that it is "the study of the system underlying the especially formal features of a language, as the sounds, morphemes, words, or sentences; a theory specifying the manner in which all sentences of a language are constructed."[9] From the same source comes this definition of usage—"the customary manner in which a language or a form of a language is spoken or written: English usage; a grammar based on usage rather than on arbitrary notions of correctness."[10] Schiller, one of the authors of a new language series states that grammar is a body of knowledge—something you know about language. He speaks of $Grammar_1$ as the system, $Grammar_2$ as some kind of description and explanation of the system, and $Grammar_3$ as usage since the systems vary in syntax, vocabulary, and/or pronunciation.[11]

If a study of grammar is a way of finding out how a system operates then there is an infinite number of grammars possible but the study of grammar in an eclectic, systematic way seems most likely to meet the needs of today's children. The concern of teachers should be with the ways in which an understanding of the language can help children improve their own oral and written expression. Research supports the conclusion that very little teaching of grammar as it has traditionally been done has helped children speak or write more effectively. The increasing amount of knowledge about children and how they learn or acquire language; the contributions to the thinking about language from

---

7. Jenkins, *op. cit.*, p. xvii.
8. Mauree Applegate, *Easy in English* (Evanston: Row Peterson and Company, 1960), p. 25.
9. Jess Stein, editor, *The Random House Dictionary of the English Language* (New York: Random House, 1966), p. 614.
10. Stein, *op. cit.*, p. 173.
11. Andrew Schiller, "A Few Words About Grammar in General and This Book in Particular," *Language and How We Use It* (Glenview, Illinois: Scott Foresman and Company, 1969), Book 5, p. x.

sociologists, linguists, social psychologists and others interested and concerned with language development; the technological media; and the multiplicity of materials for use in helping children develop language are all responsible for modification and change in the language programs in elementary schools.

An effective teacher knows and uses the understanding he has of language as an essential part of the growth process; he knows that emphasis should be placed on real experiences with meaning and purpose for the youngsters who live and learn through them; and he knows that materials and methods should fit each individual child—not all children need the same material or need to be taught in the same way. Children from varying cultures have varying patterns of usage and differing vocabularies and need teachers who can and will modify language experiences in the classroom so as to exhibit respect for different dialects. Practice is needed but only after understanding is there. Often, in the past, rules were learned and practiced with little or no understanding. Generalizations can be formed by children themselves if there are many opportunities to do useful speaking and writing. A teacher knows that language experiences are good for learning only if the learner has feelings and attitudes that allow and encourage him to learn. In no part of the curriculum is it more obvious that a person learns only that which he feels is necessary to learn or that which he wants to learn than in the field of language.

Varying Approaches to the Teaching of Grammar

What grammar should be taught? This is a question which is not easily answered. To approximate an answer, one needs time, imagination, knowledge and an understanding of the process of education. These, plus a wise use of words, are a necessity. There are differing views as to the most effective way of teaching grammar. Some authorities have denied that there is as wide a difference between what has been called traditional grammar, structural grammar, transformation-generative grammar, stratificational grammar,[12] and tagmemic-generative grammar,[13] as the proponents of each might have us believe.

If the purpose of teaching grammar is to help children develop their

---

12. For a discussion of stratificational grammar, see Lamb, *Outline of Stratificational Grammar.*
13. For a description of tagmemics, see Hughes, *Linguistics and Language Learning,* Bolinger, *Aspects of Language* and the 69th NSSE Yearbook, *Linguistics in School Programs.*

own language abilities to the utmost of their capabilities, then what kind of grammar will accomplish it? An elementary teacher needs to have some knowledge of varying viewpoints so that he can make judgments with some degree of knowing. It may be an oversimplification to discuss only three of the many types of grammars; however, many authors list traditional, structural, and transformational grammar as those most widely used in elementary schools.

Traditional Grammar

Traditional grammar has been maligned and excluded by some and praised by others who appear to be more conservative. The diagramming of sentences which was intended to show the relationship of parts of speech in a sentence and was purported to improve the diagrammer's writing was held in high favor by those who believed in traditional grammar. Such practices as diagramming sentences and "filling in blanks" in English exercises are of questionable utility for a person learning to write. In some instances, systematic study, formal, and nonfunctional grammar have been regarded as synonymous terms. Traditional grammar has as its objective the achievement of certain grammatical abilities. Considered important are a knowledge of the parts of speech; the ability to define and recognize structural elements of sentences such as subjects, predicates, complements, and modifiers of all types; the ability to choose preferred forms of usage; knowledge of grammatical terms such as case, number, voice, tense, mood, agreement, and comparison; the ability to diagram sentences and to recognize sentence faults which are associated with predication, pronoun reference, parallelism, placement of modifiers and tense sequence. Most research studies prior to 1960 have negated the consistently held belief that an understanding of grammar is related to skill in speech and writing. Grammarians used Latin as their model when they tried to fit English into the pattern of Latin grammar. Many of the rules being taught are those which hold true for Latin grammar but not for the English language since English has lost most of its inflectional endings.

Because children learn their language through imitation and are able to use structures of the language and to produce these in sentence form without the knowledge of its structure, an analytical approach to understanding seems to meet no need of a child. On the other hand, a well-developed grammar does have value in describing the structural system of the language. If there is understanding of the function of the system and the ability to work within it, there is value because it helps a child to use his language effectively.

Traditional grammar has also been called conventional, formal, systematic, prescriptive and normative. Shane and Mulry have listed representative writers who seem to sympathize with a thoroughgoing emphasis on grammar.[14] Some writers do not advocate a return to language drills but do favor a better job of teaching grammar. On the other hand, there is research which shows little correlation between certain factors in grammar and in the ability to write or speak with more facility.

Structural Grammar

In 1933, Leonard Bloomfield's *Language* was published and it generated interest in a more intensive study of English. Structural linguists emphasized the analysis of the spoken language since the techniques of the development of structural grammar were used often in the analysis of unwritten language. The importance of word order and the concept of word classes were introduced into the thinking of those interested in teaching grammar. Pioneer studies by Whitehall, Smith and Trager, Hill, Lloyd and Warfel, and Roberts are reported in an October 1959 issue of *Elementary English* by John J. DeBoer.[15] These have added to information about the basic forms and patterns of speech.

Linguistics is concerned with basic components of a language and the patterns in which these components operate. To understand structural grammar, one needs to understand that phonemes are the smallest distinctive speech sounds and morphemes are the smallest meaningful units of sound. The word boy contains two phonemes, /b/ and /oy/. These two phonemes make up one morpheme. An actual utterance or sentence contains both morphemes and phonemes as well as other linguistic concepts. Classes of words or parts of speech, word arrangement, sentence patterns and signals which indicate meaning are further concerns of linguists. Linguistics attempts to describe language by showing how items combine whereas conventional grammar is concerned with classification.[16]

Lefevre has subdivided language as a whole into the following signal-

---

14. Harold G. Shane and June G. Mulry, *Improving Language Arts Instruction Through Research* (Washington: National Education Association, 1963), p. 89.

15. John J. DeBoer, "Grammar in Language Teaching," *Elementary English* 36 (October, 1959): 413-421.

16. Wilmar Trauger, *Language Arts in Elementary Schools* (New York: McGraw-Hill Book Company, Inc., 1963), p. 149.

ing systems: intonation, sentence patterns, structure words and word-form changes. He included levels of pitch, stress or accent, and junctures or pauses as parts of the overall intonation pattern. There is little agreement on the number of sentence patterns which are commonly found in the language of English speaking people. Lefevre has stated that there are four important sentence patterns but that these may be varied by inversion, by substitution, and by pattern transformation. Function or structure words are the standard, interchangeable parts of sentence patterns. Such words as determiners or noun markers (a, an, the, our, my); intensifiers (very, just, less, more); auxiliaries or verb makers (can, could, might); clause markers (because, if, since or when, that); phrase markers or prepositions (in, down, toward, with, under); question markers (how, what, where, which, who); and conjunctions or connectors (and, but, for, or, now, yet, so) are known as structure words. The final signaling system is that of word-form changes. This system includes grammatical inflections of the four word classes and derivational prefixes and suffixes. Nouns and verbs are inflected by endings indicating plurals, and the verb forms which are classified as past, past participle, and present participle have the following inflections: The -ed ending for past, the -ed/-en ending for the past participle, and the -ing ending for the present participle. Comparative and superlative adjective and adverb endings are inflectional changes also. A derivational change such as adding -able to peace makes the noun become an adjective. In the same manner, a verb may be changed to an adjective, e.g., -able added to adapt to make adaptable.[17]

Finally, structural grammar gets at meaning through structure and emphasizes the need for children to learn to become consciously aware of the sentence patterns which they use so easily in speech. Sentences can be grammatical and nonsensical, that is, as far as word form and orders are concerned, the sentence which follows is grammatically correct.

Tall buildings skip merrily down the street.

No one agrees that the above is a meaningful or truthful statement. But it does follow the rules of English grammar. Hence, it is grammatical, though nonsensical.

Gradually children will learn that the formal patterns can be ex-

---

17. Helen Lefevre and Carl Lefevre, *Writing by Patterns* (New York: Alfred A. Knopf, 1965), p. 4.

panded and changed in an infinite number of ways. Infinite variety means choice and choice enables a person to grow in his own way.

There have been researchers who have attempted to determine the values inherent in the structural grammar approach. Kraus compared three methods of teaching sentence structure and concluded that all classes made significant gains in reducing errors and detecting weaknesses in sentence structure and that one group achieved greater gain in less time by identifying errors in their own writing and having further instruction as needed.[18]

A review of research in language arts during 1968 reported by Sheldon and Lashinger listed 76 studies. Many were in the area of reading; however, there is an increase in research in other aspects of language arts. The *Journal of Verbal Learning and Verbal Behavior* reported some 200 studies on verbal learning, psycholinguistics and other related verbal processes.[19]

Structural studies of language emphasize the importance of the formal structure of an English sentence. Some of these are the studies of Hook and Matthews, Fries, Loban, and Glanzer as reported by Squire.[20] Squire has reviewed selected research with respect to processes of perception and his comments in the April 1965 *Elementary English* on form consciousness in the teaching of language are extremely provocative.[21]

More recently, Ruddell and Graves investigated the relationship between the degree of syntactical language development and socio-ethnic status of beginning first grade children. A test of syntax administered individually to high socio-economic Caucasians and low socio-economic Negro children yielded an error rate that was analyzed. There was a significant positive correlation between error rate and socio-ethnic status. They concluded that the difference in error rate on familiar items was a reflection of the high socio-economic Caucasian group's exposure to standard English used by adult language models during preschool years.[22] In a study in Detroit, Shuy determined the features

18. Silvy Kraus, "A Comparison of Three Methods of Teaching Sentence Structure," *English Journal* 46 (May, 1957): 275-285, 311.

19. William Sheldon and Donald R. Lashinger, "A Summary of Research Studies Relating to Language Arts in Elementary Education: 1968," *Elementary English* 46 (November, 1969): 866-885.

20. James R. Squire, "Form Consciousness, An Important Variable in Teaching Language, Literature, and Composition," *Elementary English* 42 (April, 1965): 379-390.

21. Squire, *op. cit.*, pp. 381-383.

22. Robert B. Ruddell and Barbara W. Graves, "Socio-ethnic Status and the Language Achievement of First Grade Children," *Elementary English* 45 (May, 1968): 635-642.

which characterized the speech of different social groups, races, age groups and sexes. He tape recorded and analyzed 700 interviews from all parts of the city. His conclusions were:

1. Each social dialect had a structure adequate for its users.
2. Specific phonological and grammatical features and processes which characterize different groups are observable.[23]

Such research emphasizes the importance of early language models and the necessity to recognize the validity of dialectical differences.

The English Sentence

Since the structural approach to grammar is based upon the premise that English syntax can be explained by isolating and identifying phrases, clauses, and sentences, a definition of a sentence would seem to be in order. A sentence is not always a complete thought—it may be an expression such as, "Hi!," "What a day," or "Not yet," in response to "Have you eaten yet?" Lamb, writing in *Linguistics in Proper Perspective* states that " 'The basic English sentence seems to be the simple declaration, having as its immediate constituents a subject and a predicate!' "[24] Authors differ in their definitions of a sentence but many seem to include the idea that a simple sentence has two main parts, a subject or noun phrase and a predicate or a verb phrase. In order to understand and make use of the structure of the English language, it is necessary to know what an utterance or a sentence is and what part words play because of their forms. Structural linguists seem not as much concerned with meaning as with the classification of form classes or parts of speech and the order within an utterance which determines their function.

Francis has said that every construction found in a grammatical English sentence belongs to one of the following types: it is a modification (white house); it is a predication (birds have been singing); it is a subordination (along the street); it is a complementation (cutting the grass); or it is a coordination (peace and prosperity). He also maintains that every constituent is either a construction or a single word and that no

23. Roger W. Shuy, "Detroit Speech: Careless, Awkward, and Inconsistent, or Systematic, Graceful, and Regular," *Elementary English* 45 (May, 1968): 565-569.
24. Pose Lamb, *Linguistics in Proper Perspective* (Columbus, Ohio: Charles E. Merrill Publishing Company, 1967), p. 108.

string of words which does not constitute a construction can be a constituent of a larger construction.[25]

The most familiar definition of a sentence is that a sentence is a group of words that expresses a complete thought. Sledd uses, "It is.", as an example of words which can be called a sentence. This conclusion is not based on the familiar definition, however. One could find sentences in which the terminal is indicated by a different pitch, i.e.,

Did you go?

I think he left.

But this alone will not identify a sentence. Variance in pitch is sometimes difficult to hear. Another means is by testing what seems to be a sentence to determine whether there is a complete subject and a complete predicate. There are also "sentence fragments" which are correct English utterances. But these do not meet the requisites. A third condition is to determine whether the sentence contains at least one independent clause.[26]

Sentence Patterns

Common sentence patterns are basic and individuals use them automatically if they have learned English as a native speaker. A child learns a limited set of rules from which he can build and comprehend an infinite set of sentences.

Roger Brown and his associates have collected data on the development of syntax in children's speech. Researchers worked out the children's grammar at every stage of their development. The evolution of syntactic rules and sentence types was similar from one child to another.[27]

Children normally learn single words and use these as sentences up to about a year and a half. This is followed by "telegraphic speech"—a sort of child memorization of adult sentences with the grammatical elements and unstressed words omitted. Individual children use "pivot words"—these are words of high frequency and they occur in the initial position combined with words that are in the remainder class. These may match adult classes of words. After the pivot system, children grow

---

25. W. Nelson Francis, *The English Language: An Introduction* (New York: W.W. Norton and Company, 1965), p. 20.

26. James Sledd, *A Short Introduction to English Grammar* (Chicago: Scott, Foresman and Company, 1959), p. 166.

27. Jean Berko Gleason, "Language Development in Early Childhood," in *Oral Language and Reading,* edited by James Walden (Champaign: National Council of Teachers of English, 1969), p. 19.

rapidly in grammatical development and know a limited set of rules by the age of four or four and a half. These are the rules governing the patterning of sentences.

Structural linguists have grouped sentences by patterns but not all are precisely the same. Paul Roberts has a widely used grouping. He uses the following ten patterns:

1.	N	V	(Adv.)			Dolls dance (nicely).
2.	N	V	Adj.			The cabin seems damp.
3.	N	V-transitive	N			Bill found a letter.
4.	N	V-become	N			Ann became a bride.
5.	N	V-give	N	N		The man gave my mother a picture.
6.	N	V-consider	N	N		He considered Sally a beauty.
7.	N	V-elect	N	N		They elected Bill the president.
8.	N	V-be	Adv.			The crowd was outside.
9.	N	V-be	Adj.			The day was hot.
10.	N	V-be	N			They were farmers.

The experimental materials from the Nebraska Curriculum Development Center[28] list five basic patterns as the early structural approach:

1.	N	V	(a) adverb	
2.	N	V	A	
3.	N	be	N	
4.	N	V	N	
5.	N	V	N	N

Lefevre lists the following basic patterns:

Pattern I

N	V		Your letter	came.	
N	V	Adv.	Bill	has worked	all day.
N	V	Adj.	The group	arrived	hungry.

Pattern II

N	V	N	I	flew	the airplane.

(According to the author, this is the most common pattern.)

---

28. Nebraska Curriculum Development Center, *A Curriculum for English: Language Explorations for Elementary Grades* (Lincoln: The University of Nebraska, 1966), pp. 95-96.

Pattern III

N	V	N	N	Dad	thought	me	a tomboy.

(call, choose, consider, elect, think,
give, bring, buy, do, cause and others)

Pattern IV

N	LV (linking verb)	N	Mary	will be	a housewife.
N	LV	Adj.	The candy	was	sweet.
N	LV	Adv.	Tom	is	in the house.[29]

Borgh, in 1963, gave five variations of the simple declarative sentence.

	Subject	Predicate
I	(d) N or Pro	V-int + (Adv)

Where d is a determiner
N is a noun
Pro is a pronoun
V-int is an intransitive verb
Adv is an adverb

	The baby	sleeps.
II	(d) N[1] or Pro[1]	(Aux) V-t + (d) N[2] (Adv)
	The clown	took the circus seriously.
III	(d) N[1] or Pro[1]	be or Lv (d) N[1] or Pro[1]
	He	was the speaker.
IV	(d) N or Pro	be or Lv Adj.
	The night	seemed dark.
V	(d) N or Pro	be Adv. (place, time)
	The president	is here.[30]

Postman indicated basic sentence patterns by using numerals rather than initials. For instance, his four sentence patterns are:

---

29. Lefevre, *Writing by Patterns,* pp. 11-13.

30. Enola Borgh, *Grammatical Patterns and Composition* (Madison: Wisconsin Council of Teachers of English, 1963), pp. 4-6.

1. 1	2	1	Girls like boys.
2. 1	2L	1	Girls are people.
3. 1	2L	3	Girls are loving.
4. 1	2	4	Girls cry easily.[3][1]

Tibbett's "The Grammatical Revolution That Failed" is an article which questions whether the New Grammarians have "won" the revolution in English grammar. He states that the new grammarians made mistakes in theory; they failed to derive practical applications from their theory; and they failed to acknowledge the importance of language as a civilizing force. In illustrating the above points, he indicates that one can take the definition of the term sentence as a case in point. Traditional grammarians were concise and to the point with a useful definition that could be used in a school room while the New Grammarians either constructed their definitions from a base of philosophical reasoning that confused the student; they were often wordy; or there was no attempt to define the term at all.[3][2]

A recent language series which advocates a logical, systematic approach to the teaching of grammar and which is admittedly eclectic presents the following patterns or formulas:

$$NP + Vi + \begin{Bmatrix} adv. \\ prep.\ phr. \end{Bmatrix}$$

$$NP + V_t + NP + \begin{Bmatrix} adv. \\ prep.\ phr. \end{Bmatrix}$$

$$NP + V_t + NP_1 + NP_2 \begin{Bmatrix} adv. \\ prep.\ phr. \end{Bmatrix}$$

$$NP + be + \begin{Bmatrix} adv. \\ prep.\ phr. \\ adj. \\ NP \end{Bmatrix} + \begin{Bmatrix} adv. \\ prep.\ phr. \end{Bmatrix}$$

$$NP + V_L + \begin{Bmatrix} adj. \\ NP \end{Bmatrix} + \begin{Bmatrix} adv. \\ prep.\ phr. \end{Bmatrix}$$

31. Neil Postman, Harold Morine and Greta Morine, *Discovering Your Language* (New York: Holt, Rinehart and Winston, Inc., 1963), p. 151.

32. A.M. Tibbetts, "The Grammatical Revolution that Failed," *Elementary English* 45 (January, 1968): 44-50.

where NP = noun phrase
V_i = intransitive verb
V_t = transitive verb
adv = adverb
prep. phr. = prepositional phrase
NP_1 = noun phrase (indirect object)
NP_2 = noun phrase (direct object)
V_L = linking verb[33]

The above examples of basic English sentences are ways of delineating English syntax. Syntax is an important aspect of the study of the English language.

The Parts of Speech

Form classes or parts of speech have generally been classified into four categories by structural linguists. In the English language, there are usually these four: Form Class 1, nouns; Form Class 2, verbs; Form Class 3, adjectives; and Form Class 4, adverbs. Four considerations of words help to determine the characteristics of the form classes. (1) inflectional and derivational endings, (2) word order, (3) structure or function words and (4) stress.

Both nouns and verbs accept the inflectional ending -s but this does not designate a word definitely, i.e., girl, jump. The noun also can be inflected by adding -'s or -s'. So, -s, -'s and -s' describe the words we call nouns. Verbs can be classified by the endings -s, -ed and -ing. But derivational affixes also must be considered. Work classifies the same as jump because -s, -ed, and -ing can be added to either. But work will also accept -er, which will, in turn, make workers, worker's and workers'. Suffixes of the noun include many combinations: -eer, -ent, -ian, -ess, -ment, and -ism to mention only a few. Verbs can take both prefix and suffix markers—part can be either a noun or a verb. But if the prefix -im is added, the word impart is now in the verb form class. Derivational suffixes that mark verbs are: -ate, -ize; -fy, -ish, -en. Adjective inflectional suffixes are -er and -est. Examples of derivational endings for adjectives are -y, -able, -ful, -less, -ive, -en, and -ing. An -ly added to a noun marks an adjective whereas -ly added to an adjective marks an

---

33. From *Language and How to Use It,* Teachers edition, Book 5 by Andrew Schiller, et al. (Chicago: Scott, Foresman and Company, 1969).

adverb. Other derivational suffixes marking adverbs are -wise and -ward (s) and also, -a which is a derivational prefix.

Characteristics of Nouns and Verbs

Characteristics of words in the order in which they appear in sentences indicates the parts of speech also. For example, the following, "Did you ever see a pen play?" is hardly the same as "No, but I have seen a play pen." "The dog bit the man," is not the same as "The man bit the dog," although the words are exactly the same. A good method of testing word order for classifying parts of speech is to make a test frame. Examine the way in which "girl" patterns in this sentence:

The *girl* can work.

Any word which patterns or fits into the same spot or any word that is equivalent of girl + x may be said to be a noun. Substitutions can be made. She is a substitute because it does not take the -s ending. Verbs will also follow a pattern. Using the verb jump, a test frame can be made.

The boy *jumps.*

Any word which patterns in the same way or will accept the inflectional endings -s or -ed can be said to be a verb.

Characteristics of Adjectives

Words which end in -er and -est or those which accept these endings are adjectives and come before nouns so this is another way of testing for a noun. In the following test frame

The   *sweet*   girl

words which pattern like sweet are adjectives and indicate the appearance of a noun. Adjectives sometimes follow the predicate verb so if we expand this test frame the same word (an adjective) could be placed in each slot.

The   *stronger*   boy seems   *stronger.*

Characteristics of Adverbs

Adverbs are movable. They are not always found at the end of a sentence. An adverb may be found at the beginning or even in the middle of a sentence—thus:

The boy ran *rapidly.*
Rapidly the boy ran.
The boy *rapidly* ran.

Characteristics of Structure Words

Structure or function words also help determine word classes. Structure words indicate the relationships that exist among form class words in sentences. There are five kinds of structure words—connectives (and, but, or) determiners (the, all, several) auxiliaries, (shall, should, may) intensifiers (very, quite, least) and a miscellaneous group including negatives (never), expletives (there, it) sentence openers (oh, well, yes, no) and question words (which, how, where, why). *The* is a determiner or structure word or noun marker as in *the* girl. Any word used in the same way is a determiner for a noun. Examples of such words are: your, our, my, one, each, no and others. Verbs also have structure words which mark their form class. If the verb ends in -ing, it is usually preceded by am, is, was, are, were, as well as can, may, shall, will, etc. with the base verb.

Another term for an intensifier is the word qualifier. A qualifier will position after the determiner and before the adjective. Examples of qualifiers are: very, somewhat, most, so, too. However, these qualifiers can also appear with adverbs. Function and structure words are necessary parts of the language for they provide cohesion and lend rhythm to the language. These words are called both function and structure words since they may provide the structure to build sentences and also provide the function of relating other words to each other.

Characteristics of Stress

Stress permits the differentiation of nouns from words which are the same but are used as other parts of speech. For instance the stress pattern $/ / \backslash /$ in a word such as suspect signifies that it is a noun while the stress pattern $/ \backslash / /$ marks the word as a verb. Stress enables one to distinguish between a noun phrase (orderly room, a room that is orderly) and a nominal compound (orderly room, a room for orderlies). The stress pattern for a noun phrase is $/ \backslash / /$, and the stress pattern for a nominal compound is $/ / \backslash /$. The stress method may also help differentiate between certain adverbs and prepositions. The word *in* is an example. *"The doctor will be in on Wednesday,"* is an example of a primary stress on the word in which in is an adverbial. The sentence *"The doctor was in the store,"* is an example of *in* occuring as a preposition with a weak stress.[34]

Transformational Grammar

Transformational grammar came into being during the 1950's with the work of Zellig Harris of the University of Pennsylvania and Noam Chomsky of the Massachusetts Institute of Technology who developed the theory of transformational analysis. Transformational analysis assumes that there are a small "kernel" of sentence types, rules for transforming these types, and a list of morphophonemic rules which can be applied to the "structural strings" obtained by applying the transformational rules to the kernel sentences. Kernel sentences comprise a relatively small number of basic sentence types which are the core of grammar. Kernel sentences are those which cannot be derived from any sentence or sentence types underlying them. Transformational analysis also demonstrates that immediate constituent analysis applies only to kernel sentences. The concept of IC (immediate constituents), a product of American linguistics in the 1930's and 40's, views sentences as being made up of two-part constructions on a series of levels.[35]

Transformations are rules that give directions for changing, substituting, adding, deleting and combining the structures provided by the phrase structure rules to produce an endless variety of English sentences. The following sentence is an example of a kernel sentence which can be divided into immediate constituents.

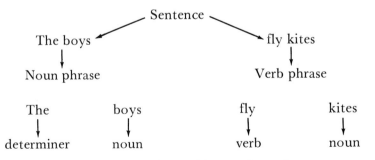

The above sentence may be transformed in a variety of ways.

---

34. *Ibid.,* pp. 73-78.
35. Roberts, *Teacher's Manual,* pp. 9-10.

Kites are flown by the boys. (a passive statement)
Do the boys fly kites? (a question in active form)
Are kites flown by the boys? (a question in passive form)
The boys do fly kites. (an emphatic statement)
The boys do not fly kites. (a negative statement)
Don't the boys fly kites?[36] (a negative question)

Tree diagrams[37] indicate certain types of information about noun phrases and verb phrases. The basic formula is

Sentence→ Noun Phrase + Verb Phrase

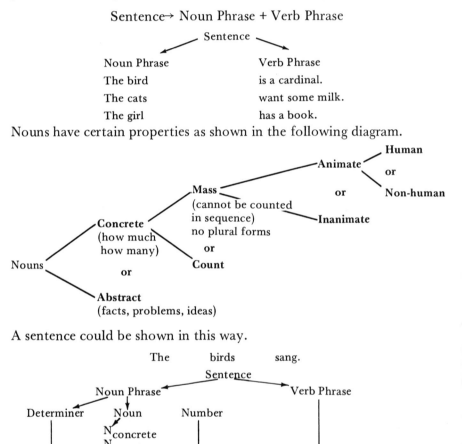

	Sentence
Noun Phrase	Verb Phrase
The bird	is a cardinal.
The cats	want some milk.
The girl	has a book.

Nouns have certain properties as shown in the following diagram.

A sentence could be shown in this way.

36. Enola Borgh, "The Case for Syntax," *Elementary English* 42 (January, 1965): 28-34.
37. Lamb, *Linguistics*, pp. 123-126.

The verb phrase contains an auxiliary and a main verb. Verb phrases may be present, past or perfect tense. These are combinations of auxiliary parts—will, must, have, has. The main verb might be:

(1) be and predicate
(2) linking verb + predicate
(3) mid-verb (look, have) and noun phrase
(4) transitive verb (see, hit) and noun phrase
(5) intransitive verb (walk, be)

The sentence "The children have taken a trip" could be tree diagrammed as follows:

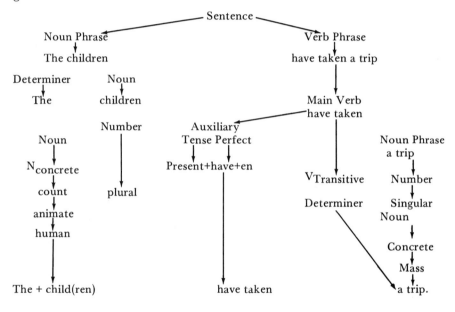

Transformational grammar assumes a meaning of deep structure level and a pronunciation or surface level. Sentences may also be transformed by expansion of the noun phrase or the verb phrase, by the use of coordination as a method of syntax, or by subordination to show relative importance of ideas.

The big boys who live on the hill fly kites. (an expanded noun phrase)

The boys fly enormous red kites high in the sky all day. (an expanded verb phrase)

The big boys who live on the hill fly enormous red kites in the sky all day. (expansions in both subject and predicate)

Boys and girls fly kites.

Boys fly kites and girls make cookies. (coordinations)

Since the boys who lived in the city did not know how to make and fly kites, the boys who lived in the country did fly kites. (subordination)

Terminology is often confusing. There are references made to generative grammar, to transformational grammar, to generative-transformational grammar and to transformational-generative grammar. Generative is a term used to discuss the purpose of grammatical study. This purpose is to formulate a kind of grammar that will generate all the grammatical sentences of the language but none of the ungrammatical ones. The generative part of generative-transformation grammar describes the basic sentence structure of the language. Transformation is concerned with technique rather than purpose. The term generative-transformational is awkward and so it is usually shortened to transformational grammar.

Types of grammar such as most of those described in the preceding section have at least one thing in common. The aim of studying grammar with any approach is to help children understand language structure so that their speech and writing may be as clear and powerful as possible. Learning isolated rules and definitions has seemed to fall short of this goal; functional grammar often has become accidental rather than planned opportunity; structural linguistics would seem to have exciting possibilities. One drawback is the lack of teachers with enough understanding to actually use this approach. Transformational grammar seems to embody some concepts of the more traditional type but also offers avenues of approach which have not heretofore been tried. And no approach can be fully subscribed to until a teacher can estimate the needs of a particular group of individual children. Denby advises, "Words of caution lest the manipulation of traditional grammar be replaced by equally irrelevant manipulation of the new grammar systems.[38]

---

38. Robert V. Denby, "Linguistic Instruction in Elementary School Classrooms," an NCTE/ERIC Report, *Elementary English* 46 (January, 1969): pp. 29-35.

Teaching Grammar in the Elementary School

One of the problems in deciding how and what to teach in the area of grammar is found in the different dialects and different levels of usage with which children come to school. Since children learn their language through imitation—and since all families do not have the same opportunities and experiences, it stands to reason that children from lower socioeconomic backgrounds or children from highly educated parents or children who are a part of a mobile population or children who are bilingual or children with any one of a dozen differences, will be vastly unequal in their understanding and use of language. Children from a school district in which parents are fairly young, fairly well educated, and possibly upper middle class will rarely say:

"There wasn't no paper," or
"Me and him brung it."

Roberts makes reference to Grammar 1 and Grammar 2. Examples of Grammars 1 and 2 are:

1. Henry brought his mother some flowers.
2. Henry brung his mother some flowers.

The first sentence is used by those who are educated and the second by those people we call uneducated. But who can defend the "better" way of telling what Henry did? There is no difference in the grammaticalness of the two statements. It is not a question of clarity or of a rule about verb endings. The sound of bring is no better than brung—but Grammar 2 is used largely by people who are not well educated and who are not very influential. It is perhaps sufficient to say that a person bent upon entering the business and professional world should have mastered Grammar 1.[39]

Categories of Usage

In the matter of usage, there is no place for absolutes. Shrewsbury states that "language constantly changes, that change is normal, that the spoken language is the primary language, that correctness in language depends upon usage and that usage is a relative matter."[40] In an article entitled "Let's Dump the Uptight Model in English," Goodman

39. Roberts, *English Sentences*, p. 8.
40. James B. Shrewsbury, "Linguistics and the Elementary Teacher: A Call for a Change in Certification Requirements," *Elementary English* 46 (March, 1969): 342-346.

encourages teachers to see that communication problems stem from differences, not deficiencies. A child's language is important because it is his. His self image, his self-respect and his attitude toward who he is and the group to which he belongs are all tied up in his use of language. "Education can help kids increase their efficiency, effectiveness, and ability to communicate, but it should never undermine what they already have."[41] There is need to cherish the language of all children—cherish, not just accept or tolerate it. Teachers often respond to a child's use of language rather than to the child and what he is saying. And though this cherishing of language differences is important—one must also remember that there are some times when so-called "front-door English" may be a necessity and essential to a person's well-being.

Pooley has divided usage into other categories. There are six levels of language use described as follows: (1) the illiterate level, (2) the homely level, (3) the informal standard level, (4) the formal standard level, (5) the literary level, and (6) the technical level. These are not mutually exclusive and any single person may use one or more depending upon what a situation calls for.[42]

Elementary teachers are most concerned with helping children move from the illiterate level to the homely level and having all children use the informal standard level when the occasion demands it. From the illiterate level come such examples as:

1. I seen, done, come
2. growed, climb
3. drownded, attackted
4. Us boys went.
5. She sings beautiful.
6. Two girls was going.
7. We ain't got no milk.

Some authors have suggested that usage should be divided into two categories: standard and substandard speech with slang as a sort of stepchild in between.

---

41. Kenneth Goodman, "Let's Dump the Uptight Model in English," *Elementary School Journal* 70 (October, 1969): 1-13.
42. Robert C. Pooley, "The Levels of Language," *Educational Method* 16 (March, 1937): 290.

Criteria for Determining "Good" English

Since teachers are concerned with the use of "poor" English it is essential that they and children alike have some notion of what constitutes "good" English. Teachers need to realize that language is not static; it is constantly changing and so what may have been "good" usage a quarter of a century ago hardly fits today's need in language. Teachers must also realize that there are many dialects or variations which do not per se indicate "poor" English just because they are different. Today's teachers also need to recognize that appropriateness of expression is determined by the purpose, the place and the group in which a particular type of language is being used. There are social levels of speech which range from the intimate speech between two people who need few words to the formal literary style which requires an entirely different type of usage. An understanding of "good" English also requires that teachers know something of the historical development of the language.

In other words, an arbitrary set standard for "good" or correct English cannot be acceptable to those concerned with the development of individuals, all of whom have worth.

Applegate has said that an elementary school has no need of definitions learned by heart; it is a place where definitions should be experienced and grown up with. She also intimates that formal grammar is needed but not at the elementary level. Children need to live with correct grammatical forms which places the responsibility for being a good model on the elementary teacher.[43]

Strickland comments that a child can tell you three things by way of his use of language. It indicates the language of his home and the cultural level of his parents; his own vocabulary gives you an insight into his experiences; and his attitude toward language and whether or not he has an easy use of language, tell you of his self-image. The concern should be with "living language in the lives of real people."[44]

Desirable Directions for Growth

In *Children and the Language Arts* Nemec and Pooley have stated that growth in speech forms and manners, growth in the conventions

43. Applegate, *Easy in English,* p. 447.
44. Ruth G. Strickland, "Trends and Emphases in Elementary English," *The Range of English* (Champaign, Illinois: National Council of Teachers of English, 1968), pp. 114-115.

required in written expression and growth in appropriate word usage should be the major points of emphasis in the elementary school.[4][5] In other textbooks such as that written by Dawson, Zollinger and Elwell, the major aim in instruction in correct usage and grammar is the development of good language habits.[4][6]

The language program, according to Greene and Petty, has two major goals: (1) development of effective expression in language activities, and (2) the development of the related attitudes, abilities, and skills contributing to expressive efficiency. Educators should emphasize a child's clear presentation of thought.[4][7]

From such statements as the foregoing, an elementary teacher can recognize his responsibility for understanding the language, its history and its structure and for understanding the needs which a child has for easy use of language.

Grammar as an Editorial Tool

Most children in the elementary school have an unconscious understanding of what happens to language to cause words to become sentences. However, what many children learn from an entire elementary school program in language may never come close to a real understanding of sentence elements or a recognition of the quality of sentences. Children may reach sixth grade level without being able to construct good clear sentences either orally or in writing. What is probably more detrimental to the child's expression is his inability to examine and edit his sentences critically.

A sentence fragment may have meaning when used between two people who know each other intimately but children need to realize that many misunderstandings come about because not enough was said to express a thought completely. The listener becomes confused and must guess at what interpretation to place upon the speaker or writer's intended meaning. Some children seem not to realize that there must be two parts or predication as well as a subject, as a necessary element in a sentence. Run-on sentences need to be edited also. Children need to be taught that a sentence must make sense. Often a child thinks he knows

---

45. Lois G. Nemec and R.C. Pooley, "Children's Experiences with Usage and Functional Grammar," in Virgil Herrick and Leldan Jacobs, *Children and the Language Arts* (Englewood Cliffs, New Jersey: Prentice-Hall, Inc., 1955), p. 289.

46. Mildred A. Dawson, Marian Zollinger and Ardell Elwell, *Guiding Language Learning* (New York: Harcourt, Brace and World, Inc., 1963), p. 377.

47. H.A. Greene and Walter Petty, *Developing Language Skills in the Elementary Schools* (Boston: Allyn and Bacon, Inc., 1967), pp. 114-115.

a subject so well that he fails to use the language skills he has to put across his ideas. He may simply have no sentence sense.

The Learning Environment

If children live in a warm, accepting, supportive school climate and have active, adequate instruction, they will start early to develop the ability to tell experiences, events and facts in structurally complete sentences. Children need much work formulating oral sentences so that they have a background for constructing good written sentences. Many direct experiences give meaning to new vocabulary. Charleton Laird has given us some thoughts on the nature of language learning which might well be incorporated into the learning environment. He states that small children learn language in an atmosphere of happiness and playfulness—not in one where fear and embarrassment are present. Often language is learned in context, as games, or in conjunction with something, as ritual. We should surround the child with excellent conditions—an adult or adults to listen to and converse with, someone who will talk to the child but who will also listen. Laird states that a child who is loved and kept relatively happy might possibly learn language better and faster. Perhaps teachers also need to ask themselves whether they understand the language, whether they can trust children to learn some things about language without help and whether they can help children learn what they need most.[48] As language maturity increases, a child grows in his ability to:

1. Vary word order
2. Sense relationship which eventually become subordinate parts of sentences
3. Develop thoughts fully
4. Use connectives effectively
5. Eliminate run-on sentences

Aspects of Effective Expression

Greene and Petty have selected several factors which need to be present in the speaking and wrting of individuals if understanding is to be complete. An individual must be perfectly clear and unconfused

---

48. Charleton Laird, "Seen But Not Heard: Language Learning and Language Teaching," *The Range of English* (Champaign, Illinois: National Council of Teachers of English), pp. 76-103.

himself if his sentences possess *clarity*. One can be clear and unconfused only if thinking is based on a wide background of experience and knowledge of what he is talking about. In order to develop clarity, children need to learn that modifiers should be placed next to or as close as possible to the words they modify and that pronouns need to be placed so that they indicate their antecedents. Such sentences as "She saw three houses coming down the street." or "Tom decided to put the letter to his mother in the mailbox." indicate the need for more thought about modifiers and pronouns.[49]

Oral and written expression should have *unity*. That is, each sentence should have unity within itself but it should also have no content that is not related to the principal thought. Each paragraph should be related to the main idea being expressed. Words and phrases in each sentence and the sentences themselves should have the proper sequence so that the idea is expressed logically and clearly.

Children need to learn that rarely does the communication process keep working if there is no interest. Communication breaks down quickly if the speaker is not interested in what he is saying; if the language he uses is unacceptable or if the structure is out of line. Boys and girls need to learn to use colorful and interesting words and a variety of structures to keep up *interest*.

Content may be interesting to the listener or reader but an effective speaker or writer uses illustrations, anecdotes, metaphors and colorful and forceful words to keep interest alive. A good speaker or writer chooses to say things concisely and concretely which also helps to keep an audience from disappearing altogether—at least, mentally.

Organization is another facet of a good presentation. Learning to organize ideas means making use of grammar as an editorial tool. First in importance is learning to stick to the point. Then, limiting the scope of the topic and relating ideas and thoughts to the topic; presenting material in the most effective sequence; giving attention to the beginning and ending sentences; and learning to outline, all contribute to effective organization.

If teachers are to help children be colorful in their use of words, less boring to their contemporaries and more clearly understandable, all teachers must help them to experience the fascination of words. A wide vocabulary not only challenges one's audience but a rich, colorful, con-

---

49. Greene and Petty, *Developing Language Skills*, p. 257-259.

cise vocabulary increases one's self-respect and the satisfaction one gets from having said something well. So the final aspect of effective expression is *vocabulary*. It is probably obvious that a wise choice of words for particular occasions and a continuing addition of new words to one's store are both important for helping to keep a vocabulary effective, alive and growing.

In using grammar as an editorial tool then, children need sentence sense, clarity, unity, interest, organization and an effective vocabulary.

Improving English Usage in the Elementary School

Most authorities agree that usage—the way in which people speak—is of more importance than a formal grammar program for six-to-twelve-year-olds; having something to say and being willing to say it is more important than form; and nothing is of more importance than realizing the satisfaction derived from wanting to speak and write and doing it well.

Children bring a wide variety of usage habits to school. A large number of boys and girls enter school with undesirable speech patterns and habits. The problem in usage instruction at the elementary school level is to find ways in which to help children substitute more desirable habits. Not everyone agrees as to the best approach. Some teachers think children will improve more readily by learning grammatical definitions and rules. Others contend that, according to the psychological principles of learning, children need to have errors corrected and then have much practice. Some contend that ear practice is a good way to improve speech habits.

Programs of intervention or compensatory education have tried to fill the gap in language development for some youngsters in our society. But do we know the answer as to the way in which environment helps the process of language development? Little children do not learn language through correction or reinforcement of the learning of grammar. Mothers usually simplify their language; however, when they talk to their children in conversation that has meaning and about something that is personally important to the child, their children learn. Some early childhood programs have failed to demonstrate that we know enough about the communication problems of children to meet their needs.[50]

---

50. Courtney B. Cazden, "Suggestions From Studies of Early Language Acquisition," *Childhood Education* 46 (December, 1969): 127-131.

Habit formation is dependent upon motivation, on having a clear impression repeated over and over with no intervening use of incorrect forms and then putting the correct form into correct use. Language habits can be changed only through drill that is fairly constant. Very few new habitual responses such as "I saw" for "I seen" can be firmly established within a given period of time-even as long as a year in the elementary school. In order to develop a single skill, the following series of stages may be of help:

1. awareness and understanding of alternate forms
2. trying alternate forms in appropriate settings
3. using old and new forms with equal ease
4. letting old forms sink into disuse as pupils' needs change.[51]

If a child feels that making a real effort is worth it, he will attempt to make a basic change in his language patterns. Gross errors are usually a barrier if a person is interested in moving upward from one socio-economic level to another. School experiences in speaking and writing must be truly important to children if they prompt children to want to change.

There are a variety of ways to attack a problem in usage. The following sequence of steps is adapted from a similar list by Hatchett and Hughes.

1. Find what your group needs. What abilities, what experiences, what interests, and what weaknesses does the group possess?
   Procedures:
   Note most conspicuous errors.
   Listen to children during all types of oral language activities. Listen for language patterns.
   Listen to children in out-of-school situations, i.e., playground, lunchroom, organization meetings.
   Examine written work for errors that are common.
   Make inventories from either standardized or teacher-made tests to find out what children need.
2. Determine which errors should be attacked.
   Procedures:
   Help children incidentally,
   Make an individual diagnostic rating sheet.
3. Select errors to attack.
   Procedures:
   Check class errors against generally recognized usage errors.
   Make a composite chart showing types of errors and members of the group.

---

51. Kenneth S. Goodman, "Let's Dump the Uptight Model in English," *Elementary School Journal* 70 (October, 1969): 1-13.

4. Give individual help.
   Procedures:
   Give specific help when needed by an individual.
   Group children by common problems.
5. Help child find his most outstanding errors in his own speech and writing.
   Procedures:
   Use a tape recorder to help him spot speech errors.
   Help child keep a notebook of his own errors.
   Teach child to proofread for errors.
6. Expand language experiences.
   Procedures:
   Encourage audience situations such as
      reading
      listening to stories
      dramatizing
      sharing poetry
   Give praise for good use of language.
   Read good literature. Listen to good literature.
   Enjoy choral speaking.
   Select and view good television shows.
   Use reference charts and posters.
   Use cartoons to illustrate actions of verbs, power of adjectives and adverbs.
   Display children's written work.
7. Help children evaluate.
   Procedures:
   Set up standards with children.
   Take time to evaluate work during and after an activity.
   Use an opaque projector to show written work to group.
   Use an overhead projector to illustrate errors and corrections.
   Copy a part of written work on chalkboard for class to discuss and evaluate.
   Give children help where it is needed when they are proofreading.
8. Guide children in practice.
   Procedures:
   Use skills periods for common errors.
   Use oral situations.
   Use devices to interest children in usage practice.
   Use language games.
   Use workbooks as they are needed in small groups or pairs.
   Use textbooks as resource books.[52]

A teacher is most successful with usage teaching if the children are highly cooperative. Such cooperation rests upon the interpersonal relationships existing in the classroom. Children respond to corrections made quietly and with regard for their feelings.

In her usual succinct way, Applegate has made her point regarding speech patterns. She has said that to help children change speech pat-

---

52. Ethel Hatchett and Donald Hughes, *Teaching Language Arts in Elementary Schools* (New York: The Ronald Press Company, 1956), pp. 147-157.

terns, first of all there must be a "rich wanting" on the part of the child. Using sarcasm and ridicule in correcting children will never promote a "rich wanting" to change. A child must know what sounds right and he must have a great deal of "good" speech practice.[53]

Grade-Placement Practices

Many textbooks in language concentrate on the same types of learning for any one grade level. More recent textbooks concentrate on oral language and on much more absorbing content. The following seem to be the points of grammar, uasage and other material which are considered important, however. These are stated in behavioral terms insofar as it is possible.

First Grade

Eliminate gross examples of non standard usage
(ain't and hain't, brung, growed, knowed)
Recognize a sentence in manuscript
Express ideas so that audience will listen

Second Grade

Eliminate additional examples of non standard usage
(hisself, theirselves, them books, this here)
Put self last
Learn that a sentence tells or asks
Express ideas so that others understand

Third Grade

Learn standard usage
(see, do, go, run, come, bring, and burst
has for *has got* and *have* for *have got*)
Put self last
Use those and them correctly
Make sentences complete thoughts
See need for statements, questions and commands
Try to eliminate run-on sentences and use of "and" between sentences
Use well-made and original sentences
Use name, describing and action words
Understand word order and how it functions in grammar
Construct sentence patterns
Recognize nouns, noun markers and pronouns and their functions
Understand what verbs are

---

53. Applegate, *Easy in English*, pp. 154-155.

Fourth Grade

Master the standard forms of common verbs
Understand the terms noun and verb
Understand singular possessive noun -'s
Understand the subject, predicate and word order
Begin to understand coordination and subordination
Understand the noun phrases, nouns with noun markers
Understand the verbs and verb markers
Understand the adjectives and their inflections
Understand the adverbs of place, time and manner

Fifth Grade

Use verbs
(begin, blow, break, fly, give, and so on)
Use a and an correctly
Understand:

  the function of a noun
  common and proper nouns
  singular and plural nouns
  singular and plural possessive nouns

Understand:

  present and past tense of verbs
  subject and predicate
  different kinds of predicates
  double negatives
  the function of conjunctions—coordination

Know basic sentence patterns
Know about inflection, derivation and functional shift

Sixth Grade

Use standard forms
Use standard prepositions
(at—to: in—into, among—between)
Use adverbs and adjectives correctly
Choose correct forms of pronouns
Understand the function of prepositions and conjunctions—subordination
Understand the agreement of subject and verb
Use grammatical terms functionally
Use a variety of sentence patterns
Understand what a morpheme is
Understand a transformation
Use transformations to produce compound and complex sentences
Use negative, interrogative, negative-interrogative and passive transformations
Understand relationship between intonation patterns and meaning and intonation patterns and punctuation

The following listing of punctuation and capitalization skills are those commonly taught at each grade level:

Grade	Punctuation		Capitalization
First grade	Use period and question for sentence endings		Know forms of capital and small letters, Capitalize: name of person name of pets first word in sentence street school town
Second grade	Use comma in date Copy letter correctly using commas Put periods after numbers in a list Put commas in alphabetized list of names		Capitalize: Mr. Miss Mrs. Teacher Principal Pets
Third grade	Use period:	statement, command abbreviation, Mr. Mrs. initials	Capitalize: Heading on papers First word in sentence First line of verse
	Use comma:	greeting, closing date, address	Word I
	Use question mark Use apostrophe in singular possessive		Proper names Common holidays Buildings In titles: book, report story, poem, list, outline
Fourth grade	Maintain what has been taught Period: After numbers in a list or outline		Capitalize: All above Topics in an outline
Fifth grade	Review all punctuation Review use of comma		Review all uses First word of a quotation Name of an organization
	Use comma to: separate parts of a sentence separate word or address from rest of sentence Hyphen at the end of the line Apostrophe in contractions and possessives Quotation marks		

Grade	Punctuation	Capitalization
Sixth grade	Review all punctuation Learn: Comma; words in series Exclamation point Comma: compound or complex sentences Quotation marks Hyphen in compound words (check dictionary)	Review Capitalize: proper adjectives regions of country

Ways of Working With Children

Language experiences are among the most necessary types of experiences for children in today's world. Grammar and usage are two facets of expressional activities that are a day-long concern. Interrelating all such expressional activities, at least for elementary children, is one of the major goals of a good language arts teacher.

Opportunity is Essential

A child's language develops in direct proportion to the opportunities he has for actual use of words and sentences. Children are extremely active linguistically before they ever attend school—and it is an amazing amount of language that many children learn in preschool years. But as one thinks of language development, one must be aware of the fact that children who live in an environment with adults who speak extremely well, will learn "good" grammar and correct usage while just the opposite is true if they are accustomed to living in an environment of low linguistic level. Whatever power a child has in language will be equaled by his power in thinking. Deeper understanding, better organization of ideas, and seeing relationships in time or complexity all accompany advances in language ability. As a child develops in language, he also begins to have a means of dealing with his growing self-concept and with meeting the demands of his social world.

As a teacher understands children and has insight into the intricacies of the nature of language, so he plans and develops a program which reflects the attitudes, the understandings and the values which he as a teacher, holds.

That the four major aspects of language are interrelated, and that growth in one affects growth in the others are supported by much research. Children depend upon their experiences for ideas and opportunity to use words. There is a close relationship between growth in language and these same experiences. Growth in language is also related to mental ability, sex, socioeconomic level and sibling status. Besides these, any language learning situation requires a social situation with purposes and communication needs. Also involved is a variety of related language media and there are always related mechanics, skills and usage agreements and certain conventions—etiquette of usage.

Arranging a Satisfactory Sequence

Determining what comes next in a program or, in other words, in what sequence these things should be taught, is a serious problem. It is difficult and almost impossible to separate the grammar and usage from many language learning activities. And that is as it should be if six-year-olds or nine-year-olds or twelve-year-olds really use the structure, vocabulary, and ideas that are important to them.

In language arts programs, we use some findings from child development to help in planning the activities. For example, one may identify things and activities that children like, find out how rapidly they achieve within the program, and develop some judgment on the maturity level at different grade levels.

A fixed, arbitrary program of certain skills or activities for certain grade levels does not take into account the wide difference in language facility or the fact that children of six or ten need the same things in language. One major difference is in degree of depth.

A child's developmental pattern and his own progress in language can be used for judging his adequacies and inadequacies in language. Evaluation, then, can become the means of helping children find better and more effective ways to meet their educational needs and their communication needs as well.

Lifelike experiences in language should be offered children through the elementary grades to encourage growth in attitudes, abilities and skills. An example of an attitude is the willingness on the part of the child to participate. Without cooperative attitudes, little else can be accomplished. Certain courtesies should be a vital part of language experiences. Children need experiences in selecting and organizing content; they also need to acquire a vivid vocabulary and sentence sense. Speech, usage and written mechanics consist of skills which children need in order to communicate effectively.

Levels of Language Experience

Examples of oral language experiences at each grade level give an idea of the scope of oral language activities in which children participate.

In kindergarten, a bag of all kinds of shoes afforded much conversation and motivation for guessing for five-year-olds. There was much discussion after it was opened. Vocabulary was used. Children talked as they used their thinking skills. A first grade dictated original stories to anyone who would listen and write them down. They were made into a book. A group of seven-year-olds decided to make puppets and dramatize the story of *Goggles*. Learning to speak clearly and loudly enough for an audience helped children as they performed for their peers.

Book reports in a third grade afforded many learnings in language. Children could write, tape, draw, dramatize or discuss books they had read. They became "salesmen" of good books to read.

A fourth grade interested in a study of space listed what they knew about space and space travel, wrote words, phrases or sentences about some aspect of space, wrote the information in notebooks, held discussions of the scientific principles involved and used oral language in a functional "method of discovery."

Children in a fifth grade studied television programs. They wished to interview primary level children and formulated a questionnaire for upper elementary children for making recommendations for viewing. They compiled their materials and formed generalizations. Finally, they ended their study by making recommendations for themselves and their schoolmates.

Sixth graders formed committees to select, classify, mount, and file materials from a supervisor's accumulation of current magazines. Children of the sixth grade interviewed teachers and children in all grades to discover what topics would be a value to each room. Some committees set up an expandable file for the use of the whole school. They read, marked, clipped, mounted and filed hundreds of items. Discussion and evaluation of plans went on daily. They eventually explained the project to parents, the school staff and even to prospective teachers.[54]

---

54. Helen Mackintosh, editor, *Children and Oral Language* (Washington, 1964), p. 25.

Summary

A reiteration of the information in this chapter will not guarantee that the reader now knows more about grammar and usage. However, to know that language is a vital force in a child's life and that teachers have an edge over most other adults in getting to know children from a professional standpoint, in attempting to diagnose strengths and weaknesses in a child's language habits and in influencing their growth for good was the underlying purpose of this chapter.

Before one can teach he must know himself, the children and the content. This is surely true in the areas of grammar and usage. A grammar can stand alone and be useful to those interested in the science of language but, in the elementary school, children need a concerned, sensitive teacher. In what better way can acceptable language habits be understood and practiced by children?

EXTENDING YOUR LEARNING

1. As you think of yourself in the role of a teacher and the importance of being a good model, what specific usage difficulties do you have? How can you eliminate these and change your language habits? Will taping your own conversation, a discussion or an interview help you to determine any difficulties?
2. As you think about the ways of teaching grammar, how would you defend structural or transformational grammar to teachers who prefer the traditional approach?
3. As you think about teaching formal grammar, where in the scheme of a curriculum should it be placed? Why? Would you use this approach?
4. As you think about your own experiences with grammar, talk with adults not in school, your peers, and children to find out what their impressions and memories of grammar are? If their ideas about grammar are negative, why do you think they are? How do you think attitudes could be changed?
5. As you think about teaching children, what choices do you see as you might use multi-media for instruction in the English language?
6. As you think about trying to improve children's language habits, what common errors would you start with? Listen to children. Can you find errors that need to be eliminated? How would you eliminate one flagrant error?
7. As you think about "good" and "poor" habits in our use of language, listen to television and radio shows, read comic strips and newspapers and collect the errors of usage for a period of a week.
8. As you think about materials for teaching grammar and usage, examine five different textbooks in elementary school English. Compare the suggestions for teaching sentence structure.
9. As you think about making decisions about textbooks, read the information on the Roberts English Series in the April 1970 issue of *Elementary English*. What conclusion can you reach?

BIBLIOGRAPHY

Books

Anderson, Paul S., *Language Skills in Elementary Education*. New York: The Macmillan Company, 1964. 447 pp. Chapter 9.

Applegate, Mauree, *Easy in English*. Evanston: Row, Peterson and Company, 1960. 564 pp. Chapters 5, 9, 10, and 11.

Bolinger, Dwight, *Aspects of Language*. New York: Harcourt, Brace and World, Inc., 1968. 326 pp.

Borgh, Enola M., *Grammatical Patterns and Composition*. Oshkosh, Wisconsin: Wisconsin Council of Teachers of English, 1963. 44 pp.

Crosby, Muriel, et al. *The World of Language. Teachers' Edition, Books 1-6*. Chicago: Follett Educational Corporation, 1969.

Francis, W. Nelson, *The English Language, An Introduction: Background For Writing*. New York: W.W. Norton and Company, 1965. 273 pp. Chapters 1 and 2.

Frost, Joe L. and G. Thomas Rowland, *Curricula for the Seventies*. Boston: Houghton Mifflin Company, 1969. 454 pp.

Greene, Harry A. and Walter T. Petty, *Developing Language Skills In The Elementary Schools*. Boston: Allyn and Bacon, Inc., 1967. 572 pp. Chapter 12.

Grommon, A.H. *The Range of English*. NCTE Distinguished Lectures, 1968. Champaign, Illinois: National Council of Teachers of English, 1968. 125 pp.

Hughes, John P., *Linguistics and Language Teaching*. New York: Random House, 1968. 143 pp.

Lamb, Pose, *Linguistics in Proper Perspective*. Columbus, Ohio: Charles E. Merrill Publishing Co., 1967. 147 pp.

Mackintosh, Helen K., *Children and Oral Language*. Joint Publication of Association for Childhood Education International, Association for Supervision and Curriculum Development, International Reading Association and National Council of Teachers of English, 1964. 38 pp.

Marckwardt, Albert H., *Linguistics and the Teaching of English*. Bloomington: Indiana University Press, 1968. 151 pp.

Moffett, James, *A Student-Centered Language Arts Curriculum Grades K-6: A Handbook for Teachers*. Boston: Houghton Mifflin Company, 1968. 274 pp.

Nebraska Curriculum Development Center. *A Curriculum for English: Language Explorations for Elementary Grades*. Lincoln: The University of Nebraska, 1966. 179 pp.

Postman, Neil and Charles Weingartner, *Teaching as a Subversive Activity*. New York: Delacorte Press, 1969. 219 pp.

Roberts, Paul, *English Sentences*. New York: Harcourt, Brace and World, Inc., 1962. 294 pp. Teachers' manual.

Roberts, Paul, *Modern Grammar*. New York: Harcourt, Brace and World, Inc., 1968. 439 pp.

Schiller, Andrew, et al., *Language and How to Use It. Teachers' Edition Books 1-6*. Glenview, Illinois: Scott, Foresman and Company, 1969.

Strickland, Ruth G., *The Language Arts in the Elementary School*. Boston: D.C. Heath and Company, 1969. 464 pp. Chapter 15.

Tiedt, Iris M. and Sidney W. Tiedt, *Readings on Contemporary English In The Elementary School*. Englewoods Cliffs, N.J.: Prentice-Hall, Inc. 376 pp.

Tiedt, Sidney W., *Teaching the Disadvantaged Child*. New York: Oxford University Press, 1968. 248 pp.

Walden, James (ed.), *Oral Language and Reading*. Champaign, Illinois: National Council of Teachers of English, 1969.

Periodicals

Borgh, Enola M., "The Case for Syntax," *Elementary English* 42:28-34, January, 1965.

Brown, Roger and Ursula Bellugi, "Three Processes in the Child's Acquisition of Syntax," *Harvard Educational Review* 34:133-151, Spring, 1964.

Cazden, Courtney B., "Suggestions from Studies of Early Language Acquisitions," *Childhood Education* 46:127-131, December, 1969.

Denby, Robert V., "Linguistic Instruction in Elementary School Classrooms—An NCTE/ERIC Report," *Elementary English* 46:29-35, January, 1969.

Ervin, Susan M., "Imitation and Structural Change in Children's Language" in Lenneberg, Eric H. (ed.) *New Directions in the Study of Language*. Cambridge, Massachusetts: The MIT Press, 1966, 163-189.

Goodman, Kenneth S., "Let's Dump the Uptight Model in English," *Elementary School Journal* 70:1-13, October, 1969.

McDavid, Raven I., Jr., "The Cultural Matrix of American English," *Elementary English* 42:13-21+, January, 1965.

Sheldon, William D. and Donald R. Lashinger, "A Summary of Research Studies Relating to Language Arts in Elementary Education," *Elementary English* 46:866-885, November, 1969.

Staiger, Ralph C., "Language Arts Research: 1964," *Elementary English* 42:433-445, April, 1965.

Tibbitts, A.M., "The Grammatical Revolution That Failed," *Elementary English* 45:44-50, January, 1968.

Focus

It would be easy to be very defensive about the current position of Foreign Language in the Elementary School. Except for a few well established programs, FLES is having difficulty holding its own. New programs have been few in number within the past five years. There are many reasons for this. School system budgets are unusually stringent. Bond issues are failing at an unprecedented rate all over the United States. When faced with budget cuts, school administrators are *not* likely to add FLES specialists to their staffs. Elementary teacher preparation programs are full, crowded, and few provide options which will permit prospective teachers to take the necessary course work which will equip them to do an adequate teaching job with a foreign language. The value of foreign language study at an early age continues to be questioned, especially by administrators who are faced with problems of teacher supply, which language or languages to include, and for whom FLES programs should be designed—all the students or chosen groups.

Elizabeth Ratté has maintained a positive and hopeful perspective concerning FLES however. She cites some new and compelling reasons for adding the study of a foreign language to the elementary curriculum. She, too, has felt the influence of linguists. It may very well be true as she writes, that a child cannot fully understand his own language, in any of its systems—structural, phonological, syntactic, unless he understands the systems of another language. She restates, very convincingly, the reasons for studying a foreign language in the elementary school which were put forth in the beginning days of FLES, following the second World War. These relate to the relative ease of acquiring a second language prior to adolescence, due to a combination of neurological and psychological factors, and the benefits which accrue to a child who knows a culture other than his own. Because a language is such a significant part of a culture (some of the most prominent early linguists were anthropologists) a child will more adequately understand a culture if he knows the language of those whose culture he's studying.

A final and very compelling reason for involving elementary school pupils in the study of a foreign language relates to a definition of the term "fluency." The acquisition of fluency in an individual's native language takes a number of years—a ten year old frequently provides illustrations of non-fluency. Can one really expect fluency in a language *not* one's native language as a result of two years study in the secondary school?

It is hoped that the reader will conclude study of this chapter with a better understanding of the rationale for FLES, as well as an awareness of the attendant problems.

Elizabeth H. Ratté

chapter ten

foreign language
in the elementary school

The place of foreign language in the elementary school (FLES), has taken on new dimensions within the past decade. This has been the outcome of years of experience since the FLES movement took on impetus in the 1950's. Outstanding programs of some duration, usually five to ten years or more, have been sources of reliable information concerning the value of FLES to the development of the individual student, to the effectiveness of the entire long-sequence foreign language program, and as an important contribution to the modern curriculum. Pillet of the University of Chicago, an active leader in this field since he started a program at the University Elementary School in 1955, expressed the favorable and optimistic conviction that "on the basis of experience we are in a position to provide increasingly for a better experience (in foreign language learning) for a greater proportion of our population.... The long language sequence experienced by a vast majority of the pupils in our school has had an impact on our high school foreign language program and has led to the asking of fundamental educational questions pertinent to all areas of the curriculum."[1] Evidence of positive results and evaluation of student achievement can also be found in a number of reports and studies now available.[2] The

---

1. Roger A. Pillet, "The Impact of FLES: An Appraisal," *Modern Language Journal* (December, 1968).

2. See Mildred R. Donoghue, *FLES: Effects and Instructional Arrangements According to Research*, ERIC Focus Report no. 3, New York: MLA-ACTFL Materials Center (1969); and Gladys Lipton and Edward Bourque, editors, *Research, Relevance, Reality: The Three R's of FLES*, MLA-ACTFL Materials Center (1969).

degree of success in these programs depends greatly on the amount of careful planning done and the quality of teaching provided.

A study dealing specifically with the students in elementary school foreign language programs presents the following facts concerning the impact of this learning experience. FLES–trained students are likely to choose to continue foreign language study in junior and senior high school. Their skills are often superior to those who started foreign language in secondary school. Accurate pronunciation and speech patterns, an intuitive sense for the grouping and choice of words, a wider active and passive vocabulary are among the frequently mentioned capabilities and achievements of these students. Development of an early interest in foreign languages and an awareness of other cultures are additional values of FLES reported by former students.[3]

Another notable and quite recent development on a national as well as a local scale, has been the organized meetings of elementary school and foreign language specialists for the purpose of relating the foreign language program to contemporary modes of learning and recent curriculum developments in the elementary school. To provide the most meaningful experience possible for the student, FLES education must be integrated horizontally into the total elementary school curriculum as well as vertically into the long language sequence. Language arts is one of the areas of the curriculum to which foreign language can make a vital and enriching contribution. The language arts program need no longer be limited to the mother tongue. Nor is a monolinguistic approach desirable if linguistic concepts, including an understanding of the nature of language, are considered essential objectives of the program.[4] To understand what language is requires going beyond the confines of one's mother tongue. In this sense, "language" is plural. The student who never has the experience of effective oral communication in a language other than his own has missed an important linguistic and cultural experience. Without this experience, it will be difficult to understand that language is individual as well as collective, that each language is an expression of the attitudes, beliefs, and ideas of the cultural environment of its native speakers.

It is through the foreign language experience that the child becomes

---

3. Virginia Spaar, "FLES in Retrospect," *The FLES Student,* Edward Bourque, editor (Philadelphia: Chilton Books, 1968), pp. 65, 68.

4. *New Dimensions in the Teaching of FLES,* "Language Arts," report based on the 1968 National FLES Symposium, New York: MLA-ACTFL Materials Center (1969), p. 36.

aware that each language is an arbitrary system of communication having many unique characteristics not similar to English. He discovers also "that other peoples, other nations, express themselves differently, but just as effectively. He suddenly comes to the realization that all thought is not cast into English molds. Since words shape thoughts, the pupil comes to the second realization, even more important, that other people think different thoughts. It is a shock to the boy or girl raised in a 100% American environment to discover that another nation may have thoughts which are so different as to be at times contradictory, but they are at the same time as logical, reasoned, profound, and intellectual as our thoughts. . . . Slavery to a single vocabulary and syntax is bondage indeed."[5]

A Rationale for FLES

Changes in foreign language teaching in the United States in the 1950's and 1960's resulted from two basic assumptions. The first involved a radical shift in emphasis from the reading aim which had been prevalent for many years. It was assumed that foreign language learning should provide the student with skills of communication, primarily that of oral communication. The second assumption was that acquiring this new set of skills was largely a matter of habit formation. Consequently, time and practice were essential. The case for starting at an early age is well founded in terms of the objectives of this new approach to foreign language teaching. The ability to give automatic, accurate response to the stimulus of spoken language is partially a motor skill, and, like learning to skate or play a musical instrument, demands continued practice over a long period of time. The Foreign Language Institute of the Department of State established, through experience with adults studying in intensive programs, the average time required for a functional mastery of French, German, or Spanish as 600 class hours plus home study ranging from 15 to 24 hours weekly. A child starting a foreign language in the third grade, getting twenty minutes of instruction daily and continuing through sixth grade, will have about 240 hours of the language. Add to that a continuing program in grades 7 through 12, and he will receive a total of approximately 1,140 hours of instruction. He should also have a good control of the language.[6]

5. Stephen A. Freeman, "Individual Development in the Second Language Experience," Modern Language Association, FL Discussion Pamphlet No. II (1959), p. 4.

6. Information obtained from, "It Takes Time," *Modern Foreign Languages and Your Child,* Washington: USOE, Bulletin OE 27020 (1964), pp. 29-31.

The audio-lingual approach emphasized at the beginning stages of learning a foreign language consists mainly of listening and speaking practice. Reading, when introduced, reinforces what has already been learned audio-lingually. At the elementary school level, introduction to the printed word may be delayed a year or two depending on the age of the students. At higher levels, junior-senior high school and college, reading is an essential part of each unit, but usually follows the audio-lingual phase of each unit during the first year or two of instruction. Experience has shown that the adolescent and young adult may not react favorably to modes of learning considered essential to habit formation such as memorization of basic sentences or dialogues and repetition drills. This approach to learning is not objectionable to the elementary school child.

Early Beginning Capitalizes on Natural Ability

Starting foreign language study in the elementary school not only provides for a span of time that makes a degree of language skill feasible, but also takes advantage of the young child's natural ability to learn language with ease and pleasure. During the preadolescent period, children do not have the self-conscious inhibitions that often make learning the spoken language an unpleasant task at high school age. The young students of elementary school age enjoy imitation and repetition. They memorize easily and enjoy dramatizing. They are naturally curious about people in other countries. They can remember what they have heard and repeat it without seeing the written word. Purely auditory memory becomes difficult for the adolescent and sometimes impossible for the adult. Preadolescent children take pleasure in the type of teaching and language content suitable to the early stages of learning a foreign language. Simple vocabulary and childish concepts, objectionable to the adolescent, are readily accepted in the lower grades. Children like to learn with the aid of action and sensory aids. They enjoy pantomime, songs, dances, and simple rhymes—all activities suitable to elementary school teaching techniques.

The Optimum Age for Beginning Study

Experts in the areas of neurology, psychology, and child development have provided interesting evidence concerning the optimum age to begin the study of a second language, all pointing to the desirability of this experience starting no later than at the age of ten. One of the most frequently quoted experts is Dr. Wilder Penfield, Director of the Montreal Neurological Institute who has studied in depth and detail the function of the human brain related to speech. He identifies the cerebral cortex as a thick layer of gray matter covering the outer surface of the brain. Certain parts are used only for sensory and motor purposes. There is a large area which is "uncommitted" at birth, however, and this area is in time used for language and perception. Dr. Penfield writes: "Before the child begins to speak and perceive, the uncommitted cortex is a blank slate on which nothing has been written. In the ensuing years, much is written and the writing is never erased. After the age of ten or twelve, the general functional connections have been established and fixed for the speech cortex—The brain of the twelve-year-old is prepared for the rapid expansion of the vocabulary of the mother tongue and of other languages he may have learned in the formative period. If he has heard these other languages, he has developed also a remarkable switch mechanism that enables him to turn from one language to another without confusion, without translation, without mother-tongue accent—(but) the uncommitted cortex must be conditioned for speech in the first decade."[7]

Psychologically the elementary school child is ready to learn a second language. He is intrigued by words, accepts a new language system without the need for translation or analysis. The new language is not strange or embarassing to him as long as it effectively fulfills his urge to communicate. Studies have shown that there is little danger that the elementary school child will confuse the second language with his mother-tongue, because he will by that time have mastered the basic sound and structural systems of his native language. In fact, there has been evidence that learning a foreign language enables the student to understand his mother-tongue better.[8] Studies and experiments carried out in the schools of St. Paul, Minnesota, Champaign, Illinois, and New York City all indicated that the time taken from other areas during the school day for foreign language instruction resulted in no detrimental effect upon achievement in those areas. These students did as well as, and some times better than, those who did not add foreign languages to their studies.

---

7. Wilder Penfield, M.D., "The Uncommitted Cortex—The Child's Changing Brain," *The Atlantic Monthly* (July, 1964).
8. Mildred R. Donoghue, *Foreign Languages and the Elementary School Child* (Dubuque, Iowa: Wm. C. Brown Company Publishers, 1968), p. 13.

The Objectives of Foreign Language Instruction

The ultimate objectives of a long-sequence foreign language program are twofold: linguistic and cultural. The linguistic objective implies the attainment of proficiency in the four skills of listening, speaking, reading, and writing. At elementary school level, the degree of skill in each area will depend much on the grade level at which instruction is started and the number of contact hours with that language during the elementary school program. A "FLES graduate" should have as his equipment for continued study of the foreign language in junior and senior high school (1) the ability to understand standard native speech uttered at a normal rate of speed; (2) a mastery of the basic sound and structural systems of the language; (3) an adequate vocabulary to carry on simple short conversations on subjects regarding everyday situations presented in class at his level of interest and (4) the ability to read material in recombinations made up of orally familiar language containing a minimum of new words. Some of the students may also be able to write dictation or simple answers to questions based on material previously practiced orally and read in class.

The cultural phase of the program, especially at the beginning stages, forms a part of the linguistic content. It is found in the behavior patterns that are inseparable from authentic language. Among the more evident "patterns" that indicate characteristic attitudes or mannerisms of a people are forms of address, expressions of courtesy and tact, proverbs, exclamations, and the gestures accompanying speech. During the early phases of language learning, the children take part in the cultural patterns as expressed by the language itself rather than hearing or talking about the culture. Oral communication in a foreign language makes a unique cultural contribution not possible in any other area of the curriculum. It is important that the child learn to imagine himself in situations illustrating another culture. Teaching dialogues in which the students dramatize a situation is an effective procedure.

Visual aids are also essential to help the students imagine themselves in a setting that represents the country where the language is spoken. These aids will be of cultural value only if they are authentic illustrations of the country. When this type of learning is meaningful and pleasurable, it is probable that the children's interest in the foreign country and its people will increase. Young students will learn, as well, to accept the strange sounds and patterns of the language as another way of talking and not "odd" or "silly" as older children are apt to do.

In these ways, the program will contribute to fulfilling cultural objectives that are not only part of the foreign language program, but also part of elementary school's attempt to extend the child's world beyond the confines of his local environment and geographical boundaries.

Linguistic Achievement

To be realistic about the linguistic objective of a FLES program, it is essential to take into account certain limitations which in the past have often been ignored. There is no doubt that there are many advantages to an early start in language learning, but this does not mean that no difficulties will be encountered by these students. It does not mean, either, that second language learning even at FLES level is exactly like learning one's mother tongue. First of all, fluency to the point of near bilingualism will take longer than the three or four years of FLES training in a school situation. The limited amount of daily contact with the foreign language in the classroom cannot be compared with the constant contact that the children had with their native language when they learned to speak. Second, there is interference from the habits formed in learning one's mother tongue. In spite of the fact that the young children usually have a much greater facility for the development of audio-lingual skills than their older brothers and sisters, they will still have to acquire a new set of habits in learning a second language. Formation of these habits may be hindered by their experience in learning and speaking the mother tongue. The science of linguistics has revealed, by comparative studies of the foreign language and the student's first language, the points of interference or differences in sounds and structures that will give students trouble. The well-informed teacher must be aware of these areas of difficulty and plan materials and techniques accordingly. It is not enough merely to present the language to the students. There must be a planned approach that makes them aware of the structure of the language.

The need for a cognitive approach to language learning at the elementary school level is slowly being accepted. In the early years of the FLES movement, it was assumed that children would acquire language skills simply by hearing and repeating. Too often instruction in the foreign language stopped with the memorization of dialogues and the practice of simple pattern drills. Little or no attempt was made to lead the students to the discovery of the system of the new language. The result, in this case, has been that the FLES student was not able to generate speech for purposes of self-expression. Two outstanding specialists have expressed alarm at this failure to give the elementary school child linguistic knowledge through comparison and contrast of the mother tongue and the foreign language. One suggests that programs could be designed which would stress practice and yet provide procedures so that children could be led to see systematic ways in which languages function. Teachers guides could make provisions for generalizations following the practice of specific structures, as well as for some judicious contrasting of the two language systems.[9] The other states that once the learner has been made aware of a linguistic fact, and once he has assigned it its proper place in the linguistic system, he can then slowly free himself from the memorized material and take small steps in creating original and authentic utterances. The objectives of a beginning language course should make provisions for both practice and knowledge.[10]

Importance of Cumulative Language Learning

If the language learning experience is truly cumulative, it will contribute to the ultimate objectives of the school foreign language program. This means two things in planning the program. Teachers at the elementary school level must be aware of the ultimate objectives and plan accordingly. Those responsible for foreign language teaching in the secondary school must build on and reinforce the skills acquired by the FLES students. The ability to understand the language and to speak it are of prime importance in the elementary school. But the introductory phases of reading and a very limited degree of writing—mostly in the form of copying and dictation—also form a part of the program. These are the skills that the secondary school teacher should continue to develop in the students. Just as this teacher has a responsibility to understand the elementary school program, so the FLES teacher must make her course a solid foundation for the continuing study of language. Only in this way will each level of instruction work toward the degree of proficiency which is the aim of the long-sequence program, namely, the ability to receive and communicate ideas and information in the foreign language on a mature level.

9. Virginia Garibaldi (Allen), *The Development of a Broader Rationale for FLES* (Doctoral Dissertation); Ohio State University, 1968, p. 41.
10. Filomena P. del Olmo, "FLES in Search of Discipline and Content," *The DFL Bulletin* VI, no. 3 (March, 1967): p. 10.

Relationships to the Total Curriculum

Second-language teaching is still regarded as a newcomer to the elementary school curriculum. Its acceptance as a regular part of the teaching program has often been questioned in light of the fact that it is an extra, an addition to the well-established curriculum. The struggle to find its place and lay a claim to "belonging" continues. On the other hand, much progress has been made, and well-established FLES programs have pointed out the way to others on uncertain terms with curriculum planners who are reluctant to welcome them. By its very nature, the effective FLES program contributes to the basic principles and procedures of the elementary school program. As shown in the description of its values, linguistic and cultural, it enriches the development of the individual child. It recognizes that children learn by doing. It focuses on the use of the language in simple, everyday situations that are familiar and of interest to young students. It makes the language meaningful by encouraging its use as a means of communication at various times during the school day, in addition to the time devoted to the foreign language lesson. It relates the foreign language experience to other areas of the curriculum.

Functional Aspects Essential to Meaning

It is this functional aspect of language which makes it meaningful to the students and motivates them to learn. To maintain the high degree of interest and motivation usually characteristic of the first year or two of learning, foreign language must assume a new, vital role as soon as possible. To be meaningful to the students it must be related to their immediate environment and it has to be useful in some way. At this time, our society rarely provides occasions for young people of pre-high school age to use foreign language outside the confines of the language class. It is therefore up to those planning the program to provide such occasions. For the elementary school level, there are two ways that this can be done. Incidental use of the foreign language during the day is highly recommended, provided the classroom teacher has the linguistic ability. It can also be used in correlation with other areas of the curriculum.

There are numerous possibilities which the alert and industrious teacher can develop. Songs in the new language can be practiced as part of their music lesson. Games which are a part of their foreign language learning can be used in the physical education program. Arithmetic drills can be conducted in the foreign language, a procedure that children usually enjoy. Some children who have difficulty telling time "catch on" easily to the method of telling time used in the foreign language. A careful study of the social studies curriculum at various grade levels can reveal many occasions for related projects involving cultural and linguistic phases of the foreign language program. It has been predicted that in the social studies teaching of the 1970's, the cross-cultural dimension involving children in studies of other families and communities throughout the world will occur at primary level as well as in the intermediate grades.[11] Opportunities to relate the foreign language with the development of social concepts are numerous.

As soon as the proficiency of the student allows, it would be desirable to have some area or areas of the curriculum taught in the foreign language. This would not only be a strong motivating factor for the improvement of skills in the foreign language, but it would also be a very practical and meaningful way of giving the students the opportunity to continue developing their proficiency. Such an extension of the role of second-language learning may not as yet be feasible in most of our schools. It is hoped that in the future it will enter into the plans of those designing curriculum for tomorrow's schools. On this subject, Dr. Emma Birkmaier wrote in a publication of the Association for Supervision and Curriculum Development regarding new curriculum developments: "Much thought is being given to the teaching of other disciplines in the foreign language at the advanced levels in the six and nine-year modern language sequences. Some school systems are teaching world geography and world affairs in Spanish and biology in German. Such projects are usually conducted by a teacher who has a major in another field besides an excellent mastery of the foreign language."[12]

Contributions to the Language Arts Program

As stated previously, the foreign language learning experience can be an extension and enrichment of the language arts program. It contributes to the student's understanding of what language is and rein-

11. *New Dimensions in the Teaching of FLES,* "Social Studies," New York: MLA-ACTFL Materials Center (1969), p. 32.

12. Emma M. Birkmaier, "Foreign Languages," *Using Current Curriculum Developments,* Chapter 4 (Washington, D.C.: Association for Supervision and Curriculum Development, National Education Association, 1963).

forces his linguistic knowledge by making him aware of the "system" of languages—his mother tongue and another. In addition, FLES helps to develop and strengthen other skills that are part of the language arts program.

Of primary importance among these skills is the ability to listen attentively and discriminately. The foreign language student is oriented from the very beginning to the idea that listening is the basic skill from which he can acquire the other language skills. During his initial experience with the foreign language, the development of auditory discrimination and auditory memory involves concentrated effort in distinguishing and recognizing sounds and intonation patterns. He must also develop the ability to recall with understanding a sequence of sounds and eventually a sequence of utterances.[13]

Literature is another part of language arts that can be enriched by the foreign language program even at elementary school level. Reading in FLES is limited mostly to material based on language already learned audio-lingually. But there is one type of literature that can be read aloud in the foreign language and enjoyed and appreciated by the children. That is poetry. Poems should be selected which suit the child's maturity, experience, and interest. Vocabulary and structures should be those which the children can comprehend in the foreign language. In using poetry in the foreign language, it should be remembered that poetry is for enjoyment, for fun, for pleasure. It should be read aloud and savoured; not assigned for memorization. For the beauty of poetry lies as much in its cadences, rhythms, and sounds as in its imagery.[14]

Reading in English about the children and country where the foreign language is spoken should also be encouraged. This can be a joint project of the two programs. Another phase of literature in language arts may include genres such as fables and folk tales of foreign lands and foreign peoples. The elementary school student may not yet be linguistically ready to read this literature in its original language, but an appreciation of such fables and folk tales in English can enrich both areas of study. Basic concepts of the people and culture developed in the foreign language program may also contribute to a greater understanding of the attitudes, morality, and values expressed in this literature.

---

13. Elizabeth H. Ratte, "Foreign Languages and the Elementary School Language Arts Program," *French Review* (October, 1968).

14. Virginia Garibaldi (Allen), Doctoral Dissertation, pp. 72-76. Comments on literature in the FLES program.

Teaching Techniques and Materials

The foreign language program, like any other area of the curriculum, must be planned according to the basic principles of motivation, habit formation, reward, and success. Consideration must be given to the characteristics of children at these age levels (for FLES usually ages 8 to 12) and recognize their urge to communicate and their need for active participation.

Assumptions Underlying FLES Programs

An effective approach to teaching a second language in the elementary school is based on the following assumptions: (1) that the second language is to be used as normal speech with oral communication as the primary objective; (2) that language learning is primarily a matter of habit formation and the acquisition of a new set of skills; (3) that there will be points of interference or difficulty in learning a second language even for the elementary school children; (4) that language learning is meaningful only when the language is used in familiar, real-life situations within the understanding and interests of the students; (5) that preadolescent children have a remarkable ability to hear and imitate accurately and to memorize; (6) that the elementary school students enjoy activity and learn best by doing.

Essentiality of Auditory Memory and Discrimination

The development of the skills of auditory discrimination and auditory memory must not be taken for granted. The teacher should plan the practice and drills needed to enable the students to hear the sounds of the language accurately, otherwise they will not be able to produce them. Auditory memory is usually acquired more easily by the young student than by the high school or college student. He does not feel the urge to analyze the sounds he hears or to identify them by seeing them. Provided the utterance is not too long, is generally understood and meaningful, the FLES student usually is capable of and enjoys auditory memorization of the new language.

Much of this initial stage of learning is based on the observation of how language is learned in general. A child begins to talk after hearing the language spoken around him for a considerable period of time. He continues to develop his speech habits surrounded constantly by the sounds of his mother tongue. It is impossible to reproduce these conditions in second language learning in a school situation, but certain procedures can be used in the classroom which will facilitate the use of the second language as normal speech. First of all, the foreign language must be the language of the classroom. On the other hand, the judicious use of the mother tongue by the teacher to explain very briefly the lesson of the day or the dialogue or narrative to be memorized is permissible. In fact, it is preferable to the total exclusion of the mother tongue to the point where misunderstandings and confusion occur because the students do not understand what is to be learned. But, and this is important to note, the use of English must be kept to a minimum and the students should not be allowed to use their mother tongue during the foreign language lesson.

Educational Uses of a Cultural Island

Creating a cultural island in the classroom is also essential to the formation of correct habits and attitudes toward learning the language. At all times the students must realize that they have to try to understand and respond through the use of the new language. To make this cultural island authentic, the model used should be near-native. If the teacher does not have a near-native pronunciation and intonation (which are highly desirable), then the model for hearing and imitating should be provided on discs or tape. The material should be recorded by native voices, preferably boys and girls, as well as both male and female adults. At the beginning stages, it is important to give the students the opportunity to listen to the spoken language with numerous repetitions of the material they are expected to understand, learn, and reproduce orally. Much of the language which they hear in the first few months will be passive vocabulary. This passive or "understanding" vocabulary will be much larger than their active vocabulary.

Teaching Foreign Language as Oral Communication

Among the generally accepted techniques for teaching languages as oral communication are dialogues, narratives, action series, and short dramatizations. The dialogue is favored as the most natural use of the language because it provides for an exchange of conversation between two or more people. The dialogue also lends itself well to creating lifelike situations within the experience and interests of the students. For young children such topics as "at the dinner table," "buying a pet dog," "going to the circus," and "a day in the country," provide situations in which they can identify themselves in the foreign language as well as in English. Both the narrative and the action series are a form of short monologue in which a student describes or talks about somebody or something. For example, the narrative might be an oral description of one's family or one's house. The action series might consist of telling what one does during the day, the emphasis being on verbs and expressions of time. Dramatizations of familiar children's stories or fairy tales usually appeal to young students in grades 1 to 4. Such dramatizations can combine the use of language with action very effectively in a play-acting situation. They should be short, lively, and carefully chosen or prepared, keeping in mind the language level of the students.

In addition to these contrived situations which create in the classroom a make-believe scene for the use of the language, there are many occasions to talk about real, everyday matters in class. It is important for the teacher to be aware of the background and activities of the children so that he can make appropriate conversation at the right time. For example, birthdays are always a welcome subject for discussion, or the arrival of a baby in the family, or the family vacation, or simply the reason why somebody in the class is absent. This may be called the incidental use of the foreign language, either during the language class or any time during the school day. Other common subjects for this type of everyday conversation would be the weather, the date, the time, and health. The conversation will usually start with a question or remark from the teacher to which one or more students respond. Then the students should be encouraged to ask each other questions, creating a conversation among themselves. At the early stages the teacher may have to direct this exchange by telling the student what to ask or say. For example, the teacher may say: "John, ask Henry if he has a cold" or "Alice, tell Joe that today is your birthday." This type of practice is called directed dialogue.

Guides to Emphasis on Pattern or Structure

The use of pattern or structure drills to teach at FLES level should always be in a meaningful situation, related to a dialogue or narrative learned or to the reality of the classroom. The manipulation of language in drills is desirable only to a limited extent at this level. The drills must be short and take only a few minutes of the class time. Visual aids help to make a drill meaningful and interesting. It is advisable to use only the simplest of drills such as substitution or rejoinders. The two sample drills that follow are based on English structures. The first is an elementary substitution drill. The structure is — It's a —

It's a (dog)   (Teacher holds up one picture at a time)
It's a (house)
It's a (car)
It's a (train) etc.

Practice in giving the correct rejoinder might concentrate on this structure:

Is he happy?   (Yes, he is.)
Is he intelligent?   (Yes, he is.)
Is he brave?   (Yes, he is.) etc.
Are they happy?   (Yes, they are.)
Are they hungry?   (Yes, they are.)
Are they tired?   (Yes, they are.) etc.

The purpose of these drills is to develop accurate, automatic response when using a difficult structure. Usually drills help the student overcome what has already been identified as points of interference or difficulties resulting from differences in structure between the foreign language and the student's mother tongue.

Songs and games in the language provide variety and an element of fun essential to motivating children in elementary school. These are desirable activities and worthwhile teaching techniques as long as the learning of language is the prime objective. Most children like to sing. They learn the words to a song with ease and enjoyment. The meaning of the song must be made clear. Some of the vocabulary may be taught with the aid of pictures or other visual aids. It is not necessary or desirable, however, to try to explain all the vocabulary in a song or in a poem. Music and rhythm facilitate memorization of the words which young children can produce orally with remarkable accuracy. As for games in the foreign language, they serve also as an effective means of motivation and provide a change of pace in classroom activity. A game wisely chosen promotes the use of language closely related to the lesson content. When properly presented and controlled, games can make drill and review a profitable, pleasurable learning experience. Numerous suggestions for language games can be found in teacher guides and books on methodology.

The importance of well-structured, professionally prepared teaching materials cannot be too strongly emphasized. A successful program depends to a great extent on the curriculum guide and teaching materials put into the hands of the foreign language teachers. Of course skilled teachers are indispensable to a good program, and this will be discussed in more detail later. It is sufficient to point out here that good teaching materials, including a well-written guide with detailed suggestions for teaching procedures, can be invaluable to the inexperienced teacher or to the teacher whose language background is somewhat inadequate.

There is now available a good number of professionally prepared guides and materials for FLES.[15] These should be examined carefully before a choice is made. A special word of advice to those who would like to prepare their own materials. It is best to avoid experimenting or creating materials until those concerned with the program are thoroughly familiar with existing materials and are well informed about the acceptable theories and practices of successful FLES programs. A chapter entitled "How Should Materials Be Prepared?" in a recent book on teaching children foreign language provides a check list for curriculum writers and states that "preparation of instructional materials is a cooperative effort. . . . Working together as a team, many persons should prepare the curriculum and accompanying materials for a FLES program. A native speaker, several classroom teachers, secondary school staff members, and wherever possible, a person with a knowledge of linguistics should cooperate in the development of a curriculum."[16]

Criteria for Judging Instructional Materials

Whether the teaching materials are bought commercially or prepared locally by competent professionals, they must fit the philosophy and needs of the community and the school. FLES programs vary considerably from one district to another in such matters as the grade level where the program starts, provision for continuity, available teachers—classroom or specialists—and, of course, the budget. Differences of this sort are to be expected and, fortunately, there is a variety of materials available. Variety in materials is advisable, however, up to only a certain point. There are basic criteria to determine desirable materials. Experi-

---

15. See the bibliography at the end of this chapter.
16. Mary Finocchiaro, *Teaching Children Foreign Languages* (New York: McGraw-Hill, Inc., 1964), pp. 155-157.

ence has indicated the following important considerations: (1) Do the materials provide the means to attain the linguistic and cultural objectives of the program? (2) Is there a carefully planned sequence for instruction through all the grades of the elementary school—and preferably beyond? (3) Does the teacher's guide contain detailed instructions for classroom procedure? (4) Are adequate audio-visual aids provided? (5) Is the language authentic and idiomatic? (6) Are the recordings on discs or tapes done by native voices at a natural rate of speech? (7) Have the materials been carefully structured for the progressive development of skills? (8) Is the content within the interests and maturity of the students? Unless most of these criteria can be checked off affirmatively, the materials can be said to be substandard and undesirable.

Materials which contain the elements just mentioned are sometimes referred to as "integrated materials." They provide teacher's guides for each level, reading material or student's book when needed, and all the audio-visual aids. (See the bibliography for a list of integrated materials.) They are prepared by a group of experts which usually includes experienced teachers, outstanding authorities in the field of language learning and linguistics, and native speakers. For the teacher, experienced or inexperienced, highly competent in the language or limited in language proficiency, such materials are the answer to many problems that one very busy teacher cannot possibly solve satisfactorily alone in a short space of time. Among these is the availability of teaching aids correlated with each lesson, providing visuals that are authentic and recordings that are well made. In addition, these materials are usually structured in accordance with the principles of linguistics and planned for the progressive development of language skills.

Uses Made of Audio-Visual Aids

Visual aids are indispensable to the teaching of language by direct oral communication without recourse to translation. In order to minimize identification or meaning by use of the mother tongue, visuals must serve to illustrate and explain the people, things, and concepts expressed by the foreign language. The visual aids in the integrated materials play a vital role in the teaching procedure. Such aids include films, filmstrip, illustrated pupils' books, posters, cutout figures, and objects. For the teacher who does not use integrated programs containing these components but who needs visual aids, there are available commercially prepared sets of language wall charts, flash cards, and filmstrip that can be used as desired—to help teach material in the course of study or to supplement it. Such aids relieve the teacher of the constant search for appropriate objects and pictures often difficult to find. They also have the advantage of a professional visual presentation, containing only what needs to be illustrated in a desirable form, color, and size. Pictures, wall charts, filmstrip and films, if authentic illustrations of the country where the language is spoken, can be used effectively to present elementary culture concepts.

Although the use of a language laboratory is not usual at elementary school level, recorded materials do form an important part of the classroom program. If the teacher's pronunciation and fluency are adequate, his voice may be the model for the children to imitate most of the time. Yet the use of discs or tapes should not be excluded. When all or most of the modelling and oral drill is done by the teacher, he may soon tire. Distortions of the language then can result. A wise teacher, no matter how proficient, will use the content of the lesson professionally recorded by native or near-native voices as a supplement to his "live" lesson. Such recorded materials are indispensable to the teacher who needs a native model for practice in preparing his lesson, and to the teacher who prefers to use native voices as the first model for the children to imitate. In any case, the students should be exposed to a variety of voices using the language—male and female, adults and children. The language should be standard and not typical of any one region.

At the beginning stages of learning the students need to be surrounded by the oral language as much as possible. Tapes and discs can act as an extension of the language lesson at other times during the day in school or in the form of take-home lessons. The teacher who understands the nature of language learning cannot ignore the value of audio aids. The constant practice, which is the only way to form correct language habits and to develop audio-lingual skills, makes demands on the teacher's time and patience beyond what he can afford to give—no matter how willing and skilled he may be. Recorded material is an essential "little teacher's helper" to be used at his discretion. For classwork, recordings on tape are preferable to those on discs. The tape recorder allows easy stopping, starting, and repeating at will. When the students are to listen or listen and repeat by themselves during free time in the school day or at home, discs are the best choice.

Television as an Instructional Aid

A discussion about audio-visual aids would not be complete without reference to teaching by television. This teaching procedure is still a relatively new addition to the school curriculum. In the area of foreign languages, research and experimentation have revealed pertinent facts for those considering television as a means of instruction. Television programs can bring to large numbers of students a master teacher having native or near-native pronunciation, a professionally prepared presentation of the language, and cultural material filmed in the country or countries where the target language is spoken. As a result of research done in three large televised FLES programs,[17] the following evaluation was noted: (1) television instruction without teacher follow-up is ineffective (Modern Language Project, Boston—*Parlons Francais,* and Denver-Stanford Project); (2) at least 30 minutes of follow-up per week is needed for desirable results in student achievement (Modern Language Project); (3) enthusiastic and conscientious handling of follow-up by skilled classroom teachers, even though they are limited in language ability, can give satisfactory results (Modern Language Project); (4) the use of specialists is likely to improve student achievement in speaking skills but not necessarily in listening and reading comprehension (University of Illinois Foreign Instruction Project); (5) practice or follow-up sections using recorded materials and carefully worked out procedures in which the classroom teacher directs the practice but does not personally give the model utterances in the foreign language can give adequate results (University of Illinois Foreign Instruction Project); (6) use of tape recorders for listening and recording of the children's voices is a recommended supplement to the televised lessons and teacher follow-up (Denver-Stanford Project); (7) instructional procedures for follow-up (recordings, a second viewing of the television lessons, or entirely teacher-directed activities without special aids) should be chosen according to the teacher's prior training and experience in the foreign language and (8) a second viewing of the televised lesson at home with the parents present has a strong motivating effect (Denver-Stanford Project).

The use of educational television has been an important factor in the expansion of FLES instruction throughout the country. It has been

17. Condensed from a paper entitled "Research Results in Three Large Televised FLES Programs," prepared by Dr. Earle S. Randall, Purdue University, for the International Conference on Modern Foreign Language Teaching, held at Berlin, August 31–September 5, 1964.

estimated that the *Parlons Francais* program alone has given instruction through educational television stations to over 2,000,000 students in various sections of the country. As research and experimentation have shown, however, it is not a cure-all for proposed programs where FLES teachers will not be available. There must be adequate and effective follow-up in the classroom by either specialists or the classroom teacher. In addition, there should be help for the classroom teacher who needs work in methods and the opportunity to better his oral language skills. This help may be found in special workshops, either in-service or at a nearby institution of higher learning, and in the availability of a foreign language specialist or supervisor employed by the school system.

The Role of the Teacher

The saying that a program is as good as its teacher is a self-evident truth. When speaking about the FLES teacher, this implies two basic qualifications—the ability to be effective in the elementary school classroom and the ability to teach or to present the foreign language to the children. "Presenting" the foreign language may appear to be the same as "teaching" the foreign language, but there is a difference. In the case of the classroom teacher who feels somewhat inadequate in the foreign language, there are ways of presenting the language to the students by the judicious use of integrated materials including films, filmstrip, recordings, and television, as has already been mentioned. The teacher's role is to plan the follow-up using the available aids. His role, in this case, may be more of a selecting and guiding process than actual teaching of the lesson. During the period of shortage of adequately trained teachers, this use of the classroom teacher has at times given desirable results. On the other hand, it must be assumed that the classroom teacher is enthusiastic, willing to take all the means possible to make his role in the FLES program effective, and conscientious in the careful planning of the follow-up class lesson. A teacher who has training adequate to handle the level of FLES assigned to him can be said to truly "teach" the foreign language. Such a teacher is the hope for the continued development of foreign language instruction in the elementary school.

In view of the critical need for FLES teachers, the Modern Language Association presented the following statement: "Ideally, he (the FLES teacher) should be an expert in the foreign language he teaches, with near-native accent and fluency, and also skillful in teaching young children ... If a teacher's foreign language accent is not good, he should make every effort to improve it, and meanwhile he should rely on discs or tapes to supply authentic model voices for his pupils. But since language is communication, and a child cannot communicate with a phonograph or a tape recorder, no FLES learning can be wholly successful without the regular presence in the classroom of a live model who is also an expert teacher. The shortage of such doubly skilled teachers is the most serious obstacle to the success of FLES. To relieve this shortage, every institution that trains future elementary-school teachers should offer a major in one or more foreign languages."[18] Unfortunately, the past decade has brought about a very limited response to this appeal made to elementary school teacher training institutions. The shortage of qualified teachers remains a major problem.

Identification of the role of the FLES teacher and the qualifications needed were subjects of controversy for some time.[19] The tendency to favor specialists was tempered somewhat by budgetary considerations and concern for close correlation of foreign language with the rest of the curriculum. "Specialist" here refers to the teacher who teaches only foreign language in the elementary schools. The role of the specialist also varies depending on the needs of the school system. In some cases, the specialists do all the teaching of the foreign language. In others, they give demonstration lessons or teach some of the lessons on a regular basis, and the classroom teacher does the follow-up. The specialist may also plan and set up the program of instruction as well as act as a resource person to the classroom teachers. Sometimes, the experienced specialist is called upon to supervise the whole program, and, if qualified, to coordinate FLES with the high school foreign language program.

It is evident that in contemporary and future FLES programs the teacher can have varied roles, depending on the structure of the program in his school system and on his individual qualifications. The tendency is to use a team of teachers, so that their combined abilities

18. *Foreign Languages in the Elementary School: A Second Statement of Policy* (New York: Modern Language Association, 1961).

19. For different opinions see *Foreign Languages in the Elementary School,* M Eriksson et al., pp. 98-99; *Teaching Children Foreign Languages,* M. Finocchiaro, pp. 11-12; and *Foreign Languages and the Elementary School Child,* M. Donoghue, pp. 363-368.

will provide instruction that is suitable to the elementary school child and linguistically correct and near-native in quality.

Teamwork is Essential

The foreign language program in the elementary school will be a worthwhile enterprise only if the attitudes and relationship of all the school staff members concerned are favorable. Unless there is a common philosophy and acceptance of the program that unites their efforts, the chances for a workable situation are not very good. Much depends on how the program is initiated and whether all the staff concerned are invited to be members of the team. Even the classroom teacher who does not teach the language, but whose class receives instruction by a specialist, needs to be informed about the nature of language learning and the aims of the program. The regular classroom teacher can do much to create favorable attitudes in his students toward learning a foreign language. He should be urged to remain in the classroom and observe the language class. This teacher may want to make incidental use of the foreign language during the day because of his interest and background in the language. It is up to the coordinator or specialist to encourage and help him to do so. The specialist teacher has an obligation to consult with the regular classroom teacher in order to become well acquainted with the children's background and general scholastic ability. He must also work with the classroom teacher on the best possible ways to correlate the foreign language program with the rest of the curriculum.

When the classroom teachers do much of the foreign language teaching, helped perhaps by specialists, television, or integrated materials, there should be provision for guidance and in-service workshops to improve or maintain their skills. This usually is the responsibility of the coordinator or supervisor who visits the classroom teachers regularly and is aware of their needs. The coordinator or supervisor will also hold frequent meetings with these teachers to discuss techniques, materials, and plans for the integration of FLES with other areas of the school program.

Since foreign language in the elementary school is considered part of a long sequence, the initial planning and continued operation of the program requires the coordinated efforts of administration and teachers at both elementary and secondary school level. This can be accomplished only if there are frequent meetings and mutual consultation of the elementary and high school foreign language staff. The FLES teacher must be aware of the skills expected and the objectives to be attained by the time the students finish the program in the elementary school. The high school teachers must have an understanding of the FLES program, its procedures and aims, and should plan to build their program on the background of the "FLES graduate," using similar techniques to continue development of audio-lingual skills. In other words, it is absolutely essential for all concerned with this long-sequence program to accept the same long-range objectives and to practice similar basic techniques of teaching.

Bilingualism

Effective FLES instruction as part of a long-range foreign language program (9-10 years) makes it possible for an increasing number of Americans to approach that degree of proficiency which is called bilingualism. This is desirable in terms of the national interest as well as individual development and preparation of the student for his world. In the past, the second language, a foreign language, was usually taught to students who were monolingual and whose mother tongue was English. This will, of course, continue to be the situation in our schools. However, a new approach to bilingualism is slowly but surely invading the schools.

Language experts[20] have, for some time, been concerned about our neglect of the many Americans who hear and speak a foreign language at home. A historical study of the situation reveals that the need to be "Americanized" caused many immigrants, particularly the young, to avoid use of a foreign language. The result was a loss to the individual and to the nation. An attempt is now being made to encourage these individuals to maintain and improve their proficiency in the foreign language, thereby improving their self-image as first-class citizens with a desirable skill that is part of their heritage. In addition, English is taught as the second language to enable them to function effectively in an English-speaking environment. The Bilingual Education Act of 1968 is also causing states to change their laws so that other languages besides English may be used to teach various areas of the curriculum.

The establishment of bilingual schools brings another new, exciting dimension to the foreign language program, especially at elementary

---

20. A.Bruce Gaarder et al., "The Challenge of Bilingualism," *Northeast Conference Report,* New York: MLA-ACTFL Materials Center, (1965). According to this report, it was estimated that over three million school-age individuals in the continental United States retain the use of a non-English mother tongue, p. 95.

school level. According to one of the outstanding leaders in foreign language education, bilingual education adds at least three new principles that are applicable to FLES. First, bilingual schooling begins in pre-school classes, in kindergarten, or in first grade—where FLES should have started in the first place. Secondly, two languages are used as a media of instruction thus suggesting that the second language is a real language and not just a school subject. And, thirdly, the teachers in bilingual programs are usually native speakers and authentic representatives of their culture.[21]

In addition, there is a fourth educational factor of major importance affecting student motivation and interest. That factor is the use of language to communicate with one's peers in a bilingual situation where language is a tool as well as a skill. This situation begins to approximate the meaningful and usually very successful experience that children have when they learn to use a second language in the country where it is spoken. So we may look to bilingual education as a promising means of offering to a large number of our school population the rewarding human experience to be had in an exchange of ideas, beliefs, and feelings, through the medium of another person's language.

EXTENDING YOUR LEARNING

1. Select a panel to discuss these topics.
   a. The advantages of second language learning at elementary school level.
   b. The place of FLES in the language arts curriculum.
2. Outline a plan for the correlation of French, Spanish or German with other areas of the curriculum in grades 3 to 6.
3. Prepare a written or oral report evaluating a set of FLES teaching materials. Note the basic criteria suggested in this chapter.
4. Conduct a question and answer period with questions prepared in advance by the students. These questions are to be answered by other students during the class period. The following topics are suggested:
   a. The nature of second language learning.
   b. Auditory skills.
   c. The formation of language habits.
   d. Techniques for teaching oral language.
   e. Audio-visual materials.
   f. Bilingualism.
5. If possible, visit local or nearby FLES classes. Divide into small groups, each group visiting one class. Try to arrange for visits at various grade levels. Give oral reports of the class activity and teaching techniques observed, followed by a general discussion period.

---

21. Theodore Andersson, *Foreign Language in the Elementary School: A Struggle Against Mediocrity* (Austin: University of Texas Press, 1969), p. 187.

BIBLIOGRAPHY
Texts, Bulletins, Reports

American Council for the Teaching of Foreign Languages and the Indiana Language Program. *New Dimensions in the Teaching of FLES.* New York: MLA-ACTFL Materials Center, 62 Fifth Avenue, 1969.

Andersson, Theodore. *Foreign Languages in the Elementary School: A Struggle Against Mediocrity.* Austin: University of Texas Press, 1969.

Bourque, Edward and Gladys Lipton (editors). *The FLES Student: A Study.* Philadelphia, Chilton Books, 1968.

Donoghue, Mildred R. *Foreign Languages and the Elementary School Child.* Dubuque, Iowa: Wm. C. Brown Company Publishers, 1968.

Dunkel, Harold B. and Roger Pillet. *French in the Elementary School: Five Years Experience.* Chicago: University of Chicago Press, 1962.

Eriksson, Marguerite, Ilse Forest and Ruth Mulhauser: *Foreign Languages in the Elementary School:* Englewood Cliffs: Prentice-Hall, Inc., 1964.

Finocchiaro, Mary. *Teaching Children Foreign Languages.* New York: McGraw-Hill Book Co., 1964.

Garibaldi, Virginia (Allen). *The Development of a Broader Rationale for FLES* (Doctoral Dissertation) Ann Arbor: University Microfilms, 1968.

Johnston, Marjorie and Elizabeth Keesee. *Modern Foreign Languages and Your Child.* Bulletin OE-27020 Washington: U.S. Government Printing Office, 1964.

Lipton, Gladys and Edward Bourque (editors). *FLES: Projections into the Future,* 1969. *Research, Relevancy, Reality: The Three R's of FLES,* 1970. New York: MLA-ACTFL Materials Center.

Miller, Helen, *An Annotated Bibliography of Integrated FLES Teaching Materials.* Bloomington: Indiana Language Program, Indiana University, 1969. To be available in 1970 from the MLA-ACTFL Materials Center.

Modern Language Association. *FLES Packet* (Over 20 articles on the rationale, problems, recommended solutions, studies and research). New York: MLA-ACTF Materials Center (revised), 1967.

Northeast Conference Reports, MLA-ACTFL Materials Center, Conrad J. Schmitt (editor) "Foreign Languages in the Elementary School," 1964. Gaarder, A. Bruce et al. "The Challenge of Bilingualism," 1965.

Pillet, Roger (editor). *FLES and the Objectives of the Contemporary Elementary Schools:* Philadelphia: Chilton Books, 1967.

Stern, H.H. *Foreign Languages in Primary Education: The Teaching of Foreign or Second Languages to Younger Children.* (Report of an international meeting.) Hamburg, Germany: UNESCO Institute for Education, 1963.

Strickland, Ruth. *The Language Arts in the Elementary School,* 3rd ed. Boston: D.C. Heath, 1969.

———, "Language Arts" pp. 35-39. *New Dimensions in the Teaching of FLES.* New York: MLA-ACTFL Materials Center, 1969.

INTEGRATED TEACHING MATERIALS

A partial listing of programs for three or four levels of continued instruction, containing audio-visual components and teacher guides or manuals.

1. *Children of the Americas Spanish Series.* San Francisco, California: Harr Wagner Publishing Co. Oral introduction to the series followed by six books all containing pictures and reading, discs, picture vocabulary cards, teacher's guides.

2. *Elementary French and Spanish Series—Bonjour, Buenos Días.* Boston, Mass.: Allyn and Bacon, Inc. Six student books, the first two with pictures only and the others with reading material. Tapes, teacher's editions of the books with suggestions for teaching procedures.

3. *En Avant.* (The Nuffield Introductory French Course) Boston: Houghton Mifflin Co. Four Stages for grades 4 through 8, plans for continuation through upper grades. Developed in England, reports, evaluation available. Teacher's manuals, tapes, flash cards, flannelboard figurines, wall charts, reading cards, posters, student readers and workbooks, games. Tests to be developed.

4. *Introducing French, Introducing Spanish.* New York: Holt, Rinehart and Winston. A series of materials for four levels with student picture books, readers, discs, tapes, posters, cut-out figures and objects, teacher's manuals. The complete Holt series provides a continuation at secondary school level.

5. *Languages Unlimited: French, German, Spanish.* Jamaica, N.Y.: Eye Gate House, Inc. Three levels with color film strip, flash cards, student workbooks, discs, teacher's manuals.

6. *Let's Speak Spanish, Let's Speak French.* New York: McGraw-Hill Book Co. Four levels of instruction containing student books with pictures for the first two levels and reading for levels three and four, student discs, vocabulary picture cue charts, teacher's guides. Continuing materials at secondary school level.

7. *Parlons Francais and Una Aventura Espanola.* Boston, Mass.: Heath-Raytheon Education Co. Film series for three or four levels of instruction. The *Parlons Francais* films are in color. Student discs, activity books, reader (for *Parlons Francais*), teacher practice discs, training films, guides, testing materials.

8. *Voix et Images de France, Cours Elémentaire—Bonjour, Line.* Philadelphia, Pa.: Chilton Books, Three parts, (Bonjour, Line I, II and III) for three or four levels of instruction. Color filmstrip, tapes, student discs and picture books, reading materials, teacher text suggesting teaching procedures.

Focus

References to evaluative principles and techniques have accompanied most of the chapters in this text which dealt with particular facets of the language arts. Nevertheless, in this era of "accountability" and the rush to hire business firms to either teach and be paid on the basis of some measure of pupil's success in learning, or, at least, to supervise the testing program, so parents can *believe* the results, good or bad, it was considered particularly important to include a separate chapter dealing with evaluation.

Dr. Montebello begins the chapter with a definition of evaluation, which she considers a broader, more comprehensive term than "testing" or "measurement." She notes that evaluation must begin from a base of clearly stated objectives—to do otherwise is to start out on a journey without a destination and complain when the journey ends that one isn't where he wanted to be!

While its impossible to treat an area as comprehensive, and as controversial, as behavioral objectives thoroughly in a chapter which must include a general treatment of evaluative techniques, the author provides a very good introduction to this field. It is clear that writers of educational objectives can no longer use such terms as "to understand" or "to appreciate" (particularly the latter) with impunity. Mager and others have forced educators to be more specific and to have more clearly in mind what we hope to accomplish as we teach.

This chapter includes checklists which should be very helpful to a classroom teacher who understands *why,* and perhaps *when,* but not *how.* When such checklists aren't included, specific guidelines are suggested which should enable a classroom teacher to more precisely gauge a child's progress toward clearly established goals.

Elementary schools, in general, and elementary teachers, in particular, are being asked to provide evidence that they are performing their very important tasks, for which the American taxpayer is paying what he considers a very high price, at a high level of competence, with good results. If educators don't provide the guidance which will make "accountability" a sensible, acceptable concept to professionals and non-professionals as well, then evaluation will take directions which the author of this chapter specifically, and most other educators as well, consider unwise and narrowly conceived.

Mary Montebello

chapter eleven

evaluation

The specific instruments and techniques for measuring and evaluating the results of instruction in the language arts program are discussed in this chapter.

Evaluation is the process of determining the extent to which objectives have been achieved. It includes all of the procedures used by the teacher, children, principal and other school personnel to appraise outcomes of instruction, and it involves such steps as (1) formulating goals as behaviors, (2) securing evidence on the achievement of goals in selected situations, (3) summarizing and recording evidence, (4) interpreting evidence, and (5) using interpretations to improve instruction.

Evaluation techniques include teacher-made paper and pencil tests, standardized tests, questionnaires, direct and informal observations, checklists, inventories, logs, diaries, themes and written work of all kinds, records of discussions and oral reports, diagnostic tests, rating scales, and any other instrument by which teachers can secure evidence of change in behavior.

No matter the technique employed, there is the need for interpreting the results. Measurement procedures are only tools. Insight skill and judgment are required in the use and interpretation of such tools.

A plan of continual observation, diagnosis and remedial guidance should be a part of the on-going instructional program.

The evaluation should include teacher evaluation, teacher-pupil evaluation, pupil-self evaluation, and pupil-pupil evaluation.

The process of measurement is secondary to that of defining objectives. The purposes to be achieved must first be formulated clearly.

The purposes held for elementary education continue to be broad, and a dual responsibility for contributing to the development of the individual and to society is clearly discernible. As has been true for a long time, the elementary school accepts a major responsibility for helping children to develop competence in the English language.

Each instructional area, in its own way, embraces goals of understanding, attitude, and skill that the child can use satisfyingly in his personal life and usefully in the life of the larger group of which he is a part. Concurrently the elementary school gives attention to a broad range of goals that are more purely related to the socialization of the child, to assist in his general enculturation. These character and personality-oriented goals become a part of the total school experience.

The most complete effort in recent years to state the objectives held for elementary education was the study published by the Russell Sage Foundation in 1953.[1] The report discusses four types of objectives—knowledge and understanding, skill and competence, attitude and interest, and action pattern.

In its most recent statement, the Educational Policies Commission[2] indicated as the central purpose of education the development of the ability to think. It supports this objective on the basis of man's rationality and a challenge that this particular objective will not be generally obtained unless the school focuses upon it.

B. Othanel Smith and others[3] suggest five criteria to be met by objectives if they are to be valid. In this system sound objectives must "(1) be conceived in terms of the demands of the social circumstances; (2) lead toward the fulfillment of basic human needs; (3) be consistent with democratic ideals; (4) be either consistent or noncontradictory in their relationships with one another; and (5) be capable of reduction to behavioristic terms."

"Behavioral objectives" are typically defined as statements of

1. Nolan C. Kearney, *Elementary School Objectives* (Beverly Hills, California: Russell Sage, 1953), 189 pp.

2. National Education Association, "The Central Purpose of American Education" *NEA Journal* (1961), p. 21.

3. B. Othanel Smith et al., *Fundamentals of Curriculum Development,* revised edition (Yonkers-on-Hudson, New York: World Book Company, 1957), 685 pp.

purpose which describe desired student behavior and indicate the content through which the behavior is to be developed. While Eugene R. Smith and others were among the earliest to use the term as such, Bobbitt and Charters expressed objectives in this fashion. As stated above, B. Othanel Smith and others require that an objective be stated in behavioral terms. Taba, Beauchamp, Goodlad and Richter, Hawthorne, McClure, Sand, Krathwohl, and Block, are among those who have utilized the idea of behavioral objectives in conceptual research and as part of curriculum development.[4] McNeil argues for behavioral objectives as the basis for supervision of instruction,[5] suggesting that teacher and supervisor agree on specific objectives to be achieved by the students with subsequent evaluation of the instruction to be based upon the extent to which the teacher accomplished what she intended to accomplish.

Ammons, in a survey of 300 school systems, found that there were no objectives of the kind described above.[6] Where there were descriptions of behaviors they either were of teacher behaviors or were of such an ambiguous nature as to obscure for whom the behavior was described.

Mager presents perhaps the most explicit description of behavior objectives and places two major qualifications on objectives not always expressed by other authors.[7] These qualifications are that the behavior must be observable and that the behaviors are to be terminal. Ammons argues for consideration of behavior which is not observable but which

---

4. Eugene R. Smith, et al., *Appraising and Recording Student Progress* (New York: Harper & Row, Publishers, 1942), 550 pp.; Franklin Bobbitt, *The Curriculum* (Boston: Houghton Mifflin Co., 1918), 295 pp.; W.W. Charters, *Curriculum Construction* (New York: The Macmillan Co., 1923), 352 pp.; B. Othanel Smith, et al., *op. cit.;* Hilda Taba, *Curriculum Development; Theory and Practice* (New York: Harcourt, Brace Jovanovich, Inc., 1962), 529 pp.; George A. Beauchamp, *Curriculum Theory,* Kagg (1961), 149 pp.; John I. Goodlad and Maurice N. Richter, Jr., *The Development of a Conceptual System for Dealing with Problems of Curriculum and Instruction,* University of California at Los Angeles and Institute for Development of Educational Activities (1966), 69 pp.; Richard D. Hawthorne, "A Model for the Analysis of Team Teachers' Curricular Decisions and Verbal Instructional Interaction" (Doctoral Dissertation; University of Wisconsin, 1967); Robert M. McClure, "Procedures, Processes, and Products in Curriculum Development," (Doctoral Dissertation; University of California at Los Angeles, 1965); Ole Sand, *Curriculum Study in Basic Nursing Education* (New York: G.P. Putnam's Sons, 1955), 225 pp.; David R. Krathwohl, "Stating Objectives Appropriately for Program, for Curriculum, and for Instructional Material Development," *Journal of Teacher Education* 16 (1965): 82-92; Elaine C. Block, "Sequence as a Factor in Classroom Instruction" (Doctoral Dissertation; University of Wisconsin, 1965).

5. John D. McNeil, "Antidote to a School Scandal," *Educational Forum* 31 (1966): 69-77.

6. Margaret Ammons, "An Empirical Study of Process and Product in Curriculum Development," *Journal of Educational Research* 57 (1964): 451-7.

7. Robert F. Mager, *Preparing Instructional Objectives* (Palo Alto, California: Fearon Publishers, 1962), 62 pp.

can be inferred according to definitions agreed upon by those involved.[8] She also sees objectives as descriptions of direction rather than as descriptions of terminal behaviors. Herrick also identifies objectives as setters of direction.[9]

The authors cited in the foregoing paragraphs tend to make a distinction between objectives and other statements of goals, restricting the use of the term "objectives" to those statements which describe desired student behavior and appropriate content. Other kinds of statements of purpose may be called goals, aims, or purposes.

Among curriculum theorists, there are those who doubt the necessity of behavioral objectives. Eisner and Macdonald argue that formulation of objectives prior to instruction may not be possible.[10] Eisner also questions the usefulness of objectives.

Bloom and Krathwohl and others have published taxonomies of educational goals.[11] Bloom's 1956 handbook was devoted to a classification of behaviors in the cognitive domain. Identified were six levels of cognitive behaviors: knowledge of specifics, comprehension, analysis, application, synthesis, and evaluation. While the authors of the taxonomy disclaim any evaluation of these different areas of objectives, they do arrange them from simple to complex. Many users have come to speak of "higher" and "lower" levels in the taxonomy, with preference for instruction and testing directed toward the higher levels.[12]

The makers and users of objective tests have long resented accusations that their tests measured only superficial aspects of educational achievement such as rote memory or recall of isolated factual details. In response, they have tended more and more to emphasize items that would be classified at higher levels in the Taxonomy. The leaflet *Multiple Choice Questions: A Close Look,* illustrates this emphasis.[13]

8. Margaret Ammons, "Evaluation: What Is It? Who Does It? When Should It Be Done?" *In Evaluation of Children's Reading Achievement,* Perspectives in Reading Monograph Series, IRA (1967).

9. Dan W. Anderson, et al., compilers, *Strategies of Curriculum Development: Works of Virgil Herrick* (Columbus, Ohio: Charles E. Merrill Publishers, 1965), 196 pp.

10. Elliot W. Eisner, "Educational Objectives: Help or Hindrance," *School Review* 75 (1967): 250-60; James B. Macdonald, "Myths About Instruction," *Educational Leadership* 22 (1965): 571-6+.

11. Benjamin S. Bloom, editor, *Taxonomy of Educational Objectives: Cognitive Domain* (New York: Longmans, Green and Co., 1956) 207 pp; David R. Krathwohl et al., *Taxonomy of Educational Objectives: Affective Domain* (New York: David McKay Co., Inc., 1964), 196 pp.

12. Christine McGuire, *Research in the Process Approach to the Construction and Analysis of Medical Examinations,* 20th Yearbook, NCME, (1963), pp. 7-16.

13. Educational Testing Service, *Multiple-Choice Questions: A Close Look,* ETS (1963(a)), 43 pp.

Classroom Questions: What Kinds? is a manual that was designed to elicit the behaviors included in Bloom's cognitive domain.[14] The second taxonomy described five levels of behavior in the affective domain: receiving, responding, valuing, organizing, and characterization. There is some concern that the affective domain will be slighted for the cognitive domain.

It seems to be increasingly recognized, that a rightful set of priorities for the elementary school in one locale and with one group of pupils may not be so in another locale and with other pupils.[15] A significant fact related to evaluation is that in a decade the educational profession has become far more aware of the individual differences that characterize the human population. In particular there is a heightened awareness of the poor fit between traditional mechanism for regulating or influencing pupil progress and the many different kinds of children whose progress, for a great variety of reasons, has usually been unsatisfactory or disappointing.

Major curriculum improvements have put a growing emphasis on process goals and other tool skills which equip children to learn, with a concomitant deemphasis on the conventional content goals. One result of this trend has been to raise many new questions about conventional approaches to the measurement and evaluation of pupil progress, and teachers have become increasingly aware of the diagnostic as well as the evaluative purposes that tests and other instruments can play in examining each child's school progress and needs.

The important relationship of evaluation procedures to the fundamental needs of learners and teachers received national attention when the Association for Supervision and Curriculum Development (ASCD) published its yearbook *Evaluation As Feedback and Guide.*[16] The argument of the ASCD yearbook is that evaluation must perform five tasks: facilitate self-evaluation, encompass all of the school's objectives, facilitate teaching and learning, generate useful records, and facilitate decision making on curriculum and educational policy. Feedback and guidance, the argument continues, are needed by a variety of persons—the pupil, his parents, and his teachers—and for a variety of purposes. They

---

14. Norris M. Sanders, *Classroom Questions: What Kinds?* (New York: Harper & Row, 1966), 176 pp.
15. National Education Association, Project on Instruction, *Deciding What to Teach* (1963), pp. 88-98.
16. Fred T. Wilhelms, editor, *Evaluation as Feedback and Guide,* Yearbook, ASCD (1967(a)), pp. 2-17.

must take a variety of forms. No simplistic, cryptic, narrow system, such as most schools now have, can possibly accomplish these tasks.

There is very strong support for the idea of emphasizing the child's own potential as the yardstick of progress and deemphasizing comparisons with other children. Parents and the children need to receive both kinds of information along the way.

> As educational theorists generally argue that children must become more self-determining learners, it becomes more obviously important for teachers to include pupils in the total process of assessing learning goals and the child's progress toward them. It seems likely that in the decade ahead, more and more attention will be paid to the teacher-pupil conference and the devices for assisting pupils in self-evaluation.[17]

Listening

Listening is recognized as an area of major importance in the field of language arts. Since this recognition has been slow in developing and because of the difficulties which have been encountered in specifically identifying the skills essential to good listening, the development of measuring instruments to determine the level of listening comprehension as well as measurable factors in the total skill has been delayed.

Broadly speaking, listening skills may be put into two classifications: (1) those concerned with accuracy of reception, and (2) those concerned with reflection upon what was received. Pratt and Greene state that the identification of the skills needed for different types and levels of listening is not yet complete.[18]

Specifically, objectives may be identified as those concerned with helping the child: (a) to become aware of the importance of listening (b) to become an accurate and responsive listener (c) to become more efficient in the specific skills of listening and (d) to become more efficient in the many types and levels of listening.

Standardized Tests

One standardized test for use in elementary schools is the "Listening Comprehension Test of the Sequential Tests of Educational Progress."[19] This test, available in forms for four levels—grades 4-6, 7-9,

---

17. Robert H. Anderson, "Pupil Progress," *Encyclopedia of Educational Research,* 4th edition (1969), p. 1060.
18. Edward Pratt and Harry A. Greene, *Training Children to Listen.* A Monograph for Elementary Teachers, No. 80 (Evanston, Illinois: Row, Peterson and Company, 1955).
19. Educational Testing Service, *Sequential Tests of Education Progress: Listening* (Princeton, New Jersey, 1957).

10-12, 13-14—attempts to measure simple comprehension, interpretation, evaluation, and application. The test is based upon oral presentation by the teacher with the pupil responding with one of four optional answers to each question given after the presentation. The pupil has a copy of the question asked and the four options; hence, certain elements of reading ability are involved.

The items on the tests relate to the following skills, which have been identified by research: identifying main ideas, remembering significant details, remembering simple sequences of information, seeing bias and prejudice in what the speaker says, judging the validity of information, distinguishing fact from fancy, judging the relevance of details to an idea, determining the organization of the spoken context, and recognizing what the speaker wants the listener to do and believe.

Teachers may use the skills listed in this test as the basis for informal testing activities for their classrooms or they may use the listing of skills identified by James I. Brown. As Brown, identified them, the skills involved in listening are as follows:

1. Identification and recall of details presented orally.
2. Ability to follow the sequence of details in the form of oral directions.
3. Retention of details long enough to answer questions about them.
4. Ability to listen reflectively for the purpose of identifying the central idea of the statement given orally.
5. Ability to draw inferences from the supporting facts presented in the statement.
6. Ability to distinguish relevant from irrelevant materials.
7. Use of contextual clues to word meanings.
8. Recognition of transitional elements in sentences.[20]

There are also a number of unpublished tests of listening which have been constructed as part of doctoral studies. The tests by Hollow and Pratt were very carefully designed and have been used as measurement instruments in a number of subsequent studies.[21] Russell suggested that a superior listening test might be constructed by using various carefully refined subtests from the many unpublished listening tests

---

20. James I. Brown, "The Construction of a Diagnostic Test of Listening Comprehension," *Journal of Experimental Education* 18 (December, 1949): 139-146.
21. Sister M. Keven Hollow, "An Experimental Study of Listening Comprehension at the Intermediate Grade Level" (Doctoral Dissertation; Fordham University, 1955); Lloyd E. Pratt, "The Experimental Evaluation of a Program for the Improvement of Listening in the Elementary School" (Doctoral Dissertation; State University of Iowa, 1953).

now in existence.[22] Lundsteen developed a test of critical listening abilities suitable for the upper elementary school grades.[23]

Remediations in the Daily Instructional Program

Duker lists four principles that should govern listening instruction at the elementary level:[24] (1) Listening should be a pleasurable, rather than a threatening, experience. (2) Daily class activities should be so planned that the amount of listening required of the children is not overpoweringly great. (3) Listening in a classroom should not be confined to listening *by* the children *to* the teacher. (4) Classroom listening should be *for* rather than *at.* Goals for the teaching of listening at the elementary school level are listed as the development of a listener who not only knows how to listen, but actually does listen, and who is selective, skillful, critical, courteous, attentive, retentive, curious, reactive, and reflective.

Early gives specific and detailed suggestions about the materials and methods for teaching a number of listening skills but emphasizes her belief that all listening skills are interdependent and thus cannot be taught in isolation.[25] Detailed lesson plans which were found to be effective in listening instruction are reported by Hollow[26] and Pratt.[27] A detailed and complete plan for teaching critical listening skills to upper-grade elementary school pupils, which was found to be effective, is reported by Lundsteen.[28] An annotated list of audio-visual materials available for the teaching of listening at the elementary as well as at other levels is given by Duker.[29]

Russell and Russell[30] and Wagner and others[31] make numerous sug-

22. David H. Russell, "A Conspectus of Recent Research on Listening Abilities," *Elementary English* 41 (1964): 262-7.

23. Sara W.R. Lundsteen, "Teaching Abilities in Critical Listening in the Fifth and Sixth Grades" (Doctoral Dissertation; Berkeley: University of California, 1963).

24. Sam Duker, "Goals of Teaching Listening Skills in the Elementary School," *Elementary English* 38 (1961): 170-4.

25. Margaret J. Early, "Suggestions for Teaching Listening," *Journal of Education* 137 (1954): 17-20.

26. Hollow, *op. cit.*

27. Pratt, *op. cit.*

28. Lundsteen, *op. cit.*

29. Sam Duker, "An Annotated Guide to Audiovisual Aids Available for the Teaching of Listening," *Audiovisual Instruction* 10 (1965): 320-2.

30. David H. Russell and Elizabeth F. Russell, *Listening Aids Through the Grades—One-Hundred-Ninety Listening Activities,* Teachers College, Columbia University (1959), 112 pp.

31. Guy Wagner et al., *Listening Games—Building Listening Skills with Instructional Games* (Greenwich, Connecticut: Teachers Publishing Corp., 1962), 132 pp.

gestions concerning specific devices for the teaching of listening at the elementary level.

The SRA Laboratories include "Listening Skill Builders" in their programs. Materials such as the Gates-Peardon Practice Exercises (Macmillan) and the Reader's Digest Skills Builder can readily be used for teaching listening skills.

Taylor has designed lessons for the development of the following listening skills:

1. Directing and Maintaining Attention
2. Following Directions
3. Listening to the Sounds of Our Language
4. Using Auditory Analysis
5. Using Mental Reorganization
6. Using Context in Listening
7. Distinguishing Relevant and Irrelevant Information
8. Listening with a Purpose
9. Finding Main Ideas and Important Details
10. Indexing an Aural Message
11. Making Comparisons in an Aural Message
12. Finding Sequence in an Aural Message
13. Making Inferences and Drawing Conclusions
14. Forming Sensory Images from Oral Descriptions
15. Sensing Emotions and Moods Through Words Used and Through Manner of Delivery
16. Critical Listening
17. Appreciative Listening[32]

Oral Communication

The skills of oral communication are prerequisite to the development of all language skills. The specific communication skill which is most critical for the fully functioning individual in modern society and for success in any academic area is proficiency in the use of oral language. A major responsibility of the teacher is helping children develop and increase the skill and fluidity that characterize language facility.

---

32. Stanford E. Taylor, *What Research Says to the Teacher: Listening*, Department of Classroom Teachers and American Educational Research Association (Washington: National Education Association, 1964), pp. 23-29.

Evaluating Progress

The desired outcomes in the development of oral language skills cannot be evaluated by any of the formalized testing procedures which are commonly used. Objectives and standards must be thought of in terms of each pupil. This means that the progress of the individual learner must be evaluated in terms of his progress from his own individual status of language development toward the goals which he and the teacher accept as reasonable, challenging, and desirable.

The learner must be involved in the process of evaluation. He will progress only as far as he sees a need to progress; his own self-determined goals are the motivating source of learning. He should be encouraged to criticize his own tape recordings, to make notes of his weaknesses and errors, to keep and use a vocabulary notebook, and to practice oral contributions to class activities in front of a mirror at times.

Teacher-pupil conferences should be used as an excellent way to help the child identify his language problems and devise plans for improvement. Pairs of children practicing with each other promote self-evaluation, too. As the child listens to his partner and tries to help, he also identifies his own needs.

If the classroom climate is one of mutual helpfulness and acceptance, constructive criticisms from members of the class may point out individual and common weaknesses which need attention. One needs to be cautious with this technique. The children who need the most help are often those who are the most sensitive to criticism, and they may not be emotionally capable of sustaining critical comments from their peers.

One effective way of evaluating and recording the progress of each child is by keeping a notebook or card file with a separate page or card for each child. Diagnosis of errors and weaknesses and comments on evidences of progress are noted. Specific needs and plans are included.

Obviously, a teacher cannot expect to write something about each child every day. By selecting a few youngsters each day and by rotating around the class a complete picture of each child's level of language usage and his particular needs will emerge. Entries should be brief, factual, and specific.

The profile of each child will be the basis for individualized instruction and for individual improvement.

Although standardized language and general achievement tests do not measure a child's spoken usage, a teacher should use them in a planned program of testing and should make use of the information provided by the tests in his subsequent teaching. The following chart will assist a teacher in analyzing the results from standardized testing.

LANGUAGE USAGE

Possible causes of low test scores	Additional evidence of deficiency	Suggested remedial treatment
1. Failure to comprehend testing technique.	1. Misunderstanding of method of recording responses to items.	1. Prepare and use drill exercises similar to those used in test. Work with pupil until he understands technique.
2. Poor control over special language usages.	2. Observation and check on daily habits of oral and written expression.	2. Check pupil's test paper to identify types of usages missed. Check with text and course of study for grade emphasis. Emphasize individual drill on specific errors. Contrast correct forms with those to be avoided. Supplement with oral drill.
3. Poor language background.	3. Careless, inaccurate usage in oral and written expression.	3. Corrective instruction is the only remedy here. Select a limited number of usages and proceed as in No. 2 above.
4. Foreign language in the home.	4. Observed foreign accents. Evidence of two languages in the home.	4. Use direct corrective instruction here. Follow suggestions in No. 2 above.
5. Poor general reading comprehension.	5. Erratic response to test items; poor reading ability in other subjects.	5. Drill on sentence and total meaning comprehension as required for general improvement in reading.
6. Low mental ability.	6. Difficulty in following directions; erratic response to difficulty with common usages; low MA and IQ shown by reliable mental test.	6. Follow general procedure as outlined in Nos. 2 and 3 above. Have pupil prepare and memorize a key sentence for troublesome usages.

Possible causes of low test scores	Additional evidence of deficiency	Suggested remedial treatment
7. Careless language habits.	7. Erratic responses to test items; carelessness in informal expression.	7. Develop self-critical attitude toward usage errors. Bring pressure to bear favoring correct usages. Stress proofreading all written work.
8. Confusion caused by emphasis on formal rather than functional usages.	8. Inaccurate responses to items emphasized mainly through rules.	8. Emphasize individual drills; stress definite habits of correct response to important usages.

From the *Manual for Interpreting the Iowa Language Abilities Test*. Reproduced with the permission of the publisher (Yonkers-on-Hudson, New York: World Book Company).

Composition

This section concerns the evaluation of written composition throughout the elementary years. Rather than treating "creative writing" as something separate from other original writing, the author assumes that an element of creativity is involved in any writing which is not merely the copying of someone else's creation.

The purpose of evaluation is to find weaknesses to be strengthened and strengths to be expanded, refined, and deepened. Any program of evaluation comes back finally to the individual. Since growth in writing is closely tied up with all other aspects of individual growth, the individual must be strengthened in order to strengthen his writing. Expanding the individual's contacts, deepening his insights, helping him to think more clearly and feel more deeply—all these will improve the content of his writing.

A great deal has been written regarding standards for the evaluation of children's writing. The key to good work lies not in the standards the school sets for the children's writing, but in the standards each child is helped to set for himself. These are the standards the child takes with himself out into life.

The art of writing as of speaking consists in having something to say and knowing how to say it. Content and style must be thought of together since in any good composition content should determine form.

Teachers who wish to help children become writers turn their attention first to what the child wishes to say and his purpose in saying it, and, last to an appraisal of the form in which the ideas are set forth. It would seem impossible to correct or improve a pupil's expression until he offers enough of it to work with. When it is flowing freely as he is capable of at the time, he is ready for help with form and correctness.

The quality of what is expressed in writing depends upon the quality of thinking that undergirds it.

Essential Types of Evaluation

Evaluation of composition in the schools requires looking at composition in a variety of ways and from a number of angles. No one type of evaluation will serve the needs of any teacher or any class or school.

There is the evaluation of a piece of writing. There is the evaluation of the growth of an individual child from day to day, within the school year, and from year to year throughout his school life.

How evaluation is done depends on the level of maturity of the writer, the purpose for which the writing is done, and the needs of the writer at the time. The emphasis placed on content and on form depends on the stage the pupil has reached. In the earliest grades children may furnish the content, but the teacher assumes full responsibility for the form in which it is set out. A desirable program of evaluation is accomplished through adjusting criteria and methods of evaluating to the level and needs of the individual.

Evaluation at the Beginning Stages of Composition

Young children's first compositions are dictated for the teacher to write. Frequently this dictation is guided by the teacher's comments and questions and thus represents both child and teacher. The teacher is responsible for the form which the material takes on the paper, its spelling, punctuation, and arrangement. The child furnishes the ideas and expresses them in his own way with a minimum of guidance. At this stage, the teacher's evaluation of the child's composition deals with the quality of the child's ideas and the evidence these offer of the richness or meagerness of his background of experience as well as with his powers of expression. The purpose of evaluation is that of determining where the child stands with regard both to content for composition and skill in expression so that the teacher knows where to start her guidance and how to proceed with it. Her comments regarding what the child dictates are designed to draw him out, to help clarify his thinking, and to aid him in expressing his meaning.

Anecdotal records help the teacher of beginners to study each child's language ability and his needs. These records tend to show the child's attitude toward himself, the freedom and ease with which he speaks, and the quality and maturity of his language and of his thinking. They make clear the child's needs so that the teacher can devise means of meeting those needs.

The child's own evaluation of his composition lies in the satisfaction he finds in watching the teacher transfer his words to the paper and the use to which his contribution is put. The message of the composition is the most important item for consideration in the mind of the child and should be kept so.

These same values should be in evidence as the child begins to write his composition for himself. Spelling, capitalization, punctuation, and arrangement on the paper are guided by the teacher as she helps the child to say in writing what he wants to say. All types of writing tend to be managed in this way as long as children need such help though emphasis on independence and the use of self-help resources—word lists, picture dictionaries, models, "helping partners" and the like—are encouraged as the child is ready for them. The teacher's evaluation of the child's progress is a continuous one. The attitudes that the child shows, the amount of help he needs, his growth in interest, in initiative, in sustained attention to the writing task, in independence, as well as in technical skills of handwriting and spelling are all a part of the evaluation. The teacher's observation of the child's behavior, her anecdotal records, and the writing the child produces form the materials for evaluation.

This early stage in learning to write is a critical one. If a child is asked to write only when he has something to write, has a purpose for writing, and can write with all the help he needs, he is on the way to becoming a writer. Unwise requirements have no place in this early critical period.

Every piece of writing produced by a child in the primary grade is a reflection of the oral work that goes on in that grade. The atmosphere and general attitude that give rise to good writing are almost always those of constant conversation and oral alertness. Evaluation of the child's level of operation in oral work must accompany evaluation of his ability to write and probably should actually precede it. The two cannot be separated because one is clearly the outgrowth of the other.

Evaluation of Composition in the Middle Grades

Children in the middle grades do a number of kinds of writing and for a widening number of purposes. The emphasis on imaginative, creative writing continues with thought given to what makes it interesting and how to achieve it. Class discussion of quality may include attention to an opening sentence or paragraph which catches attention and interest, a plot that is built up in an interesting manner, and a conclusion that is clear and satisfying. Through discussion and comparison of their own stories with those in books they become increasingly good judges of quality. Revision may follow evaluation or the child may lay aside this attempt and try to incorporate points of improvement into his next effort. Writing, sharing, evaluation by the class and self-evaluation are closely interwoven. The teacher enters into the class discussion to raise children's sights.

Personal writing that is to be shared with the group or used to serve a purpose—an anecdote, a report of experience, or possibly a personal letter may be evaluated and revised if the occasion warrants it. This may be done by the teacher with the individual child or it may serve as material for class discussion depending on the teacher's judgment of the worth of such discussion to the child or the group.

Utilitarian writing that is to serve a class or individual purpose is usually carried through several stages of refinement. After the material for the report, announcement, or business letter has been assembled, the pupil writes a rough draft, reads it for clarity, completeness and satisfactory presentation of content, reads it again for form to catch and remedy any problems of spelling, punctuation, and the like. He may then take it to the group or the teacher for reading and criticism before turning out a final, carefully executed draft.

Watts recommends the assignment of three-sentence compositions as a method of developing disciplined writing. He would require children from time to time to write all that is of interest or importance to them about a topic in no more and no fewer than three sentences. This compels children to exercise their judgment and skill for a perfectly definite purpose. They learn through this experience to get quickly off the mark, to distribute ideas among the sentences and to give thought to sentence construction and emphasis. The sentences children write differ according to age and maturity. Class discussion and evaluation of the product provide children with goals to work toward in their writing yet allow for individual differences in style as well as maturity. Watts has devised a three-sentence written composition scale for judging the maturity of such compositions.[33]

33. A.F. Watts, *The Language and Mental Development of Children* (London: George G. Harrap and Company, Ltd., 1944); (Boston: D.C. Heath and Company, 1947), pp. 141-142.

Development of sentence structure and "degree of grammaticalness" (a phrase coined by the structural linguists) enter into any appraisal of the growth of writing competence in the middle grades. As children progress in maturity they can be led to realize that sentences can be made to express thoughts with increasing clarity and interest by the addition of moveables of a variety of sorts. The simple subject-predicate sequence, "Clayton came." can be enriched by the addition of moveables which tell where, when, why, how and for what purpose, as in the following examples: "Clayton came home yesterday to visit his sister." "Yesterday, because it was her birthday, Clayton came home to visit his sister and surprise her with the gift of a new record player." Changing the verb in the predicate slot adds new possibilities as in: "Because yesterday was her birthday, Clayton flew home to surprise his sister and delight her with his unexpected visit." Children learn how to weave ideas together into well-constructed longer sentences through opportunity to play with moveables and arrange them in different positions in relation to the two essential slots, subject and predicate. With teacher guidance, they discover the fact that a change in position may alter emphasis or create a new shade of meaning. Intonation and meaning determine punctuation within the written sentence.[34]

While it is true that length of sentence and number of dependent clauses are indicative of growth beyond the simple sentence, mere increase in the number of dependent clauses must not be overweighted as evidence of progress in the use of language. It may be found that a single sentence pattern is used over and over again as it is in the folk story, "This is the house that Jack built." Use of a variety of types of subordination should be encouraged and be in evidence. As children's writing skill advances they tend to use simple sentence containing prepositional phrases and infinitive expressions in place of clauses.[35] Examples such as the following begin to appear: "To his surprise, the boy returned once again." in place of "He was surprised that the boy returned once again." or "Being very tired, he sat down to rest." in place of "He sat down to rest because he was very tired." Compression and use of fewer words may be evidence of greater sophistication and command of language than the use of a larger number of words.

34. *Ibid.* Also W. Nelson Francis, *The Structure of American English* (New York: The Ronald Press Company, 1958).
35. Watts, *op. cit.*

Proofreading

In the middle and upper grades, careful proofreading follows the writing of a first draft and making a final copy climaxes the effort of making the necessary revisions in expression of ideas, statement of fact, sequence, phraseology, and spelling. The making of the final copy provides the writer with the experience of putting every part of his work into shape that will be a credit to him. It reinforces what he learns from the corrections he has made. While these final steps may seem to some children laborious and distasteful, if the purpose for which the writing is done is one that the child can identify with, he tends to view his final product with real satisfaction.

Harmful habits of writing are certain to develop from inadequate attention to proofreading. McKee has stated this point effectively as follows:

> If he does not do this thinking and changing or rewriting, the chances are good that his first draft will have supplied him with harmful practice in writing poorly. It is by this correcting, improving, and changing or rewriting that the pupil learns to write well. He learns to write well, not so much by writing first drafts about many different topics as by the right sort of proofreading and rewriting of what he has written.[36]

Checklists of criteria can usually be found in language textbooks. The following is one example:[37]

Checklist for Proofreading

1. Have you capitalized the first word, the last word, and all the important words in the title?
2. Do all of your sentences give complete thoughts?
3. Does each paragraph tell about one topic?
4. Have you indented the first word of each paragraph?
5. Have you capitalized the first word of each sentence?
6. Have you capitalized the word I whenever you have used it?
7. Have you used the correct punctuation mark at the end of each sentence?
8. Have you checked the spelling of each word?

36. Paul McKee, "An Adequate Program in the Language Arts," *Teaching Language in the Elementary School,* Forty-third Yearbook of the National Society for the Study of Education, Part II (Chicago: The University of Chicago Press, 1944), pp. 34-35.

37. Josephine B. Wolfe, Adele J. Wright, and Lillian E. Olson, *English Your Language,* Book 5 (Boston: Allyn and Bacon, Inc., 1963), p. 25.

9. Have you used is, are, was, and were correctly?
10. Have you left neat and even margins on the left side and on the right side of your paper?
11. Is your writing easy to read?

Evaluating the Growth of an Individual

Respect needs to be shown for children's compositions. They need to be kept in some sort of permanent form which makes possible both self-evaluation by the child and evaluation by the teacher over a period of time long enough to show growth.

Selected samples of children's writing added each year to the children's folders in the official cumulative file can give a picture of the emergence of individual style. Through it one can see growth in power to compose sentences, to spell, to write and to express ideas clearly and vividly.

Many teachers arrange a folder for each child in which samples of his work are accumulated. Children find great satisfaction and real motivation in evidence they are growing in power. This is a method of helping children take pride in their growth and motivating them to seek new heights.

The teacher's evaluation of each child's progress is always with reference to himself—the distance from the point at which he started to the point which he has achieved. Children are not judged by the application of an arbitrary standard nor expected to attain an established norm. Each child's work is judged with relation to his own potential. Slow children develop pride in what they can accomplish, and gifted children are encouraged to expand their powers as rapidly as their capacity permits.

The comments on a student's paper should cause him to dig a little deeper, think through his topic, and his purpose more carefully, and put his thoughts down more clearly and accurately. Attention must include form as well as content. If the writer is clear about his purpose and knows what he has to say, he usually writes in complete sentences, but if the thinking lacks clarity the writing will present the same problem.

An evaluation of composition is a composite of appraisal of each individual's ability to communicate his thoughts and feelings in various written forms appropriate to his purpose, to the specific occasion, and to the reader whom he intends to reach. Since the language act grows out of the experience of the individual, the situation in which the act is performed, and the skill of the individual in the situation exact measurement is extremely difficult. Language power and thought power go hand in hand. One cannot be assessed without attention to the other. Language is a social instrument which cannot be isolated and measured in the same sense that spelling or arithmetic skill can be measured. However, some variables must be identified as a starting point for the building of criteria. The three variables that are almost certain to appear in any list of criteria are content, logical sequence, and mechanics of expression.

The elementary battery of the Iowa Language Abilities Tests contains five subtests on spelling, word meanings, language usage, capitalization and punctuation.[38] That battery is for use in Grades 4, 5, and 6 with optional use in Grade 7.

The language test booklet of the current Iowa Every-Pupil Tests of Basic Skills possesses considerable analytical power.[39] The skill coverage of this booklet closely parallels that of the Iowa Language Abilities Tests. The elementary booklet is designed for use in Grades 3, 4, and 5 while the advanced book is for Grades 5 to 9.

The Manual for Interpreting the Iowa Language Abilities Tests[40] presents remedial suggestions in four language areas. This suggestion can be profitably used by elementary teachers as they become aware of the language needs of their particular classrooms and plan a remedial program.

LANGUAGE USAGE

Possible causes of low test scores	Additional evidence of deficiency	Suggested remedial treatment
1. Failure to comprehend testing technique.	1. Misunderstanding of method of recording responses to items.	1. Prepare and use drill exercises similar to those used in test. Work with pupil until he understands technique.

38. Harry A. Greene and H.L. Ballenger, *Iowa Language Abilities Tests* (Yonkers-on-Hudson, New York: World Book Company, 1948).

39. E.F. Lindquist, general editor, *Iowa Every-Pupil Tests of Basic Skills, Test C* (Geneva, Illinois: Houghton-Mifflin Company).

40. Reproduced here with the permission of the publishers (Yonkers-on-Hudson, New York: World Book Company).

Possible causes of low test scores	Additional evidence of deficiency	Suggested remedial treatment
2. Poor control over special language usages.	2. Observation and check on daily habits or oral and written expression.	2. Check pupil's test paper to identify types of usages missed. Check with text and course of study for grade emphasis. Emphasize individual drill on specific errors. Contrast correct forms with those to be avoided. Supplement with oral drill.
3. Poor language background.	3. Careless, inaccurate usage in oral and written expression.	3. Corrective instruction is the only remedy here. Select a limited number of usages and proceed as in No. 2 above.
4. Foreign language in the home.	4. Observed foreign accents. Evidence of two languages in the home.	4. Use direct corrective instruction here. Follow suggestions in No. 2 above.
5. Poor general reading comprehension.	5. Erratic response to test items; poor reading ability in other subjects.	5. Drill on sentence and total meaning comprehension as required for general improvement in reading.
6. Low mental ability.	6. Difficulty in following directions; erratic response to difficulty with common usage; low MA and IQ shown by reliable mental test.	6. Follow general procedure as outlined in Nos. 2 and 3 above. Have pupil prepare and memorize a key sentence for troublesome usages.
7. Careless language habits.	7. Erratic responses to test items; carelessness in informal expression.	7. Develop self-critical attitude toward usage errors. Bring pressure to bear favoring correct usages. Stress proofreading in all written work.
8. Confusion caused by emphasis on formal rather than functional usages.	8. Inaccurate responses to items emphasized mainly through rules.	8. Emphasize individual drills; stress definite habits of correct response to important usages.

SENTENCE SENSE

Possible causes of low test scores	Additional evidence of deficiency	Suggested remedial treatment
1. Limited meaning vocabulary.	1. Low scores on vocabulary tests; observation of pupil's use of words in oral and written work.	1. Drill on meaning vocabulary. Develop different meanings of common words. Stress using words in sentences demonstrating differences in meanings.
2. Poor reading comprehension.	2. Low scores of information and on reading comprehension tests.	2. Drill on word meanings, sentences and paragraph meanings, and comprehension of total meaning of content suitable for the grade.
3. Inability to recognize subjects and predicates of sentences, and to sense what is missing in a fragment.	3. Note pupil's habits in speech and writing; individual work with pupils on analysis of sentences and fragments.	3. Drill on choosing complete subjects and predicates from pupil's own writing. Use matching exercises made up of complete subjects in one column and complete predicates in parallel column.
4. Failure to think of sentence as complete unit of expression.	4. Note pupil's spoken and written work for sentence errors.	4. Stress use of complete sentences in daily oral and written work. Point out that there are times when fragments may be used but that they must be recognized as such. Drill on completion of exercises in which subjects or predicates are missing. Drill on exercises calling for identification of fragments and sentences.
5. Use of "run-on" sentences; loose "and."	5. Analysis of pupil's expression for use of loose "and's" and "run-on's."	5. Explain and illustrate various types of incorrect sentences. Stress individual practice in writing good sentences. Drill on identifying poor sentence structure and in recasting poor sentences.

CAPITALIZATION

Possible causes of low test scores	Additional evidence of deficiency	Suggested remedial treatment
1. Lack of knowledge of capitalization situations.	1. Analysis of pupil's test paper and other written work to determine types of errors made.	1. Check specific capitalization skills missed by pupil on test paper with textbook and local course of study. Stress proofreading drills on skills in which pupil is weak.
2. Limited knowledge of exceptions and irregularities in capitalization.	2. Analysis of test paper and daily written work; note tendency to over-capitalize.	2. Give direct drill on capitalization skills taught in this grade. Point out exceptions and irregularities in the use of capitals.
3. Tendency to over-capitalize.	3. High correction for over-capitalization in test.	3. Inspect test paper and written work for excessive use of capitals. Use dictation and proofreading designed to emphasize correct use of capitals.
4. Lack of self-critical attitude toward capitalization. Poor proofreading ability.	4. Erratic and careless work in daily written expression in other subjects; limited ability to note errors in own or other written copy.	4. Emphasize need for self-critical attitude toward pupil's own written work. Drill on proofreading exercises designed to emphasize use of capitals.
5. Poorly developed sentence sense.	5. Low scores on sentence sense tests.	5. Use suggestions in remedial chart for sentence sense.
6. Carelessness in writing.	6. Analysis of handwriting characteristics in daily work.	6. Drill on distinctive characteristics of capital letters and small letters which analysis shows cause trouble.

PUNCTUATION

Possible causes of low test scores	Additional evidence of deficiency	Suggested remedial treatment
1. Lack of knowledge of specific punctuation skills.	1. Check test papers to determine types of skills missed; observation of daily written work.	1. Check punctuation items missed on test with textbook and course of study. Use proofreading drills on skills missed by pupil. Stress drills on correct punctuation, avoiding overpunctuation, and self-editing of own copy.
2. Tendency to overpunctuate.	2. Analysis test and daily work for evidence of over-punctuation, especially commas.	2. Use dictation and proofreading drills for the elimination of improper or excessive punctuation.
3. Lack of self-critical attitude toward own written work.	3. Careless punctuation in daily work; fails to note errors in own or other written copy.	3. Emphasize self-criticism of own daily written work. Use proofreading exercises to emphasize correct use of punctuation marks.
4. Poor general comprehension in reading.	4. Low scores on comprehension tests; poor reading in other subjects.	4. Drill on word meaning, sentence comprehension, and comprehension of total meaning in varied subject-matter fields.
5. Poor vision or hearing.	5. Observation of pupil at work; nurse's or doctor's examination.	5. Refer pupil to doctor for medical attention. Move pupil to front of room. Encourage pupil to make special effort to write carefully and to make punctuation marks distinctly.

Possible causes of low test scores	Additional evidence of deficiency	Suggested remedial treatment
6. Poorly developed sentence sense.	6. Observation of pupil's daily usage.	6. Explain types of sentences and the relation of sentence structure to punctuation. Stress practice in writing sentences and punctuating them correctly. Use dictation and proofreading exercises calling for punctuation.
7. Carelessness in matters of form in written expression.	7. Observation and analysis of characteristics of handwriting and punctuation.	7. Stress essentials of good form in written work. Insist that pupils edit and proofread all written work.

Any evaluation of a composition should be of such a nature so as to encourage the pupil to continue writing and to write increasingly well. It thus becomes imperative to be judicious in the use of charts and standards. The individual is all-important.

Handwriting

The commonly accepted broad goal of handwriting is to write legibly with ease and speed.

Two factors constitute the chief approaches to measurement of handwriting. These are (1) quality, or the degree of legibility, and (2) speed, or the quantity of writing produced in a given unit of time. The first of these factors usually is evaluated by means of general merit scales and diagnostic scales and charts. The second is commonly expressed in terms of the number of letters per minute at which a copy was written.

General Merit and Diagnostic Scales

The quality of the pupil's handwriting is usually determined by comparing the specimens to be evaluated with samples of established value on grade level scales. Thorndike produced the first handwriting scale in America in 1910.

The Ayres Scale, the second scale to be developed, was standardized on the basis of legibility alone.[41] This scale has been known generally

41. Leonard P. Ayres, *A Scale for Measuring the Quality of Handwriting of School Children,* Bulletin no. 113 (New York: Division of Education, Russell Sage Foundation, 1912).

as the Gettysburg Edition because the specimens were based on the first four sentences of Lincoln's Gettysburg Address. Today these two scales are used only for handwriting research.

The American Handwriting Scale, developed by Paul V. West, is one of the most comprehensive of the general merit scales.[42] The scale provides a number of features of which at least two deserve mention: (1) a separate scale is provided for each grade from two to eight; (2) the specimens have been scaled for both quality and rate, taking into account the fact that the better writing is usually done at a more rapid rate and the poorer writing at a slower rate. Separate scales are provided for Grades 2-8.

The Handwriting Evaluation Scales by F.N. Freeman[43] are similar in many respects to those developed by West. Cursive scales for each grade from three through nine present specimens classified as high, good, medium, fair, and poor. The provision of separate scales for each grade in both the Freeman and West Scales makes possible a somewhat more accurate evaluation of any quality of writing in its relation to the grade in which it is produced than is possible in a single scale.

The Conrad Manuscript Standards is comprised of two separate scales. The scale used in scoring pencil-written forms contains twelve specimens ranging in quality from the scrawl of the beginning first-grade child to excellent manuscript writing at the fourth-grade level. The scale for scoring pen-written forms comprises ten specimens ranging from beginning third-grade work in ink to excellent quality ink work produced by a sixth-grade pupil.[44]

The Freeman Scale contains manuscript scales for grades one and two. The manuscript samples in the scale are classified as high, good, medium, fair and poor.

The Metropolitan Primary Manuscript Handwriting Scale is available for grades one through three.[45]

To use all of these scales or standards of measurement, the scorer slides each sample along the scale until he finds the quality that closely

---

42. Paul V. West, *The American Handwriting Scale* (New York: A.N. Palmer Co., 1951).

43. Frank N. Freeman and the Zaner-Bloser Staff, *Evaluation Scales for Guiding Growth in Handwriting* (Columbus, Ohio: The Zaner-Bloser Company, 1958). Revised scales also accompany the new program (1969), "Expressional Growth Through Handwriting."

44. Edith U. Conrad, *Conrad Manuscript Writing Standards* (New York: Bureau of Publications, Teachers College, Columbus University, 1929).

45. Gertrude H. Hildreth, *Metropolitan Primary Manuscript Handwriting* (New York: Harcourt, Brace & World, Inc., 1933).

matches the sample in appearance, quality, or legibility. The quality value of the matching scale sample is then assigned to the pupil's handwriting sample.

A basic question regarding the value of scales is whether their use enhances reliability in judging the quality of handwriting samples. Two attempts to answer this question were reported recently. Feldt examined between-judge reliability with a set of scales used in grades one and two.[46] He found that reliability can be raised by analyzing scores from several independent sessions and by providing additional training materials for the judges. Rondinella had groups of elementary teachers rate handwriting samples from 239 pupils in grade four through six and found that the teachers tended to rate the samples subjectively and that many were unaware of the criteria for judging suggested in scales.[47] The judges mentioned fourteen different characteristics as being responsible for their judgments; this is in contrast to the single notion of general readability or the three to five characteristics suggested by most scale developers.

A justifiable conclusion seems to be that with sufficient training the reliability of teachers' judgments regarding handwriting quality can be increased through the use of scales. Nevertheless, Herrick and Okada's national survey of practices revealed that only in about one-third of the responding schools was some use made of scales.[48]

An example of a diagnostic scale is the Zaner-Bloser Chart on "Handwriting Faults and How to Correct Them."[49] It is an instrument recommended for the location of specific faults in handwriting. The Zaner-Bloser Chart contains the following excellent suggestions on ways to test handwriting copy for such elements as legibility, slant, spacing, alignment, size of letters, and quality of line. This chart is helpful because it enables the teacher as well as the pupil to discover the special handwriting weaknesses that are in need of remedial treatment and gives excellent suggestions for correcting the defects.

46. Leonard S. Feldt, "Reliability of Measures of Handwriting Quality," *Journal of Educational Psychology* 53 (1962): 288-92.

47. Oreste R. Rondinella, "An Evaluation of Subjectivity of Elementary School Teachers in Grading Handwriting," *Elementary English* 40 (1963): 531-2.

48. Virgil E. Herrick and Nora Okada, "The Present Scene: Practices in the Teaching of Handwriting in the U.S.—1960." In Virgil E. Herrick, editor, *New Horizons for Research in Handwriting* (Madison, Wisconsin: University of Wisconsin Press, 1963), pp. 17-38.

49. Frank N. Freeman and the Zaner-Bloser Staff, *Handwriting Faults and How to Correct Them* (Columbus, Ohio: Zaner-Bloser Co., 1958).

How to test legibility:	Make a letter finder by cutting a hole a little larger than the letter in a piece of cardboard. Place the hole of this finder over each letter in turn and mark the letters which are illegible. Have the pupils practice these letters separately, then write the word again and test as before.
How to test slant:	Draw slanting lines through the letters and mark all letters which are off slant. If the slant is too great, the paper is tilted too much. If the writing is too vertical, the paper is too upright and if the slant is backward, the paper is tilted the wrong direction.
How to test for spacing:	Begin each new word in a sentence directly under the ending stroke of the preceding word.
How to test alignment:	Alignment and size are closely integrated and should be studied together. Use a ruler (a diagnostic ruler is best) and draw a base line touching as many of the letters as possible. Also draw a line along the tops of the small letters. Mark the letters above or below these lines.
How to test size of letters:	Draw lines along the tops of the letters. Remember the minimum letters, i, u, v, etc., are 1/4 space high; d, t, p, are 1/2 space; capitals and l, h, k, b, d, are 3/4 space high. All the lower loop letters extend 1/2 space below the line.
How to test for quality of line:	Make a letter finder by cutting a hole a little larger than the letter in a piece of cardboard. Place the hole of this finder over each letter in turn and mark the letters which are illegible due to the quality of line. Have pupils practice these letters from their writing books separately until the letters are perfectly legible. Then have them write the whole word again and test as before.

The chart is large and an excellent visual aid for youngsters as they strive to grow in self-evaluation. The nominal price of the chart makes several copies easily available for classroom use.

Children can be guided in the use of these charts for self-diagnosis especially in the intermediate grades. Before they use a chart, however, some background discussion in the class is needed so that the members of the class will know what they are looking for, i.e., how to analyze their errors. These discussions should point up understandings of what is meant by uniform slant, even spacing, correct proportion, smooth line quality, accurate letter forms, and good alignment.

The habit of evaluation should be developed early and continually in the instructional program. Children should be encouraged to look at their practice efforts critically. They should compare their product with the chart. The teacher should lead them to see where they are making poor strokes or movements. If a child cannot see his errors, the teacher should show him. When his practice shows success in making the correction, she should recognize his accomplishment by a favorable comment, establishing at once her habit of noticing and appreciating improvement and good workmanship.

Measuring Handwriting Speed

Although speed of writing was considered a very important element in handwriting at the turn of the century, this factor has been de-emphasized in school programs in recent years. The ability to write rapidly affords the individual an important advantage in most situations, however, whether in school or outside. In note-taking, in examinations, in letter writing, the pressures of time make the advantage of speed very real.

Freeman suggests speed norms in handwriting for grades II through VIII which are based upon the number of letters written per minute. These figures represent the typical findings of a number of research studies. The Roman numerals indicate the grade; the Arabic numerals give the speed of writing in letters per minute for each grade.[50]

50. Frank N. Freeman, *What Research Says to the Teacher: Teaching Handwriting* (Washington: Department of Classroom Teachers and American Education Research Association, National Education Association, 1954), p. 4; Dan W. Andersen, "Speed," *What Research Says to the Teacher: Teaching Handwriting* (Washington: Association of Classroom Teachers, National Educational Association, 1968), p. 5; also Theodore L. Harris, "Handwriting," *Encyclopedia of Educational Research* (1960), p. 620; "Handwriting," Wayne Otto and Dan W. Andersen, *Encyclopedia of Educational Research* (1969), pp. 570-579.

GRADE	II	III	IV	V	VI	VII	VIII
SPEED	30	40	50	60	67	74	80

Norms for speed in handwriting suggested by Freeman have been widely accepted. The speeds were derived from studies of children's normal rates of writing, but speed is flexible and can usually be increased from normal rates without legibility being sacrificed. Speed and quality must be considered together because to develop one without the other is pointless.

Groff recently suggested new norms for speed of handwriting.[51] He argued that earlier norms had been developed with subjects who copied familiar sentences, whereas his subjects did not have a "set" for the sentences. Therefore, he believes that the lesser number of words per minute reported in his norms is more realistic.

Standards in speed are set largely on the basis of comparative performance. The various situations in which handwriting is used and the speed demanded in each cannot conveniently be studied.

The measurement of rate of writing is accomplished by having pupils write for a specific period selections which they have previously read and memorized. Rate of writing may be expressed in either seconds per letter or in letters per minute. The rate score is obtained by counting the total number of minutes allowed for the writing.

Handwriting samples or specimens selected for evaluation on a quality scale and for deriving rate scores are affected by three factors which must be considered when they are being collected. The first of these is the suitability or the difficulty of the copy pupils are asked to write.

The sample should contain very few spelling or vocabulary difficulties and should be understood by the pupils. The selected copy should be written on the blackboard several days prior to the test where it can be studied and where it can be seen during the writing test itself.

A second is the care with which the instructions for the writing test are given. The third factor which must be controlled in the collection of writing specimens is the time allowance. The two-minute period has been generally accepted as suitable for the writing of such samples.

Handwriting Remediation Suggestions

There is some agreement that once children have mastered the basic letter forms and sequences of producing them the bulk of instructional

51. Patrick J. Groff, "New Speeds of Handwriting," *Elementary English* 38 (1961): 564-5.

time in handwriting should be devoted to helping them to diagnose and remedy their own errors.[52] In aiding the expediting of such an approach, the information continued in a report by Quant is classic.[53] His is one of the few studies in which an attempt is made to single out and evaluate the factors which contribute to illegibility in handwriting. Once the specific causes for illegibility are known, the matter of correcting them becomes a reasonably straight-forward task. More recently, Lewis and Lewis extended Quant's analysis, which covered cursive forms only, by making an analysis of first graders' errors in the formation of manuscript letters.[54]

Enstrom and McElravy described instructional procedures for teaching handwriting to slow learners.[55] They agree on the importance of readiness and adapted pacing, and both feel that slow learners should make the transition to cursive writing, because it will enhance their self-perception.

Ediger suggests differentiated instruction for pupils with different levels of ability in handwriting and stresses the importance of motivation.[56] Sister Mary Lauriana has listed ten commandments of good handwriting directed at improving teaching.[57] A particularly noteworthy suggestion was that pupils be given timed exercises to train them for writing under pressure. Enstrom has discussed means for improving cursive writing through improved teaching.[58] Meeker, too, was concerned about the teaching of cursive writing; she stressed the need for motivation and regular practice.[59]

With regard to movement and position, the left-handed writer has received considerable attention, but little research has been done. Enstrom reviewed existing research and summarized the results of his dissertation study of the left-handed writer.[60] He reported that there

52. Wayne Otto and Richard A. McMenemy, *Corrective and Remedial Teaching* (Boston: Houghton Mifflin Company, 1966), p. 377.

53. Leslie Quant, "Factors Affecting the Legibility of Handwriting," *Journal of Experimental Education* 14 (1946): 297-316.

54. Edward R. Lewis and Hilda P. Lewis, "An Analysis of Errors in the Formation of Manuscript Letters by First-grade Children," *American Educational Research Journal* 2 (1965): 25-35.

55. Erick A. Enstrom, "Out of the Classroom; Handwriting for the Retarded," *Exceptional Child* 32 (1966(b)): 285-8; Anna McElravy, "Handwriting and the Slow Learner," *Elementary English* 41 (1964): 865-8.

56. Marlow Ediger, "Essentials in Teaching Handwriting," *Ed.* 86 (1965): 37-9.

57. Sister Mary Lauriana, "Ten Commandments of Good Handwriting," *Elementary English* 41 (1964): 854+.

58. Erick A. Enstrom, "Research in Teaching the Left-handed, *Instructor* 74 (1964(b)): 44-6+.

59. Alice M. Meeker, "Cursive Writing in the Middle Grades," *Instructor* 74 (1964): 45+.

60. Enstrom, *op. cit.*

are probably more left-handed pupils in the schools than current estimates indicate. He described an efficient writing position for left-handed pupils and concluded that the left-handers' "hooked" writing position is difficult, if not impossible to change beyond grade four. He suggested that older "hooked" writers be assisted in making minor adaptations that will permit them to write with reasonable ease and legibility.

Measuring handwriting by general merit scales and diagnostic charts, evaluating the product closely to find the elements that are detracting from its legibility and pleasing appearance, and remedying those defects are all a part of a well-organized handwriting program. The following list of handwriting irregularities and their underlying causes should aid the teacher in her program of remediation.

HANDWRITING IRREGULARITIES AND THEIR CAUSES

Slant of Writing

1. Too much slant.	1. Hand, body, pen, or pencil is out of position. 2. Paper turned too much. 3. Paper slanted too much toward the left.
2. Too nearly vertical.	1. Paper too straight up and down. 2. Incorrect body position.
3. Irregular slant.	1. Incorrect body position. 2. Hand, arm, pen, or paper out of position. 3. The child doesn't sit the same way at all times—there is a shift of body while writing. 4. Movement is not uniform.

Forms of Letters

1. Angular letters.	1. Poor visualization of the letters. 2. Poor knowledge of formations of the letters. 3. Writing is done with jerky motion instead of smooth motion. 4. The child stops at the "turns" and not at the "retraces" of letters.
2. Letters too round.	1. Writing too fast. 2. Writing too slowly. 3. Poor visualization of the letters.
3. Letters too thin.	1. Writing too slowly. 2. Incorrect motion or rhythm. 3. Too much finger movement. 4. Not enough rolling or curving motion on the upstrokes.

4. Capital letters weak.	1. Not enough arm movement. (There is more arm movement in the capital letters as a general rule than there is in the small letters.) 2. The child needs review of the movements for the letters.
5. Small letters weak.	1. Poor visualization. 2. Poor knowledge of curves, straight parts, and all the different strokes.
6. Disconnected letters in words.	1. Pen lifts within a word. 2. The child thinks in terms of parts of words and not the whole word.

Spacing of Letters

1. Spacing too wide (scattered).	1. Pencil progresses too fast to the right. 2. Too much lateral movement.
2. Spacing too crowded.	1. Doesn't leave the width of a letter between sentences. 2. Space between the letters is not about the same as the width of a letter. 3. Doesn't regulate space between words by the beginning and ending strokes of the letters in the words.

Size

1. Too small.	1. Tight and tense hand position. 2. The child needs help with rhythm and movement.
2. Too large.	1. Poor visualization of correct relationships for different grade levels. 2. The child needs motivation. 3. The child needs to see visual aids, recorders, charts, etc.

Line Quality

1. Writing too heavy.	1. Index finger pressing too heavily. 2. Writing instrument too small in diameter.
2. Writing too light.	1. Writing instrument held too straight. 2. Writing instrument too large in diameter. 3. Eyelet of pen turned to side.
3. Writing too irregular.	1. The child is putting more pressure on some strokes than on others. 2. Needs more arm action. 3. Needs to hold the pen or pencil lightly.

Alignment

1. Off the line in places.	1. Needs to look at the line as he writes.
2. Minimum letters vary.	1. Needs to rule a few lines as a crutch and practice within the lines. 2. Needs visual aids.

Research Implications for the Daily Program

A survey of practices advocated by nineteen commercial systems of handwriting instruction, which supply about 95 percent of the instructional materials currently in use in the United States, was reported in 1960.[61] Instructional practices within the schools would, of course, be expected to parallel practices advocated by the commercial suppliers of instructional materials rather closely. The salient conclusions from the survey are as follows: (1) There is substantial agreement among the systems that legibility is the fundamental objective of handwriting instruction. In operational terms, handwriting that is easily read and easily written is legible. (2) Handwriting is generally regarded in a functional role, as a tool for communication. Attempts are made, therefore, to correlate handwriting instruction with work in the skill and content fields. In some systems, handwriting performance is evaluated in application rather than within the handwriting period. (3) There is some agreement on procedures for developing the motor skills, required for handwriting. For example, arm rather than finger movements are advocated as conducive to rhythmic movements and fluent writing. (4) Systematic procedures for learning the letter forms are proposed by some systems—e.g. seeing the letter or word, hearing it, and tracing it in the air. (5) There is general agreement that practice is necessary and that it should be purposeful; but the purposes suggested range from pupil experiences (e.g. labeling and letter writing) to mastery of a particular stroke (e.g. drawing circles and making vertical and horizontal strokes). (6) Scales are introduced for use in comparing pupils' writing with standard norms, but greater emphasis is placed upon pupils' self-evaluation of their own writing. (7) There is no expectation of a uniform degree of skill in a classroom. The fact that pupils' abilities vary is recognized, and lessons are planned accordingly. (8) The fundamental principles of good writing are the same for all grades, but at the upper elementary level there is a tendency to use the instructional time for remedial work. Pupils are helped to become more proficient in identifying general and specific inaccuracies in letter forms, slant, size, spacing and alignment.

---

61. University of Wisconsin, Committee for Research in Basic Skills, *Comparison of Practices in Handwriting Advocated by Nineteen Commercial Systems of Handwriting Instruction* (Madison, Wisconsin: University of Wisconsin Press, 1960), 111 pp.

Spelling

The most widely accepted objectives for teaching spelling are to help children learn the words they will need to write as adults and the words needed in their present writing, both in and out of school. It is clearly impossible for pupils to learn in school all the words they may at some time have occasion to write. It is the central words, that is, the words most often needed in writing, that pupils should learn to spell.

Proceeding from the two broad objectives, schools need to make definite decisions on many other specific matters related to the improvement of spelling ability; which words are to be learned at each grade level; what dictionary habits and skills should be developed; what rules and other orthographical generalizations should be learned; what phonic knowledge should be acquired; what emphasis should be placed on proofreading; and how much to rely on incidental learning as well as on direct instruction.

Among the most important functions served by measurements in spelling are: (a) to show individual differences in spelling ability in the class and hence to enable the teacher to make proper adjustments to these differences; (b) to show which words each child needs to study; (c) to guide learning by depicting its success and failure; (d) to show what progress has been made during a term or year. No one test can serve all these ends.

The spelling program should include several types of evaluation. These are: (a) evaluating through the use of standardized achievement tests, (b) evaluating through teacher made tests from spelling scales, (c) evaluating through diagnostic scales and charts, (d) evaluating as a part of the daily instructional program, (e) evaluating through informal techniques.

Standardized Tests

Most general achievement or language usage batteries include subtests which attempt to measure spelling ability for particular grade levels. This type of testing has limitations with respect to measuring the effectiveness of the systematic spelling instructional program. These tests, however, are useful as a general survey.

While the majority of language achievement tests fall short of being really diagnostic, they are valuable screening devices to locate the low-achievement pupils quickly at the beginning of the term and to ascertain the general level of progress for the class as a whole.

It is imperative the teacher remember that this type of testing will not indicate how well the pupil has learned the particular words he studied in his spelling lessons from day to day during the year. The scores made on these tests therefore may not be closely related to the achievement of the specific goals set up for instruction.

A few tests of the many suitable for teacher use are:

1. *The Iowa Language Abilities Tests.* These tests are available at two levels. The elementary battery is for Grades 4, 5, and 6 with optional use in Grade 7. The elementary test booklet contains five subtests, one of which is Spelling.[62]

2. *Iowa Tests of Basic Skills: Test C.* The elementary booklet is designed for use in Grades 3, 4, and 5. The advanced booklet is designed for use in Grades 6, 7, and 8. Spelling is one of the language arts tested.[63]

3. *California Language Test.* This test is available at the primary, elementary, and intermediate levels. Grades 1-3, and 4-6. Spelling is one of the language arts tested.[64]

4. *Morrison-McCall Spelling Scale.* This scale is for use in Grades 2-8. The teacher may use any one of eight lists of fifty words each. The lists are based on the work of Thorndyke and Ayers.[65]

In addition to the tests listed, most of the achievement test batteries contain subtests in spelling. Separate spelling tests are available also from most commercial publishers of standard tests. For a more complete listing and description of these, the reader may wish to consult *Tests in Print.*[66]

Tests Constructed from Standardized Spelling Scales

The nature of spelling ability makes it extremely difficult to guarantee the validity of a standardized spelling test. The words tested must

62. Harry A. Greene and H.L. Ballenger, *Iowa Language Abilities Tests* (Yonkers-on-Hudson, New York: World Book Company, 1948).

63. E.F. Lindquist, general editor, *Iowa Tests of Basic Skills, Test C.* (Boston: Houghton Mifflin Company, 1955-1956).

64. Ernest W. Tiegs and Willis W. Clark, *California Language Test* (California Test Bureau, 1957).

65. Cayce Morrison and William A. McCall, *Morrison-McCall Spelling Scale* (New York: Harcourt, Brace and World, Inc., 1923).

66. Oscar Krisen Buros, editor, *Tests in Print* (Highland Park, New Jersey: The Gryphon Press, 1961).

be selected from those presented for instruction. This means naturally, that the most common and useful measures of spelling are those constructed locally by the classroom teacher if the construction is done properly.

It is important that the content of a spelling test be chosen from properly validated writing vocabulary lists comprised of words that are now and will be ultimately of greatest usefulness to the pupil's writing. Many early sources of such word lists, such as the one by Anderson used by Ashbaugh in constructing the *Iowa Spelling Scales*, Horn's *Basic Writing Vocabulary*, and Bixler's *Standard Elementary Spelling Scale*, have been used in the development of commercial spelling textbooks.[67] A valuable source of socially-evaluated and difficulty-rated material for this purpose is *The New Iowa Spelling Scale*. If the directions accompanying the scale are followed, this scale can be used as a source of material for spelling tests that will provide valid and reliable measures of spelling efficiency.

Teachers who are using no spelling textbooks or who are using texts whose vocabulary content is of unknown social importance will find these spelling scales valuable sources for use in selecting valid content for their own spelling tests. Words included in a spelling test should, of course, be selected from those comprising the list studied by the pupils. "The most valid types of spelling words on which to test a pupil are also those words that have relatively high social usage. Thus, a cross check of the words common to the local spelling text and to a standardized spelling scale will reveal the high social frequency words that the pupils have had a chance to study and will at the same time give the teacher a measure of the relative difficulty of the words from their values in the scale itself."[68]

Words selected from a socially validated vocabulary source such as *The New Iowa Spelling Scale* should be in the list studied by the pupils and should be selected in terms of their known spelling difficulty.[69] The words included in a test for any grade should be adapted as closely as possible to the average ability of the group to be tested.

67. W.N. Anderson, *Determination of a Spelling Vocabulary Based Upon Written Correspondence.* Studies in Education, vol. II, no. 1. (Iowa City: State University of Iowa, 1917); E.J. Ashbaugh, *The Iowa Spelling Scale* (Bloomington, Illinois: Public School Publishing Company, 1919); Ernest Horn, *A Basic Writing Vocabulary.* Monographs in Education, First Series, no. 4 (Iowa City: State University of Iowa, 1926); H.H. Bixler, *The Standard Elementary Spelling Scale* (Atlanta: Turner E. Smith and Company, 1940).

68. Harry A. Greene, A.N. Jergensen and J.R. Gerberich, *Measurement and Evaluation in the Elementary School* (New York: Longmans, Green and Company, 1953), p. 442.

69. *Ibid.*

The principle of sampling commonly used in all other testing applies equally well in the field of spelling. The number of words required for reliable results depends largely upon the purpose the test is to serve. For a survey of the status of spelling in an entire school system, a list of twenty-five carefully selected words may be sufficient. A much larger list of words is required in a test intended to reveal the spelling ability of individual pupils, while fifty words may be adequate for use with a complete class group.

Diagnostic and Remedial Scales and Charts

It is important to discover, as early as possible, pupils who are doing poor work in spelling, to diagnose their difficulties, and to give them help. A teacher recognizes rather easily a pupil with a spelling disability. Recognition is easier, however, than the discovery of the causes underlying the difficulty. Diagnostic tests aid in the discovery of the types and causes of spelling difficulties.

One series of individual diagnostic tests is the *Gates-Russell Diagnostic Series*.[70] The teacher who has administered a diagnostic test will have more accurate information as to the causes of the pupil's difficulty. Consequently, she can more accurately give remedial help.

The areas of the Gates-Russell Series are:

1. Spelling Words Orally.
2. Word Pronunciation.
3. Giving Letters for Letter Sounds.
4. Spelling One Syllable.
5. Spelling Two Syllables.
6. Reversals.
7. Learning to Spell Hard Words.
8. Auditory Discrimination.
9. Visual, Auditory, Kinaesthetic, and Combined Study Method.

By utilizing all of the data secured through the foregoing tests, as well as the information in the child's cumulative school record, the teacher will gain a more complete understanding of the pupil and guide him more effectively. "Spelling disability is seldom or never the result of a single causal factor."[71]

Gates and Russell also have delineated remedial suggestions in their diagnostic manual. The six classifications of deficiencies and the accom-

---

70. Arthur I. Gates and David H. Russell, *Gates-Russell Diagnostic Series* (New York: Bureau of Publications, Teachers College, Columbia University, 1937).

71. Gates and Russell, *Diagnostic and Remedial Spelling Manual,* p. 29.

panying remedial suggestions are produced below. In addition, thirty-seven activity suggestions are given in Chapter VI of that publication. Teachers will profit from consulting that chapter.[72]

1. General Verbal and Linguistic Retardation: When a pupil is referred for spelling disability, it is sometimes discovered that he is backward in all language activities. To meet such a difficulty, the teacher should: (a) Explore possibilities of enrichment in the pupil's environment outside school. (b) Initiate a general program of word study skills which will apply to reading, spelling, and language. More and better reading tends to improve spelling. A program of word-form study which correlates reading and spelling techniques can be most valuable to such a pupil. (c) Provide special opportunities for work with words in the form of letters to the home, considerable oral language experiences and activities to give a background of ideas such as pictures, movies, or excursions.

2. Pupil Misses Word Entirely: This difficulty is shown when a pupil writes "dark" for "baby," "look" for "seen," etc. The remedial work should: (a) Check vision and hearing carefully. (b) Check the pupil's school history for the first two or three years. Is there a record of absence, illness, changing schools, etc.? That is, did the pupil ever receive any systematic, continuous instruction in word study? If not, the regular primary reading and language programs may be started. (c) Use remedial devices calling attention to the relationships between letters and sounds and the form of words.

3. Difficulties in Giving Letter Equivalents of Sounds and Syllables: This is a difficulty in a primary skill which requires, at first, very simple procedures, such as knowing the alphabet and the common sounds of each letter, being able to blend two or three sounds, and being able to recognize common phonograms such as "in," "ol," "st," "de," and the like.

4. Difficulties in Certain Parts of Words: Difficulties in certain parts of words may involve particular letters such as the silent "e" or a number of phonograms such as the "tion" and "sion" forms; or they may lie in certain sections of words generally. In the latter case most errors are likely to be in the center of words and to the right of center. There are usually twice as many errors in the third syllable as in the first, and the letters e, a, i, and u are the most difficult. This difficulty

---

72. Arthur I. Gates and David H. Russell, *Diagnostic and Remedial Spelling Manual: A Handbook for Teachers* (1940), pp. 13-17, 41-50.

calls for special help in word study, such as taking plenty of time to see the entire word, getting each syllable definitely in mind, and pronouncing each part of the word clearly.

5. Pupil Uses a Letter-by-Letter Method: Pupils using this method have never learned to see word-parts. For example, spelling the word prison p-r-i-s-o-n may be a relatively inactive process compared to saying pri-son. The pupils who can use syllabication, who see pronunciation units in words, who recognize common phonograms or other words within longer words, and who have a rhythm in oral or written spelling, have skilled techniques which the remedial teacher should help the letter-by-letter speller to acquire.

6. Pupil Has an Apparently Restricted Method for Word Study: By watching their classroom practices and by Test 9 of the Diagnostic Series, some pupils are discovered who learn to spell words in only one way. It is probably an advantage to be able to use a variety of methods in studying words, so if a pupil uses only one type of attack, a remedial teacher will: (a) Look for physical defeats in sensory apparatus. (b) Explore the possibility of using more techniques. If a pupil uses only auditory methods, for example, it is well to see if he has the necessary basic information and skills for using visual and kinaesthetic methods. He may lack only a little guidance in these. (c) Use methods of word study adapted to the "special ability" of any pupil if there seem to be definite constitutional difficulties with the others.

Another invaluable aid for teachers would be diagnostic and remedial charts. The following was adapted by Greene and Petty from a current language test manual.[73] The chart provides an excellent summary of the many causes of spelling deficiency as well as remedial suggestions for the classroom teacher.

DIAGNOSTIC AND REMEDIAL CHART FOR SPELLING

Possible causes of low test scores	Additional evidence of deficiency	Suggested remedial treatment
1. Lack of experience with the testing technique.	1. Low score on test contrasted with high score when words are given on dictation test.	1. Drills on choosing correct spellings from lists of errors of same word, choosing correct forms from long lists, some correct, some incorrect; proofreading on written work.

73. Harry A. Greene and Walter T. Petty, *Developing Language Skills in the Elementary Schools* (Boston: Allyn and Bacon, Inc., 1963), pp. 546-548.

2. Emphasis on different or wrong vocabulary.	2. Low scores on test in contrast with good record for daily work.	2. Check words not taught in your course with lists of known social utility.
3. Failure to develop a critical attitude toward spelling.	3. Indifference to spelling errors in daily written work.	3. Emphasize proofreading of own work. Drill on choosing correctly spelled forms in lists. Check pupil's certainty of his judgment of correctness of spelling.
4. Lack of teaching emphasis on individual's own spelling difficulties.	4. Observation of pupil's misspellings in daily work.	4. Have pupils keep lists of misspellings in daily work as basis for individual study. Focus on pupil's own errors. Try for transfer to all written work.
5. Special learning difficulties: a. Faulty pronunciation by the teacher.	5. a. Observation of speech habits; informal pronunciation tests based on spelling vocabulary.	5. a. Look up word in dictionary. Pronounce it distinctly for pupil. Have him repeat it while looking at word to associate sight and correct sound.
b. Limited power to visualize or "see" word forms.	b. Observation test. Have pupil try to visualize a 3-in. cube painted red. Ask questions: number of faces; number of planes necessary to cut it into 1-in. cubes; number of small cubes; number painted on one side, two sides, three sides, not painted, etc.	b. Emphasize the practice of looking at the word; closing eyes, and attempting to recall the word, as part of every spelling study period.
c. Difficulties in seeing or in hearing.	c. Observation; doctor's or nurse's examination.	c. Refer to nurse or medical service. Move pupil to front of room near window and blackboard. Stand near him in tests and spelling exercises. Make special effort to speak and write clearly.

d. Failure to associate sounds of letters and syllables with spelling of words.	d. Individual interview; analysis of spelling errors in tests and in daily work.	d. Go over words with child while he studies them. Teach him to analyze words himself.
e. Tendency to transpose, add, or omit letters.	e. Analysis of spelling papers; observation of daily work; pronunciation tests.	e. Emphasize visual recall of words. Have pupil practice writing the words, exaggerating the formation of the letters. Underline individual hard spots.
f. Tendency to spell unphonetic words phonetically.	f. Note types of errors made in spelling tests, especially insertion or leaving out letters.	f. Show that all words are not spelled as they sound. Each word must be learned individually. Emphasize steps in learning to spell. See h below.
g. Difficulties in writing; letter formation.	g. Observation of daily written work and spelling papers. Check writing with Ayres or Freeman writing scales.	g. Practice difficult letter formations and combinations. Emphasize need to avoid confusing letter forms, as i, e, r, and t.
h. Failure to master method of learning to spell.	h. Low scores on daily tests; observe the pupil's method of study in spelling; test on steps in learning to spell.	h. Check pupil's method of learning spelling. Teach steps in learning to spell until he uses them. Steps; (1) look at word, (2) listen to teacher pronounce it, (3) pronounce it by syllables then say the letters, (4) use it in a sentence, (5) close eyes and visualize it, (6) write it, (7) close eyes and recall, (8) write word. Repeat steps as necessary.

The Role of Tests in the Daily Program

For instructional purposes, evidence indicates that the modified sentence-recall form is the most valid and economical test: that is, the teacher pronounces each word, uses it in an oral sentence, and pronounces it again. The students then write the word.[74] Such preliminary tests are sometimes criticized on the erroneous assumption that initial errors are likely to persist. Evidence indicates that, with a five-periods-per-week plan, a negligible percentage of errors made in the Monday test were duplicated in the Friday test, if they had been immediately corrected on Monday.[75] Evidence reported earlier indicated that such tests before study appeared to be less effective in Grade 2 than in higher grades:[76] later evidence indicates that test-study procedures are equal to or superior to study-test procedures for Grade 2 as well as other levels.[77]

Attention should be given in the spelling instruction to the correction of the tests. Tests should be regarded as learning exercises as well as measures of spelling achievement.

The corrected-test technique is by far the most efficient single procedure for learning to spell if the students (1) clearly understand the purposes of the pretest; (2) immediately correct their errors with care; and (3) understand that alert correction of the "pretest" contributes greatly to the reduction of errors.[78] Horn states that "when corrected by the pupils and the result properly utilized, the test is the most fruitful single learning activity per unit of time that has yet been devised."[79] To utilize the testing procedure properly, the teacher should show children how testing identifies the words they need to learn to spell, how it is a learning exercise that calls their attention to how a

74. David S. Brody, "A Comparative Study of Different Forms of Spelling Tests," *Journal of Educational Psychology* 35 (1944): 129-44; Walter W. Cook, "The Measurement of General Spelling Ability Involving Controlled Comparisons Between Techniques," *University of Iowa Student Education* 6, No. 6 (1932): 1-112; Stanley D. Nisbet, "Non-Dictated Spelling Tests," *British Journal of Educational Psychology* 9 (1939): 29-44.

75. Paul G. McKee, *Language in the Elementary School,* revised edition (Boston: Houghton Mifflin Company, 1939), 500 p.

76. Arthur I. Gates, "An Experimental Comparison of the Study-Test and Test-Study Methods in Spelling," *Journal of Educational Psychology* 22 (1931): 1-19.

77. Ruth C. Cook, "Evaluation of Two Methods of Teaching Spelling," *Elementary School Journal* 59 (1957): 21-7; James A. Fitzgerald, *The Teaching of Spelling* (New York: Bruce Books, 1951(b)), p. 233; Thomas D. Horn, "Some Issues in Learning to Spell," *Education* 79 (1958): 229-33; Thomas D. Horn, "Spelling and Children's Written Composition." Reprinted from *Elementary English NCTE* (1960), pp. 52-63.

78. Norman Hall, "The Letter Mark-Out Corrected Test," *Journal of Educational Research* 58 (1964): 148-57; Thomas D. Horn, "The Effect of the Corrected Test on Learning to Spell," *Elementary School Journal* 47 (1947): 277-85; Ivernia M. Tyson, "Factors Contributing to the Effectiveness of the Corrected Test in Spelling" (Doctoral Dissertation; Iowa City: State University of Iowa, 1953).

79. Ernest Horn, "Spelling" in *Encyclopedia of Educational Research,* Third Edition (New York: The Macmillan Company, 1960), pp. 1337-1354; see also "Spelling" section in 1969 edition.

word is spelled and calls for the necessary recall that is spelling. Pupils should correct their own tests and record their own scores with occasional rechecking by the teacher to see that the pupil's checking has been carefully done.

Any successful spelling program should give attention to the individual needs of pupils and challenge each according to his ability. This is not as difficult a problem as it is often thought. Pupils should study only those words of actual written communication usefulness that they cannot spell. Thus if the list of words has been carefully selected, and if a child can correctly spell these words on the pretest, he need not study the words of a particular lesson. When a child has great difficulty with spelling, the number of words he is asked to spell should be reduced from the total presented to the majority of the class in order to develop the proper attitude toward spelling and to teach him how to study.

Children may be grouped for spelling instruction in a manner similar to the grouping for reading and mathematics instruction. The first step in instituting groups should be the administering of a quarterly, semester, or yearly pretest of twenty-five to seventy-five words (depending upon the abilities of the pupils to handle the mechanics of writing). The words on this test should be randomly selected from the words to be taught for the particular quarter, semester, or year. Children misspelling none or very few of these words may be considered the high achievers, those misspelling ten to fifty percent should be labelled the average group, and those pupils misspelling more than fifty percent of the words may be considered the slow spellers.

The high and average groups may be tested for each lesson on all the words of a lesson, though some enrichment words may be added to the list for the high group if they are carefully selected for their need in writing. For the slow group, one-half or fewer of the lesson words should be selected. The actual number chosen should be sufficient to challenge but not so great as to frustrate these pupils.

Spelling occupies a minor, though important, place in the present-day school curriculum. Early statements of dissatisfaction with spelling methodology at the turn of the century gave rise to the issue of whether or not supplanting direct instruction by incidental methods of learning would be desirable.[80] The controversy persisted through the

---

80. Oliver P. Cornman, *Spelling in the Elementary School: An Experimental and Statistical Investigation* (Boston: Ginn and Company, 1902), p. 98; J.M. Rice, "The Futility of the Spelling Grind," *Forum* 23 (1897): 1963-72.

1930's and into the World War II years.[81] The post-Sputnik impact on the curriculum, with increasing emphasis upon science, mathematics, and eventually the humanities, forced a new look at the optimum ways in which direct instruction and incidental learning could complement each other. So-called linguistically based reading materials sought to incorporate spelling instruction more closely in reading development. Evidence concerning the contributions to spelling improvement in Grades 2 and 3 of varying combinations of direct and incidental (functional) instruction has been inconsistent from grade to grade.[82] This suggests that how well a method is implemented may be more crucial than the nature of the methods used in the investigation.

The extent to which the 3,000 to 4,000 word security segment of the spelling curriculum may be learned through activities outside the regular spelling period may be determined by tests using sample words from the security list. Through testing, the pupil knows which, if any, words he needs to study; the teacher is aware of individual pupil progress, including pupils in need of special help; mastery of the security segment is not left to chance; and the individual student is released from unnecessary study of words he has learned through other activities.

Additional techniques of day-by-day evaluation are:

1. Recognition-type test: Several incorrect forms of a word are presented with one correct form. The student marks the correct form. However, marking the correct form does not mean a student can spell the word correctly. This is also a useful test of visualization.
2. Completion-type test: A sentence is written with a word left out. The student fills in the blank with the correctly spelled word. This is also a test of meaning.
3. Essay-type test: The teacher constructs a simple paragraph or short story which contains many of the words to be taught later to a class. The student writes it as it is dictated. Misspelled words are checked. At a later date when all test words have been taught, the paragraph is again dictated and marked for misspellings.

81. Arthur I. Gates et al., "A Modern Systematic vs. An Opportunistic Method of Teaching," *Teacher's College Record* 27 (1926): 679-700; Ernest Horn, "The Incidental Teaching of Spelling," *Elementary English R.* 14 (1937): 3-5, 21; Ernest Horn, "Research in Spelling," *Elementary English R.* 21 (1944): 6-13.

82. Hale C. Reid, "Evaluating Five Methods of Teaching Spelling-Second and Third Grades," *Instructor* 75 (1966): 77, 82; Hale C. Reid and A.M. Hieronymus, *An Evaluation of Five Methods of Teaching Spelling in the Second and Third Grades.* Cooperative Research Project no. 1869 (Iowa City: State University of Iowa, 1963), p. 111.

4. Recognition of errors printed in word lists.

5. Proofreading for errors in context: Some words are spelled incorrectly and pupils are expected to recognize them.

6. Detection of errors in written composition: The pupil is required to detect spelling errors and correct the misspelled words. This technique makes greater demands on the pupil than either "1" or "5."

7. Copying test: A test in straight copying does much to sensitize the pupil to the "hazard" of carelessness.

8. Dictionary tests: Tests in the use of the dictionary are a necessary part of the evaluation program. Anderson has done an excellent job of compiling numerous testing and activity suggestions related to abilities to use the dictionary.[83]

Efficient dictionary use is basic to any spelling program and is crucial for accommodating individual differences.[84]

Research Implications for Remediation

Of the many factors that condition spelling ability, the following have been shown to be amenable to instruction or remedial measures: motivation, work habits, and special abilities and disabilities in vision, hearing, and speech.[85]

Motivation in spelling is affected by teacher and pupil attitudes and interests, the level of pupil motivation, the set to learn and remember, work habits, instructional methods and their utilization, and self-confidence.

Probably the most important source of interest and motivation is the child's awareness of progress.[86] Games and special devices would also appear to enhance motivation in spelling.[87]

83. Paul S. Anderson, *Resource Materials for Teachers of Spelling* (Minneapolis: Burgess Publishing Company, 1959), pp. 78-96.

84. Thomas D. Horn, *Encyclopedia of Educational Research,* 4th edition, p. 1289.

85. Glenn M. Blair, *Diagnostic and Remedial Teaching* (New York: The Macmillan Company, 1956), p. 409; Leo J. Brueckner and Ernest O. Melby, *Diagnostic and Remedial Teaching* (Boston: Houghton Mifflin Company, 1931), p. 598.

86. Sister Mary Columba, *A Study of Interests and Their Relations to Other Factors of Achievement in Elementary School Subjects* (Washington, D.C.: The Catholic University of America Press, 1926), p. 35; Charles M. Diserens and James Vaughn, "The Experimental Psychology of Motivation," *Psychology Bulletin* 28 (1931): 15-65; Ernest Horn, "Teaching Spelling," *In What Research Says to the Teacher, NEA* (1967), p. 32; Paul G. McKee, *Language in the Elementary School,* revised edition (New York: Houghton Mifflin Company, 1939), p. 500; Edward L. Thorndike, *The Psychology of Wants, Interests, and Attitudes* (New York: Appleton-Century-Crofts, 1935), p. 301.

87. James A. Fitzgerald, *The Teaching of Spelling* (New York: Bruce Books, 1951(b)), p. 233; Arthur I. Gates and Frederick B. Graham, "The Value of Various Games and Activities in Teaching Spelling," *Journal of Educational Research* 28 (1934): 1-9; Gertrude Hildreth, *Teaching Spelling* (New York: Holt, Rinehart & Winston, Inc., 1955), p. 346.

The development and maintenance of desirable attitudes toward spelling may be accomplished by "(1) showing the student that the words taught are those most likely to be needed by him now and in the future; (2) limiting the student's study to those words which tests have shown him to be unable to spell; (3) providing the student with a definite and efficient method of learning; (4) emphasizing individual and class progress; and (5) encouraging in the class the spirit of mutual pride and cooperation in spelling achievement."[88]

Closely related to levels of motivation, poor study habits are one of the most common causes of poor spelling achievement.[89] The failure of pupils to learn and utilize approved methods of learning to spell new or difficult words is one of the chief causes of poor achievement in spelling. Certainly, this is not always the fault of the pupil. Frequently he is not taught how to study, or the methods he is taught are not effective. Frequently little more than general observation is required to reveal whether or not the pupil makes a systematic attack on his learning of new or difficult words. Does he definitely center his attention upon the word, does he try to visualize the word, i.e., close his eyes and attempt to recall its appearance, does he say the letters of the word softly to himself, does he pronounce the word correctly syllable by syllable and try to recall how each syllable appears, does he compare the word with the correct written or printed copy, does he watch for silent letters, double letters, different vowels having the same sound, and for different combinations of letters, does he recall the word repeatedly until he has mastered it, does he develop the meaning of the word by using the dictionary, and fix it in his experience by using it in sentences?

Special abilities and disabilities condition learning to spell. They may be categorized as: (1) visual, (2) auditory, (3) oral, and (4) modes of learning.

88. Ernest Horn, "Spelling." In Chester W. Harris, editor, *Encyclopedia of Educational Research*, 3rd edition (New York: The Macmillan Company, 1960), pp. 1337-54.

89. James A. Fitzgerald, *The Teaching of Spelling* (New York: Bruce Books, 1951(b)), p. 233; Arthur I. Gates, *The Psychology of Reading and Spelling With Special Reference to Disability* (New York: Teachers College Press, Columbia University, 1922), p. 108; Ernest Horn, "Teaching Spelling," *In What Research Says to the Teacher*, NEA (1967), p. 32; Paul G. McKee, "Teaching and Testing Spelling by Column and Context Forms" (Doctoral Dissertation; State University of Iowa, 1924); David H. Russell, *Characteristics of Good and Poor Spellers* (New York: Teachers College Press, Columbia University, 1937), p. 103; David H. Russell, "A Second Study of Characteristics of Good and Poor Spellers," *Journal of Educational Psychology* 46 (1955): 129-41; Edmund G. Williamson, "Mental Abilities Related to Learning to Spell," *Psychology Bulletin* 30 (1933(a)): 743-51; Edmund G. Williamson, "The Relation of Learning to Spelling Ability," *Journal of Educational Psychology* 24 (1933(b)): 257-65.

Spelling ability has been shown to be strongly related to visual perception, visual discrimination, and visual memory.[90] Improvement of perceptual analysis may apparently be achieved through training.[91] Therefore, provision of exercises for strengthening visual perception and discrimination should be provided.

Significant relationships have also been found between spelling and sound perception and discrimination.[92] However, these correlations appear to be lower than those between visual factors and spelling.[93]

90. Ira E. Aaron, "The Relationship of Auditory-Visual Discrimination to Spelling Ability") (Doctoral Dissertation) (Minneapolis: University of Minnesota Press, 1954); Margaret M. Adkins, "Relationships Involving Particular Groups of Syndromes; Factors Related to School Success," *Monogr. Soc. Res. Child Development* 8 (1943): 503-22, 583-638; Joseph F. Comerford, "Perceptual Abilities in Spelling" (Doctoral Dissertation; Boston University, 1954); John J. DeBoer, "Oral and Written Language," *Research in Educational Research* 25 (1955): 107-20; Luther C. Gilbert and Doris W. Gilbert, "Training for Speed and Accuracy of Visual Perception in Learning to Spell," *University of California Public Education* 7 (1942): 351-426; Esther Mack, "An Investigation of the Importance of Various Word Analysis Abilities in Reading and Spelling Achievement" (Doctoral Dissertation; Boston University, 1953); Bertha M. Newton, "A Study of Certain Factors Related to Achievement in Spelling" (Doctoral Dissertation; Columbia, Missouri: University of Missouri Press, 1960); David H. Russell, *Characteristics of Good and Poor Spellers* (New York: Teachers College Press, Columbia University, 1937), p. 103; David H. Russell, "A Diagnostic Study of Spelling Readiness," *Journal of Educational Research* 37 (1943): 276-83; David H. Russell, "A Second Study of Characteristics of Good and Poor Spellers," *Journal of Educational Psychology* 46 (1955): 129-41.

91. Luther C. Gilbert, "An Experimental Investigation of Eye Movements in Learning to Spell Words," *Psychology Monograph* 43, no. 3 (1932): 81; Luther C. Gilbert, "A Genetic Study of Growth in Perceptual Habits in Spelling," *Elementary School Journal* 40 (1940): 346-57; Luther C. Gilbert and Doris W. Gilbert, "Training for Speed and Accuracy of Visual Perception in Learning to Spell," *University of California Public Education* 7 (1942): 351-426; Jess S. Hudson and Lola Toler, "Instruction in Auditory and Visual Discrimination as Means of Improving Spelling," *Elementary School Journal* 49 (1949): 466-9.

92. Henry F. Bradford, "Oral-Aural Differentiation Among Basic Speech Sounds as a Factor in Spelling Readiness," *Elementary School Journal* 54 (1954): 354-8; Thelma L.J. Damgaard, "Auditory Acuity and Discrimination as Factors in Spelling Competence" (Doctoral Dissertation; Stanford, California: Stanford University Press, 1956); Arthur I. Gates, *The Psychology of Reading and Spelling With Special Reference to Disability* (New York: Teachers College Press, Columbia University, 1922), p. 108; Arthur I. Gates, "A Study of the Role of Visual Perception, Intelligence, and Certain Associative Processes in Reading and Spelling," *Journal of Educational Psychology* 17 (1926): 433-45; Jess S. Hudson and Lola Toler, "Instruction in Auditory and Visual Discrimination as Means of Improving Spelling," *Elementary School Journal* 49 (1949): 466-9; David H. Russell, *Characteristics of Good and Poor Spellers* (New York: Teachers College Press, Columbia University, 1937), p. 103; David H. Russell, "A Diagnostic Study of Spelling Readiness," *Journal of Educational Research* 37 (1943): 276-83; David H. Russell, "A Second Study of Characteristics of Good and Poor Spellers," *Journal of Educational Psychology* 46 (1955): 129-41; David H. Russell, "Auditory Abilities and Achievement in Spelling in the Primary Grades," *Journal of Educational Psychology* 49 (1958): 315-9; Mildred C. Templin, "Phonic Knowledge and Its Relation to the Spelling and Reading Achievement of Fourth Grade Pupils," *Journal of Educational Research* 47 (1954): 441-54; Empress Y. Zedler, "Effect of Phonic Training on Speech Sound Discrimination and Spelling Performance," *Journal of Speech, Hearing Disorders* 21 (1956): 245-50.

93. Bertha M. Newton, "A Study of Certain Factors Related to Achievement in Spelling" (Doctoral Dissertation; Columbia, Missouri: University of Missouri Press, 1960); David H. Russell, "Auditory Abilities and Achievement in Spelling in the Primary Grades," *Journal of Educational Psychology* 49 (1958): 315-9.

Available evidence indicates that sound discrimination can be improved.[94]

Again, there are implications for the daily instructional program.

> Very frequently words are misspelled because they are spelled the way they are heard or pronounced. Improper pronunciation by the pupil himself is more likely to result in misspellings than is mispronunciation by the teacher either in teaching or in testing. Imperfect hearing or improper pronunciation or enunciation of the words by his associate thus becomes a contributing cause. It is, therefore, imperative that children form proper habits of pronunciation and enunciation.[95]

All learners use varying amounts of visual, auditory, and kinesthetic imagery when attempting to spell correctly. Individuals who are blind or deaf must obviously compensate for their loss by sharpening the sensory modes of learning and perception that are left to them. Indeed, deaf children have been shown to make fewer errors than children with normal hearing. Since the identification of individual imagery types has proved extremely elusive for psychologists, learning experiences which involve all imagery types should be most fruitful.[96] It may well be that one reason for the efficiency of the corrected test technique[97] in learning to spell is that it utilizes all three types of imagery, with emphasis on the visual and auditory during pupil self-correction.

A Final Word

Few educators today, if any, consider the 3,000 to 4,000 words found in most spelling series as anything more than the security segment of the spelling curriculum. Although the role of spelling in practical writing is different from its purpose in creative writing, where the flow of thought is the prime consideration, both of these instructional areas provide the means for greatly expanding students' writing vocabularies. It is very probable that spelling ability is best developed and

---

94. Jess S. Hudson and Lola Toler, "Instruction in Auditory and Visual Discrimination as Means of Improving Spelling," *Elementary School Journal* 49 (1949): 466-9; Empress Y. Zedler, "Effect on Phonic Training on Speech Sound Discrimination and Spelling Performance," *Journal Speech, Hearing Disorders* 21 (1956): 245-50.

95. Harry A. Greene and Walter T. Petty, *Developing Language Skills in the Elementary Schools*, Third Edition (1963), p. 352.

96. Ira E. Aaron, "The Relationship of Auditory-Visual Discrimination to Spelling Ability" (Doctoral Dissertation; Minneapolis: University of Minnesota Press, 1954); Mabel R. Fernald, "The Diagnosis of Mental Imagery," *Psychology Monograph* 14, no. 1 (1912): 169; Leta S. Hollingworth, *The Psychology of Special Disability in Spelling* (New York: Teachers College Press, Columbia University, 1918), p. 105; Robert S. Woodworth and Harold Schlosbert, *Experimental Psychology* (New York: Holt, Rinehart & Winston, Inc., 1954), p. 948.

97. Thomas D. Horn, "The Effect of the Corrected Test on Learning to Spell," *Elementary School Journal* 47 (1947): 227-85.

maintained in the long run through stimulation of, and careful attention to, the writing that children do. On the other hand, there is as yet no field-tested substitute for direct instruction on the basic core of high-frequency words needed in child and adult writing.

In the final analysis, everything we do is with the permeating hope that he will care enough to spell correctly today, tomorrow, and always.

A Concluding Philosophy

Diagnosis, evaluation and remediation are the keys to an effective language arts program. The teacher must analyze growth and then make provisions for problems.

A classroom teacher must constantly diagnose difficulties and then adjust instruction to fit the needs of the individual. In one sense, a teacher is diagnosing almost 100 per cent of the time that she is teaching. She diagnoses as she questions the class, grades papers, and leads discussion. She knows which individual student needs to be taught or re-taught a specific task. She knows when the whole class is responding at a particular level. Therefore, it is time to go on to the next teaching level.

We don't have all of the answers for the many questions related to diagnosis, evaluation, and remediation. Each student brings his own unique problems. A teacher will be searching for answers for as long as she teaches. Just as she thinks she knows the answers, she will have a student come in who has all new problems and the things that she has done before with others will not work for this student.

The following are guiding principles for a program of diagnosis, evaluation, and remediation:

1. It is just as important to find out what a pupil knows as it is to learn what he doesn't know.
2. Remedial instruction is just as important as finding out the causes of the problem.
3. Testing should be kept to a minimum for two reasons: (a) Testing is time-consuming. The time might be better spent in remedial instruction and (b) Tests may submit the youngster to another failure experience. This is the last thing he needs.
4. There is not a set solution. There are no tried-and-true materials. What works for a particular student is good. What doesn't work is

bad. Thus, the teacher needs to be creative and try lots of things. If it works, keep it. If it doesn't work, discard it.

5. No two students are alike. Therefore, one cannot generalize for remedial instruction.

6. Use machines whenever possible for drill. Although they do not do anything that you as the teacher could not do without them, they do have a motivating and exciting effect on students for they are "new" to students and seem advanced. Use machines to help note roots of words, word peculiarities, spellings, as one example.

7. Use tape recorders with headsets as often as possible. They are extremely valuable and versatile. They are excellent for listening, reading, speaking, and self-evaluation activities.

8. Success is imperative. We must insure success. For some youngsters, at first, prescribed materials should be too easy.

9. Very often have, youngsters in need of remedial work have short attention-spans. The fact needs to be remembered in diagnostic evaluation and remediation.

10. Show respect for the student's ideas. In many cases, this is the first time that anyone has acted like he is important.

11. Most students have a very poor self-concept and he will be successful to the degree that you can raise his self-concept.

12. Individual differences and self-evaluation must be continually characteristic of the total language arts program and, the remedial program should be one of hope and success. Not one of despair.

BIBLIOGRAPHY

Evaluation and Objectives

Ammons, Margaret. "An Empirical Study of Process and Product in Curriculum Development." *Journal of Educational Research,* 57:451-7; 1964.

————. "Evaluation: What Is It? Who Does It? When Should It Be Done?" *In Evaluation of Children's Reading Achievement.* Perspectives in Reading Monograph Series. IRA, 1967.

Anderson, Dan W., and others. (Compilers). *Strategies of Curriculum Development: Works of Virgil Herrick.* Merrill, 1965. 196 pp.

Anderson, Robert H. "Pupil Progress." *Encyclopedia of Educational Research,* 4th Edition, p. 1060.

Beauchamp, George A. *Curriculum Theory.* Kagg, 1961. 149 pp.

Block, Elaine C. "Sequence as a Factor in Classroom Instruction." Doctoral dissertation. University of Wisconsin, 1965.

Bloom, Benjamin S. (ed.) *Taxonomy of Educational Objectives: Cognitive Domain.* London: Longmans, Green and Co., 1956. 207 pp.

Bobbitt, Franklin. *The Curriculum.* New York: Houghton Mifflin Co., 1918. 295 pp.

Charters, W.W. *Curriculum Construction.* New York: The Macmillan Co., 1923. 352 pp.

Educational Testing Service. *Multiple-Choice Questions: A Close Look.* ETS, 1963(a). 43 p.

Eisner, Elliot W. "Educational Objectives: Help or Hindrance." *School Review,* 75:250-60, 1967.

Goodlad, John I., and Richter, Maurice N., Jr. *The Development of a Conceptual System for Dealing with Problems of Curriculum and Instruction.* University of California at Los Angeles and Institute for Development of Educational Activities, 1966. 69 pp.

Hawthorne, Richard D. "A Model for the Analysis of Team Teachers' Curricular Decisions and Verbal Instructional Interaction." Doctoral dissertation. University of Wisconsin, 1967.

Kearney, Nolan C. *Elementary School Objectives.* New York: Russell Sage Foundation, 1953. 189 pp.

Krathwohl, David R., and others. *Taxonomy of Educational Objectives: Affective Domain.* New York: David McKay Co., 1964. 196 pp.

———. "Stating Objectives Appropriately for Program, for Curriculum, and for Instructional Material Development." *Journal of Teacher Education,* 16:83-92; 1965.

Mager, Robert F. *Preparing Instructional Objectives.* Palo Alto, California: Fearon Publishers, 1962. 62 pp.

Macdonald, James B. "Myths About Instruction." *Educational Leadership,* 22:571-6+, 1965.

McClure, Robert M. "Procedures, Processes, and Products in Curriculum Development." Doctoral dissertation. University of California at Los Angeles, 1965.

McGuire, Christine. *Research in the Process Approach to the Construction and Analysis of Medical Examinations.* 20th Yearbook. NCME, 1963. p. 7-16.

McNeil, John D. "Antidote to a School Scandal." *Educational Forum,* 31:69-77; 1966.

National Education Association. *The Central Purpose of American Education.* Washington: NEA, 1961. 21 p.

———. Project on Instruction. *Deciding What to Teach,* Washington: National Education Association, 1963. p. 88-98.

Sand, Ole. *Curriculum Study in Basic Nursing Education.* New York: G.P. Putnam's Sons, 1955. 225 pp.

Sanders, Norris M. *Classroom Questions: What Kinds?* New York: Harper and Row, 1966. 176 pp.

Smith, B. Othanel, and others. *Fundamentals of Curriculum Development.* rev. ed. New York World Publishers, 1957. 685 p.

Smith, Eugene R., and others. *Appraising and Recording Student Progress.* New York: Harper and Row, 1942. 550 pp.

Taba, Hilda. *Curriculum Development: Theory and Practice.* Harcourt Brace Javanovich, 1962. 529 pp.

Wilhelms, Fred T. (ed.) *Evaluation as Feedback and Guide Yearbook.* ASCD, 1967(a). pp. 2-17.

BIBLIOGRAPHY

Listening

Brown, James I. "The Construction of a Diagnostic Test of Listening Comprehension." *Journal of Experimental Education,* 18:139-146, December, 1949.

Duker, Sam. "Goals of Teaching Listening Skills in the Elementary School." *Elementary English,* 38:170-4, 1961.

———. "An Annotated Guide to Audiovisual Aids Available for the Teaching of Listening." *Audiovisual Instruction,* 10:320-2, 1965.

Early, Margaret J. "Suggestions for Teaching Listening." *Journal of Education,* 137:17-20, 1954.

Educational Testing Service, *Sequential Tests of Educational Progress: Listening.* Princeton, New Jersey, 1957.

Hollow, Kevin, Sister M. "An Experimental Study of Listening Comprehension at the Intermediate Grade Level." Doctoral dissertation, Fordham University, 1955.

Lundsteen, Sara W.R. "Teaching Abilities in Critical Listening in the Fifth and Sixth Grades." Doctoral dissertation. University of California at Berkeley, 1963.

Pratt, Edward and Greene, Harry A. *Training Children to Listen.* A Monograph for Elementary Teachers, No. 80. Evanston, Ill.: Row, Peterson and Company, 1955.

Pratt, Lloyd E. "The Experimental Evaluation of a Program for the Improvement of Listening in the Elementary School." Doctoral dissertation. State University of Iowa, 1953.

Russell, David H. "A Conspectus of Recent Research on Listening Abilities." *Elementary English,* 41:262-7, 1964.

Russell, David H., and Russell, Elizabeth F. *Listening Aids Through the Grades— One-Hundred-Ninety Listening Activities.* New York: Teachers College Press, 1959.

Taylor, Stanford. *What Research Says to the Teacher: Listening.* Department of Classroom Teachers and American Educational Research Association. Washington: National Education Association, 1964, pp. 23-29.

Wagner, Guy, and others. *Listening Games—Building Listening Skills with Instructional Games.* Greenwich, Connecticut: Teachers Publishing Corp., 1962, 132 pp.

BIBLIOGRAPHY

Oral Communication

Manual for Interpreting the Iowa Language Abilities Test. Yonkers-on-Hudson, New York: World Book Company.

BIBLIOGRAPHY

Composition

Greene, Harry A. and Ballenger, H.L. *Iowa Language Abilities Tests.* Yonkers-on-Hudson: World Book Company, 1948.

Lindquist, E.F., general ed. *Iowa Tests of Basic Skills, Test C.* Geneva, Illinois: Houghton-Mifflin Company.

McKee, Paul. "An Adequate Program in the Language Arts." *Teaching Language in the Elementary School,* Forty-third Yearbook of the National Society for the Study of Education, Part II. Chicago: The University of Chicago Press, 1944, pp. 34-35.

Nelson, Francis, W. *The Structure of American English.* New York: The Ronald Press Company, 1958.

Watts, A.F. *The Language and Mental Development of Children.* London: George G. Harrap and Company, Ltd., 1944. Boston: D.C. Heath and Company, 1947, pp. 141-142.

Wolfe, Joseph B., Wright, Adele J., Olson, Lillian E. *English Your Language,* Book 5, p. 25. Boston: Allyn and Boston, Inc., 1963.

BIBLIOGRAPHY

Handwriting

Ayres, Leonard P. *A Scale for Measuring the Quality of Handwriting of School Children.* Bulletin No. 113 New York: Division of Education, Russell Sage Foundation, 1912.

Conrad, Edith U. *Conrad Manuscript Writing Standards* New York: Bureau of Publications, Teachers College, Columbia University, 1929.

Ediger, Marlow. "Essentials in Teaching Handwriting." *Education* 86:37-9; 1965.

Enstrom, Erick A. "Out of the Classroom: Handwriting for the Retarded." *Exceptional Children,* 32:285-8; 1966(b).

Enstrom, Erick A. "Research in Teaching the Left-handed." *Instructor,* 74:44-6+ 1964(b).

Feldt, Leonard S. "Reliability of Measures of Handwriting Quality." *Journal of Educational Psychology*

Freeman, Frank N., and the Zaner-Bloser Staff, *Evaluation Scales for Guiding Growth in Handwriting* Columbus, Ohio: The Zaner-Bloser Company, 1958.

——. *Handwritten Faults and How to Correct Them* Columbus, Ohio: Zaner-Bloser Co., 1958.

——. *What Research Says to the Teacher: Teaching Handwriting* Washington: Department of Classroom Teachers and American Educational Research Association, National Education Association, 1954, p. 4.

Groff, Patrick J. "New Speeds of Handwriting." *Elementary English,* 38:564-5; 1961.

Harris, Theodore L. "Handwriting," *Encyclopedia of Educational Research,* 1960, p. 620.

Herrick, Virgil E., and Okada, Nora. "The Present Scene: Practices in the Teaching of Handwriting in the U.S.—1960." In Herrick, Virgil E. (ed.) *New Horizons for Research in Handwriting.* Madison: University of Wisconsin Press, 1963. p. 17-38.

Hildreth, Gertrude H. *Metropolitan Primary Manuscript Handwriting* New York: Harcourt, Brace and World, Inc., 1933.

Lewis, Edward R., and Lewis, Hilda P. "An Analysis of Errors in the Formation of Manuscript Letters by First-grade Children." *American Educational Research Journal,* 2:25-35; 1965.

McElravy, Anna. "Handwriting and the Slow Learner." *Elementary English* 41:865-8; 1964.

Laurianna, Sister Mary. "Ten Commandments of Good Handwriting." *Elementary English* 41:854+; 1964.

Meeker, Alice M. "Cursive Writing in the Middle Grades." *Instructor*, 74:45+; 1964.

Otto, Wayne, and McMenemy, Richard A. *Corrective and Remedial Teaching*, New York: Houghton Mifflin Co., 1966. 377 pp.

Quant, Leslie. "Factors Affecting the Legibility of Handwriting." *Journal Experimental Education*, 14:297-316; 1946.

Rondinella, Oreste R. "An Evaluation of Subjectivity of Elementary School Teachers in Grading Handwriting." *Elementary English* 40:531-2; 1963.

University of Wisconsin, Committee for Research in Basic Skills. *Comparison of Practices in Handwriting Advocated by Nineteen Commercial Systems of Handwriting Instruction*. Madison: University of Wisconsin Press, 1960. 111 pp.

West, Paul V. *The American Handwriting Scale* New York: A.N. Palmer Co., 1951.

BIBLIOGRAPHY

Spelling

Allen, Robert L., Virginia F. Allen, and Margaret Shute. *English Sounds and Their Spellings*, New York: Thomas Y. Crowell and Company, 1966.

Anderson, Paul S. *Resource Materials for Teachers of Spelling*, Minneapolis: Burgess Publishing Company, 1959.

Bradford, Henry F. "Oral-Aural Differentiation Among Basic Speech Sounds as a Factor in Spelling Readiness," *Elementary School Journal*, 54:354-8, April, 1954.

Brothers, Arleen, and Cora Holsclaw. "Fusing Behaviors into Spelling," *Elementary English*, 46:25-28, January, 1969.

Greene, Harry A., Gerberich, J.R., and A.N. Jergensen. *Measurement and Evaluation in the Elementary School*, New York: Longman's Green and Company, 1953, p. 442.

Hall, Robert A. *Sound and Spelling in English*, Philadelphia: Chilton Company, 1961.

Hanna, Jean S., and Paul R. "Spelling As a School Subject: A Brief History," *The National Elementary School Principal*, 38:8-23, May, 1959.

Hodges, Richard E. "The Psychological Bases of Spelling," *Elementary English*, 42:629-635, October, 1965.

Hodges, Richard E., and E. Hugh Rudorf. "Searching Linguistics for Cues for the Teaching of Spelling," *Elementary English*, 42:527-533, May, 1965.

Horn, Ernest. *What Research Says to the Teacher: Teaching Spelling*, Washington, D.C., The National Education Association, 1967.

Horn, Thomas D. "Spelling," in *Encyclopedia of Educational Research*, Robert L. Ebel, editor, New York: Macmillan Company, 1969, pp. 1282-1299.

Personke, Carl and Albert H. Yee. "A Model for the Analysis of Spelling Behavior," *Elementary English*, 43:278-284, March, 1966.

———. "The Situational Choice and the Spelling Program," *Elementary English*, 45:32-37, 40, January, 1968.

Yee, Albert H. "The Generalization Controversy in Spelling Instruction," *Elementary English*, 43:154-161, February, 1966.

index

405